The Future of the Natural Gas Market in Southeast Europe

The Future of the Natural Gas Market in Southeast Europe

THE WORLD BANK

PPIAF

PUBLIC-PRIVATE INFRASTRUCTURE ADVISORY FACILITY

ISBN: 978-0-8213-7864-9
eISBN: 978-0-8213-7998-1
DOI: 10.1596/978-0-8213-7864-9

Library of Congress Cataloging-in-Publication Data
The future of the natural gas market in South East Europe.
    p. cm.
  ISBN 978-0-8213-7864-9—ISBN 978-0-8213-7998-1 (e-version)
  1. Gas industry—Balkan Peninsula.

  HD9581.B312F88 2009
  382'.4228509496—dc22

                                                              2009041882

Cover design: Naylor Design, Inc.

CONTENTS

MAPS

TABLES

ACKNOWLEDGMENTS

This study was made possible by the generous contribution of funds from the Energy Sector Management Assistance Program (ESMAP), the Public-Private Infrastructure Advisory Facility (PPIAF), and KfW Entwicklungsbank; and it was overseen by staff from the World Bank and KfW.

The financial and technical support of ESMAP is gratefully acknowledged. ESMAP, a global knowledge and technical assistance partnership administered by the World Bank and sponsored by official bilateral donors, assists low- and middle-income countries, its clients, to provide modern energy services for poverty reduction and environmentally sustainable economic development. It is governed and funded by a consultative group comprising official bilateral donors and multilateral institutions, representing Australia, Austria, Canada, Denmark, Finland, France, Germany, Iceland, the Netherlands, Norway, Sweden, the United Kingdom, and the World Bank Group.

PPIAF is a multidonor technical assistance facility focused on helping developing countries improve the quality of their infrastructure through private involvement. For more information on the facility, see the Web site, http://www.ppiaf.org.

KfW Entwicklungsbank (KfW development bank), on behalf of the German government, provides funds and expertise for projects and programs within the scope of financial cooperation. The objective of Germany's development cooperation is to improve the economic and social situation of people in developing countries and economies in transition. For more information, see the Web site, http://www.kfw-entwicklungsbank.de.

The consulting firm Economic Consulting Associates (ECA) prepared the report under the leadership of Stephen Wilson, with contributions from Penspen, Energy Institute Hrvoje Požar (EIHP) and Untergrundspeicher- und Geotechnologie-Systeme GmbH (UGS).

Contact details for further information on the study:

- **Franz Gerner,** Senior Energy Economist
  Sustainable Development, Europe and Central Asia Region
  The World Bank
  1818 H Street, NW
  Washington, DC 20433, USA
  fgerner@worldbank.org
  www.worldbank.org

- **Jens Drillisch,** Senior Project Manager
  KfW Entwicklungsbank
  LIII a 3 – Energy and Transport
  Europe and Caucasus
  Palmengartenstrasse 5–9
  D-60325 Frankfurt am Main, Germany
  jens.drillisch@kfw.de
  www.kfw.de

- **Alfred Schuch,** Senior Gas Expert
  Energy Community Secretariat
  Am Hof 4, Level 6
  Vienna 1010, Austria
  alfred.schuch@energy-community.org
  www.energy-community.org

- **Stephen Wilson,** Director
  Economic Consulting Associates Ltd.
  41 Lonsdale Road
  London NW6 6RA, UK
  stephen.wilson@eca-uk.com
  www.eca-uk.com

ABBREVIATIONS

AAQ   actual annual quantity
ACQ   annual contract quantity
Bcm   billion cubic meters
          [used here for billion standard cubic meters (Bscm)]
Btu   British thermal unit
CCGT   combined-cycle gas turbine
CIF   cost, insurance, and freight
EC   Energy Community
ECA   Economic Consulting Associates
ECSec   Energy Community Secretariat
EIA   Energy Information Administration
EIHP   Energy Institute Hrvoje Požar, of Croatia
ERGEG   European Regulator's Group for Electricity and Gas
ESMAP   Energy Sector Management Assistance Program
ETP   electronic trading platform
EU   European Union
EU25   25 members of the European Union
FOB   free on board
GDP   gross domestic product
GIE   Gas Infrastructure Europe
GIS   Southeast Europe Generation Investment Study
GUEU   Georgia-Ukraine-EU
HP   high-pressure
IAP   Ionian-Adriatic pipeline
IEA   International Energy Agency
IGI   Italy-Greece Interconnector

kbpd	thousand barrels per day
KfW	KfW Entwicklungsbank
kWh	kilowatt-hour
LNG	liquefied natural gas
LPG	liquefied petroleum gas
LRMC	long-run marginal cost
Mcm	thousand cubic meters
	[used here for thousand standard cubic meters (Mscm)]
MDP	maximum demand penalty
MDQ	maximum daily quantity
MMBtu	million British thermal units
MMcm	million cubic meters
MMscm	million standard cubic meters
MPa	megapascal
Mt	megatonne
MW	megawatt
MWh	megawatt-hour
NBP	National Balancing Point
NDPI	mineral resources production tax
NEGP	North-European Gas Pipeline
NGIIR	New Gas Infrastructure Investment Regulations
OCGT	open-cycle gas turbine
OPEC	Organization of the Petroleum Exporting Countries
PEGP	pan-European gas pipeline
PPIAF	Public-Private Infrastructure Advisory Facility
RGS	regional gasification study
RMI	risk mitigation instrument
SCP	South Caucasus pipeline
SEE	Southeast Europe
SI	*Système international d'unités* [International System of Units]
TAG	trans-Austria Gasleitung [trans-Austria pipeline]
TAP	trans-Adriatic pipeline
Tcf	trillion cubic feet
Tcm	trillion cubic meters [used here for trillion standard cubic meters (Tscm)]
TGI	Turkey-Greece-Italy pipeline
TPO	transmission project operator
TPP	take-or-pay penalty
TPQ	take-or-pay quantity
UGS	underground gas storage
UN	United Nations

UNMIK	United Nations Interim Administration Mission in Kosovo
VAT	value added tax
WTI	West Texas Intermediate

All amounts are presented in U.S. dollars, unless otherwise indicated.

A Note on Units

The gas industry is well known for its large variety of both imperial and metric units, and for its nonstandard abbreviations of metric units. The general practice in Europe is to favor metric units, and so those are used throughout this report. However, in the gas industry, the standard *Systeme Internationale* (SI) prefixes usually used elsewhere with the metric system (for example, kWh, MWh, GWh or kJ, MJ, GJ) tend not to be used. This is a carryover from the old prefixes used in the imperial system (for example, Mcf, MMcf, Bcf, Tcf). An explanation of the SI and imperial prefixes and an example for the volumetric units used in this report are shown here:

Multiple	Exponential	SI prefix	Gas industry (imperial) prefix	Example
Thousand	10^3	k, kilo	M (Roman numeral thousand)	Mcm (thousand cubic meters)
Million	10^6	M, Mega	MM (thousand thousand)	MMcm (million cubic meters)
Billion	10^9	G, Giga	B (billion)	Bcm (billion cubic meters)
Trillion	10^{12}	T, Tera	T (trillion)	Tcm (trillion cubic meters)

This system creates the potential for confusion or ambiguity when referring to cubic meters. If these are abbreviated "cm," they can be confused with the abbreviation for the common unit "centimeter." If abbreviated "c.m." or "cu.m.," the formatting appears inconsistent with Mcm, MMcm, and so firth. The other alternative is "m^3," which is unambiguous but inconsistent from a formatting point of view. In this report, we have decided to use cubic meter.

In the case of underground storage, a further distinction needs to be made between physical volumetric units (for example, the space within a salt cavern), which are measured in m^3 and standard cubic meters of gas. A single m^3 of storage (or pipeline) volume can hold many standard cubic meters of gas under pressure.

OVERVIEW

A consulting team led by Economic Consulting Associates (ECA) of the United Kingdom was appointed to execute the Regional Gasification Study for Southeast Europe (SEE). The World Bank and KfW Entwicklungsbank are the joint managers and sponsors of the study, and the study is partly funded by the Energy Sector Management Assistance Program and the Public-Private Infrastructure Advisory Facility. For the sponsoring agencies, the overall objective of the study is to identify regional, cross-border, and country-specific gas infrastructure projects that are economically, financially, and technically sound. The study also analyses and makes proposals for the institutional and policy issues relating to funding and implementing gas infrastructure projects.

The study examines sources of gas supply from Russia, the Caspian region, and other current and prospective producer-countries through Turkey and other transit routes (including liquefied natural gas [LNG]); and it assesses costs of supply and gasification prospects in these nine gas markets in the Southeast Europe region:

- Albania
- Bosnia and Herzegovina
- Bulgaria
- Croatia
- Kosovo
- the former Yugoslav Republic of Macedonia
- Montenegro
- Romania
- Serbia.

All of these markets are signatories to the Athens Memoranda of 2002 and 2003, which commit the participants to regional cooperation in electricity and gas. In 2005, the participants formed an Energy Community (EC), whose Secretariat was subsequently established in Vienna, Austria.

It is recognized that the small size of these markets (excepting Romania) makes it difficult to establish new bulk transmission lines to supply them alone. However, the fact that there are a number of proposals for major transmission lines that will cross the SEE region en route to supplying major markets in Western Europe opens the possibility for spur lines to augment existing supplies to the SEE countries to meet their projected demand up to the year 2025.

The following issues are this study's main subjects of investigation:

- the rate at which gas demand would grow in the SEE markets if potential users had access to gas, with a particular focus on markets that are not gasified at present (Albania, Kosovo, and Montenegro); and whether this growth would be sufficient to justify major new transmission pipelines
- prospects for Caspian gas competing effectively with Russian gas in supplying markets in Southeastern and neighboring Western Europe; and prospects for other supply sources, including LNG
- the feasibility of meeting demand in each of the SEE markets through regional transmission pipelines supplied by major transmission systems traversing the region, and the identification of the most promising infrastructure configuration to meet those requirements
- the main institutional and policy issues affecting the feasibility of implementation and operation of these new pipelines and new markets.

The work has been contracted in two phases covering the nine main tasks in the terms of reference. This document covers tasks in both Phase 1 and Phase 2. The full list of tasks is presented in table 1.

How This Report Is Organized

The main report following this overview is divided into five main chapters, with supporting appendixes at the back of the book:

1. the introduction, study background, and discussion of the methodology
2. demand-side assessments
3. supply-side options
4. institutional framework and implementation issues
5. conclusions and key findings.

Table 1 Study Tasks, Phase 1 and Phase 2

Task/phase	Description of task
Task 1, Phase 1	Provide long-term SEE gas demand forecasts (chapter 2)
Task 2, Phase 1	Provide a perspective on the economics of SEE gasification, based on gas supply from Russia (chapter 3)
Task 3, Phase 1	Provide a perspective on the cost of new gas pipelines linking Turkey with SEE and Western Europe (chapter 3)
Task 4, Phase 1	Provide a perspective on the economics of new gas transmission pipelines (chapter 3)
Task 5, Phase 2	Provide a perspective on the economics of SEE gasification, based on increased LNG imports (chapter 3)
Task 6, Phase 1	Provide a perspective on the gas price at the Turkish border (chapter 3)
Task 7, Phase 2	Provide a perspective on the relationship between SEE gasification and Western European gas markets (chapter 3)
Task 8, Phase 1	Provide an overview of the economics of SEE gasification, based on Caspian gas (chapter 2)
Task 9, Phase 2	Review the institutional framework for SEE gas market development (chapter 4)

Source: Authors' compilation.
Note: LNG = liquefied natural gas; SEE = Southeast Europe.

How the Report Has Been Distributed

The main report and each relevant market report have been distributed to representatives of each of the nine markets involved in the study. The main report and all of the individual market reports have been given to the World Bank and KfW Entwicklungsbank, the sponsors of the study, as well as to the EC Secretariat in Vienna. The documents are available to other interested parties on request, and can be downloaded from the EC Secretariat Web site.

Demand-Side Assessments

The demand-side assessments principally covering the development of long-term demand scenarios for each market were developed initially in the inception phase of the project. Those analyses and scenario projections are further elaborated here to provide the link to the supply-side analysis of pipeline options. The demand-side assessment covers

- examination of the breakeven price for gas to compete with alternate fuels in the main sectors, using netback pricing analysis
- development of a scenario of demand growth in each market
- assessment of the incremental demand that would need to be met by new gas supply, and the buildup of demand.

Projecting Demand for Gas

Six of the markets already use natural gas, with supplies coming primarily through imports from Russia (transiting Ukraine), although two markets have a significant proportion of demand met from domestic supplies (Croatia and Romania) and two others have small-percentage shares of domestic gas (Bulgaria and Serbia). In projecting future demand for gas, one of the main issues is the extent to which the availability of gas would make possible the displacement of other fuels in various categories of demand—notably, power generation and residential, commercial, and industrial applications. Relative prices of competing fuels lie at the heart of the analysis, although potential growth in demand for gas also will be driven by other factors—including convenience, environmental aspects, and national policies (as reflected in taxes, incentives, and so forth).

Competitive Gas Prices, Relative to Other Fuels and Current Russian Gas Imports

The gas price that is equivalent to the international marker prices of fuels that incremental gas imports would need to displace varies among fuels and with the conversion efficiency, and hence will vary with the consuming sector/technology. Prices also will vary over time, particularly with movements in crude oil prices. Table 2 shows the values for liquefied petroleum gas (LPG) (using propane as a proxy), diesel, light fuel oil (solar), and heavy fuel oil (mazut) at six selected crude oil price points, using partial calculation from the netback methodology.

Gas price formulas typically have a base gas value on a particular date, which is then adjusted for movements in the prices of a basket of oil products, according to an agreed weighting of each fuel. The price ranges in the last column of table 2 reflect an estimate of typical price indexation formulas for long-term imports of gas from Russia, notionally for delivery of gas on the western Ukraine border near Uzhgorod. The second-last and third-last columns show the results of two supposed formulas: each assuming a base price of $87 per thousand cubic meters (Mcm) at the start of January 2000,

Table 2 Equivalent Gas Border Prices, Relative to International Marker Prices

Brent ($/bbl)	Petroleum products				Weighted[a]		Estimated Russian gas border price
	LPG	DSL	LFO	HFO	0:50:50	30:35:35	
Thermal efficiency (%)[b]	92	88	88	88	n.a.	n.a.	92
International Marker Prices ($/USgal)							
150	2.29	4.47	2.56	2.66	n.a.	n.a.	n.a.
125	1.93	3.72	2.15	2.23	n.a.	n.a.	n.a.
100	1.57	2.97	1.73	1.80	n.a.	n.a.	n.a.
75	1.21	2.22	1.31	1.37	n.a.	n.a.	n.a.
50	0.85	1.47	0.90	0.94	n.a.	n.a.	n.a.
25	0.49	0.72	0.48	0.51	n.a.	n.a.	n.a.
Equivalent natural gas prices[c] ($/Mcm)							
150	831	1,140	624	639	461	494	460~490
125	701	948	523	536	386	413	385~410
100	570	757	421	433	311	332	310~330
75	440	566	320	330	237	251	235~250
50	309	374	218	226	162	170	160~170
25	178	183	117	123	88	89	85~90

Source: Economic Consulting Associates' analysis, using information on gas prices in Southeast, Central, and Eastern Europe and data from the Energy Information Administration.
Note: ~ = approximate range; bbl = barrel; DSL = diesel; HFO = heavy fuel oil; LFO = light fuel oil; LPG = liquefied petroleum gas; Mcm = thousand cubic meters; n.a. = not applicable; USgal = U.S. gallon. Marker prices used are the Mont Belvieu, Texas, propane spot price free on board as a proxy for LPG; U.S. Gulf Coast No. 2 diesel; Amsterdam/Rotterdam/Antwerp 1.0% sulfur light fuel oil; and Singapore 3.5% sulfur heavy fuel oil.
a. The order of the weighting is diesel to light fuel oil to heavy fuel oil.
b. Efficiency of converting the fuel to heat at the burner tip.
c. These are the equivalent prices at the border, taking into account the net calorific values and typical combustion efficiencies of the various fuels at the burner tip.

but with different weightings of the indexed fuels. The estimated border prices are lower than the strict gas price equivalent of the indexed fuels because the competitive prices netted back from the burner tip also are affected by relative transport costs (and taxes) on both the gas and competing fuel sides of the market.

Shipping, transport, distribution, and local delivery, and excise and other taxes (or any subsidies) vary from market to markets for the fuels that gas would compete away and for gas. Table 3 shows the range of gas price estimates across the nine SEE markets that would be competitive with each fuel at the burner tip, using available data on local prices to arrive at estimates of local final fuel prices under the three oil price scenarios.

The lower part of table 3 shows the estimated competitive final gas price in each oil price scenario in each market, when weighted across the estimated prices of the various fuels in each market in each of the relevant oil price scenarios. Note that LPG is not included in the weighting. In most cases, its inclusion would increase the price. Conversely, the weighted price shown would be more than competitive with LPG in most of the markets.

Table 4 shows the margins for transmission, distribution, and supply (and any local taxes on gas). These margins have been calculated by subtracting the assumed border prices shown in the table from the competitive burner tip gas prices shown in table 2. It is notable that, although the values are dependent on the oil price, the range of values is considerably narrower than the factor of 6.0 across the range of oil prices and the factor of about 5.5 across the range of gas border prices.

The margins for fuel oil, particularly heavy fuel oil, are significantly lower than for the higher-grade fuels, following the expected pattern of margins being inversely related to volume. Many large prospective gas customers would be transmission connected and, therefore, would pay no distribution costs. Gas probably would need to compete on convenience and environmental benefits, rather than on price, to capture heavy fuel oil users with distribution-connected gas supply.

Projected Incremental Demand to Be Met by New Infrastructure

In addition to relative price considerations, the demand-side assessments have been made on the basis of the following factors:

- demographic and economic projections for each market
- comparison with gas consumption intensities in other (more economically developed) markets
- current consumption of fuels that gas could displace
- current and projected overall energy intensities in the target markets.

The present situation is one in which the SEE markets have very high energy intensities. Long-term energy growth in relation to GDP growth will be affected by the changing structure of production in the economies, more energy-efficient technologies being adopted and environmental

Table 3 Competitive Netback Prices at the Burner Tip, by Fuel and Market

Fuel/weight *(%)*	Sector	Brent *($/bbl)*					
		25	**50**	**75**	**100**	**125**	**150**
		Natural gas *($/Mcm)*					
Market price	Western Ukraine border	90	170	250	330	410	490

Range of burner tip prices for each fuel (max~min in 9 markets, rounded)

LPG (0)	Residential, some commercial	1,309 ~526	1,440 ~657	1,571 ~787	1,701 ~918	1,832 ~1,049	1,962 ~1,179
DSL (30)	Commercial, some industrial	889 ~665	1,081 ~857	1,272 ~1,048	1,463 ~1,239	1,655 ~1,431	1,846 ~1,622
LFO (35)	Industrial, some commercial	783 ~261	885 ~363	986 ~464	1,087 ~565	1,189 ~667	1,290 ~768
HFO (35)	Electricity, large industrial	290 ~105	393 ~208	496 ~312	599 ~415	703 ~518	806 ~621

Burner tip prices in each market, based on local fuel prices (weighted 30:35:35 by fuel, rounded)

Albania	All, weighted	360	490	620	750	880	1,010
Bosnia and Herzegovina	All, weighted	500	630	760	890	1,020	1,150
Bulgaria	All, weighted	490	620	750	880	1,000	1,130
Croatia	All, weighted	390	520	650	780	900	1,030
Kosovo	All, weighted	480	610	730	860	990	1,120
Macedonia, FYR	All, weighted	460	580	710	840	970	1,100
Montenegro	All, weighted	640	770	900	1,030	1,160	1,290
Romania	All, weighted	480	610	730	860	990	1,120
Serbia	All, weighted	480	610	730	860	990	1,120
Minimum	n.a.	360	490	620	750	880	1,010
Mid	n.a.	500	630	760	890	1,020	1,150
Maximum	n.a.	640	770	900	1,030	1,160	1,290

Source: Economic Consulting Associates' analysis, using information gathered on local fuel prices and taxes (with estimates where required).
Note: ~ = approximate range; bbl = barrel; DSL = diesel; HFO = heavy fuel oil; LFO = light fuel oil; LPG = liquefied petroleum gas; max = maximum; Mcm = thousand cubic meters; min = minimum; n.a. = not applicable.

Table 4   Margins for Transmission, Distribution, and Supply, Indicated by Netback Analysis

Market price	Western Ukraine border	Brent crude ($/bbl)					
		25	50	75	100	125	150
		Natural gas ($/Mcm)					
Weight	Sector	90	170	250	330	410	490
Transmission and distribution margin, by fuel							
(burner tip – border price, min~max in nine markets)							
Liquefied petroleum gas, 0%	Residential, some commercial	1,219 ~436	1,270 ~487	**1,321 ~537**	**1,371 ~588**	1,422 ~639	1,472 ~689
Diesel, 30%	Commercial, some industrial	799 ~575	911 ~687	**1,022 ~798**	**1,133 ~909**	1,245 ~1,021	1,356 ~1,132
Light fuel oil, 35%	Industrial, some commercial	693 ~171	715 ~193	**736 ~214**	**757 ~235**	779 ~257	800 ~278
Heavy fuel oil, 35%	Electricity, large industrial	200 ~15	223 ~38	**246 ~62**	**269 ~85**	293 ~108	316 ~131
Transmission and distribution margin, by country							
(burner tip – border price, weighted by fuel, rounded)							
Albania	All, weighted	270	320	**370**	**420**	470	520
Bosnia and Herzegovina	All, weighted	410	460	**510**	**560**	610	660
Bulgaria	All, weighted	400	450	**500**	**550**	590	640
Croatia	All, weighted	300	350	**400**	**450**	490	540
Kosovo	All, weighted	390	440	**480**	**530**	580	630
Macedonia, FYR	All, weighted	370	410	**460**	**510**	560	610
Montenegro	All, weighted	550	600	**650**	**700**	750	800
Romania	All, weighted	390	440	**480**	**530**	580	630
Serbia	All, weighted	390	440	**480**	**530**	580	630
Minimum		270	320	**370**	**420**	470	520
Midpoint		410	460	**510**	**560**	610	660
Maximum		550	600	**650**	**700**	750	800

Source: Economic Consulting Associates' analysis, using information on gas prices in Southeast Europe and Central and Eastern Europe and data from the Energy Information Administration.
Note: ~ = estimated range; bbl = barrel; Mcm = thousand cubic meters; Boldface type indicates the most likely scenarios; currently, the forward price curve is in this range, out to 2017.

considerations gaining more influence on fuel choices. The displacement of other fuels by gas is superimposed on this complex picture. Using 2005 as a base, projections of total demand have been made to 2025. These projections are shown in table 5, which is ordered by population size of the nine markets.

Table 5   Projected Demand and Supply Gap, 2005–25

Market	Total demand (Bcm)			2010–25 average annual growth[a] (%)	Supply gap (Bcm)		Main end-use sectors driving incremental demand (descending order)
	2005	2010	2025		2015	2025	
Romania	17.3	19.9	25.6	1.7	9.5	18.3	Residential, commercial, power
Bulgaria	3.2	3.9	6.3	3.2	1.5	3.1	Power, industry, residential
Serbia	2.5	2.7	3.6	1.9	0.5	1.2	Power, heating, residential
Croatia	2.7	3.6	4.2	1.0	0.6	2.0	Power, industry, residential
Bosnia and Herzegovina	0.3	0.6	1.4	6.1	0.6	1.1	Heating, industry
Macedonia FYR	0.1	0.7	1.2	3.8	0.7	1.1	Power, industry, residential
Albania	0.1	0.6	1.0	10.2	0.7	1.0	Power, industry, residential
Kosovo	...	0.1	0.9	15.5	0.3	0.9	Heating, transport
Montenegro	...	0.6	0.7	1.0	0.6	0.7	Power, industry
Total	26.2	32.8	45.0	2.6	15.0	29.4	Power, industry, residential

Source: Authors' compilation.
Note: ... = no gas available; Bcm = billion cubic meters. Supply gap is the supply (in 2015 and 2025) required relative to 2005, taking into account both demand growth and decline in gas production in markets where it is relevant.
a. The growth rate is based on the 15 years from 2010 to 2025 because 2010 is the earliest possible time for new gas developments and because growth rates cannot be calculated with reference to zero, which is the 2005 demand in some markets.

Figure 1 illustrates the buildup of demand in five-year intervals. The over-all picture is one in which the mature gas markets are projected to grow at relatively modest rates, while demand in the other cases grows rapidly from a low base as gas penetrates new markets. The overall weighted average annual rate of growth that emerges from the analysis is 2.6 percent, which suggests that the projections of growth prospects are on the conservative side. It is important to appreciate that the projected levels of demand are contingent on the investment in infrastructure necessary to deliver these incremental gas volumes to the markets, some of which have no gas infrastructure at present.

For the design of new supply systems, it is assumed that the new sources of gas imports would supply new demand, and that Russian and indigenous gas would continue to supply existing (2005) demand. Therefore, the incre-

Figure 1   Projected Gas Demand in Nine SEE Markets, 2005–25

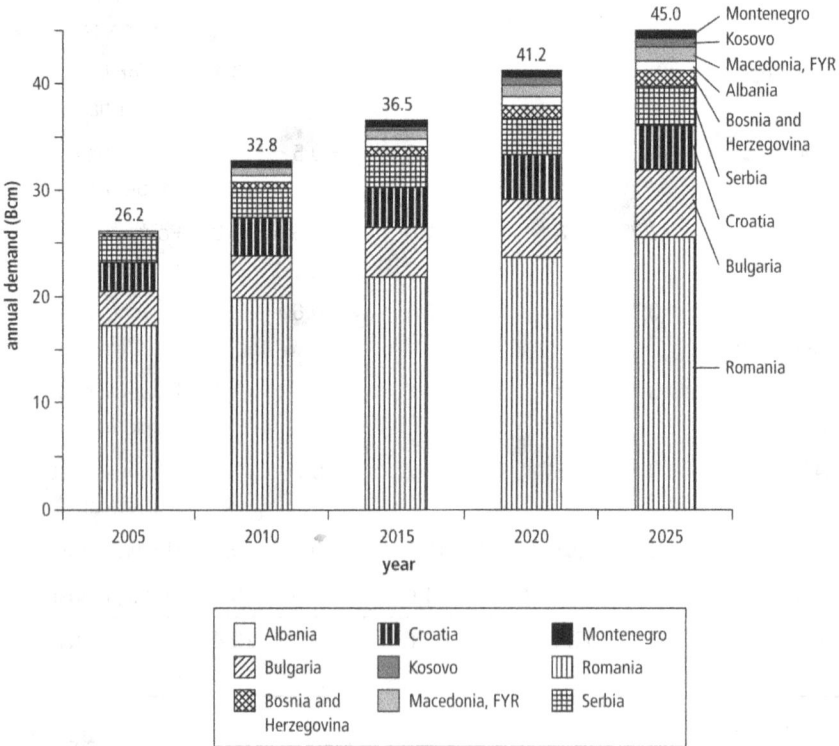

Source: Economic Consutling Associates' projections from country data.
Note: Bcm = billion cubic meters.

mental volumes that new imports would be required to serve are calculated as the projected growth in demand, relative to 2005, less any change in indigenous gas production. The resulting figures for 2025 are given in table 5, and the buildup in five-year intervals is illustrated in figure 2.

Demand Buildup and Anchor Loads

The rate of buildup of demand will be an important determinant of the viability of transmission line investments. As pipelines incur the major expenditure up front, rapid buildup of demand is required to cover the financing costs in the early years. It is typical that pipeline investment can go ahead when a significant share of the total volume can be guaranteed by a few large loads—"anchor loads."

Figure 2   Projected Supply Gap in Nine SEE Markets, 2005–25

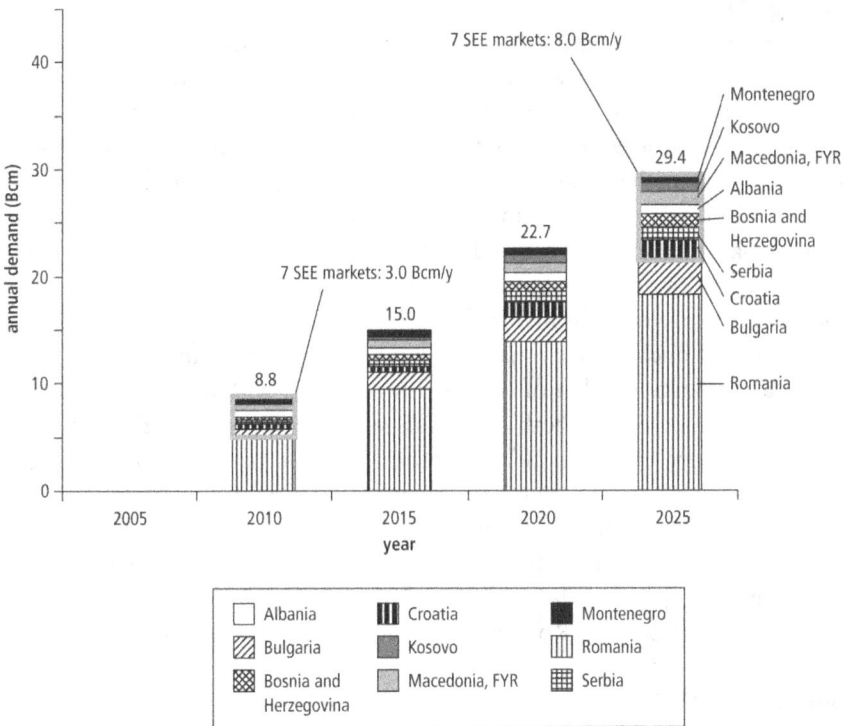

Source: Economic Consutling Associates' projections from country data.
Note: Bcm = billion cubic meters per year; SEE = Southesast Europe.

The demand projections that form the basis of the indicative pipeline designs have incorporated anchor projects in each market sufficient to ensure

- that there is enough up-front baseload to justify the main network investments early in the planning period
- that the transmission and distribution network achieves sufficient penetration into the region to give end users who should be using gas (on economic and/or environmental grounds) access to gas supply.

For the purpose of engineering designs and costing, anchor loads (predominantly, for power generation) equivalent to half of the projected 2025 demand are assumed to be in place so that their timing is coordianted with the availability of gas transmission. This timing is shown notionally as 2011; and the design is based on 2025 capacity requirements, with the other 50 percent of capacity being taken up progressively over the period 2011–25.

Storage Demand
The greatest demand for new storage capacity is expected to arise along with the growth in demand associated with gasification in the seven westernmost markets of Southeast Europe: Albania, Bosnia and Herzegovina, Croatia, Kosovo, FYR Macedonia, Montenegro, and Serbia. To the extent that it leads to the growth of residential and small commercial loads, further gasification in Bulgaria also will lead to increased demand for storage. Romania is a more mature market, already relatively well served by storage. The demand for storage is driven by seasonal swing and daily variability. Both of those factors are expected to be low in the early years, when demand is dominated by the initial anchor loads that will have a fairly flat load shape. In later years, as the large number of small loads builds up with the development of distribution networks, both seasonal swing and daily variability will increase. Figure 3 shows the expected long-term load-duration curve for Southeast Europe, which will drive the need for storage.

Storage capacity of 2.0–2.5 billion cubic meters (Bcm) should be sufficient to meet the needs of the seven markets of Southeast Europe that currently are not part of the European Union (EU). Additional capacity is required in Bulgaria and Romania, and much of it already exists.

Supply-Side Options
The supply-side analysis is concerned primarily with the options that may be available for connection to transmission pipeline infrastructure to enable increased volumes of gas to be delivered to the markets of Southeast Europe.

Figure 3 Expected Long-Term Load-Duration Curve in Southeast Europe

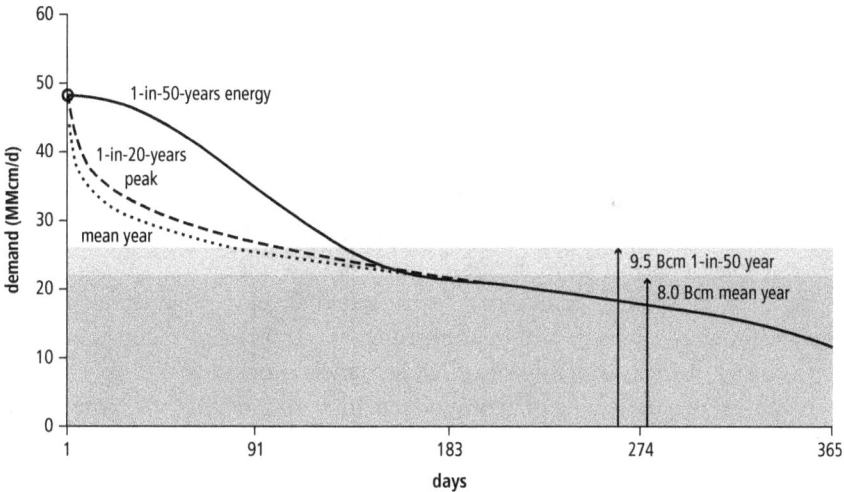

Source: Economic Consulting Associates' storage model.
Note: Bcm = billion cubic meters; MMcm/d = million cubic meters per day.

The full value chain back up to the producer countries is considered in the netback analysis of prices.

Objectives and Approach of the Supply-Side Analysis

The supply-side analysis seeks to determine the costs of meeting the projected incremental demand via spur lines from the major transmission systems that are planned to cross the SEE region. In addition, this study has proposed the concept of the EC Gas Transmission Ring, which would link any or all of the major import pipeline options. The analysis is complicated by uncertainty over which of these many transmission options will materialize; and by related uncertainty about the relative price of gas from Russia, the Caspian region, and other possible sources of supply.

Therefore, the supply-side options include a number of potential new, major import pipeline routes, as well as LNG imports and the branch transmission pipelines that will supply or interconnect each market. The branch transmission options will differ somewhat, depending on whether development is by the more traditional radial branches telescoped down toward the ends, or by constant-diameter pipelines to be connected to the EC Ring. The steps in the supply-side analysis are different for pipeline gas and LNG. These are the steps to compare pipeline sources:

- identify and analyze the gas import supply options—both sources and routes
- identify the network nodes that will form the supply price reference points for comparing alternate supply costs
- compare pipeline gas supply costs (principally Russian versus Caspian) to establish the potential competitive position of new sources
- make assumptions for pipeline design for the regional branch pipelines to supply each market from the major transmission lines
- perform economic analysis of each regional branch pipeline, taking account of the incremental investment costs, gas price at the offtake from the major transmission pipeline, and incremental demand
- compare alternative regional branch pipelines and identify the most promising options.

For potential LNG supply, these are the steps:

- identify alternate locations for an LNG regasification terminal to supply Southeast Europe
- examine the possible sources of supply and the costs of the LNG value chain to determine the costs of supply to Southeast Europe
- assess the international competition for LNG and the likely prices of LNG delivered to Southeast Europe
- evaluate the likely contribution of LNG to SEE markets and the possible projects.

Gas Pipeline Import Scenarios

The gas resources and main import pipeline routes to Southeast Europe are shown in map 1, highlighting the existing and future Russian and Caspian gas routes. Of the gas import scenarios considered in this study, the five scenarios of most immediate interest are

1. imports of Russian gas via existing routes
2. imports of Russian gas via new routes (for example, new onshore pipelines supplied via South Stream or Blue Stream II)
3. imports of Caspian gas via the trans-Adriatic pipeline and/or the Ionian-Adriatic pipeline
4. imports of Caspian and other gas from various sources via Nabucco
5. imports of Caspian or Russian gas via the Italy-Greece Interconnector, which is part of the larger Turkey-Greece-Italy project.

Map 1 Gas Sources of Interest to the Nine SEE Markets

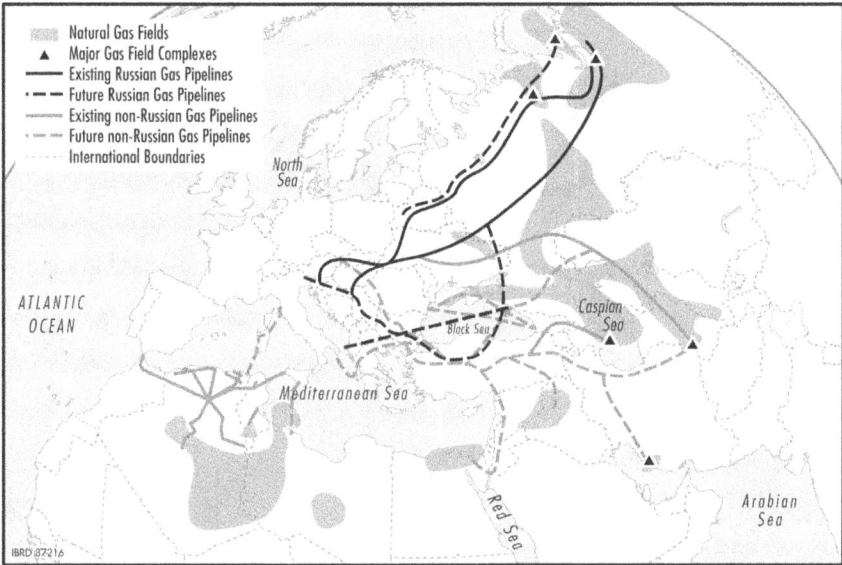

Sources: World Bank, compiled with reference to GIE, WinGas, and other published pipeline maps.

The new routes are highlighted in map 2. The Georgia-Ukraine-EU (or White Stream) proposed pipeline would deliver Caspian gas into the Romanian system or into the Ukrainian transmission system, which then could deliver gas to Southeast Europe via the same transit routes followed by Russian gas through the Ukraine.

South Stream would deliver Russian gas across the Black Sea to Bulgaria and then into Central Europe (the Nord option), Baumgarten, northern Italy or southern Italy (the Sud option), or some combination of those destinations.

LNG Supply Options

There is a possibility that some of the gas supplies for increased gasification in Southeast Europe could come from LNG, rather than all the needed gas supplies coming from Russia or the Caspian.

Perhaps a third of the additional gas supply needed for SEE region could come from LNG, although this would make it a relatively small LNG project by international standards. Whether LNG actually will supply this need depends on many factors, including pricing, the prospects of transmission access to existing available receiving terminal capacity in the early years,

Map 2 Potential New Pipeline Routes

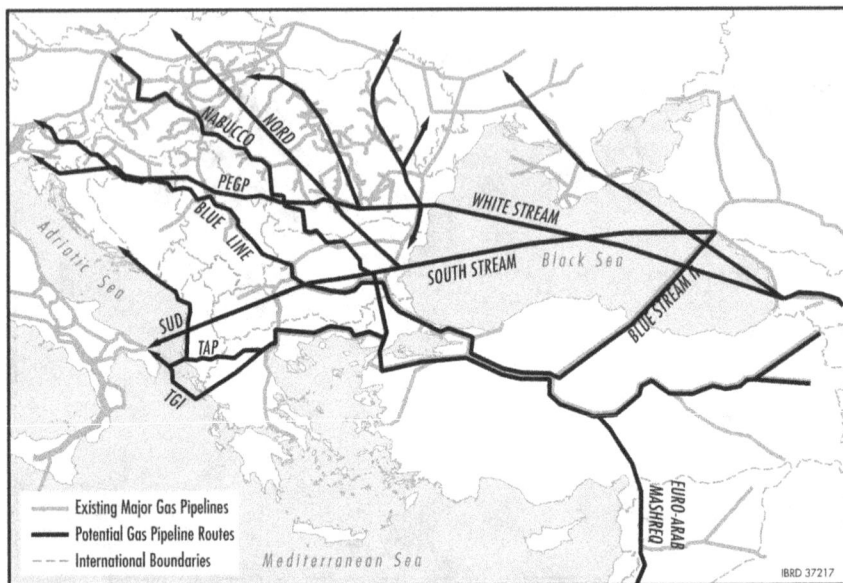

Sources: World Bank, compiled from pipeline companies' published information and with reference to GIE, WinGas, and other published pipeline maps.

political will, resources to enable a new terminal to be built, and the credit-worthiness of the gas buyers.

A key issue for Southeast Europe is that the potential volumes are relatively small in each of the countries, so flows would need to be aggregated to provide an anchor load to support the financing of a regasification terminal. That could make an LNG project more difficult to achieve.

Worldwide, total gas volumes delivered via LNG are much smaller than volumes delivered via the pipelines. However, the global LNG market continues to grow rapidly, at around 7 percent a year. Because LNG markets worldwide increasingly are influenced by the ability of LNG to be delivered over long distances—either to Japan and other markets in East Asia, to Europe, or to the United States—there is increasing price convergence among international markets. Historically, the price of LNG in both the Pacific and Atlantic markets has been linked to oil prices. Now the direct link is more to pipeline gas, but both prices are correlated strongly with oil prices.

LNG is characterized by very high fixed costs, and it is extremely capital intensive. Long-term contracts are required to secure financing for LNG projects.[1] Costs are related to the size of projects (smaller projects are more costly). However, the distance-related component of the cost of transport would help offset the economic disadvantage of small volumes in Southeast Europe, bearing in mind that the most likely supply sources would be nearby North African and Middle East producers. The costs of the supply chain for delivering LNG (on top of the wellhead price of the gas) are expected to be on the order of $85/Mcm.

However, LNG suppliers might not find it as attractive to import LNG into Southeast Europe if they can achieve higher netback prices elsewhere (in East Asia and the United States, for example). If a higher market risk is perceived in Southeast Europe, it might make development of the SEE LNG market more difficult—or, at least, the LNG price might not be lower than for other LNG importers.[2]

In either case, unless Southeast Europe is prepared to pay a small premium to gain geographical diversity of gas supplies, the price of LNG into the region is likely to be capped by the price of local pipeline gas. This is could make LNG sales into Southeast Europe unattractive, relative to sales elsewhere in the world where pipeline gas prices may be higher.

Finding a location for an LNG terminal also presents difficulties. An LNG terminal is a large, industrial facility located on the coastline. There were objections on environmental grounds to the original proposal for an LNG terminal on the Island of Krk in Croatia. The revived proposal by the Adria LNG consortium has not yet obtained government approval, and environmental impact assessments of five potential sites in Croatia have been commissioned by the Croatian government.

In selecting the site for an LNG terminal, the geology and topography of the area must be studied to ensure a sound geographical base over which the plant foundations can be built. The concerns relating to LNG terminals relate to the assessment of risk of explosion or fire resulting from a catastrophic engineering failure or from terrorist action. Even though these risks are low, developers generally seek locations well away from sensitive activities and populations.

The Black Sea coast of Bulgaria and Romania is considered effectively off limits to the development of LNG receiving terminals because LNG tankers would be unable to receive permission to navigate the Bosporus.

---

[1] In general, an LNG project requires simultaneous financing of the whole supply chain: the liquefaction terminal, tankers, and the regasification terminal facilities.

[2] In the period just before oil prices spiraled upward in 2005, two landmark LNG deals were concluded for the sale of LNG to China and to India, at very low prices. However, this low "new entry" price is unlikely to be offered to a small market like Southeast Europe.

Existing LNG terminals nearest to the Adriatic are ENI's Panigaglia terminal near Genoa (3.3 Bcm/y) and the Revithoussa terminal near Athens in Greece. The Revithoussa terminal's send-out capacity currently is being expanded with a third storage tank, after which the site is understood to have no room for subsequent expansion. Two terminals on the Italian side of the Adriatic are expected to begin operations in 2008.

The possibility of developing other nearby terminals, especially in northern Italy, would present a competitive threat to the development of a new LNG terminal in Southeast Europe. Such terminals might compete away both supplies and the market for regasified gas, thereby prejudicing the commercial viability of a new SEE terminal. The competitive threat is particularly evident at the proposed new Adria terminal in Croatia, which is close to an existing terminal in northern Italy—particularly if the costs of developing a greenfield LNG receiving terminal in Southeast Europe are higher than installing a second train at an existing site, such as Porto Levante.

However, the existing LNG receiving terminal at Revithoussa is largely unutilized. The unused capacity there could present a threat to a new LNG receiving terminal in Southeast Europe, if gas could be delivered from it to the region. Turning the threat around, it becomes an economic and commercial opportunity for Southeast Europe: there is no need to incur the cost and risk of developing an LNG terminal in Southeast Europe in the short- to medium-term if SEE markets can access existing spare terminal capacity.

It should be possible for SEE markets to access 2.0–2.5 Bcm of capacity for power station anchor demand in the 2010–15 period by backhauling LNG from Revithoussa against the prevailing north-to-south flow in the Greek system.

Based on the review of LNG options, the most promising options are these:

- contract for LNG deliveries to Revithoussa in Greece to use its available capacity to meet demand in the southern markets in Southeast Europe (possibly by backhauling)
- backhaul LNG from terminals in northern Italy into the northern markets of Southeast Europe, particularly Croatia
- contract for a share of LNG delivered to the Krk Island Adria LNG terminal, if its development goes ahead.

However, the delivered price of LNG is not expected to be below the cost of pipeline gas, and it is more likely to be at a slight price premium.

Key Transmission Network Nodes
For simplicity's sake, imported gas arriving in Southeast Europe via alternate transport routes can be assumed to enter through a number of key nodal

points. Map 3 shows the following key nodes for gas import prices on the international gas transmission system:

- Baumgarten, Austria, near the border with the Slovak Republic
- three import/transit points near Uzhgorod, Ukraine, to
  - Velke Kapusany, on the border with the Slovak Republic
  - Beregdarock on the border with Hungary
  - Mediesu Aurit, on the border with Romania.

Also indicated are the following four existing import points to the nine SEE markets for Russian gas:

- Rogatec, on the Slovenia-Croatia border
- Kiskundorozsma, on the Hungary-Serbia border
- Mediesu Aurit, on the Ukraine-Romania border
- Isaccea, on the Ukraine-Romania border.

Map 3   Key Existing and Potential Transmission Network Nodes for Southeast Europe

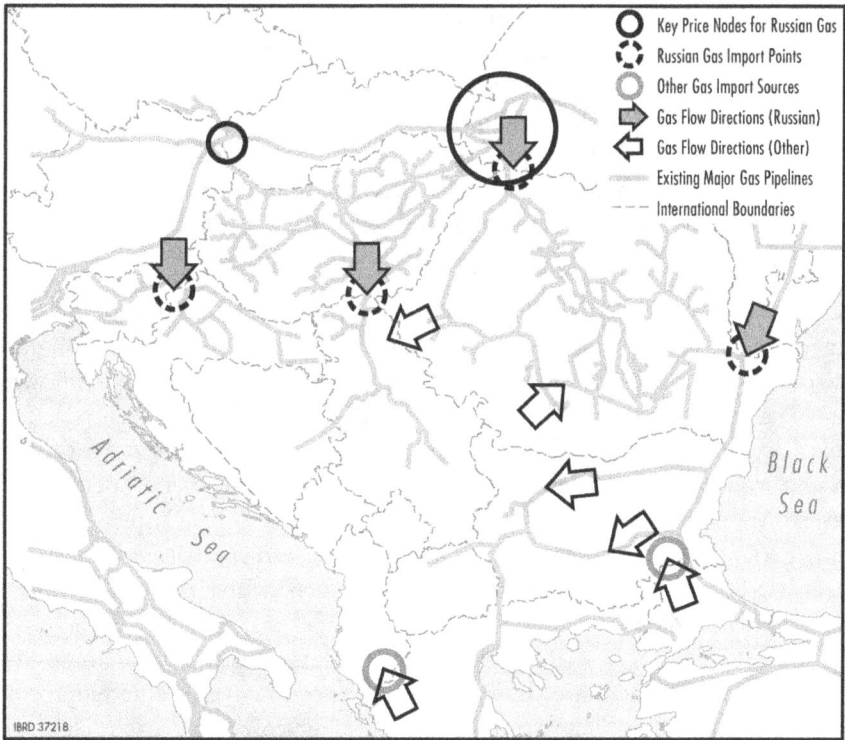

Sources: World Bank, compiled with reference to GIE, WinGas, and other published pipeline maps.

The potential future import point near Malkoclar, on the Turkey-Bulgaria border, for Caspian Sea gas delivered via Nabucco is indicated; and there is an approximate point on the Greece-Albania border for imports of either Caspian or Russian gas via the Italy-Greece Interconnector or the trans-Adriatic pipeline. Branching flows from Nabucco to or through Bulgaria and Romania also are indicated in the map.

Distribution Economics

The estimates from the 20 case study cities show that costs vary inversely with population, as expected. The three largest cities—Tirana, Pristina, and Skopje—would have the lowest estimated distribution costs: around $25/Mcm. The smallest town—Horezu, Romania—would have the highest distribution cost: almost $500/Mcm (which is not likely to be economic). Costs for most of the cities are between $65/Mcm and $110/Mcm. Transmission would add $26/Mcm. All of these values are based on discounting 20 years of projected volumes building up linearly from zero to the long-run demand over 10 years, at a discount rate of 10 percent a year. These results suggest that there is sufficient margin for most distribution costs around these levels, although the transmission and distribution costs in a number of cities exceed the margin for heavy fuel oil; transmission-connected heavy fuel oil customers, however, could switch to gas in some cities.

Although changing the buildup to 15 years and discounting just 15 years of revenues at 15 percent a year would more than double the transmission and distribution charges necessary to recover the investment, the margins appear large enough for this in many cities (based on the modeling of upstream prices and the available data on local fuel prices).

Comparison of the Upstream Value Chain for Russian and Caspian Gas

In considering the gasification of Southeast Europe, availability of gas resources is not a major issue in the medium term because there are known large-scale gas reserves in the vast arc from Russia, through Central Asia and the Caspian region, to the Middle East and North Africa. (North Africa has the shortest shipping distances for LNG supply to Southeast Europe.) However, one important issue in this study is the extent to which Caspian gas and other sources can compete with gas from Russia and can penetrate the SEE market. This issue may have price benefits as well as diversity and security-of-supply advantages.

In the Caspian region, the main field Shah Deniz is rich in condensates. It is estimated that there are sufficient condensates to cover the development costs of the field and that the marginal economic cost of the gas is close to zero or even may be negative, depending on the oil price after netting off the value of condensates. A comparison of the upstream value chain for Russian gas and Caspian gas thus indicates that Caspian gas delivered via the Nabucco pipeline is likely to be highly competitive with Russian gas. This indicates that the future gas price at the key transmission node near Ankara. Turkey, well may be set by Caspian rather than Russian gas.[3]

This economic advantage will not necessarily translate into significantly lower import prices for importers in the nine SEE markets because the competing importers may need to undercut Russian gas and other fuel prices by only a small margin to gain a competitive advantage.[4] The advantage, however, does suggest that gas should be in a strong position to displace petroleum products in the nine SEE markets, even if low oil prices prevail, because gas prices should be able to follow oil prices downward and still be profitable for the producers.

Assumptions and Approach to Regional Pipeline Design

The next step in the analysis is to cost the possible spur lines from the main transmission routes or the EC Ring. The design capacities of the regional branch pipelines are based on estimated daily peak flows corresponding to the projected annual volume in 2025, with the assumption of a 65 percent annual load factor. This assumption was arrived at from the following approximate estimation approach:

- half of the annual volume would be consumed by electricity generation (power) and industrial customers, with an annual load factor of 80 percent
- half of the annual volume would be consumed by commercial and residential customers, predominantly in the winter (that is, with a strong seasonal swing), with an annual load factor of 50 percent.

The worst-case (most conservative) assumption for the power and industrial load is that it has a seasonal peak that coincides with the commercial and residential seasonal peak. For an 80 percent load factor, this means the average summer demand would be about two thirds of the average winter demand.

Seasonal fluctuations could be catered for by developing underground storage at the downstream end. At a 65 percent annual load factor, the pipeline is considered to have reached capacity when it hits its limit in the winter; but this leaves about half again as much spare capacity in the summer. Underground annual storage at the downstream end of a pipeline

---

[3] It is believed that the first deliveries of Azeri gas via the South Caucasus pipeline to Turkey undercut the price of Russian gas delivered to Turkey via Blue Stream and via Bulgaria.

[4] Consideration of security-of-supply issues indicates that some markets might be prepared to pay even a little more for non-Russian gas to obtain the security-of-supply diversification.

(or connected anywhere to the EC Ring) would allow this capacity to be used. The capacity benefit would occur on all pipeline segments upstream of the underground storage.

The decision to invest in underground storage would depend on the economics of the storage facility in question, compared with the economics of building an additional pipeline. The pipeline designs and engineering cost estimates do not allow for storage options, although it should be noted that seasonal storage may be able to meet the winter-summer demand swing at a lower economic cost than would be incurred in purchasing flexibility on supply contracts, as well as the incremental transmission capacity upstream of the underground storage facility.

Economics of Regional Branch Transmission Lines

The economics of regional branch transmission lines requires that we consider two main factors:

1. incremental transmission costs to deliver gas to the SEE markets
2. gas price at the offtake point from the major transmission pipeline.

Comparing the incremental transmission costs to each city or node on the regional branch transmission pipelines from Nabucco versus the onshore extensions of Blue Stream II (Blue Line) shows differences in transmission costs, mainly in the range of $5/Mcm to $20/Mcm, mostly in favor of the latter option. These two routes would follow generally similar alignments upstream of the nine SEE markets, through Bulgaria and Turkey, as far as a point just east of Ankara where the route of the pipeline from the Blue Stream outlet would converge with the route of the Nabucco pipeline from Erzurum.

In view of the conclusion that Caspian gas probably will be the price setter for gas at the key node near Ankara, Turkey, the indication is that the relatively small transmission cost advantage of the Blue Line is likely to be eclipsed by the gas price advantage of Caspian gas into Nabucco. The priority branches thus are assumed to emanate from Nabucco rather than from the Blue Line, despite the latter tending to have slightly lower costs for the transmission investments alone.

Practicalities: Phased Development of the EC Ring

The EC Ring concept, shown in map 4, was developed by overlaying the branch pipelines that would arise from each separate major import transmission pipeline, and observing that together they would form a ring connecting seven of the nongasified or less-gasified SEE markets. The EC Ring would be a major infrastructure project: the estimated capital cost is almost $ 1 billion. However, it would not necessarily need to be developed all at one time.

Map 4   Concept of the Energy Community Gas Ring in the Regional Context

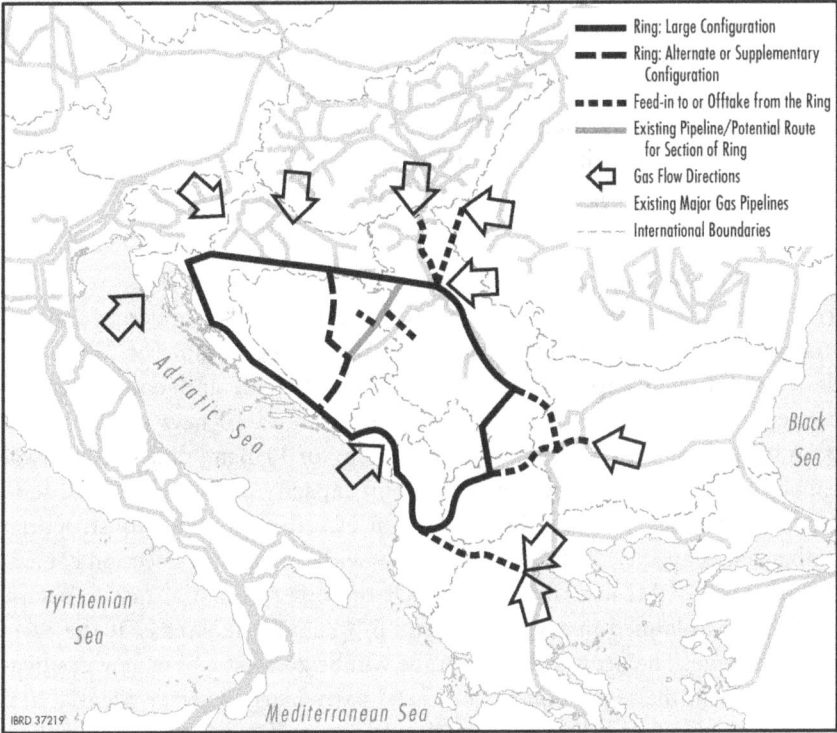

Sources: World Bank, compiled with reference to GIE, WinGas, and other published pipeline maps.

The EC Ring concept is suitable for incremental development. Under such an approach, the first stages would be developed to bring gas to new power stations in currently nongasified areas on the Adriatic coast. Those power plants, in turn, would anchor the economics and bankability of the transmission investment. Next, additional sections of the ring would be developed, gasifying new areas, connecting new entry points, and increasing the diversity of supply options and technical and commercial security of supply. Finally, the entire ring would be completed and begin delivering all of the benefits unique to a ring configuration—especially the increase of capacity (for the same, existing diameter) with each new injection point.

The potential exists for the Ionian-Adriatic Pipeline infrastructure to form the western side of the EC Ring (Albania-Montenegro-Croatia). Connection possibilities would be Greece-Albania, Greece- FYR Macedonia-Albania, or Bulgaria-FYR Macedonia-Albania, with gas supplied into Southeast Europe from the southeast.

The potential also exists for new pipeline infrastructure along the Bulgaria-Serbia-Croatia corridor to form the western part of the EC Ring, linking with the Adriatic coastal corridor in northern Croatia. The northern and southern sides of the ring then could be developed, strengthening supply to the Bosnian market and bringing supply to the Kosovan market.

Two of the key advantages of the EC Ring as a vision for SEE regional gas development are that it does not need to be developed all at one time and that there is significant scope for flexibility in both specific alignments and in the timing.

Regional Underground Gas Storage

The nine markets in Southeast Europe have 10 existing underground gas storage (UGS) facilities. They offer a total working volume of 3.78 Bcm, daily withdrawal capacity in excess of 12 MMcm, and daily injection capacity of about 10 MMcm. Four expansion and 10 new projects have been identified, with a total working capacity of 11 Bcm, daily withdrawal capacity of 46 MMcm, and daily injection capacity of roughly 29 MMcm. Of these facilities, just one (Banatski Dvor in Serbia) is under construction, with a final capacity of 0.8 Bcm and daily withdrawal and injection capacities of 9 and 7 MMcm, respectively. Of the other potential new capacity, 3.56 Bcm is planned in seven sites, and 6.7 Bcm at six sites is at the early concept stage. The need for new storage will be greatest where new gasification occurs in the seven non-EU markets, particularly when residential and commercial loads build up with the development of distribution networks.

The study identified six promising sites. In approximate descending order of likely commercial development and attractiveness from a regional perspective, they are

- Banatski Dvor, a depleted gas field in Serbia
- Benicanci, a depleted oil field redevelopment in Croatia
- Tuzla-Tetima, working salt mines in Bosnia and Herzegovina
- Dumrea, an undeveloped salt formation in Albania
- Okoli, a depleted oil field UGS expansion site in Croatia
- Divjaka, a depleted gas field in Albania.

Map 5 shows the 10 existing and numerous potential UGS sites in the nine SEE markets, relative to the position of existing and potential transmission infrastructure. The existing facilities have a total working capacity of 3.78 Bcm. Most of this (3.20 Bcm) is in Romania, with a small amount in Bulgaria; the remaining 0.58 Bcm is at one facility in Croatia. Banatski Dvor in Serbia soon will have working capacity as it is filled with cushion and working gas over the coming years.

Map 5   Existing and Potential UGS Sites in Southeast Europe

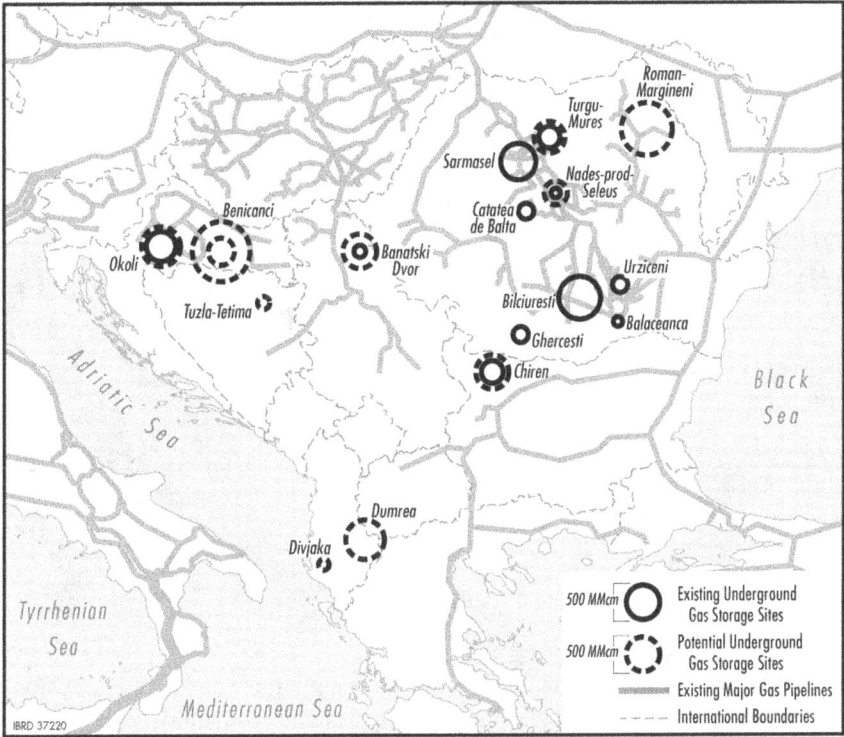

Sources: World Bank, compiled with reference to GIE, WinGas, and other published pipeline maps.
Note: UGS = underground gas storage.

Economic analysis based on engineering cost estimates showed that, from a regional perspective, the economically preferred UGS facilities in Southeast Europe are Banatski Dvor, Benicanci, and Dumrea. In the long run, these sites would provide well over 2 Bcm of working gas storage capacity, which would be sufficient for the expected requirements of the seven non-EU gas markets in Southeast Europe over the period until 2025. Table 6 summarizes the key results of the economic cost analysis for these UGS facilities.

In assessing alternatives to UGS—including customer interruption, building larger-diameter transmission pipelines to use the additional line-pack for storage, using LNG for seasonal and peak supply, and contracting for increased flexibility—we found that all options had estimated opportunity costs higher than the estimated costs of underground storage under reasonable assumptions and for the provision of comparable balancing services.

Table 6   Preferred Near- and Medium-Term UGS Options in Western Southeast Europe

Factor	Banatski Dvor	Benicanci	Dumrea	Total
Geological type	Field	Field	Salt formation	n.a.
Capital cost ($ million, discounted at 10% per annum)	142	116	102	360
Capacity (MMcm)	800	500	1,120	2,420
Withdrawal rate (MMcm/d)	9.0	6.2	6.0	21.2
Capacity cost ($/Mcm)	74	83	82	n.a.
Number of cycles per year	1.25	1.25	2.00	n.a.
Volume cost ($/Mcm)	77	84	60	n.a.

Source: Economic Consulting Associates' storage model, using underground gas storage engineering cost estimates that are based on data from national experts.
Note: Mcm = thousand cubic meters; MMcm = million cubic meters; n.a. = not applicable; UGS = underground gas storage.

Figure 4 shows the demand outlook and supply options for regional storage in Southeast Europe (not including Bulgaira and Romania), with the preferred options from table 6 overlaid. The large capacity variant of Dumrea development suitable for regional storage and transit services is shown.

Further analysis revealed that the use of alternative or secondary backup fuels in industry and power stations is likely to be more attractive than underground storage, particularly for low-frequency use on the coldest days and where these backup facilities need to be maintained anyway. Dispatching gas-fired plants in a counterseasonal manner when distribution loads build up also is likely to be economically attractive. These options cannot be expected to have sufficient potential to replace the need for UGS capacity in Southeast Europe, but their potential to reduce the amount of UGS capacity required in there should be explored thoroughly.

Interactions with Western European Gas Markets

Production in Western Europe was just over 265 Bcm in 2006, leaving an import requirement of just under 160 Bcm. If Western Europe's gas production declines as expected, and demand grows as expected, the import requirement will open up to about 250 Bcm by 2010, to over 450 Bcm by

Figure 4 Storage Demand Outlook and Supply Options in Non-EU Southeast Europe

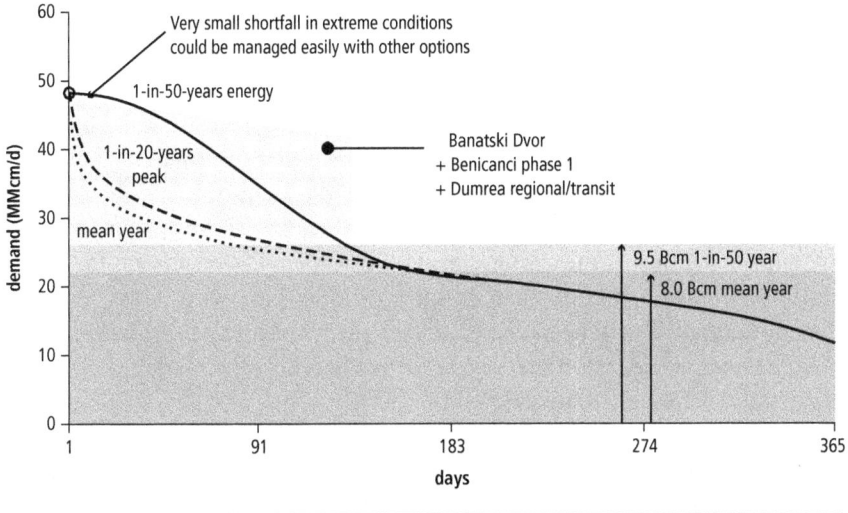

Source: Economic Consulting Associates' storage model.
Note: EU = European Union; MMcm/d = million cubic meters per day.

2020, and to roughly 600 Bcm by 2030. A less-rapid decline in Western European indigenous production and/or slower demand growth would result in a smaller import requirement.

Regardless of the precise outcome, it seems clear that Western Europe will be looking to all of the gas sources in the vast arc sweeping from the North Sea to the Russian Arctic, through western Siberia to the trans-Caspian states, the Caspian Sea, and the Middle East (including the Islamic Republic of Iran and Iraq), through Egypt, across North Africa, and down to West Africa in an effort to meet its future import requirements. Both new pipelines and LNG developments will be required to close the supply gap.

The Baumgarten gas-trading hub in Austria will become increasingly important for price formation in Southeast Europe. The price of Nabucco offtake to Southeast Europe would be expected to be the Baumgarten price, minus the cost of the transmission distance saved from Baumgarten back to the SEE offtake point, plus the cost of transmission from that point to the region. LNG backhauled from Krk Island also may be traded at Baumgarten.

But the Italian gas market is expected to exert an equally strong or stronger influence on price formation in the SEE markets. Italy currently imports gas from the North Sea via the Switzerland-Italy border, from Russia via the trans-Austria pipeline to the Austria-Italy border, from Algeria via the trans-Mediterranean pipeline, and from Libya via the Green Stream pipeline to Sicily. In the future, Italy is expected to import additional gas from Qatar via LNG to the Rovigo terminal; from the Caspian Sea (and/or Russia) via Turkey; through the Greece-Italy Poseidon pipeline from Algeria via Sardinia and landed on Italy's western coast; and from other North African countries (possibly including Egypt) and perhaps West African countries (such as Nigeria) via LNG to proposed terminals around the coast.

This means that, at the margin, physical flows of gas from sources in all five supply regions of the vast arc around Europe will be entering Italy: the North Sea, Russia, the Caspian Sea, the Middle East, and North Africa.[5] Therefore, they all will be expected to face the same price in the Italian market. The price terms in long-term contracts will reflect the market conditions at the time the prices are negotiated.

That principle would be expected to apply to both piped gas and LNG, and it suggests that Italy's virtual hub for gas trading—the Punto di Scambio Virtuale—is likely to emerge as a key location in Europe, as the LNG and European gas markets mature and trading becomes more liquid. Therefore, price netbacks from Italy and the SEE markets to a common point on the common upstream supply route should be equal. This effect is expected to be particularly strong for the seven westernmost SEE markets, but also will be relevant for Bulgaria and Romania.

Institutional Framework and Implementation Issues

Chapter 4 of the report addresses a problem for complex regional gas infrastructure projects: they often are difficult to bring to fruition, even when they have very strong economic fundamentals and are considered strategically important. Three key areas are identified to bring cross-border gas projects to fruition:

1. **National gas market**— The markets involved should have well-developed gas policies and stable, predictable regulatory frameworks.
2. **Cross-border framework**—Harmonized mechanisms for investment in and operation of cross-border gas pipeline projects should be in place.
3. **Financing**—A strategy to minimize and/or mitigate financing risks should be available.

---

[5] The number of sources would increase to six, including West Africa, if Nigerian LNG were sold into the Italian market in the future, as it has been in the past. As table 3.30 will show, Turkey was the only European or Mediterranean market that bought Nigerian LNG in 2006.

In Southeast Europe, addressing these three requirements is a vigorous, ongoing process. With the support of the EC Secretariat and other institutions, such as the European Regulator's Group for Electricity and Gas, a great deal has been achieved already, but much remains to be done.

National Gas Markets
To facilitate rapid growth of the gas sector, individual markets need to provide a stable and predictable environment that encourages investment in the sector. Conditions conducive to business for the gas sector will be met best by implementing the requirements of European Union Gas Directive 2003/55/EC. Members of the Energy Community committed themselves to compliance with the Gas Directive within one year of accession to the Energy Community Treaty. In practice, the requirements of the directive are difficult to meet; and the process has been extended over a longer period. Table 7 indicates progress in different dimensions in each market. As of late 2008, the overall level of implementation was about 50 percent, up from about 30 percent 18 months earlier, indicating steady progress.

The list of provisions covered in the table is as follows:

- third-party access
- monitoring of security of supply
- unbundling provisions and access to accounts
- technical rules
- public service obligation and customer protection
- market opening
- new infrastructure and exemptions
- cross-border trade mechanism.

Cross-Border Framework
The challenges to be met in the cross-border environment are harmonization of operations (access, allocation, interoperability, transparency, balancing, gas storage, LNG, and so forth) and agreement on cross-border investment issues (such as tariffs, open-season procedures, regulatory requirements, and a standardized approach to exemptions from third-party access requirements). The EC's New Gas Infrastructure Investment Regulation (NGIIR), currently under discussion, addresses these issues.

Building on the experience of successful cross-border pipeline projects elsewhere, the starting point of the NGIIR is recognizing the need for a

Table 7 Progress on Implementation of EC Treaty Provisions in the Nine SEE Markets, Late 2008

Market	Third-party access	Security of supply	Unbundling provisions and access to accounts	Technical rules	Public service obligations and consumer protection	Market opening	New infrastructure and exemptions	Cross-border trade mechanism	Progress (%)
EC markets already in the EU and currently served by gas:									
Bulgaria	■	■	■	■	○	○	◆	●	70
Romania	■	■	○	■	○	■	■	●	80
EC markets currently served by gas:									
Croatia	■	■	■	■	■	■	■	◆	90
Serbia	■	■	○	■	○	■	●	●	65
EC markets with limited gas import and capacity:									
Bosnia and Herzegovina	●	●	●	●	●	●	●	●	0
Macedonia, FYR	○	◆	◆	◆	◆	◆	◆	●	33
EC markets currently without any gas infrastructure:									
Albania	○	○	○	◆	○	◆	○	●	50
Kosovo	○	◆	○	◆	○	◆	■	●	50
Montenegro	●	●	●	●	●	●	●	●	0
Progress (%)	65	60	55	55	55	55	55	0	50

Source: Analysis by Economic Consulting Associates, using data from the Energy Community Secretariat, presented in Ljubljana, Slovenia, on October 10, 2008.
Note: ● = getting started; ◆ = some provisions available; ○ = some provisions missing; ■ = all provisions available; EC = Energy Community; EU = European Union.

seamless cross-border operational regime. The NGIIR approach is grounded on two key concepts:

1. The transmission project operator (TPO) is to be the single transmission system operator responsible for negotiating, implementing, and operating an international pipeline project.
2. The TPO is to offer a one-stop-shop facility so that shippers of gas need deal with only one entity, with the assurance that there will be uniform operational arrangements despite the fact that the gas may be transported over several different legal jurisdictions.

The central concerns of the NGIIR revolve around third-party access and capacity allocation. The default regulatory regime is one in which a third-party access exemption has not been granted. Rules for the regulated third-party access regime are provided in an annex to the NGIIR. These rules establish a harmonized framework for contractual relationships, entry/exit regimes, tariff setting, firm capacity, backhauling, open-season requirements, nomination procedures, congestion management, prevention of capacity hoarding (including the use-it-or-lose-it principle), and interoperability.

In practice, all new cross-border investment projects (such as the Balgzand-Bacton Line) have required a waiver from the third-party access requirements. Another NGIIR annex provides regulations for exemptions. This annex constitutes guidelines to standardize the approach by which EC members apply the provision of the Gas Directive that allows for exemptions (that is, Article 22).

Underground Gas Storage
The main issues with which regulators will be concerned with respect to UGS are its efficient development and use, nondiscriminatory access, the need for a regional perspective, transparency, and publication of operational data. The Gas Directive has a number of requirements regarding UGS. It allows a degree of regulatory discretion with respect to regulated versus market-based approaches to storage. Because not all markets have geological potential for UGS development, there must be a regional approach to storage. Such an approach will enable storage to be developed and used in the most economically efficient way, and hence will allow the most attractive commercial returns to reward investors' risk in undertaking storage development. It is likely that a market-based approach to storage will be more suitable for Southeast Europe than will a regulated approach. Under either approach, the cross-border framework will be particularly important to

allow regional access to storage because some SEE markets have neither UGS facilities nor identified geological potential for new ones.

Under a market-based approach, any investor would be free to develop potential storage sites and to set the price of storage, according to market supply and demand, via published, nondiscriminatory tariffs. Doing so still would require a set of rules to be implemented that were not only consistent with the provisions of the Gas Directive embodied in the EC Treaty, but also consistent across the EC in their operational details.

The alternative approach would be for regulators to decide when and which storage facilities could be built and to set regulated prices for storage services. This would be less likely to result in economically efficient outcomes. Considering that the region is characterized by many small and developing markets—some with no known storage potential—this approach would require an extremely high degree of coordination among regulators in all of the interconnected markets of Southeast Europe. Such coordination almost certainly would be much more complex than would a market-based approach.

Strategic storage has been discussed between EU member-states, but there are no obligations in the Gas Directive or the EC Treaty to establish strategic gas storage for security-of-supply purposes. It is up to the governments in individual markets whether to follow Hungary and Italy in doing so.

In Hungary, annual gas demand is about 15.0 Bcm. There is 1.2 Bcm of underground storage capacity (equivalent to about 8 percent of annual gas demand) mandated by Hungarian Act #26 of 2006 ("on strategic storage of natural gas") to hold strategic gas reserves under development by the company MMBF (for completion in 2010). Until recently, the total UGS capacity was 3.50 Bcm; but by 2010, it will be 5.85 Bcm. MMBF is 62 percent owned by MOL and 38 percent owned by the Hungarian Hydrocarbon Stockpiling Association. The legal obligation to hold strategic gas reserves rests with the members of the Hungarian Hydrocarbon Stockpiling Association, and the costs of doing so are passed through to consumers, via the tariff structure. The association has a long-term service agreement with MMBF (a special-purpose vehicle, established by MOL, in which the association now has a minority share) to hold the strategic gas reserves on its behalf. The strategic storage contract was won by MOL after a competitive tendering process in which E.ON Földgáz storage (the owner of all other underground storage in Hungary) was the only other bidder.

In Italy, annual gas demand is about 80 Bcm. There is a storage capacity of 5.1 Bcm (equivalent to about 6 percent of annual demand) for holding strategic reserves, out of a total storage capacity of 13.6 Bcm (Carnevalini 2008). There are regulated tariffs for storage used by gas producers; for strategic storage; and for peak, daily, and seasonal modulation. Italy is a major gas importer with limited indigenous production, but it benefits from diverse supply sources and routes. This diversity brings Italy into contrast with Hungary, which increasingly is import dependent on a single source (Russia) and a single route (via Ukraine).

Financing of Regional Gas Investments

Regional gas investments, whether in transmission pipelines or LNG facilities, are highly capital intensive. In the past, such investments were undertaken by the public sector, either through direct investments from the state budget or through budgetary subventions and/or sovereign guarantees to support the investment programs of state enterprises. Increasingly, governments are seeking to reduce demands on the national budget by financing infrastructure through structured project finance, involvement of the private sector, and support of external agencies through equity provision and/or risk mitigation.

In the context of the developments envisaged in this report, the involvement of the private sector is much less likely in the case of the major transmission investments, including the EC Ring, than it is in the upstream power plant investments needed to provide the gas anchor loads and the downstream distribution investments to provide access for retail customers. For this, regulatory systems that grant concession licenses with built-in financial incentives to invest in the distribution network and connect new customers at an agreed rate over time are needed.

The principal requirements for financial closure of large infrastructure projects are these:

- **Good project design**—The project must be designed to match supply with demand in an efficient and cost-effective manner. Tariffs should be cost reflective; and projected revenues should be adequate to cover all costs, including financing requirements.
- **Properly structured contractual framework**—Commercial risk, particularly volume risk, is of particular concern for gas projects. Requiring offtakers to commit to take-or-pay contracts is one of the basic ways to reduce this risk. In the case of regional projects, a complex set of interlocking contractual arrangements is likely to be necessary, as illustrated by the recently commissioned South Caucasus pipeline. The leading offtake candidates for take-or-pay contracts are electricity generators, who almost certainly would require take-or-pay electricity contracts for their output. Even with independent power producers as the gas offtakers, the creditworthiness and general financial health of the power sector (indicated by such metrics as energy billed and bills collected) will be very

important. This is recognized as an area with room for improvement in some of the SEE markets.

- **Predictable gas sector regulatory environment**—a coherent framework for the gas sector must be in place to ensure that tariffs and operating conditions are predictable. As table 7 shows, significant work remains to be done on this in some SEE markets, particularly those with no gas industry at present (Albania, Kosovo, and Montenegro) or with limited gas imports and capacity (Bosnia and Herzegovina and FYR Macedonia).
- **For a regional gas project, a TPO must be in place**—Having a TPO with a one-stop-shop mandate enhances the transparency and predictability of arrangements from the viewpoint of investors and financiers. However, incremental development of the EC Ring is likely to involve multiple project operators.
- **Legal recourse in the event of disputes**—If there is a breach of contract, it is important that agreed dispute resolution procedures and mechanisms are in place.
- **Risk mitigation instruments in place**—Most of the main project risks would be catered for if all of the above requirements were met in full. In practice, significant remaining elements of risk (as well as others not yet alluded to) can be ameliorated to some degree by risk mitigation instruments (RMIs).

Including RMIs in the negotiations is often a crucial step in reaching financial closure. Risks can be considered to fall into two broad categories, political risks and commercial risks. There are two types of project participants seeking RMIs: equity investors (project sponsors, exposed to investment risk) and the providers of loans (debt holders, exposed to credit risk).

Multilateral development institutions, such as the World Bank, KfW Entwicklungsbank, and other international financial institutions, often are willing to provide risk coverage for large infrastructure projects. Bilateral agencies and private institutions also offer RMIs on varying terms and with differing eligibility criteria. Recent cross-border gas pipeline projects that demonstrate that financial closure can be reached when there are RMIs in place are the Southern Africa Regional Gas Pipeline and the West African Gas Pipeline. In Southeast Europe, compliance with the EC regulatory framework is likely to ease the way to obtaining RMIs as part of the financing package for gas infrastructure.

Implementation of the EC Ring
This study has identified benefits for SEE countries from intensifying regional cooperation in a mix of projects that range from relatively modest

bilateral projects to reinforce existing or to build new transmission lines to ambitious proposals for the EC Ring. On the face of it, the rational approach would be to schedule projects so as to move progressively toward completing the ring. However, from the viewpoint of accelerating SEE gasification, the earlier the ring is in place, the better. This is because the EC Ring would link currently nongasified areas with mature gas markets, facilitating supply diversity and providing favorable prospects for security of supply (among other means, by providing access to regional underground storage facilities). The EC Ring would foster regional cooperation by promoting constructive interdependence among seven markets of the region.

For this reason, it is relevant to consider what will be required to implement a project of the size and complexity of the proposed EC Ring. Having seven markets involved is important in terms of maximizing the benefits; but from an institutional viewpoint, the number of countries greatly increases the challenges of structuring and financing the project. Moving to the multicountry EC Ring project strengthens the case for urgent attention to be given to aligning national gas markets with EU norms and the case for harmonizing operational and third-party access waiver procedures in cross-border contexts.

The key starting point for defining the cross-border framework, identifying a TPO, and negotiating financing for the EC Ring is to establish an institutional structure for the project. One option would involve seven or more partners having equal shares in an EC Ring holding company, with wholly owned individual subsidiary companies in each of the participating markets. The holding company would offer a one-stop-shop for the ring's users, and would be responsible for engineering designs and project financing; the subsidiary companies would construct, own, and maintain the infrastructure within their own territories.

Conclusions and Key Findings

The SEE markets are small in terms of current and future gas consumption. This makes the prospect of developing and financing infrastructure for new gas consumption in the region more challenging. The city distribution case studies have shown that expansion of distribution generally will be economic in current conditions, provided the gas can be brought into the region at reasonable cost.

Increased gasification requires large up-front investments in transmission infrastructure to bring the gas to the markets concerned. Conversely, up-front investment in transmission infrastructure requires creditworthy offtakers with a sufficiently large quantity of demand (that is, anchor loads) immediately after the construction is completed to make the investment al and bankable.

One solution is to coordinate parallel, up-front investments in gas-fired power stations to come online at the same time. When the transmission infrastructure is in place, distribution investment can follow, building the smaller loads on top of the power generation anchor load.

Modestly increased use of gas in the power sector is likely to be economic in the SEE region (and would be sufficient to provide the anchor loads for new transmission investment); but the quantity of gas-fired power generation is highly sensitive to the future gas price, especially compared with the price of coal/lignite. This study uses the gas price and power development scenarios included in the *Development of Power Generation in Southeast Europe: Update of Generation Investment Study, Final Report* (SEE 2007) to estimate the amount of gas demand there could be from the power sector.

In reality, development of gas-fired power generation is very unlikely to follow the economically optimal plant construction sequence precisely. To make the gas investments viable in the first place, one key finding is that some of the gas-fired generation capacity scheduled for later years would need to be brought forward (and some non-gas-fired plants correspondingly slipped backward in the schedule) to provide a minimum of 2.0–2.5 Bcm of anchor demand from the first year of operation of the new gas transmission infrastructure.

To achieve this, governments in each market would need to develop a policy for gas distribution in advance of the development of the transmission infrastructure so that investors are prepared for the development of distribution networks without delay, when the gas is available on the transmission system.

The EC Ring concept provides a vision for such development. It would deliver a large number of benefits, including these:

- establishing strong regional cooperation based around the principles of the Stability Pact, the EC, and the Energy Charter Treaty
- enabling the pipeline infrastructure to be sized just large enough to deliver gas to the initial anchor loads (along a linear configuration, prior to completion of the ring)
- allowing flexibility in the development of major proposed pipeline projects and LNG options, with imports of gas from various sources
- enabling markets with no known or with limited geological possibilities for developing UGS to access storage services in neighboring markets
- enhancing both diversity and technical security of supply
- allowing incremental development of transmission capacity with each additional injection point, as and when required.

Distribution networks can be developed when the regional transmission infrastructure is in place, anchored by power station loads. Buildup of the many small loads on distribution networks will increase both the seasonal swing on the gas system and the peak response to low temperatures. Therefore, serving distribution demand will require the development of UGS. Because of the quite long lead times required for developing some of the potential storage sites identified in the region—especially for leaching salt caverns—it will be particularly important for good coordination of storage development with distribution development as part of regional gasification. The World Bank, KfW Entwicklungsbank, and other international financial institutions could play an important role in this effort. The analysis suggests that 2.0–2.5 Bcm of capacity will be needed in the seven markets of the region not currently part of the EU. A decision to set aside storage capacity for strategic reserves for use in the case of supply interruption would further increase the storage capacity required.

The EC Treaty provides the blueprint for implementing the institutional and regulatory framework in each market. Such implementation would be expected to be a prerequisite to qualify for international financial institution and donor funding of new gas infrastructure and commercial financing. There are roles for both private and public investors within the main investment areas of gas transmission, power plants, and gas distribution. Leveraging private sector financing in those parts of the system where the private sector is best able to contribute will enable scarce public sector financing, together with donor support, to be focused on the remaining areas—especially on major transmission investments and projects with a regional dimension.

1.

INTRODUCTION

This document is the *Draft Final Report* for the Southeast Europe Regional Gasification Study. The World Bank and KfW Entwicklungsbank, joint managers of the study, appointed a consulting team, led by Economic Consulting Associates (ECA) of the United Kingdom.[1] The World Bank, KfW, the Energy Sector Management Assistance Program (ESMAP), and the Public-Private Infrastructure Advisory Facility (PPIAF) provided funding.

The study examines sources of gas supply from the Russian Federation, the Caspian region, and other producer countries through Turkey and other transit routes; and assesses costs of supply and gasification prospects in these nine gas markets in the Southeast Europe (SEE) region:

- Albania
- Bosnia and Herzegovina
- Bulgaria
- Croatia
- Kosovo[2]
- the former Yugoslav Republic of Macedonia

---

[1] This study was conducted in two phases. The World Bank and KfW jointly managed and funded Phase 1, and additional funding was provided by ESMAP and PPIAF. Phase 2 was overseen solely by the World Bank, with funding from ESMAP and PPIAF. The Phase 1 tasks, first presented in the April 2007 *Interim Report,* were completed in parallel with the Phase 2 tasks, so KfW was involved throughout the course of the study.

[2] Kosovo currently is under the administration of the United Nations Interim Administration Mission in Kosovo (UNMIK), according to the terms of UN Security Resolution 1244 of June 1999. The Special Representative of the UN Secretary General has signed the Energy Community of Southeast Europe Treaty on behalf of UNMIK.

- Montenegro
- Romania
- Serbia

ECA managed the consultants' team and carried out the economic analyses and integration of the results. The study team included Penspen of the United Kingdom, which was responsible for the pipeline engineering analyses and city distribution case studies; the Energy Institute of Croatia; and a team of local consultants for the nine gas markets.

This *Draft Final Report* presents the study's conclusions, building on the preliminary findings presented in the *Interim Report* submitted in April 2007, which followed the September 2006 *Inception Report*. It was circulated to representatives of the nine SEE markets and other participants for discussion at the Gas Forum held at Maribor, Slovenia, on November 9, 2007. Following feedback received from discussion at the forum, revisions agreed by the World Bank and KfW were included in the *Final Report*.

Study Background and Objectives

Recognizing the potential benefits from increased gas competition, and as part of a wider movement to deepen regional integration, Albania, Bulgaria, Bosnia and Herzegovina, Croatia, FYR Macedonia, Montenegro, Romania, Serbia, and the United Nations Interim Administration Mission in Kosovo agreed to develop a regional gas market. The agreement was reached through the Athens Process and the 2002 and 2003 Athens memoranda of understanding; and it culminated in the Treaty establishing the Energy Community,[3] which was signed by the European Union (EU) and nine contracting parties in Athens on October 25, 2005. The treaty recalls "the contribution of the Stability Pact for South East Europe that has as its core the need to strengthen co-operation amongst the states and nations of South East Europe and to foster the conditions for peace, stability, and economic growth."

Through the treaty, the contracting parties resolve to establish an integrated market in natural gas and electricity, based on common interest and solidarity. The formal mechanism for the establishment of the integrated market is the adoption of the requirements of EU Gas Directive 2003/55/EC and Electricity Directive 2003/54/EC.[4]

---

[3] Available at http://www.energy-community.org/pls/portal/docs/36298.PDF.

[4] Within the EU internal market, the 2003 directives have been superseded by the 2009 directives as part of the Third Energy Package. A decision of the Council of Ministers from the Energy Community contracting parties will be required before adoption of the new directives becomes the basis for the regional market in Southeast Europe.

Currently, the level of gasification in Southeast Europe is relatively low, with combined gas demand from Albania, Bosnia and Herzegovina, FYR Macedonia, and Serbia at less than 1 billion cubic meter per year. Gas supply comes from Russia, either directly from Gazprom or through intermediaries. Increased gas competition, resulting in increased volumes traded at lower prices, would support increased gasification in Southeast Europe. There is scope for increased competition, given the possibility that Caspian and Middle East gas could be imported to the region.

Turkey currently imports pipeline gas from Russia and Iran and liquefied natural gas (LNG) from Algeria and Nigeria; it will import from Azerbaijan and later (possibly) from Turkmenistan. Over time, scope is expected for significant exports of gas from Azerbaijan, Central Asia, the Islamic Republic of Iran, Iraq, and Egypt through Turkey to Southeast and Western Europe. A number of projects are being developed to support westward exports from gas sources that would be new for Europe. Given the geography of the region, it is possible that SEE countries could benefit from these projects, through either offtake of gas or transit fees (or through both). The focus of the present study was to assess the scope for increased gasification in Southeast Europe, based on the scope for gas market development in the region.

Background

Two of the key initial drivers for the study were concern for the security of the region's gas supply and interest in examining the prospects for gas supplies that would serve as alternatives to those from Russia (particularly Caspian gas). A further major interest was in finding ways to develop the gas sector in markets that had little or no current use of gas because they lacked the needed infrastructure. The study implicitly recognized that a regional perspective on gas development is necessary because of the very-large-scale investments needed to bring gas into the region through large-capacity pipelines.

Under the auspices of the Stability Pact for Southeast Europe, an EU initiative with Southeast Europe, the governments of the nine markets plus Greece and Turkey signed the 2002 Athens Memorandum. By signing, they agreed to adopt EU Directive 2003/54/EC (the Electricity Directive) and to set up a structure to monitor the operation of the electricity market. In 2003, the signatories to the memorandum decided to extend this approach to natural gas in the framework of Directive 2003/55/EC. For that reason, another Memorandum of Understanding, covering natural gas as well as electricity, was signed in Athens in 2003. This memorandum recognized the potential benefits of increased cooperation in gas market development and gas competition, and of being part of a wider movement to deepen regional integration.

On October 25, 2005, a treaty establishing the Energy Community (EC) was signed by the governments of Albania, Bosnia and Herzegovina, Bulgaria, Croatia, FYR Macedonia, Montenegro, Romania, Serbia, and the Special Representative of the Secretary General on behalf of UNMIK. Within the treaty establishing the EC, an Energy Community Secretariat (ECSec) was set up, an entity mainly responsible for seeing that the signatories properly fulfilled their treaty obligations and for reviewing and assisting the European Commission in its effort to coordinate the activities of donors, the Ministerial Council, the Permanent High Level Group, the Regulatory Board, and the Fora. The ECSec has been set up in Vienna, Austria.

The governments responsible for the nine markets therefore have taken a formal step toward the full integration of their energy markets into the EU energy market. Potential transit routes for gas from the Caspian Sea region (and in the future, possibly from other sources south of Turkey) pass through Southeast Europe. The prospect of these gas deliveries extending to Western Europe creates a further potential for increased gasification of the SEE markets.

Beyond the large regional gas import projects requiring major transmission lines crossing one or more countries, there are clear needs for investment in cross-border branch transmission pipelines, for relief of transmission bottlenecks, for new transmission network connections in SEE countries, and for seasonal storage to meet peak (winter) demands as economically as possible. The government in each of the markets is likely to perceive the potential benefits of coordinated action to reduce cost at the regional level. Using as a basis the specific demand and supply analyses for each of the SEE markets, the study indicates the transmission developments that will facilitate gasification and organic growth within the existing network and that may require additional infrastructure development in some countries.

Instead of serving simply as a collection of individual country analyses, the study itself takes a regional perspective. It indicates how each country could "piggyback" its gas development on existing and future regional gas transmission pipeline developments. The study involves scoping out transmission system expansions rather than detailed studies, which would require a full and comprehensive model of the network. (A full least-cost gas system expansion study for each country is beyond the scope of the present work). In this respect, it is worth noting that a least-cost or most-economic *regional* pipeline development may be very different from the least-cost gas pipeline development and supply option for each SEE market viewed individually.

Objectives

The overall objective of the study for the World Bank and KfW is to assess the scope for increased gasification in Southeast Europe, based on the scope for gas market development in the region. The study also analyzes and makes proposals for institutional and policy issues relating to funding and implementing gas infrastructure projects.

ECA was contracted to conduct the study in two phases. According to the terms of reference, the study aims to

- assess the economics of increased SEE gasification based on Russian gas
- assess the economics of increased SEE gasification based on pipelines linking Turkey with Western Europe
- consider the economics of increased SEE gasification through increased LNG imports
- outline reform steps that would support increased gasification in Southeast Europe.

A further part of Phase 1 is to identify opportunities for gas distribution investments in the nine SEE markets, taking account of the current and potential sources and costs of gas supply.[5] Specifically, this study assesses the economics of gasification in 20 cities in the region.

The full list of study tasks in both phases is presented in table 1.1.

Study Methodology and Approach to Analysis

The very broad geographical and temporal scope of the study, extending upstream to the countries producing and supplying the gas and downstream to the neighboring Western European markets, limits the extent to which it would be practicable to apply comprehensive system modeling or to carry out optimal system expansion analyses. The study instead has adopted a scenario analysis approach.

Scenario Analysis Approach

The core of the scenario approach to assessing the economic prospects for regional gasification includes the following main efforts:

- Develop demand scenarios for each market, taking into account the economic trends, current fuel use, and relative competitiveness of gas.

---

[5] Although full-scale distribution investment study in each market is not part of the present investigation, this study does include a more limited examination of the opportunities through a small number of typical case studies focusing on sample cities in each of the nine markets.

Table 1.1 Study Tasks, Phase 1 and Phase 2

Task/phase	Description of task
Task 1, Phase 1	Provide long-term SEE gas demand forecasts
Task 2, Phase 1	Provide a perspective on the economics of SEE gasification, based on gas supply from Russia
Task 3, Phase 1	Provide a perspective on the cost of new gas pipelines linking Turkey with SEE and Western Europe
Task 4, Phase 1	Provide a perspective on the economics of new gas transmission pipelines
Task 5, Phase 2	Provide a perspective on the economics of SEE gasification, based on increased LNG imports
Task 6, Phase 1	Provide a perspective on the gas price at the Turkish border
Task 7, Phase 2	Provide a perspective on the relationship between SEE gasification and Western European gas markets
Task 8, Phase 1	Provide an overview of the economics of SEE gasification, based on Caspian gas
Task 9, Phase 2	Review the institutional framework for SEE gas market development
Phase 2	Provide additional short reports summarizing the analysis and findings for each market.

Source: Authors' compilation.
Note: LNG = liquefied natural gas; SEE = Southeast Europe.

- Make wholesale gas price projections at key reference points in the regional transmission pipeline system.
- Make wholesale gas price projections for each border entry point (from each supply country and transit route) into the SEE region.
- Identify the pipeline options for each market, based on the alternative major regional import and transmission pipelines, and assess the most promising option(s).
- Estimate the transport costs from the border to each of the nine markets and the relevant offtake points (for example, the case study cities).
- Estimate the cost of gas distribution network development and the delivered cost of gas to typical consumer categories.

- Assess the competitiveness of gas, compared with alternative fuels, to final consumers; and evaluate the consequent prospects for gasification (noting the links among the nine markets related to alternative regional transmission development options).

The analysis is described separately for each of the two main components of the study—the demand side and the supply side—but there is considerable iteration between these two components.

Demand-Side Analysis

Chapter 2 presents projections of potential gas demand in the nine SEE markets for the purpose of developing notional transmission pipeline designs that could deliver gas to the region. Ideally, estimates of potential future gas consumption would be based on current and projected consumption of the main competing fuels--in turn, developed from reliable data on the historical consumption of those fuels and on economic indexes. Unfortunately, such data are unavailable, unreliable, or incomplete in many of the SEE markets. In some cases, particularly in the former Yugoslavia, war severely affected fuel consumption in the 1990s; therefore, historical data do not provide a reliable basis for projecting future consumption.

Given the limited information that is available, estimates of potential future gas demand in the SEE region have been developed from three sets of factors:

- demographic and economic projections for each market
- comparisons with gas consumption intensities in other (more economically developed) markets, with a view to the medium- to long-term development of the SEE economies and gas sector
- current consumption of fuels that gas could displace
- current and projected overall energy intensities in the target markets.

The main gas consumption sectors considered are the power sector and industrial and domestic gas demand. The prices of fuels with which gas would compete in each market, taxes and subsidies, and the assumptions adopted about future fuel prices also are discussed in the context of determining the competitive position of gas and the likelihood that it will penetrate various consumption sectors. Appendix A develops a detailed analysis of the costs of Russian gas supply.

Supply-Side Analysis

The demand in the nine SEE markets is not sufficiently large by itself to attract investment in dedicated long-distance transmission pipelines to supply gas all the way from the wellhead, particularly for new developments.

Therefore, the focus of the method used to evaluate the supply-side options is on the development of pipeline branches from major transmission pipeline projects proposed to pass through or near the nine SEE markets.

The method for analyzing the supply options considers notional regional transmission pipelines that would be required to supply the SEE markets by branching from each major transmission pipeline project.

The method for calculating engineering costs for proposed pipelines is set out in appendix C. The economics of gas supply to the nine SEE markets were developed through the following steps:

- Adopt projections of potential gas demand to 2025 in each market and deduct indigenous production and existing supply[6] to arrive at the incremental supply required to meet the projected demand to 2025, as described in chapter 2.
- Develop notional branch pipeline routes, with distances distinguished according to whether the terrain is easy or hard for laying pipeline.
- Calculate from the annual volumes the daily peak flows in 2025 for the relevant SEE markets along each notional route into and through each market and, hence, calculate the design capacities required for each new pipeline.
- Calculate the diameters and compression required for the specified design capacity of each pipeline route.
- Estimate the capital expenditure required in each case, based on pipeline route lengths, terrain, required sizes, and system facilities (compression, metering and regulation, and pressure reduction stations).
- Assume a profile for the annual demand buildup over the years to 2025.
- Discount the annual volumes associated with that demand buildup.
- Calculate the levelized economic cost for each transmission segment.
- Calculate the levelized economic transmission cost, by market.

Overview of the Work Program and Report Content

As already noted, the complete work program originally set out in the terms of reference was split into two phases for contractual purposes.

This draft final report presents the following information:

- demand-side assessments for the nine SEE markets (chapter 2), including
  - an overview of the economies in the region as a backdrop to the factors driving growth in potential demand for gas, including a summary of

---

[6] It is assumed for the purposes of this analysis that supply from existing sources delivered via existing infrastructure (although almost certainly not contracted out to 2025) will have incumbent economic advantages over new sources requiring the development of new infrastructure.

the energy sector in the region, the current fuel mix, and a discussion of the region's gas sector
- projections of potential gas demand, indigenous production, and import contracts to define incremental gas import requirements
- a discussion of future fuel price scenarios
- an analysis of prices from the demand-side perspective, applying a simplified netback pricing analysis from the costs of using those fuels with which gas would be expected to compete
- supply-side options (chapter 3), covering
  - an analysis of prices from the supply-side perspective, including typical formulas in existing long-term Russian gas contracts and a discussion of the gas prices at the borders of the nine SEE markets
  - a discussion of potential gas sources and supply routes to the SEE markets
  - a review of LNG markets and the potential for LNG supply to Southeast Europe
  - a description of current and possible future transmission supply routes and scenarios
  - a description and economic analysis of the EC Gas Ring—the recommended regional transmission infrastructure for the seven westernmost markets in Southeast Europe[7]
  - a review of the economics of distribution networks, based on a case study analysis of 20 cities in the nine SEE markets
  - an analysis of the gas value chain
  - a discussion of interactions to be expected between SEE and Western European gas markets
  - the implications of the supply analysis for each SEE market
- institutional framework and implementation issues, (chapter 4), including
  - a discussion of the institutional framework for the SEE gas market, based on the EC treaty
  - a presentation of existing regional initiatives
  - lessons from international examples
  - the requirements of each country's gas market
  - a discussion of the cross-border framework
  - a discussion of ideas for financing regional gas investments
- conclusions and key findings (chapter 5).

---

[7] Appendix C describes the pipeline costing methodology, including engineering estimates of the unit capital costs of transmission pipeline and facilities investments. Appendix D includes an indication of the most promising regional transmission branches, taking into account the estimated cost of regional transmission branches and the costs at the offtake point on the major transmission pipeline implied by market prices and the value chain upstream of the offtake point.

2.

DEMAND-SIDE ASSESSMENTS

The demand-side assessment covers the following three main steps:

1. examining the breakeven price for gas to compete with alternate fuels in the main sectors, using netback pricing analysis, and comparing the competitiveness of new supply sources (such as Caspian gas) with gas from the Russian Federation
2. developing a scenario of potential gas demand growth in each market, contingent on
   a. development of the gas transmission supply pipelines
   b. competitiveness of gas delivered to the market, in relation to other fuels
3. assessing the incremental demand that could be met by new gas supply and the buildup of demand.

To provide the background to development of the growth scenario, this chapter starts with a brief overview of the macroeconomic context and the current gas sector activity and structure in each of the nine markets.

Background: The Economic and Energy Sector Contexts
A brief review of the economies in Southeast Europe is provided, before a consideration of the energy sector in the region.

Overview of the Regional Economies
The tables presented in this section give some of the basic data used in the calculations and a summary of our estimates of current and projected demand for natural gas in the Southeast Europe (SEE) region. The tables are based on studies of each of the markets.

The tables are arranged in descending order by the size of the urban population and the degree of urbanization. As shown in table 2.1, the largest market in terms of population is Romania (21.8 million people) and the smallest is Montenegro (0.6 million). The total population of the nine markets is 55 million, roughly equivalent to the population of France, Italy, or the United Kingdom. It is unfortunate that the definition of "urban" is from national sources, so there is no assurance of uniformity or cross-country comparability of the urban population and percentage figures given in the table. With that caveat, it appears that the most urbanized markets are Bulgaria and FYR Macedonia; and the least urbanized are Kosovo, Albania, and Bosnia and Herzegovina.

In 2004, the total GDP of the region was about $180 billion,[1] with the four largest economies accounting for 86 percent of the total. Croatia has the highest per capita income, followed by Romania, Montenegro, Bulgaria, and FYR Macedonia. On a purchasing power parity basis, which is intended to overcome variations in purchasing power due to different price levels, Montenegro's per capita ranking falls and those of Bosnia and Herzegovina and FYR Macedonia rise.

The final column of table 2.1 gives the projected average GDP growth rate for 2005–07. The weighted average is 5.2 percent per year. The countries that are expected to grow faster than this average are Croatia, Serbia, Bulgaria, and Bosnia and Herzegovina. For a long-term study of this type, these immediate prospects well may be overtaken in due course by underlying growth rates that could be quite different in magnitude. This applies in particular to Kosovo, where the present low level of GDP growth (2.9 percent) should be replaced by rapid postconflict recovery when its future status and its economic policies are more certain.

Overview of the Energy Sector in the Region

The energy intensity indicators in table 2.2 record that the larger, more industrial economies of Romania, Serbia, and Bulgaria have very high levels of energy intensity, this level being defined as significantly higher than the corresponding figure for the United States. Energy intensity in the region is likely to change in complex ways in the short- to medium-term as the structure of economies shifts and energy efficiency/climate change initiatives are adopted. The pattern in the industrial countries has been for energy intensity to increase as industrialization deepened, with this tendency reversed as heavy industries were replaced or surpassed by high value added, low energy service activities. Starting from a typical position of highly energy-inefficient

---

[1] A billion is 1,000 millions.

Table 2.1 Basic Demographic and Economic Data for the Nine Markets, 2004

Market	Total population (million)	Urban population (million/ percent of total)	GDP ($ billion)	GDP per capita ($)	Annual GDP growth (%)
Romania	21.8	11.9/54	73.2	3,358	5.0
Bulgaria	7.8	5.4/70	24.1	3,090	5.5
Serbia	9.9	5.3/54	22.5	2,273	5.6
Croatia	4.5	2.5/56	34.3	7,622	5.7
Bosnia and Herzegovina	3.9	1.8/45	8.5	2,179	5.5
Macedonia, FYR	2.0	1.4/68	5.4	2,700	4.0
Albania	3.1	1.4/45	7.6	2,452	5.2
Kosovo	2.0	0.8/40	1.6	800	2.9
Montenegro	0.6	0.3/54	1.9	3,167	4.0
Total (weighted average)	55.1	30.9/55	179.1	3,221	5.2

Sources: UNDP 2006, indicator tables 1, 5, and 14; supplemented with International Monetary Fund (IMF) and World Bank data for Kosovo, Montenegro, and Serbia. GDP growth figures are IMF data and projections for 2005ENNN07.
Note: Differing national definitions of "urban" apply, so cross-country comparisons should be made with caution.

electricity and industrial production systems, this process is likely to be accelerated in transition economies.

The energy intensity indicators are based on the main commercial fuels—gas, oil, coal, and liquefied petroleum gas (LPG)—and exclude traditional fuels such as firewood. The countries where gas contributes significantly are Romania, Croatia, Serbia, and Bulgaria (all of which produce gas), with minor contributions from gas in Bosnia and Herzegovina and in FYR Macedonia. Oil and coal rank next in importance as primary energy sources in the region as a whole, with the ordering of gas, oil, and coal as the three major sources varying across different countries.

Table 2.2 provides the names of the regulatory agencies in the nine markets. Agencies with formal responsibility for gas have been established in

Table 2.2   Energy Profiles of the Nine Markets, 2004

Market	Energy intensity ($ GDP)	Main fuel sources[a]	Gas production (Bcm/y)	Gas regulator
Romania	Very high	Gas, oil, coal	11.60	Natural Gas Regulatory Authority
Bulgaria	Very high	Oil, gas, coal	0.30	State Energy and Water Regulatory Commission
Serbia	Very high	Gas, oil, coal	0.35	Energy Agency of the Republic of Serbia
Croatia	High	Gas, coal, oil	1.57	Croatian Energy Regulatory Agency
Bosnia and Herzegovina	High	Gas, coal, oil	0	Gas sector, but no gas regulator[b]
Macedonia, FYR	Very high	Oil, coal, LPG, gas	0	Energy Regulatory Commission of the Republic of Macedonia
Albania	High	Oil, coal, LPG	0	No gas sector and no gas regulator[c]
Kosovo	Very high	Coal, oil	0	Energy Regulatory Office, but no gas sector
Montenegro	High	Oil	0	Republic of Montenegro Energy Regulatory Agency, but no gas sector
Total	Very high	Gas, oil, coal	13.52	n.a.

Source: Authors' compilation.
Note: Bcm/y = billion cubic meters per year; GDP = gross domestic product; LPG = liquefied petroleum gas; n.a. = not applicable. "High" energy intensity signifies the same order of magnitude as U.S. energy intensity.
a. Fuel sources are presented in descending order.
b. The Ministry of Trade has policy responsibility at the state level. A key policy priority is to implement the regulatory framework in the energy sector, including enactment of a gas law at the state level. There is a proposal to widen the responsibilities of the State Electricity Regulatory Commission to include gas.
c. The responsibilities of the Albanian Electricity Regulatory Authority may be widened in future to include gas.

Bulgaria, Croatia, FYR Macedonia, Romania, and Serbia. In the remaining markets, formal gas regulation is likely to become the responsibility of existing regulators for electricity or energy.

Overview of the Gas Sector in the Region

Table 2.3 summarizes the gas sector industry structure in the nine SEE markets in 2008. Each of the six markets with gas have a single importer, and most have a single gas transmission company—with the exceptions of Bosnia and Herzegovina and Serbia. In Serbia, JugoRosGaz is the transmission company for the south and Srbijagas serves the north. Despite its small geographic size, relatively small gas market, and simple linear transmission system, Bosnia and Herzegovina has a rather complex arrangement of three gas transmission companies.

The six markets with gas all have more than one distribution company. The general trend in the region is toward a large number of small distribution companies. Some of the markets have one or several large distribution companies (for example, the two Distrigas companies in Romania and Srbijagas in Serbia), as well as other, smaller distribution companies. The small distribution companies tend to be municipally owned or cooperative enterprises (as in Croatia and Serbia). There also are privately owned distribution companies in some markets.

Demand Projections

This section describes the current and potential demand in Southeast Europe, the contribution of large anchor loads, current indigenous gas production and imports, and the projected supply gap.

Current and Projected Market Demand

Projecting future demand in the nine SEE markets has been carried out according to the methodology outlined in the "Study Methodology and Approach to Analysis" section of chapter 1. We develop an overall gas demand projection and then net off other sources to give the incremental demand that might be met through new pipelines.

It is important to appreciate that these levels of demand are contingent on the level of investment in infrastructure necessary to deliver these incremental gas volumes to the markets, some of which have no gas infrastructure at all at present. They are dependent on (1) sufficient anchor loads being in place at the outset to make the gas transmission infrastructure investment possible and (2) subsequent development of distribution networks and the connection of new customers at a rate sufficient to facilitate the buildup of smaller loads.

Table 2.3   Gas Sector Industry Structure in the Nine Markets, 2008

Market	Importers	Transmission companies	Distribution companies
EU members			
Romania	Romgaz	Transgaz	Distrigaz Nord, Distrigaz Sud, other small distribution companies
Bulgaria	Bulgargaz	Bulgargaz	Many companies
Partially gasified markets			
Serbia	JugoRosGaz[a]	Srbijagas, JugoRosGaz	Srbijagas, municipal companies or coops, JugoRosGaz
Croatia	INA	Plinacro	Many companies, mostly municipality based
Bosnia and Herzegovina	Energolnvest[b]	Gaspromet Pale, Sarajevo-Gas Lukavica, BH-Gas Sarajevo	Zvornik Stan, Sarajevo-Gas Sarajevo, Sarajevo-Gas Lukavica, Visokogas[c]
Macedonia, FYR	Makpetrol	GAMA	n.a.
Nongasified markets			
Albania	n.a.	n.a.	n.a.
Kosovo	n.a.	n.a.	n.a.
Montenegro	n.a.	n.a.	n.a.

Source: Economic Consulting Associates' research and country visits.
Note: EU = European Union; n.a. = not applicable.
a. Previously, Srbijagas was the importer. It is understood that JugoRosGaz now holds the import contracts, after the signing of the Memorandum of Understanding between Gazprom and the Ministry of Energy and Mining in Serbia in late 2006.
b. Energolnvest is the official importer of gas to Bosnia and Herzegovina. Some outstanding or disputed payments for gas delivered during the 1990s are understood to remain unresolved. BH-Gas pays the Russian side directly for gas imports under the present arrangements.
c. There also are a number of transmission-connected industrial consumers.

Anchor Loads

A number of large "anchor" projects will be required to ensure that

- there is enough up-front base load to generate a revenue stream with sufficient present value to justify the main network investments
- there is sufficient cash flow from the start of operations to make the project bankable
- the gas transmission system is extended, particularly into the currently nongasified regions of Serbia; the largely nongasified market of FYR Macedonia; and the currently completely nongasified markets of Albania, Kosovo, and Montenegro
- access to gas becomes available to end users who could be using gas on economic or environmental grounds.

The only prospective anchor loads of sufficient size in the SEE region are gas-fired power stations.[2] In the absence of large anchor loads (power stations or other), the financial viability of the investment could be undermined and the project most likely delayed. The remainder of incremental demand is expected to be driven by growth in industrial, district heating, and domestic gas use.

Using the official rehabilitation program of the electricity generation companies in the SEE markets and the central case price assumption (€206 per thousand cubic meters [Mcm] declining to €146/Mcm—about $275 declining to $195/Mcm—over the planning period 2005–20) resulted in 1,300 megawatts of new combined-cycle gas turbine (CCGT) capacity, plus 100 megawatts of open-cycle gas turbine (OCGT) peaking capacity for scenario B/case 2A2.[3] This case is described in the updated GIS (SEE Consultants 2007) as a "fully interconnected power system without any transmission constraints and partial environmental compliance." Assuming that the open-cycle plant is for peaking and runs very few hours each year, and assuming 53 percent thermal efficiency and 70–80 percent annual plant factor (equivalent to 6,100–7,000 hours per year at full load) for the combined-cycle plant, this implies gas demand of 1.4–1.6 Bcm a year.

---

[2] The *Update of Generation Investment Study, Final Report* (SEE Consultants 2007) is the source used for projections of the magnitude of this potential under various modeling assumptions.

[3] The central case gas price assumption of the *Update of Generation Investment Study* (the updated GIS) (SEE Consultants 2007) compares with €97/Mcm, increasing to €107/Mcm as used in the original GIS (about $129/Mcm, increasing to $143/Mcm) over the same period. Adjustments also were made to the assumptions of future fuel prices for oil and imported coal (higher, more so in the earlier years) and to lignite prices in the two most competitive mines in the region. The changes in fuel price assumptions are described in volume 1, annex 3 of SEE Consultants (2007).

Removing from the official program economically unjustified rehabilitation of old plants and keeping the other input the same resulted in 2,100 megawatts of CCGT capacity and no OCGT capacity. With the same assumptions as above, this implies an annual gas demand of 2.25–2.6 Bcm.

The high gas price assumptions in the updated GIS—€276/Mcm ($368/Mcm) increasing to €392/Mcm ($523/Mcm)—produced the same results as the reference case: 1,300 megawatts of CCGT and 100 megawatts of OCGT, which imply annual gas demand of 0.6–1.0 Bcm. The low gas price assumptions in the updated GIS—€188/Mcm ($250/Mcm) declining to €90/Mcm ($120/Mcm)—resulted in 4,000 megawatts of CCGT and 200 megawatts of OCGT, which imply annual gas demand of 4.3–4.9 Bcm.

Adding carbon prices of €20 per tonne of carbon dioxide was sufficient for gas turbine capacity to hit the upper constraint imposed by the modelers (7,900 megawatts of CCGT, with no OCGT), which would require some 8.5–9.8 Bcm of gas each year.

The buildup of power generation load under the three key updated GIS scenarios presented here is shown in figure 2.1.

The screening curves in the updated GIS show CCGT as lower in cost than nuclear power, at up to 85 percent plant capacity factor for 300-megawatt CCGT and at all plant capacity factors for 500-megawatt CCGT (at the 2010 base gas prices). Accordingly, a high plant capacity factor of 80 percent (7,000 hours a year) has been assumed for the justified expansion with base gas prices scenario and in the $20-per-tonne-of-carbon-dioxide price scenario adopted from the updated GIS. (The assumed availability used in the updated GIS modeling after deducting the forced outage rate and the maintenance outage rate is 90 percent). However, in the high gas price scenario, a gas-fired plant becomes uneconomic at much lower plant factors, so a plant factor of 50 percent (4,500 hours a year full load equivalent) has been assumed. (That is why the estimated gas demand under the updated GIS high gas price scenario is only 1.0 Bcm for 1,300 megawatts instead of 1.6 Bcm, as it is for the first 1,300 megawatts of capacity in the justified rehabilitation with base gas prices scenario.)

With these input assumptions, the GIS high gas price assumptions would reduce gas demand from more than 2 Bcm in the period 2015–20 to just 1 Bcm by 2020. Including a carbon price of $20 per tonne of carbon dioxide radically changes the picture, requiring almost 10 Bcm of gas before 2020.

In figure 2.1 it is clear that the potential demand for gas in the power sector is very sensitive to the gas price and to the penalty value assumed for carbon emissions.

Figure 2.1   Power Generation Capacity and Gas Demand under Three Scenarios, 2005–20

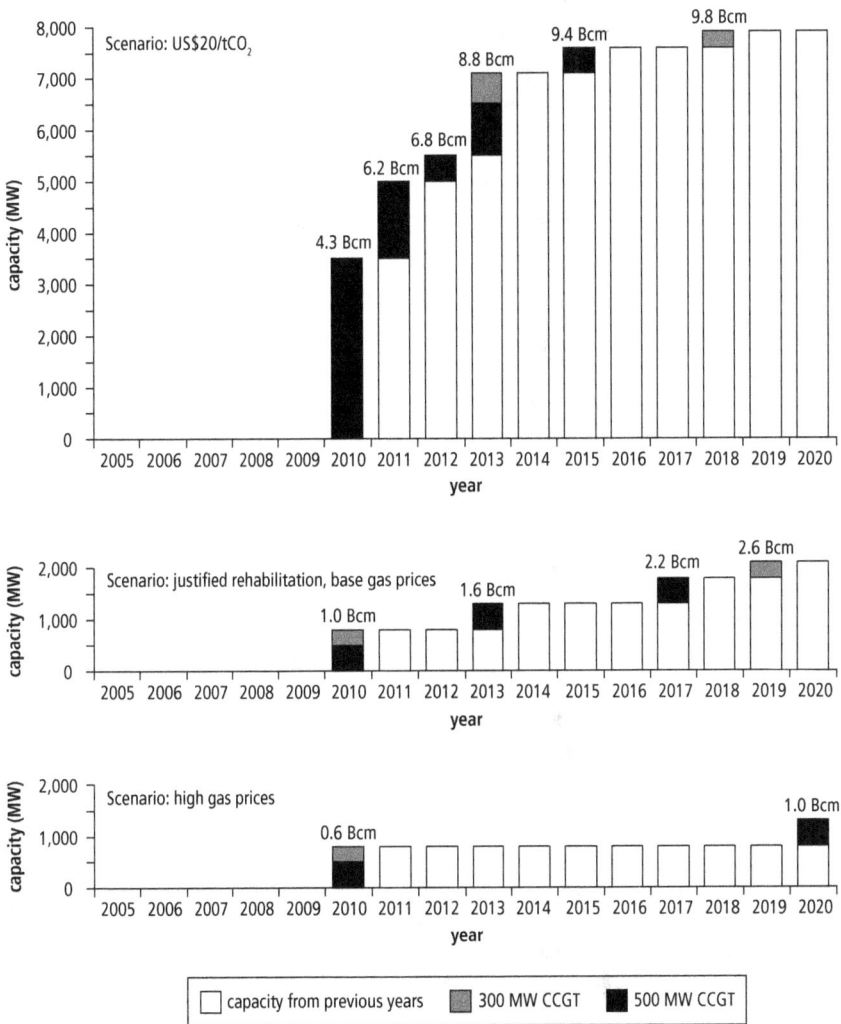

Source: Economic Consulting Associates' calculations, using results from SEE Consultants (2007).
Note: Bcm = billion cubic meters; CCGT = combined-cycle gas turbine; MW = megawatt; tCO₂ = tonnes of carbon dioxide.

Current Indigenous Production and Imports

Some of the markets have indigenous gas production. The most significant of these is Romania, where two thirds of gas was supplied from indigenous fields (11.6 out of 17.3 Bcm) in 2005. Croatia followed with more than half

(1.57 out of 2.7 Bcm) of its gas supplied from its own sources in 2005. Serbia's gas reserves are well into the production tail, supplying only a small amount (0.35 out of 2.53 Bcm) in 2005. Bulgaria also has a very small amount of indigenous gas production. In addition, a number of the markets have existing gas imports, all from Russia and transiting Ukraine.

The projected gas demand scenario is illustrated in figure 2.2.[4]

Projected Supply Gap

For the purposes of this analysis, it is assumed that supply from existing sources delivered via existing infrastructure will have incumbent eco-

---

[4] The demand scenarios and the methodology were presented at the Mini Gas Forum in Vienna on October 13, 2006.

Figure 2.2 Projected Gas Demand in Nine SEE Markets, 2005–25

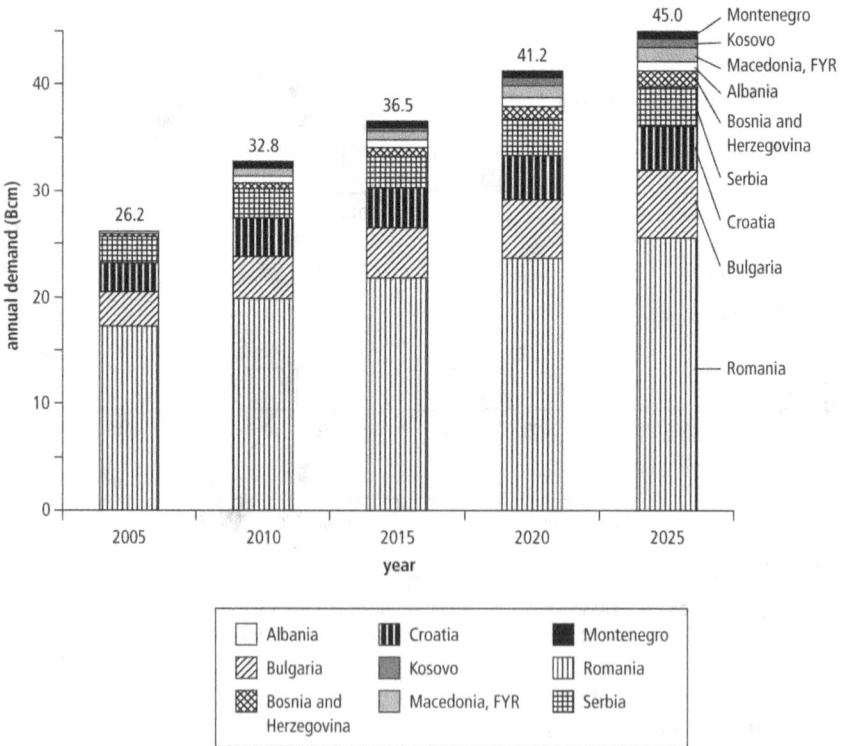

Source: Economic Consulting Associates' projections from country data.
Note: Bcm = billion cubic meters.

nomic advantages over new sources requiring the development of new infrastructure.[5] Therefore, incremental volumes that new imports would be required to serve are calculated as the projected growth in demand relative to 2005, plus the decline in indigenous gas production expected by 2025. This assumes that the new gas sources would supply new demand and that Russian and indigenous gas would continue to supply existing (2005) demand. Figure 2.3 shows the resulting incremental supply required to meet the projected demand to 2025, after indigenous production

---

[5] This assumption may be conservative, given that none of the countries currently are contracted to take Russian gas for 20 years, out to 2025. Gas companies in some countries have no long-term supply contract in place, but debts for previous gas imports complicate the financial picture.

Figure 2.3   Projected Supply Gap in Nine SEE Markets, 2005–25

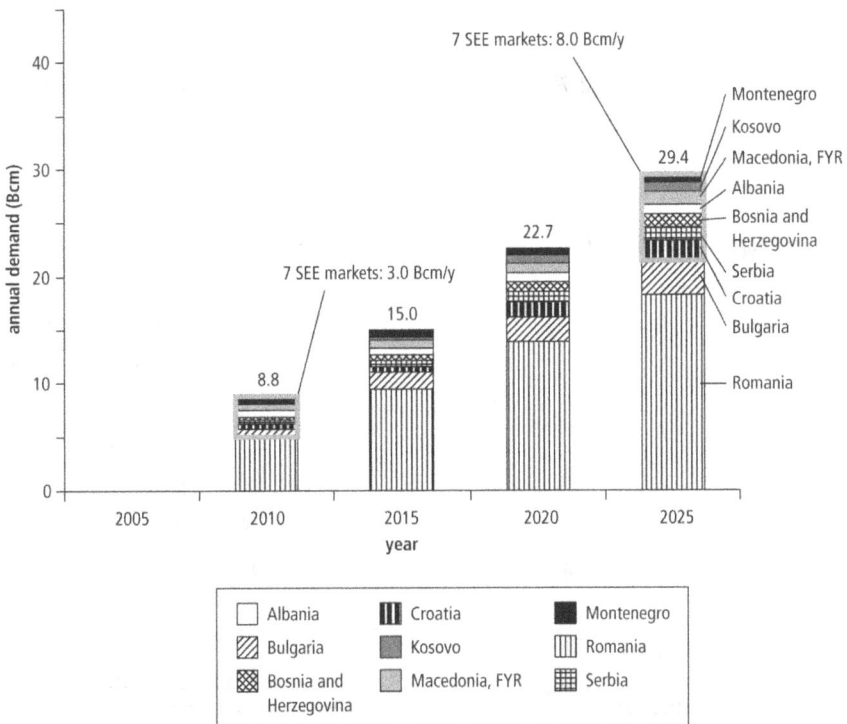

Source: Economic Consulting Associates' projections from country data.
Note: Bcm/y = billion cubic meters per year; SEE = Southeast Europe.

and existing supply have been deducted from the demand projections in figure 2.2.

The gas demand projections and the implied incremental supply that will be required in 2015 and 2025 are summarized in table 2.4. The overall pic-

Table 2.4   Projected Demand and Supply Gap, 2005–25

Market	Total demand (Bcm)			2010–25 average annual growth[a] (%)	Supply gap (Bcm)		Main end-use sectors driving incremental demand (descending order)
	2005	2010	2025		2015	2025	
Romania	17.3	19.9	25.6	1.7	9.5	18.3	Residential, commercial, power
Bulgaria	3.2	3.9	6.3	3.2	1.5	3.1	Power, industry, residential
Serbia	2.5	2.7	3.6	1.9	0.5	1.2	Power, heating, residential
Croatia	2.7	3.6	4.2	1.0	0.6	2.0	Power, industry, residential
Bosnia and Herzegovina	0.3	0.6	1.4	6.1	0.6	1.1	Heating, industry
Macedonia FYR	0.1	0.7	1.2	3.8	0.7	1.1	Power, industry, residential
Albania	0.1	0.6	1.0	10.2	0.7	1.0	Power, industry, residential
Kosovo	...	0.1	0.9	15.5	0.3	0.9	Heating, transport
Montenegro	...	0.6	0.7	1.0	0.6	0.7	Power, industry
Total	26.2	32.8	45.0	2.6	15.0	29.4	Power, industry, residential

Source: Authors' compilation.
Note: ... = no gas available; Bcm = billion cubic meters. Supply gap is the supply (in 2015 and 2025) required relative to 2005, taking into account both demand growth and decline in gas production in markets where it is relevant.
a. The growth rate is based on the 15 years from 2010 to 2025 because 2010 is the earliest possible time for new gas developments and because growth rates cannot be calculated with reference to zero, which is the 2005 demand in some markets.

ture is one in which the mature gas markets are projected to grow at relatively modest rates, while demand in the new markets grows rapidly from a low base. The overall weighted average rate of growth that emerges from the analysis is 2.6 percent a year, which suggests that the projections of growth prospects are on the conservative side.[6]

The incremental supply requirements are the increase in demand adjusted for anticipated changes in supply of gas from domestic sources—notably, a sharp decline by 2025 in production of gas in Romania and smaller declines in Croatia and Serbia. It is the incremental supply that is assumed to be met by one of the regional pipeline projects that are elaborated in the "Storage Demand" section later in this chapter.

Figure 2.4 shows the detail for incremental imports (the supply gap) to the seven westernmost markets in Southeast Europe—imports that are quite small relative to those of Romania and Bulgaria combined in figure 2.3. Included in these demand projections are 0.6 Bcm/y of anchor demand for each of four 500-megawatt power stations in Albania, southern Croatia, FYR Macedonia, and Montenegro, contributing 2.4 of the 3.0 Bcm of demand in 2010. (The actual timing of this gas supply gap will depend on the availability of new gas transmission infrastructure and power sector planning.) The remaining 0.6 Bcm in the supply gap is from a combination of organic growth in already gasified markets and decline in indigenous production.

Fuel Price Scenarios

The fuel price scenarios have been developed with reference to the benchmark prices of competing fuels, their relationship to oil prices, and the uncertainty of future oil prices.

Benchmark Prices of Competing Fuels

Increases in gas consumption in markets that already have at least some gas supply and uptake in markets to which gas is newly introduced can be attributed to the displacement of other fuels. Even gradual, incremental growth in gas demand in a mature market can be considered to be displacing (or holding out) another fuel because there is always a next-best option that would

---

[6] In the central case identified in the Regional Balkans Electricity Generation Investment Study, the annual average growth in electricity demand for the nine markets was 2.3 percent. It is reasonable that the gas demand rate should be somewhat higher than this because it is beginning from a lower base. It is appropriate to err on the conservative side because excessively bullish assumptions are made all too often in studies of this type, and such assumptions lead to formulation of unrealisable infrastructure investment plans. The *Final Report* will include a full discussion of the sensitivity analyses carried out during the study.

Figure 2.4 **Projected Supply Gap in Seven Westernmost SEE Markets, 2005–25**

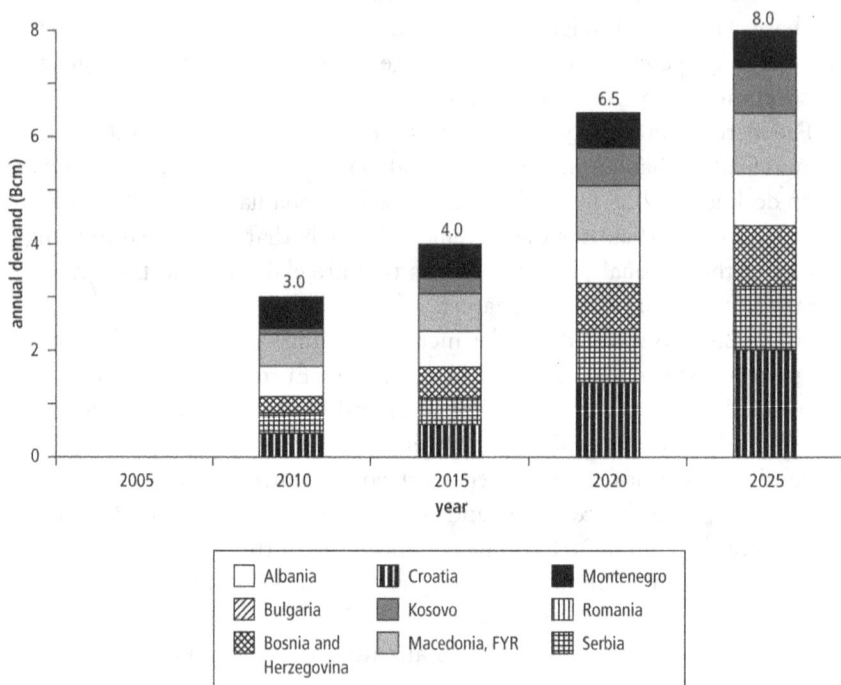

Source: Economic Consulting Associates' projections from country data.
Note: Bcm = billion cubic meters; SEE = Southeast Europe.

be adopted if the incremental gas supply was not available. The fuels that gas would seek to displace in the nine SEE markets are

- heavy fuel oil (mazut), principally used in the industrial sector and for district heating
- light fuel oil, used in the industrial sector and for district heating
- No. 2 diesel, used in industry and for combined heat and power
- LPG, used for heating, hot water, and cooking in the commercial and residential sectors
- electricity, used for heating in the residential and (possibly) commercial sectors.

The prices of most of those fuels—particularly fuel oils and diesel—move in response to international crude oil prices, with adjustment for transport costs, fuel excise and other taxes (such as value added tax [VAT]), and any

Figure 2.5   Daily Spot Prices of Crude Oil and Selected Products, 2000–09

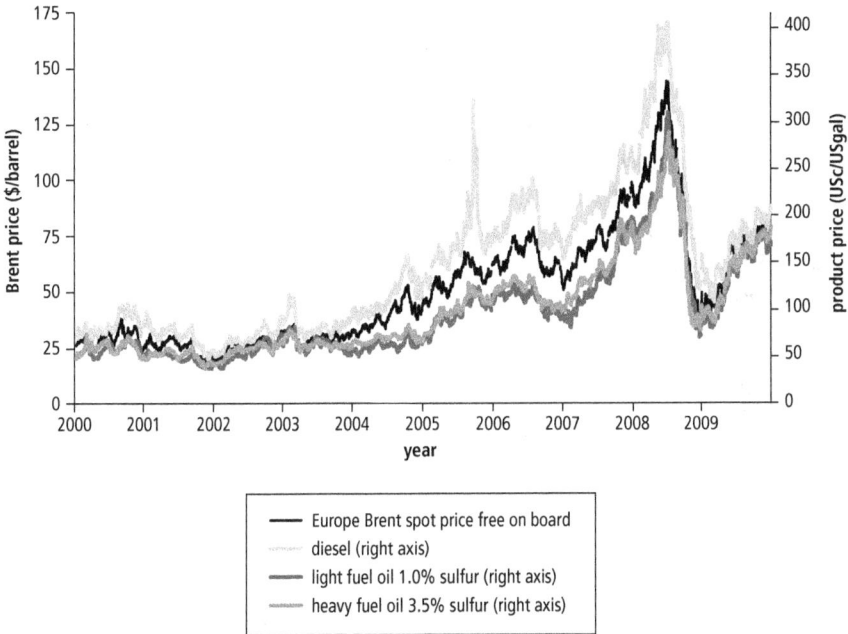

Source: Economic Consulting Asociates' illustration, using Energy Information Administration price data.
Note: Gulf Coast, heavy fuel oil is residual fuel oil 180 in Singapore and fuel oil is residual fuel oil with ≤1 percent sulfur at Rotterdam. Historical data for Mediterranean or Black Sea marker prices were not available. Price differences among locations result from shipping costs, but these differences normally are very small. The late-2005 diesel price spike on the U.S. Gulf Coast is an artifact of Hurricane Katrina.

subsidies in each local market. Indeed, the sales agreements under which Russia's Gazprom and its subsidiary companies sell gas use formulas that link the gas price to various substitute fuels, such as fuel oil and diesel oil, as well as to crude oil price indexes. The structure of the formulas generally includes time lags and sometimes floors and ceilings (caps and collars) on the gas price (or oil price indexation factors), which constrain the gas price from reflecting fully the prevailing oil spot price. Therefore, with Russia as the sole supplier, the wholesale prices of gas imported to all of the SEE markets that currently have gas (Bosnia and Herzegovina, Bulgaria, Croatia, FYR Macedonia, Romania, and Serbia) are linked via a formula to the prices of No. 2 diesel and light and heavy fuel oil. Figure 2.5 shows the daily market prices of Brent crude oil, No. 2 diesel, light fuel oil, and heavy fuel oil from January 2000 until December 2008.

The fuel price trends for the period illustrated in figure 2.5 confirm the expectation that the prices of petroleum products are correlated very closely with the price of Brent crude oil.

As figure 2.6 shows, there are some differences between the petroleum products with respect to the ratio of their prices to the price of Brent crude oil over the period from January 2000 until December 2008. In particular, the marker prices of heavy and light fuel oils have not increased in proportion with crude oil prices, but have remained at proportionately lower levels in recent years. Before 2003, these products traded at prices in a range of about 80–95 percent of crude oil prices (on a volume-for-volume basis). Since 2003, they have traded in a range of about 65–80 percent. This has been caused by the production of large quantities of residual fuel oil products, despite increasingly stringent environmental emission requirements prompting declining European and global demand for fuel oils with high sul-

Figure 2.6   Rolling Average Prices of Crude Oil and Selected Products, 2000–09

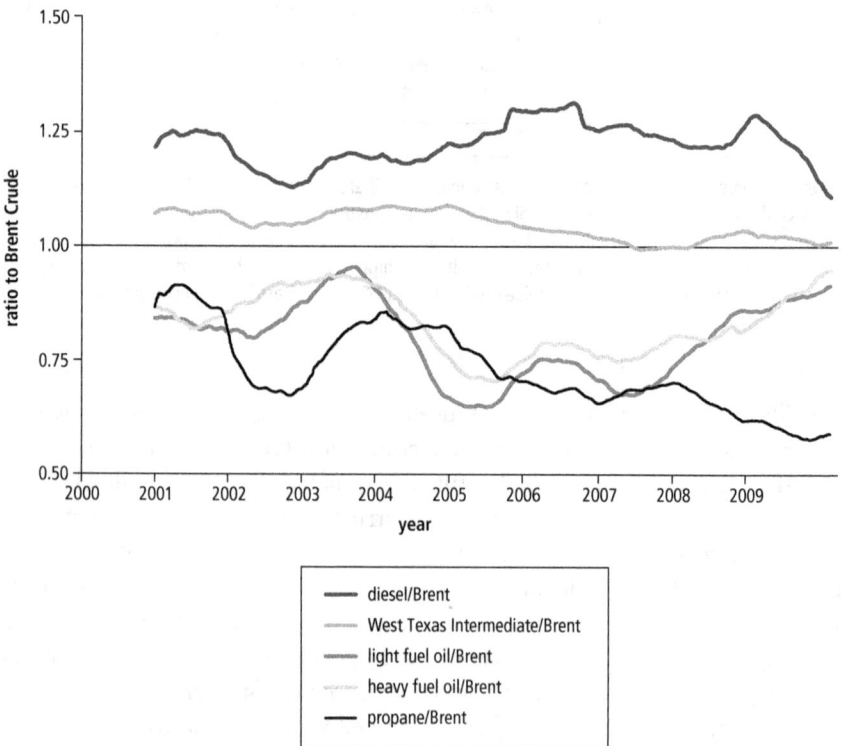

Source: Authors' calculations, using data from the Energy Information Administration.
Note: Previous year rolling.

fur content. Old refineries in Central, Eastern, and Southeast Europe—many of Russian design and technology—typically lack the flexibility to produce more highly refined products.[7]

The presence of fuel oil at low price levels may present an economic challenge for gasification in the nine SEE markets. In this respect, tightening environmental standards clearly would help the competitive position of gas, but would incur a corresponding economic cost. Relative fuel prices are not the only factor affecting gas demand. The extent to which gas transmission and distribution infrastructure is extended into the markets is a necessary precondition for future gas demand.

The economics of gasification are linked to the prices of oil products with which gas competes. All else being equal,[8] higher oil product prices would be expected to extend the economic reach of gas by making higher levels of investment in transmission and distribution infrastructure economic. But oil product prices are a continuously fluctuating moving target, as are underlying crude oil prices.

It is convenient to consider future gas prices in terms of future oil price scenarios. To make this link, it is necessary to find the relationship between gas prices and oil product prices, and then to find the relationship between those oil product prices and crude oil prices.

Uncertainty of Future Oil Prices
Oil prices currently are highly volatile, and long-term expectations are subject to a high degree of uncertainty. A World Bank workshop asked rhetorically, "Are oil prices heading toward $150 a barrel or $50 a barrel?"[9]

---

[7] Examples of such inflexible refineries in the SEE region include the Ballsh and Fier refineries and smaller refineries at several other locations in Albania (combined capacity 33 thousand barrels per day [kbpd]) and the OKTA refinery (about 50 kbpd) near Skopje in FYR Macedonia. There also are refineries at Bosanski Brod in Bosnia and Herzegovina (100 kbpd); at Urinj, Rijeka, and Sisak in Croatia (310 kbpd); at Pancevo and Novi Sad in Serbia (138 kbpd); at Burgas in Bulgaria (115 kbpd); and at Arpechim, Petrobrazi, and Ploiesti in Romania (about 264 kbpd).The privatized Petrom's refineries at Arpechim and Petrobrazi, owned by OMV of Austria, aim to produce all fuels to European Union specification by 2007 and to reduce the heavy fuel oil yield from 15 percent to 2 percent by 2010.

[8] In particular, the upstream costs of exploration and production and the midstream costs of transmission and distribution usually would be assumed to be fixed for the purposes of analysis. In fact, the upstream costs and the costs of steel for pipelines do move somewhat with oil prices; but the relationships are too complex to model, and the price movements are far less closely linked than are the movements of gas prices relative to oil.

[9] The workshop, cosponsored by the World Bank Institute and George Washington University, was titled "Oil Price Volatility, Economic Impact, and Financial Management." it served as a forum for more than 140 policy makers from central banks and from energy and finance ministries, oil company executives, representatives of heavy industrial users of oil, economists, and journalists. It was held in March 2008.

Considering the movement of the spot price in 2008, the correct answer to the question was "yes." To give some perspective to the current price environment, figure 2.7 shows the long price history since oil first was commercialized, both in dollars of the day and in inflation-adjusted 2006 dollars.

The figure shows annual average values. It should be noted that the 2008 price peak (above $140 a barrel for both Brent and West Texas Intermediate [WTI] on July 3) was for daily spot prices, not annual average values. The 2007 annual average price was $72 a barrel. (Taking into account 2007 inflation would make it lower in 2006 dollars.) Nevertheless, the annual average oil price for 2008 was close to $100, which is beyond the 95th percentile price for annual average prices in the Organization of the Petroleum Exporting Countries era ($80 in inflation-adjusted 2006 currency) and beyond the previous peak from 1980 (about $90 in 2006 currency), if not above the all-time annual average high from 1864 (more than $100 in 2006

Figure 2.7   Oil Price History, 1860–2009

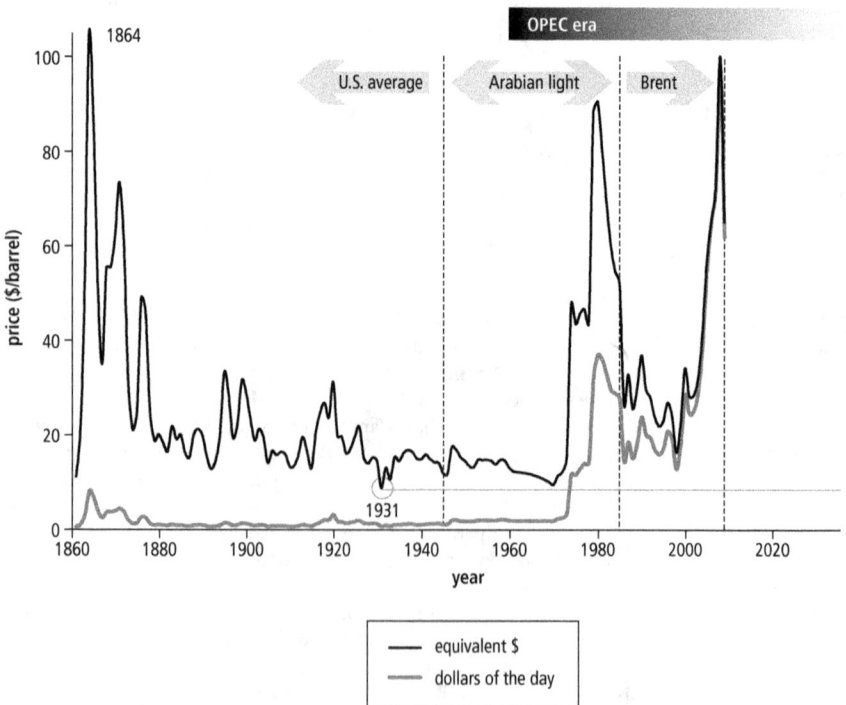

Source: Economic Consulting Associates' analysis, using data from the BP Statistical Review.
Note: OPEC = Organization of the Petroleum Exporting Countries.

currency). The economic analysis needs to be able to deal as robustly as possible with the uncertainty associated with high oil price volatility.

After a long period of stable, low dollar inflation, it is possible that we are entering a period with some similarities to the 1970s, which were characterized by large, sudden jumps in oil prices and high inflation. The price of gold then jumped to approximately $800 an ounce. The price of gold also has increased significantly in the last few years, surpassing $1,000 an ounce in mid-March 2008. (Gold would have to reach $2,500 an ounce to equal the early 1970s peak in real terms.) Figure 2.8, showing the change in oil prices in the world's four major currencies and relative to gold, suggests that the oil

Figure 2.8 Oil Price Changes, in Major Currencies and Relative to Gold, since January 2000

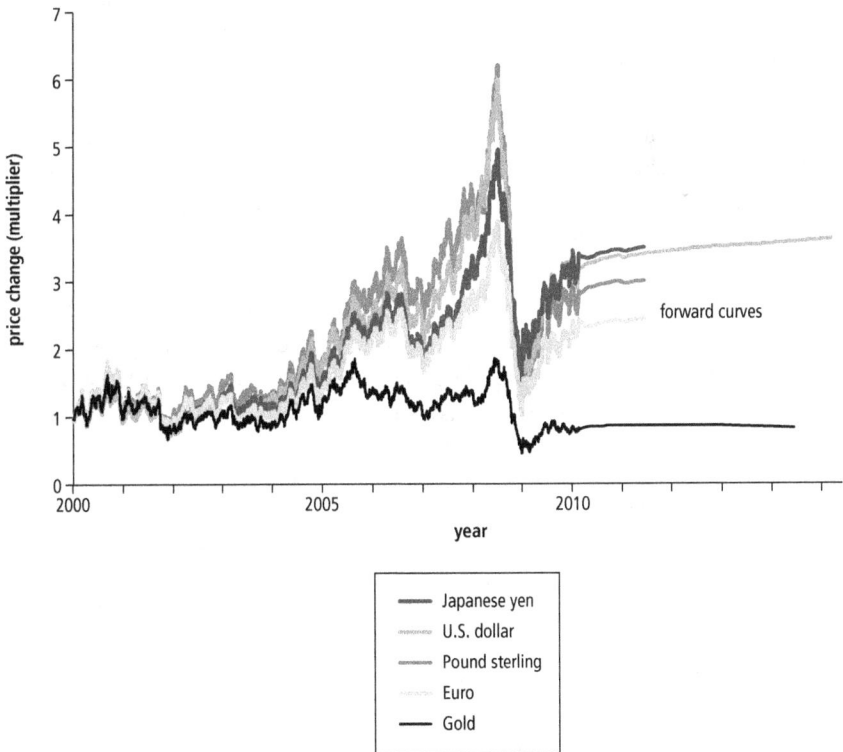

Source: Economic Consulting Associates' analysis, using oil price data from the Energy Information Administration, foreign exchange data from http://www.fxtop.com, and gold price data from http://www.oanda.com.
Note: Prices are per barrel of Brent crude oil. January 4, 2000 = 1.

price increases from 2004 to the peak of the super spike in summer 2008 resulted as much from the devaluation of paper currencies (particularly the U.S. dollar, the Japanese yen, and to a lesser extent the pound sterling and the euro) as to low real interest rates. Large amounts of borrowed money are thought to have flowed into commodities trading via highly leveraged hedge funds and investment banks. This process has gone into reverse with the credit crunch and global financial crisis, driving down the spot prices of oil and of commodities in general. The value of the dollar has strengthened relative to most other currencies (and to some extent against gold). Nevertheless, oil is priced in U.S. dollars, the global reserve currency that underpins more than 85 percent of international financial transactions, including commodity trades. The analysis in this report assumes that the U.S. dollar will retain its position as the global reserve currency for the foreseeable future.

The forward curves for oil relative to the forward curves for the selected currencies and gold also are shown in the figure. The market expectation at the end of 2008 seemed to be that the fall in spot crude prices is a short-term phenomenon and that prices will return to nearly four times their year 2000 values in the medium to long term. With long-dated futures prices well above spot prices, producers have a financial incentive to leave reserves in the ground by reducing production. This would be expected to drive up spot prices. Working against this will be the incentive for oil-exporting governments to produce more to obtain revenues in times of economic recession.

Oil prices will remain volatile, regardless of their average level. More important, oil price outlooks tend to appear quaintly outdated quite soon after publication, particularly in the current environment. (A review of the International Energy Agency's price outlooks published in the last few years' *World Energy Outlook* confirms this fact.) Therefore, rather than relying on an oil price outlook vector or even on several price paths, this study handles the uncertainty surrounding future oil prices by assessing the economics of gasification in Southeast Europe at six oil price points: $25, $50, $75, $100, $125, and $150 a barrel. The key questions are these: how sensitive to oil prices are the economics of increased SEE gasification, and in what oil price range would increased SEE gasification be economic?

Figure 2.9 shows the daily spot price history since 1990 (nominal dollars-of-the-day values) for Brent crude oil and the inflation-adjusted annual average prices for the World Bank's basket of WTI, Brent, and Dubai crudes.[10] The figure also shows five future price scenarios: three from the Energy Information Administration (EIA) of the U.S. Department of Energy, pub-

---

[10] WTI is the U.S. benchmark crude oil at Cushing, Oklahoma. "Brent" refers to the Europe spot price for Brent crude oil from the North Sea.

Figure 2.9   Oil Price Outlook, 1990–2030

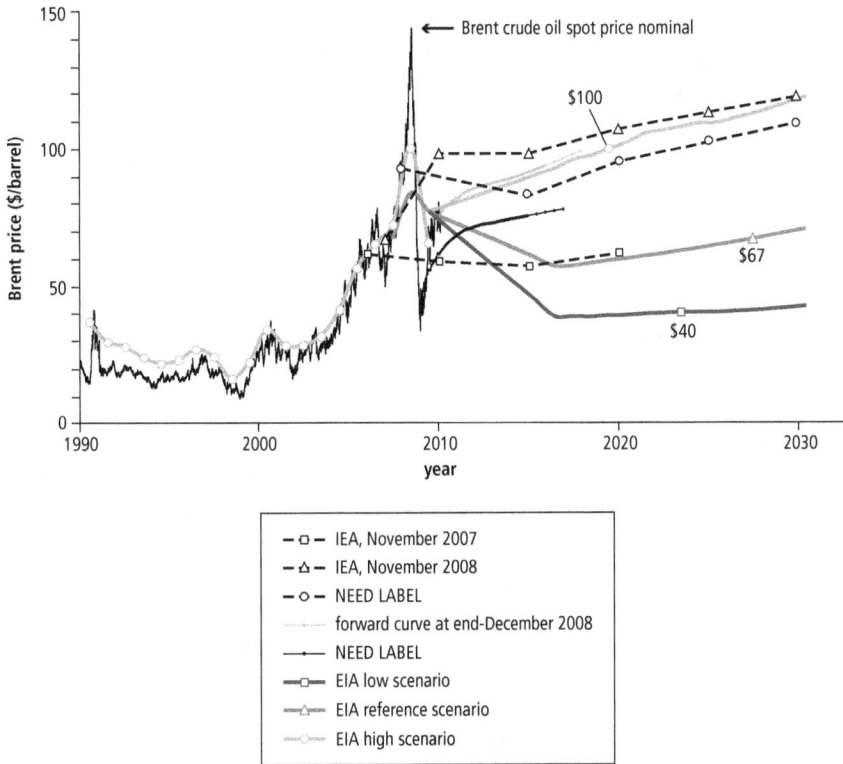

Source: EIA 2008; IEA 2008.
Note: EIA = Energy Information Administration; IEA = International Energy Agency. Prices are in constant 2006 dollars, except for the daily spot price series labeled "nominal." Prices are shown free on board, as quoted.

lished in September 2008; one from the International Energy Agency (IEA), published in November 2007; and one from the IEA, published in November 2008 (all scenarios adjusted to constant 2006 dollars).[11]

The IEA's forward oil price curve represents the fossil-fuel price assumptions used in their reference scenario modeling. It "reflect[s their] judgment of the prices that will be needed to generate sufficient investment in supply to

---

[11] The adjustment to constant currency terms is based on the World Bank's projection of the G5 MUV deflator (the manufacturers' unit value index, a proxy of developing country imports of manufactures in U.S. dollars, calculated as a weighted average of the export prices of manufactured goods from France, Germany, Japan, the United Kingdom, and the United States), provided along with the oil price projection.

meet projected demand over the *World Energy Outlook* period, taking account of market conditions. They should not be interpreted as forecasts" (IEA 2008, p. 63). However, this future price scenario could be interpreted as a reasonable approximation of the long-run marginal cost (LRMC) curve, under the global population and economic growth and supply-demand in the IEA's reference scenario.

The IEA's forward curve only extends to 2020, but it is interesting to note that it almost coincides with the EIA's reference scenario curve from about 2016. The EIA's reference scenario could be interpreted as market prices, returning to LRMC after 2015. The EIA's high scenario curve then might be thought of as representing prices remaining significantly above LRMC as a result of political or other barriers to the investment needed to bring prices down to LRMC. The EIA's low scenario curve could be thought of as representing prices falling below LRMC, either as a result of overinvestment relative to demand or as a result of overproduction relative to LRMC.

The effects of the economic downturn associated with the 1998 Asian financial crisis and the Russian sovereign debt default and of the 2001 U.S. stock market "correction" and subsequent recession can be seen clearly in the oil price history. To some extent, the dramatic run-up in oil prices since 2003 reflects the general commodity price boom and the weakening of the exchange value of the U.S. dollar (figure 2.8), as well as supply and demand in the oil market. At the time of writing, economic conditions show numerous signs of shifting toward downturn, and financial markets are going through their most turbulent and volatile period since the late 1920s. Some of this volatility can be seen in the daily oil spot price history: prices have traded in a range from about $50 a barrel near the start of 2007 to almost $150 a barrel in July 2008, returning to roughly $100 a barrel by late September 2008. In such market conditions, price scenarios are particularly important tools.

Analysis of Prices, Demand Side

Consumers have alternatives to gas. To enter a market for the first time, or to expand in a market where gas already is present, gas needs to displace those alternatives. This section explores the relationships between gas prices and oil, taking into account the equivalent gas price for several specific petroleum products, enabling the competitive gas price at the burner tip to be estimated.

Oil-Gas Price Relationships

Finding the underlying relationships among the prices of heavy fuel oil, light fuel oil, and No. 2 diesel is one of the keys to the analysis presented in this report because those are the major fuels against which gas needs to compete

BOX 2.1

Product-to-Crude Price Regressions

$P(LPG) = 1.3474.P(BrentCrude) + 16.422 \qquad R^2 = 0.9409$

$P(DSL) = 2.9748.P(BrentCrude) - 1.6081 \qquad R^2 = 0.9806$

$P(LFO) = 1.8870.P(BrentCrude) - 1.6053 \qquad R^2 = 0.9388$

$P(HFO) = 1.8388.P(BrentCrude) + 3.9947 \qquad R^2 = 0.9641$

Sources: Economic Consulting Associates' analysis, using Energy Information Administration petroleum price data from January 4, 2000 (first trading day) to December 31, 2009.
Note: DSL = diesel; HFO = heavy fuel oil; LFO = light fuel oil; LPG = propane. These equations use the units in the published Energy Information Administration data. The price of Brent crude oil is in dollars per barrel, and the prices of the oil products are all in cents per U.S. gallon.

to capture demand in Southeast Europe. Finding such relationships makes it unnecessary to predict particular future price paths in the volatile crude oil and petroleum products markets. These crude oil-to-oil product price relationships have been inferred from ordinary least squares linear regression analysis of the data shown in figure 2.5, providing the results presented in box 2.1.

Although Russian and Russian-controlled trans-Caspian gas sold by Gazexport dominates the region, there is some variation between price formulas from one market to another (Rehbinder 2006). To the extent that the price formula is attempting to reflect the different mix of fuels that gas needs to compete away in each market, this variation is to be expected. Across Europe, the weightings differ in the following typical patterns:

- *in Central and Eastern Europe*—close to 50 percent heavy fuel oil and 50 percent light fuel oil
- *in Western Europe*—50 percent light fuel oil, 30 percent heavy fuel oil, and a mix of other fuels (including the prices of gas, crude oil, coal, and electricity), as well as general inflation and fixed components
- *in some parts of Southeast Europe*—35 percent heavy fuel oil, 35 percent light fuel oil, and 30 percent diesel.

Because the various oil products all track crude oil quite closely (as box 2.1 shows), changes in the weighting do not make very much difference to the resulting gas price for the same base price assumption. Changes in the gas base price (the starting reference date) and in any floors, ceilings, or collars on the formula (and the detail of the averaging method used for the reference price inputs) will make some difference to actual gas prices paid. However, the main point is that, regardless of whether gas is priced on a formula or under market conditions, gas prices are expected to continue to reflect the price of the fuels with which gas is competing on the demand side in the final markets.

Assuming that the historical relationships among crude oil and petroleum products shown in box 2.1 will continue to hold in the future allows any Brent crude oil price to be mapped to the expected value of the corresponding product prices.[12] These product prices then can be substituted into an assumed gas price formula to give the expected gas price level at each crude oil price level.

For two different petroleum product weighting assumptions (a typical Central and Eastern European mix and a typical SEE mix), table 2.5 shows the gas import contract prices corresponding to six selected Brent crude oil price points, using the base price assumptions noted below the table.

---

[12] This inference is subject to some statistical error or uncertainty (because the R^2 value is less than 1).

Table 2.5 Oil Price Points and Corresponding Natural Gas Price Estimates

Brent crude oil price ($/bbl)	Inferred from assumed product-weighted formulas		Simple rules of thumb linked to Brent crude oil price	
	0:50:50 ($/Mcm)	30:35:35 ($/Mcm)	3•Brent + 10 ($/Mcm)	3.2•Brent + 10 ($/Mcm)
150	461	494	460	490
125	386	413	385	410
100	311	332	310	330
75	237	251	235	250
50[a]	162	170	160	170
25[b]	88	89	85	90

Source: Economic Consulting Associates' analysis, using Energy Information Administration petroleum price data and other information.
Note: bbl = barrel; Mcm = thousand cubic meters. Assumed base prices at the start of January 2000 for purposes of illustration: diesel 68 cents per U.S. gallon, light fuel oil 48 cents per U.S. gallon, heavy fuel oil 50 cents per U.S. gallon, and natural gas $87/Mcm.
a. International oil companies are using prices around this level to screen their future exploration and production investments.
b. For comparison, the median price during the Organization of the Petroleum Exporting Countries era (since 1960) is approximately $26, and the mean price is about $31. Roughly one year in 20 since 1960 has experienced an annual average price above $80, and one year in 20 has had an annual average price below $10 per barrel. All prices mentioned here are in equivalent 2005 dollars.

The result of the analysis in table 2.5 is shown in figure 2.10. The result depends on the assumed gas base price value as well as on the date selected for the base prices (that is, changing the time base used to determine the relationships would change the parameters in box 2.1 somewhat), but the final result is quite stable.[13] In practice, gas price formulas both smooth out the volatility in oil spot prices and lag those prices because the formulas are indexed to a rolling average of historical product prices. For the purposes of the present economic analysis, these dynamic effects are not important.

The fourth and fifth columns of table 2.5 also show how estimates of gas contract prices can be derived from two simple linear equations linked only to the Brent crude oil price, producing values that are quite close to the results obtained from the assumed petroleum product–indexed pricing formulas shown in the second and third columns of the table. These price estimates are convenient round-number alternatives to the values in the second and third columns, and they are more reflective of the uncertainty around the estimates.

---

[13] The assumptions used here also have been checked for reasonableness against historical European gas price data series from Heren Energy.

Figure 2.10 Inferred Relationships between Gas Prices and Crude Oil Prices

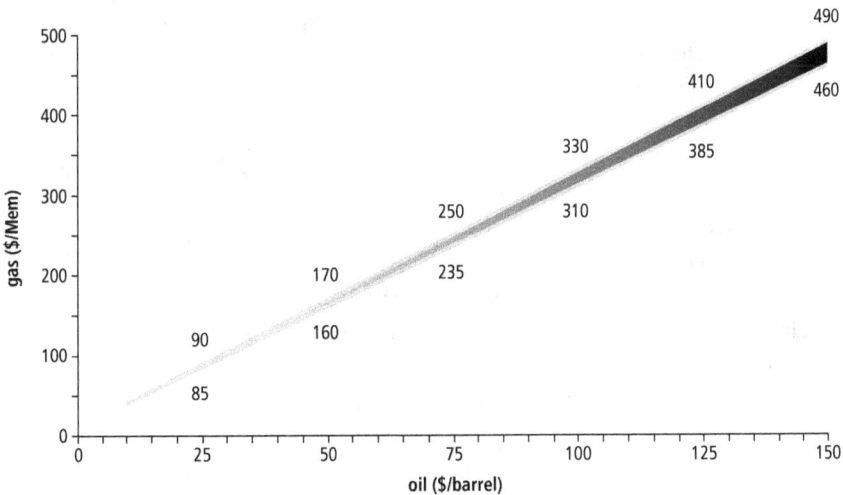

Source: Economic Consulting Associates' analysis, using Energy Information Administration petroleum price data and other information.
Note: Mcm = thousand cubic meters.

Fuel-Specific Equivalent Gas Prices

The gas price estimates in the two right-hand columns of table 2.5 may be considered to represent gas purchased at each oil price point for import to Southeast Europe at the western Ukraine border near Uzhgorod. Between the import purchase point and the burner tip, several components are added to the price, including transmission and transit to the border of the importing country, fuel taxes (or any subsidies) in the importing country, and transmission and distribution costs in the importing country. Each of these components is country specific and is discussed later in this chapter. The price at which gas breaks even with the fuels that incremental gas imports would need to displace underpins the economics of increased gasification. This price can vary from one displaced fuel to the next and from one consuming sector and technology to the next. The breakeven price also will vary over time, particularly with movements in crude oil prices.

Figure 2.11 presents schematically the economic comparison between an incumbent fuel and gas. This is a classic netback pricing comparison, with the calculation approach following the direction of the arrows. Figure 2.12 shows a simplified version of the methodology in figure 2.11, and table 2.6 summarizes the methodology's results for the part of the netback pricing calculation down to the dashed "import price—border" line in figure 2.11.

Each column in the top block of table 2.6 shows the expected international marker prices of selected petroleum products for a range of Brent crude oil price points: $25, $50, $75, $100, $125, and $150 a barrel. The selected petroleum products are LPG (using propane price as a proxy), No. 2 diesel (also referred to as gas oil, distillate, and solar or industrial diesel oil), light fuel oil (1.0 percent sulfur), and heavy fuel oil or mazut (3.5 percent sulfur). These are the product prices inferred from the linear regressions shown in box 2.1, based on their historical relationship with Brent crude oil prices between January 1, 2000, and March 18, 2008.

The corresponding rows in the bottom block of the table indicate the equivalent gas price for each of the fuels, taking into account the net calorific value and the combustion efficiency of each fuel. The assumed combustion efficiencies are 92 percent for natural gas and LPG and 88 percent for the liquid fuels.

The columns titled "Weighted 0:50:50" and "Weighted 30:35:35" show the gas prices that would result from these weightings of each oil product price, at each of the selected oil price points. The right-hand column of table 2.6 shows the range of estimated contract prices at the western Ukraine border near Uzhgorod at each of the oil price points. (These prices are discussed in greater detail in the "Analysis of Prices—Supply Side" section of chapter 3.). The gas price equivalents of the international marker prices for heavy

Figure 2.11   Comparative Netback Pricing Approach

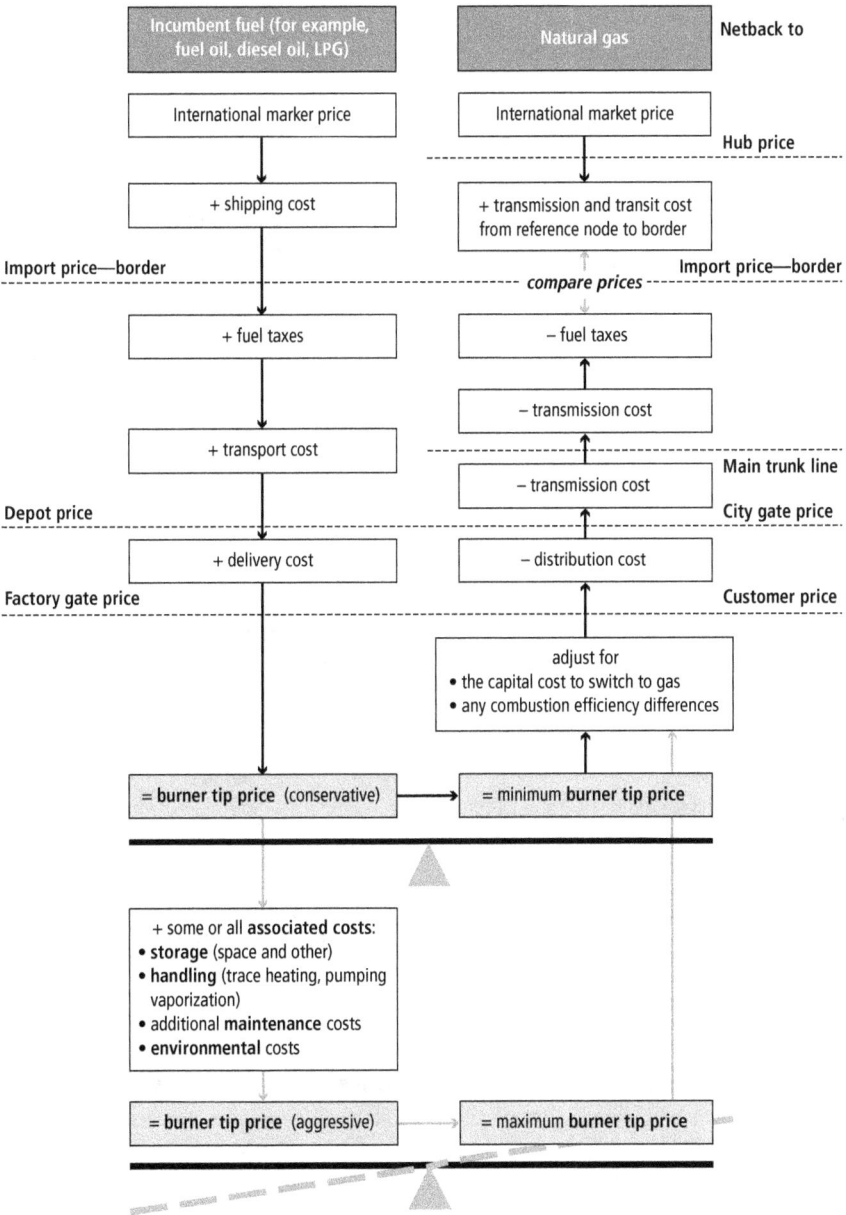

Incumbent fuel (for example, fuel oil, diesel oil, LPG)	Natural gas	Netback to
International marker price	International market price	
		Hub price
+ shipping cost	+ transmission and transit cost from reference node to border	
Import price—border	compare prices	Import price—border
+ fuel taxes	− fuel taxes	
	− transmission cost	
+ transport cost	− transmission cost	Main trunk line
Depot price		City gate price
+ delivery cost	− distribution cost	
Factory gate price		Customer price
	adjust for • the capital cost to switch to gas • any combustion efficiency differences	
= burner tip price (conservative)	= minimum burner tip price	

+ some or all associated costs:
• storage (space and other)
• handling (trace heating, pumping vaporization)
• additional maintenance costs
• environmental costs

= burner tip price (aggressive) → = maximum burner tip price

Source: Authors' illustration.
Note: LPG = liquefied petroleum gas.

Figure 2.12 Simplified Fuel Price Comparison

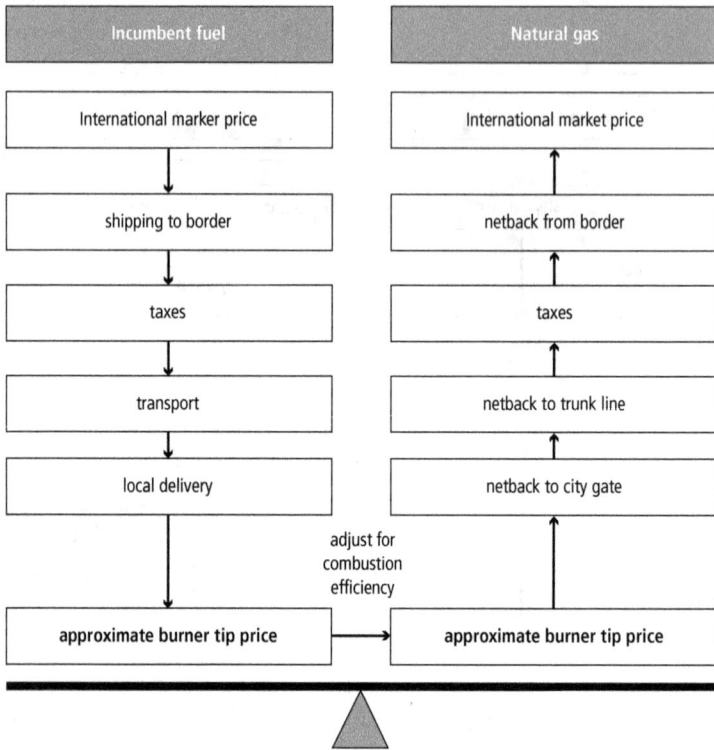

Incumbent fuel	Natural gas
International marker price	International market price
shipping to border	netback from border
taxes	taxes
transport	netback to trunk line
local delivery	netback to city gate
approximate burner tip price	approximate burner tip price

adjust for combustion efficiency

Source: Authors' illustration.

fuel oil and light fuel oil are only about 30–35 percent above these prices. This finding implies that gas can compete with heavy and light fuel oils, with a slightly higher margin to cover transit, transmission, and distribution plus taxes (that is, the parallel boxes in figures 2.11 and 2.12) and any price allowance needed to allow customers to recover switching costs.

Where gas suppliers can differentiate price among customers, or if tariff categories can be defined such that each category uses one particular fuel that gas aims to displace, then a gas import price calculated using a formula indexed to petroleum product prices could be split back out into end customer prices that reflect burner tip breakeven prices like those presented in table 2.6.

Competitive Gas Prices at the Burner Tip
For gas and for the fuels that gas would seek to compete away, shipping, transport, distribution, and local delivery costs and fuel taxes (or any sub-

Table 2.6 Equivalent Gas Border Prices, Relative to International Marker Prices

| Brent ($/bbl) | Petroleum products | | | | Weighted[a] | | Estimated Russian gas border price |
	LPG	DSL	LFO	HFO	0:50:50	30:35:35	
Thermal efficiency (%)[b]	92	88	88	88	n.a.	n.a.	92
International Marker Prices ($/USgal)							
150	2.29	4.47	2.56	2.66	n.a.	n.a.	n.a.
125	1.93	3.72	2.15	2.23	n.a.	n.a.	n.a.
100	1.57	2.97	1.73	1.80	n.a.	n.a.	n.a.
75	1.21	2.22	1.31	1.37	n.a.	n.a.	n.a.
50	0.85	1.47	0.90	0.94	n.a.	n.a.	n.a.
25	0.49	0.72	0.48	0.51	n.a.	n.a.	n.a.
Equivalent natural gas prices[c] ($/Mcm)							
150	831	1,140	624	639	461	494	460~490
125	701	948	523	536	386	413	385~410
100	570	757	421	433	311	332	310~330
75	440	566	320	330	237	251	235~250
50	309	374	218	226	162	170	160~170
25	178	183	117	123	88	89	85~90

Source: Economic Consulting Associates' analysis, using information on gas prices in Southeast, Central, and Eastern Europe and data from the Energy Information Administration.

Note: ~ = approximate range; bbl = barrel; DSL = diesel; HFO = heavy fuel oil; LFO = light fuel oil; LPG = liquefied petroleum gas; Mcm = thousand cubic meters; n.a. = not applicable; USgal = U.S. gallon. Marker prices used are the Mont Belvieu, Texas, propane spot price free on board as a proxy for LPG; U.S. Gulf Coast No. 2 diesel; Amsterdam/Rotterdam/Antwerp 1.0% sulfur light fuel oil; and Singapore 3.5% sulfur heavy fuel oil.

a. The order of the weighting is diesel to light fuel oil to heavy fuel oil.
b. Efficiency of converting the fuel to heat at the burner tip.
c. These are the equivalent prices at the border, taking into account the net calorific values and typical combustion efficiencies of the various fuels at the burner tip.

sidies) vary from market to market. Table 2.7 shows the range of gas prices that would be competitive with each fuel at the burner tip across the nine SEE markets, using available data on local prices to arrive at estimates of local final fuel prices at the selected oil price points. The table

Table 2.7 Competitive Netback Prices at the Burner Tip, by Fuel and Market

		Brent *(S/bbl)*					
		25	**50**	**75**	**100**	**125**	**150**
Fuel/weight *(%)*	**Sector**	Natural gas *($/Mcm)*					
Market price	Western Ukraine border	90	170	250	330	410	490
Range of burner tip prices for each fuel (max~min in 9 markets, rounded)							
LPG (0)	Residential, some commercial	1,309 ~526	1,440 ~657	1,571 ~787	1,701 ~918	1,832 ~1,049	1,962 ~1,179
DSL (30)	Commercial, some industrial	889 ~665	1,081 ~857	1,272 ~1,048	1,463 ~1,239	1,655 ~1,431	1,846 ~1,622
LFO (35)	Industrial, some commercial	783 ~261	885 ~363	986 ~464	1,087 ~565	1,189 ~667	1,290 ~768
HFO (35)	Electricity, large industrial	290 ~105	393 ~208	496 ~312	599 ~415	703 ~518	806 ~621
Burner tip prices in each market, based on local fuel prices (weighted 30:35:35 by fuel, rounded)							
Albania	All, weighted	360	490	620	750	880	1,010
Bosnia and Herzegovina	All, weighted	500	630	760	890	1,020	1,150
Bulgaria	All, weighted	490	620	750	880	1,000	1,130
Croatia	All, weighted	390	520	650	780	900	1,030
Kosovo	All, weighted	480	610	730	860	990	1,120
Macedonia, FYR	All, weighted	460	580	710	840	970	1,100
Montenegro	All, weighted	640	770	900	1,030	1,160	1,290
Romania	All, weighted	480	610	730	860	990	1,120
Serbia	All, weighted	480	610	730	860	990	1,120
Minimum	n.a.	360	490	620	750	880	1,010
Mid	n.a.	500	630	760	890	1,020	1,150
Maximum	n.a.	640	770	900	1,030	1,160	1,290

Source: Economic Consulting Associates' analysis, using information gathered on local fuel prices and taxes (with estimates where required).
Note: ~ = approximate range; bbl = barrel; DSL = diesel; HFO = heavy fuel oil; LFO = light fuel oil; LPG = liquefied petroleum gas; max = maximum; Mcm = thousand cubic meters; min = minimum; n.a. = not applicable.

also shows competitive final prices at each oil price point in each market when weighted 30:35:35 across diesel, light fuel oil, and heavy fuel oil, respectively.

The patterns in the results are as expected: the competitive prices increase with oil prices, and are higher for the lighter, more refined fuels and lower for the heavier, less refined fuels. The weighting is conservative (reflecting typical gas import contracts) in that LPG has a zero weight. Therefore, any LPG displaced by natural gas will provide upside for gasification (consumers and suppliers).

Local Market Price Differences, Delivery Costs, and Taxes

The difference between these values and the border price is the maximum margin available for the recovery of capital and operating costs for transmission, distribution, and supply, including the profits of the companies that would be engaged in those businesses in each market. (That margin is discussed further in the "Analysis of Prices—Supply Side" section of chapter 3).

For example, the average international marker price of heavy fuel oil for October–November 2006 was just over $1 per U.S. gallon (27.3 cents per liter),[14] which implies a competitive gas price of $221/Mcm. The heavy fuel oil price to end customers in Serbia for the same period was 38.8 cents per liter, including 18 percent VAT, which implies a competitive gas price of $314/Mcm. The difference between the international marker price and the final customer market price in Serbia—11.5 cents per liter—therefore is equivalent to a $93/Mcm difference at the burner tip to cover the costs of transit, transmission, and distribution plus taxes (and any switching costs).

The ex-VAT price of 32.9 cents per liter implies shipping, transport, and local delivery costs plus fuel excise taxes and import duties totaling about 5.6 cents per liter. VAT will be applied equally to gas and to the competing fuels. But if no fuel excise duty is applied to gas imports, then this 5.6 cents per liter price differential between market prices and the international marker price would be worth about $45/Mcm on the gas price, implying a burner tip breakeven gas price of $266/Mcm.

It is important to note that the results shown here are the *maximum* burner tip prices because they include no allowance for recovering any capital costs associated with switching to gas. Those costs are site specific but can be significant, depending on the nature of the technology at each site. Investors would be expected to allow a sufficient margin between gas and the displaced fuel to make the switch attractive to customers who face costs to switch.

---

[14] The Brent crude oil price during the October–November 2006 comparison period averaged just over $58 a barrel.

Storage Demand

In addition to meeting the annual demand for gas, the system must meet customers' aggregate demand on a seasonal, monthly, daily, and hourly basis. The criteria for being able to match gas supply and demand is the minimum delivery pressure. This in turn requires sufficient delivery capacity and gas in the transmission system.[15] (The way that this delivery capacity is provided is discussed in the "Regional Underground Gas Storage section of chapter 3.)

This section focuses on the estimates of the expected peak capacity requirements on seasonal through to daily and hourly bases. Seasonal swing is considered first, followed by daily variability. Hourly variability is considered briefly. Finally, some consideration is given to strategic gas reserves in the context of wider security of supply.

Seasonal Swing

The seasonal swing of gas demand depends to a large extent on the temperature sensitivity of customers' loads, with the most significant temperature-sensitive load being space heating (mainly in the residential and commercial sectors). Water heating also is temperature sensitive, but usually is a much smaller load than space heating. Therefore, the changing mix of customer types as gas demand builds up over time with increasing gasification will have a significant influence on the seasonal swing of the system as a whole.

Power Sector Seasonal Profile The initial 2.5 Bcm/y of transmission-connected demand shown in figure 2.13 predominantly would be the gas-fired CCGT power station anchor loads, as discussed earlier in this chapter. The buildup to 3.6 Bcm/y by 2020 also is assumed to be power sector demand, although some of this could be similarly flat industrial sector demand without affecting the conclusions from the analysis.

For the purposes of modeling gas storage needs, it is assumed that the power sector gas demand varies throughout the year in a manner consistent with the general assumptions described in this chapter's "Anchor Loads" section for the annual plant load factor. Figure 2.14 illustrates the case with an annual contract of 2.4 Bcm, giving an annual average daily contract quantity of 6.58 MMcm (million cubic meters) a day. A maximum daily contract quantity of 115 percent is shown. (Typical values range from 105 percent to more than 120 percent.) However, physical transmission capacity rather than contract terms may be the constraint, so a check for which of the two is the constraining factor was incorporated in the analysis.

---

[15] Distribution systems always are designed with diameters large enough to meet the maximum demand on the specified peak day, with a suitable safety margin, and such assumptions have been made in the notional design of the distribution systems considered in this report.

Figure 2.13 Assumed Load Buildup in Seven Non-EU SEE Markets, 2010–35

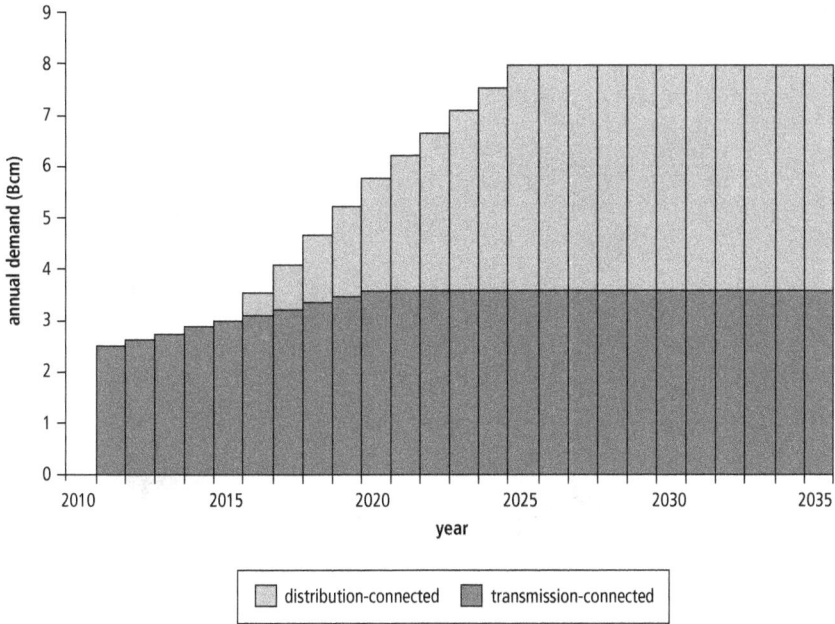

Source: Economic Consulting Associates' projections, consistent with figure 2.4.
Note: Bcm = billion cubic meters; EU = European Union; SEE = Southeast Europe. Includes all markets of Southeast Europe, except Bulgaria and Romania.

The "Regional Gas Transmission Infrastructure" section of chapter 3 describes the development of an integrated regional transmission infrastructure in a ring configuration, with a constant 24-inch diameter, providing the ability to expand peak capacity by adding new, well-spaced supply injection points. But in the short term, new pipelines would be expected to be financed on the basis of power station anchor loads in simple linear configuration with unidirectional flow from a single supply point at the branch from the upstream infrastructure.

The capacity of a 24-inch unidirectional linear transmission system (7.44 MMcm a day) would be binding over the contract constraint described above, and an 85 percent take-or-pay minimum would be exceeded comfortably. At the upper end of the assumed CCGT plant load factor range (7,000 full-load equivalent hours per year, or 80 percent plant factor), 2.6 Bcm would be needed annually, and the additional consumption would have to occur in the lower demand months, unless the transmission constraint of the 24-inch linear system with a single supply point was relieved.

Figure 2.14 Expected Annual Volume—2.4 Bcm/y Low-Swing Initial Anchor Loads

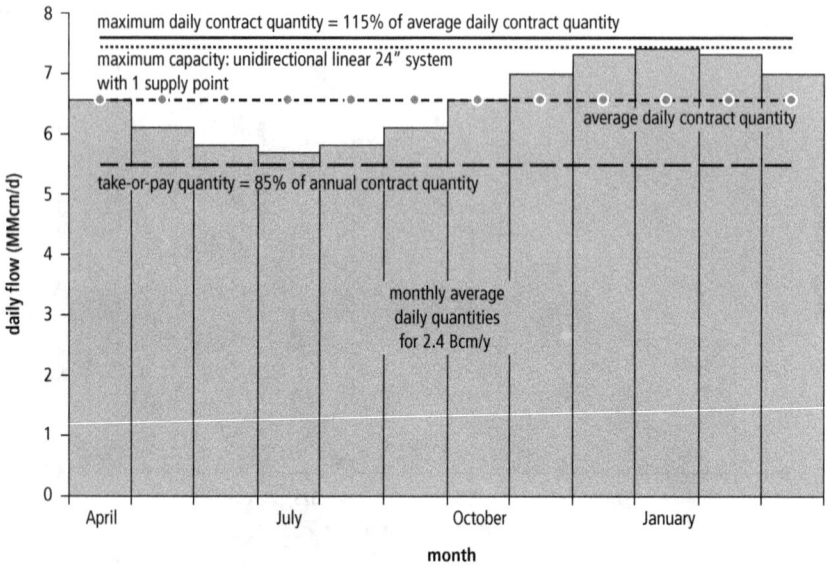

Source: Economic Consulting Associates' gas storage model, typical contract parameters.
Note: Bcm/y = billion cubic meters per year; MMcm/d = million cubic meters per day. Chart includes all markets of Southeast Europe, except Bulgaria and Romania.

Assuming an 85 percent annual take-or-pay minimum on the contract, a 2.40 Bcm/y contract would allow 2.04 Bcm/y to be consumed in a low-demand year without incurring a penalty (equivalent to 5,500 full-load equivalent hours annually, or 63 percent plant factor). This scenario, shown in figure 2.15, is well below the lower end of the plant dispatch range (6,100 hours, or 70 percent) from the "Anchor Loads" section above.

As well as allowing flexibility on annual volumes, the contract terms indicated would allow flexibility on demand variability, which is shown as increased seasonal swing in figure 2.16. The variability of power sector demand is shown here as being fully coincident with the seasonal swing of distribution-connected demands that will build up on top of the anchor loads. This is the worst-case scenario. If the variability occurs more evenly throughout the year or in a counterseasonal pattern (higher in summer and lower in winter), it would be beneficial to the system and would defer the need for transmission and storage capacity increases.

Figures 2.14, 2.15, and 2.16 show that the maximum capacity of a 24-inch unidirectional linear system with a single supply point is just less than 7.5 MMcm a day. Therefore, regional power station annual anchor

Figure 2.15   Annual Take-or-Pay Constraint—2 Bcm/y Low-Swing Initial Anchor Loads

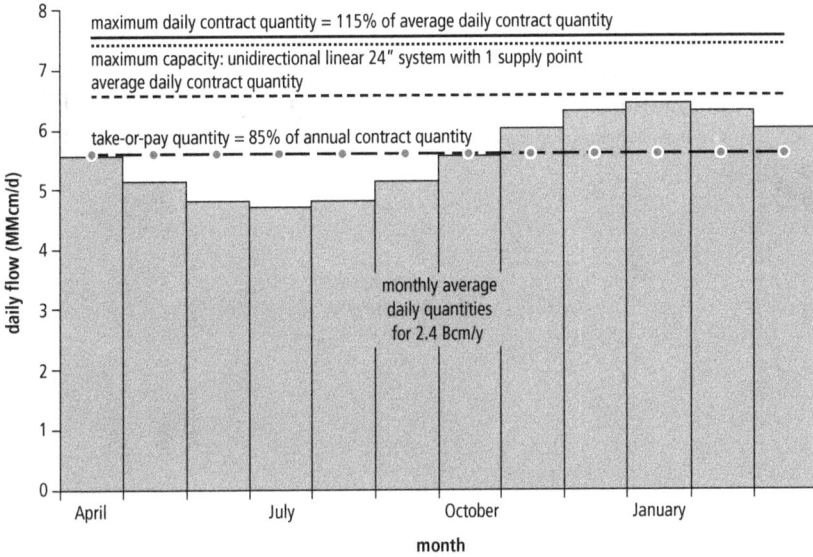

Source: Economic Consulting Associates' gas storage model, typical contract parameters.
Note: Bcm/y = billion cubic meters per year; MMcm/d = million cubic meters per day. Chart includes all markets of Southeast Europe, except Bulgaria and Romania.

loads between 2.0 Bcm with a low load factor and 2.6 Bcm with a high load factor could be served with a 24-inch pipeline before the ring configuration is completed, without the need for storage or other supply-demand balancing options. An annual volume of 2.0–2.6 Bcm corresponds to 2,100 megawatts of CCGT plants with 53 percent thermal efficiency operating between 5,500 and 7,000 hours a year. Up to 84 percent of this capacity at full load could be supplied with gas at any one time, via a linear 24-inch system from a single supply point, without storage. If the full-load thermal efficiency were higher than the assumed average 53 percent (a realistic possibility), then more gas-fired plants could generate simultaneously. Clearly, a linear system supplied from one end would be less reliable than a linear system fed from both ends or a ring.

The addition of further load would make necessary the completion of the ring (which would double its peak capacity) or the addition of a second supply point at the other end of the system.

Non-Power Sector Seasonal Profile   The annual 4.4 Bcm of long-run distribution-connected demand shown in figure 2.13 is modeled as being

Figure 2.16   Annual Take-or-Pay Constraint—2 Bcm/y High-Swing Initial Anchor Loads

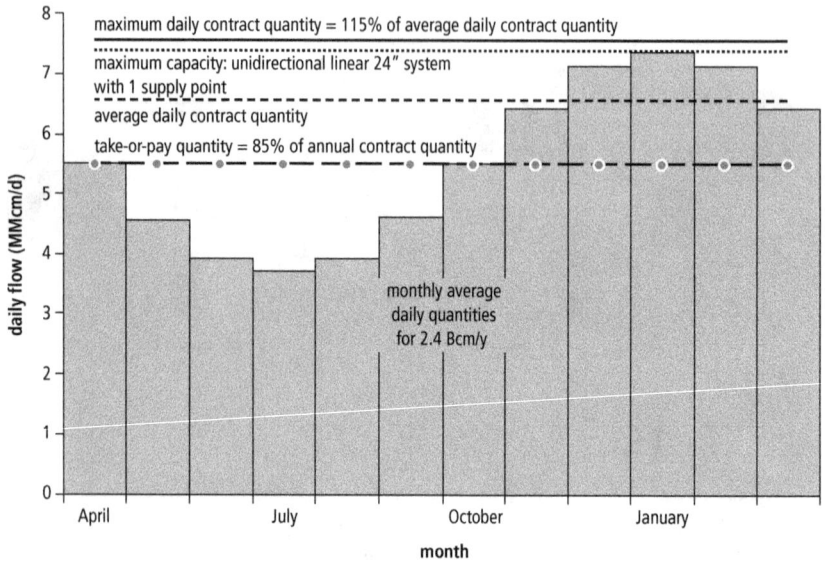

Source: Economic Consulting Associates' gas storage model, typical contract parameters.
Note: Bcm/y = billion cubic meters per year; MMcm/d = million cubic meters per day. Chart includes all markets of Southeast Europe, except Bulgaria and Romania.

predominantly temperature-sensitive residential and commercial load, with most of the consumption in the winter months. Annual consumption of 4.4 Bcm is equivalent to an average daily quantity of just over 12 MMcm. The amplitude of the total seasonal swing is modeled as 10 MMcm a day— that is, the average demand in the coldest month is assumed to be about 22 MMcm a day, and the average demand in the warmest month is assumed to be about 2 MMcm a day. Such a seasonal swing pattern is equivalent to just over 75 percent of the gas being consumed in the six coldest months.

Figure 2.17 shows the long-run total projected annual demand of 8.0 Bcm (transmission-connected power station load having grown from 2.4 to 3.6, plus 4.4 from distribution-connected seasonal loads) for the worst case: the daily 10 MMcm of seasonal swing on the distribution-connected load is modeled as 100 percent coincident with the daily 1.3 MMcm (scaled up from the 0.865 MMcm a day in figure 2.14) of swing on the power station load. The total 8.0 Bcm of annual power sector and distribution-connected demand is equivalent to an average daily quantity of just under 22 MMcm. The average day in the coldest winter month would demand just under

Figure 2.17 Contracting Based on Annual Average Quantity Showing Monthly Average Days

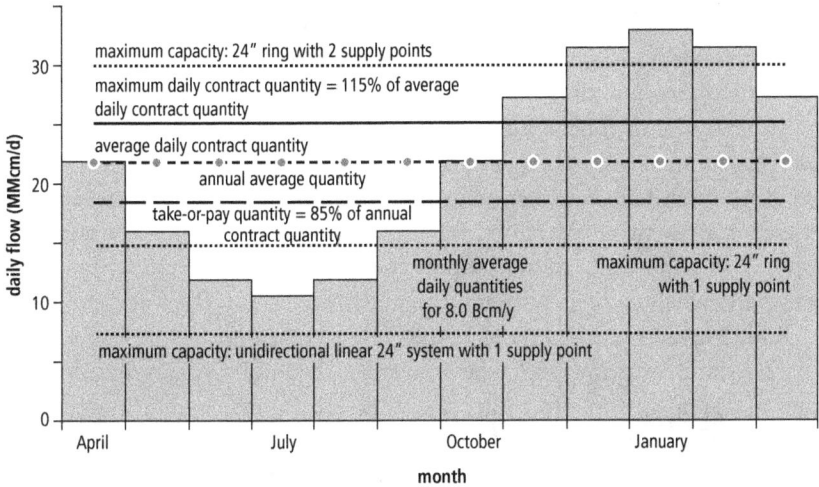

Source: Economic Consulting Associates' gas storage model.
Note: Bcm/y = billion cubic meters per year; MMcm/d = million cubic meters per day. Chart includes all markets of Southeast Europe, except Bulgaria and Romania.

35 MMcm. Figure 2.17 shows a scenario where power stations and wholesale gas suppliers have contracted for the annual average demand as their average daily contract quantity, giving some upward flexibility at the same price within the maximum daily contract quantity threshold. From this figure it is clear that a ring with at least two well-spaced supply points would be needed to meet this level of annual demand. It also is clear that storage would be required to match the contract with the demand.

Figure 2.17 also shows that both a unidirectional linear 24-inch system with a single supply point and a 24-inch ring with a single supply point would not have sufficient capacity to meet 8.0 Bcm of annual demand—even with storage to manage the flows—because the annual average quantity would be above the capacity of those system configurations. A 24-inch ring with two supply points would have more than enough capacity to meet the annual average demand, but still would be insufficient during the peak season: the capacity of just under 30 MMcm a day is less than the average daily demand in the winter months December, January, and February. Therefore, either a storage facility, which would serve as a third supply point in winter, would be required to meet the long-run projected demand, or an additional supply point would be needed. (The second option would require accepting the take-or-pay penalties.)

Figure 2.18 shows the best-case scenario: the swing on the power station load is counterseasonal, reducing the total seasonal swing on the distribution-connected loads. It also shows an alternative contracting strategy: the maximum daily quantity has been set equal to the expected average demand in the peak month. The annual average quantity happens to be just slightly below the annual take-or-pay quantity, so some penalties would be incurred. The maximum daily contract quantity is marginally above the capacity of a 24-inch ring with two well-spaced supply points. Therefore, it would be impossible for such a system to supply the winter peak demand without storage, particularly when demand on individual peak days is taken into account. Furthermore, demand would fall significantly below the take-or-pay threshold in years with below-average demand, potentially incurring penalties (unless, as is often the case, there was a clause to allow untaken volumes to be rolled over to future years). It is clear from the above analysis that some storage will be required to meet the seasonal demand as distribution loads develop in Southeast Europe.

Figure 2.18 Contracting to Keep Maximum Daily Quantity within a Monthly Average Days Constraint

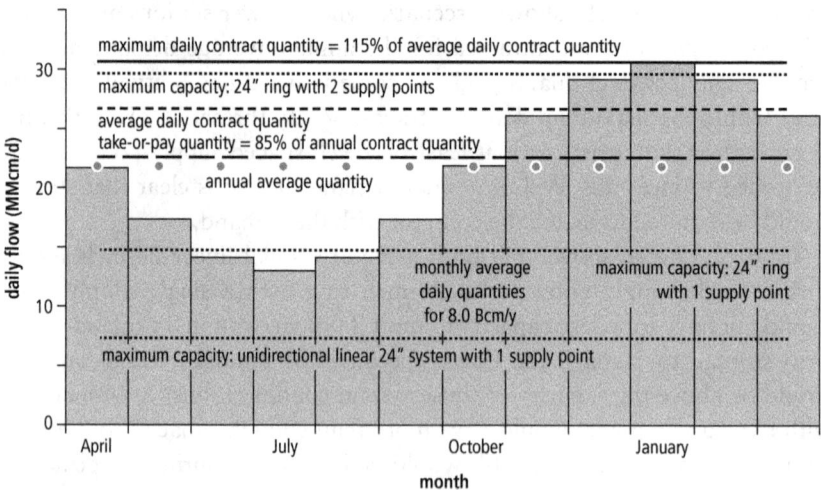

Source: Economic Consulting Associates' gas storage model.
Note: Bcm/y = billion cubic meters per year; MMcm/d = million cubic meters per day. Chart includes all markets of Southeast Europe, except Bulgaria and Romania.

Daily Variability

The analysis of seasonal swing presented above considers the average daily demand in each month. However, the actual daily demands are subject to considerable variability around these seasonal trend values. Furthermore, the daily peak demands are subject to variability from year to year. Both of those considerations are very important for gas storage. Load-duration curve parameters and data from countries in the region have been reviewed. For the nongasified parts of the region, of course, no data are available. Furthermore, what is required is a representation of the expected daily variability many years in the future for the purposes of analyzing storage needs and the corresponding economics. Therefore, a modeling approach is needed.

The daily variability is modeled using an inverse logit function of the form shown here:

$$D = A.Ln\left(\frac{1-x}{x}\right) + C \qquad \text{Eq. 2.1}$$

where D is demand, A is a vertical scale factor related to the peak load, x is a horizontal scale factor related to the fraction of the year, and C is a constant related to the annual average load.

Figure 2.19 plots the curve as modeled for Southeast Europe and compares this with the sinusoidal seasonal profile if only monthly and not daily variability were taken into account.

For storage, it is important to consider not only the average year but, more important, the peak years. Figure 2.20 shows the assumed load-duration curve for the year containing the 1-in-20-years peak demand value. A 1-in-20 year corresponds to a 5 percent probability. The curve shown is built on the assumption that this will be 10 percent higher than the peak demand day in the mean year (that is, with the expected value for the coldest day of the year).

The 1-in-20-years peak day is the criteria typically used for deliverability (for example, by National Grid in the United Kingdom). For storage, however, it is important to consider the volumes of gas required in a winter with persistently very cold periods to ensure that there is enough stored gas volume to meet such a contingency. A 1-in-50 energy year corresponds to a 2 percent probability, which is slightly more extreme than two standard deviations from the mean. Figure 2.21 shows how such a curve has been modeled.

Table 2.8 summarizes the key parameters used in the annual modeling consistent with the load-duration curves shown in figures 2.20 and 2.21. The values in the table represent the long-run load shown in figure 2.13 and the corresponding seasonal load in figure 2.17.

Figure 2.19 Long-Run Mean Year Load-Duration Curve and Seasonal Profile

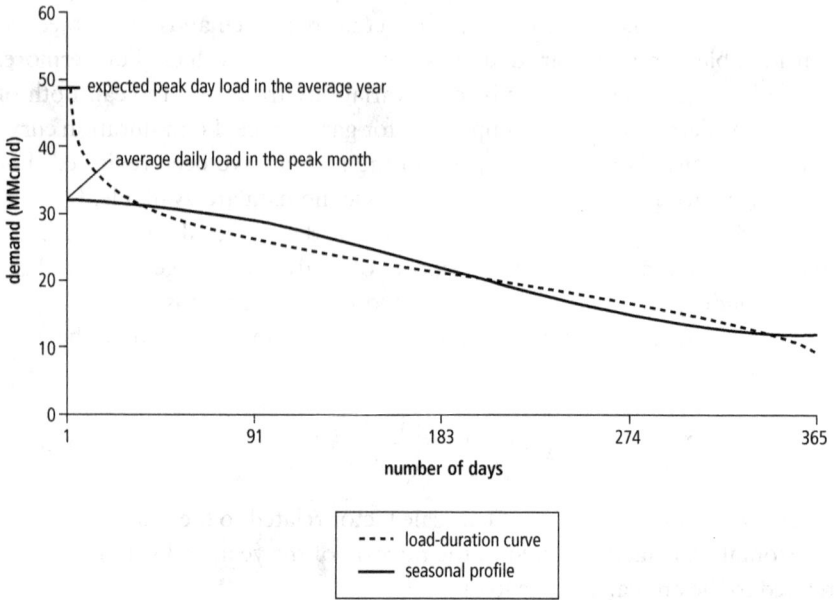

Source: Economic Consulting Associates' gas storage model.
Note: MMcm/d = million cubic meters per day. Chart includes all markets of Southeast Europe, except Bulgaria and Romania.

Both the year containing the 1-in-20-years peak day and the 1-in-50-years energy consumption are assumed to have the same peak demand. The 1-in-20-years peak demand case has the lowest load factor: 42 percent, compared with a mean of 45 percent. The 1-in-50-years energy case has a higher load factor, which an inspection of figure 2.21 suggests. All of the additional consumption in the 1-in-50-years energy case is assumed to occur in the coldest six months of the year—most of it in the coldest three months. This describes a consistently very cold year, with an extremely cold winter and colder than average autumn and spring seasons.

Hourly Variability

In addition to daily (interday) variability, gas demand varies hourly (intraday). This variability usually is managed using the pressure range between the maximum and minimum operating pressures of the transmission pipeline system (called "line-pack"). During hours of lower demand, the pressure is increased (the lines are "packed" with gas); and during hours of higher demand, the pressure is allowed to decrease. (Some discussion of line-pack available under various transmission system configurations is provided in the discussion in the "Cost of Alternatives to Underground Gas Storage" section of chapter 3.)

Security of Supply

The issue of security of supply relates to unexpected and infrequent interruptions of supply for technical, political, or other reasons. It is considered separately from seasonal and daily variability because it is different in nature and, more important, because capacity used to manage daily and seasonal variability cannot be double-counted as providing security of supply to cover the interruption of normal supply. (This issue is discussed in the "Security of Supply" section of chapter 4.)

Summary of Demand for Storage

Increased gasification in Southeast Europe will require parallel development of underground gas storage. The buildup of the many small loads on distribution networks will increase both the seasonal swing on the gas system and

Figure 2.20   Long-Run 1-in-20-Years Peak Day and Mean Year Load-Duration Curves

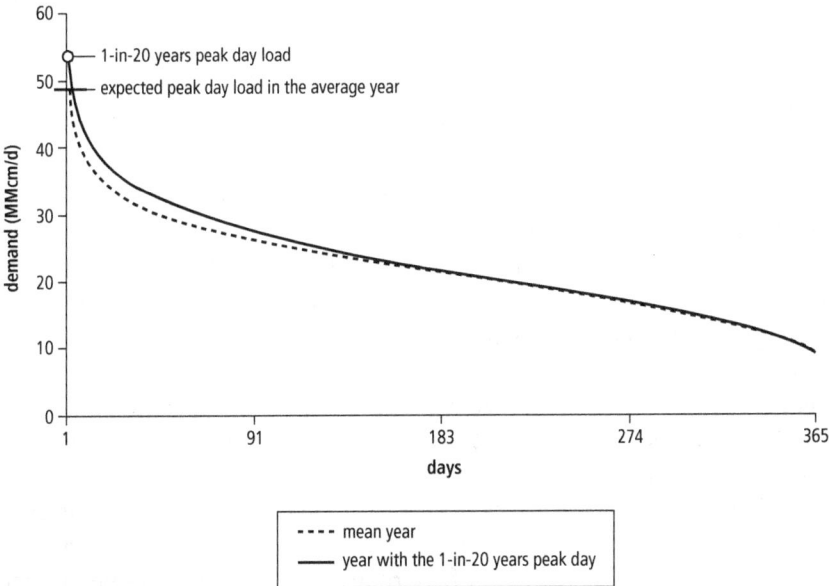

Source: Economic Consulting Associates' gas storage model.
Note: MMcm/d = million cubic meters per day. Chart includes all markets of Southeast Europe, except Bulgaria and Romania.

Figure 2.21   Long-Run 1-in-50-Years Energy and Mean Year Load-Duration Curves

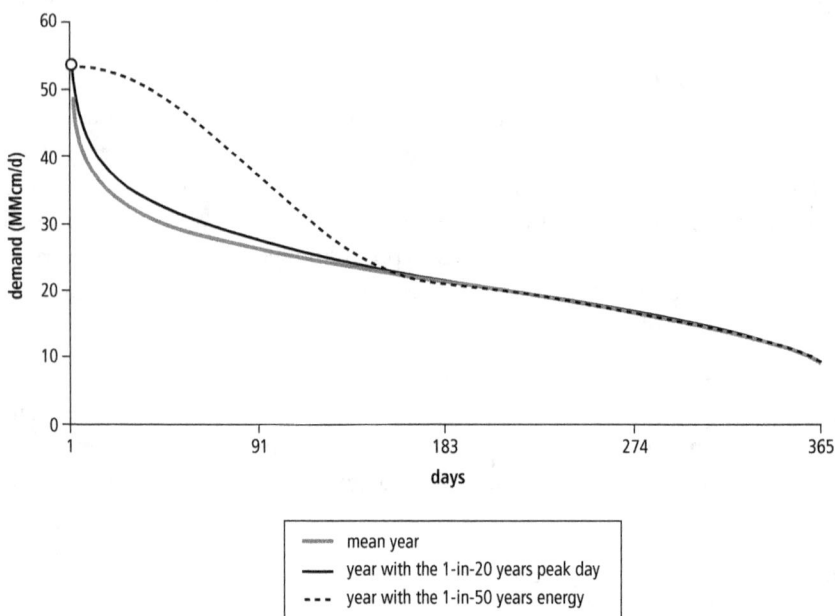

Source: Economic Consulting Associates' gas storage model.
Note: MMcm/d = million cubic meters per day. Chart includes all markets of Southeast Europe, except Bulgaria and Romania.

the peak response to low temperatures. The storage modeling indicates that 2.0–2.5 Bcm of capacity will be needed in the seven markets of the region that are not currently part of the European Union. A decision to set aside storage capacity for strategic reserves use in the case of supply interruption would increase this amount of needed capacity further.

Some 0.8 Bcm of underground storage capacity already is under development at the Banatski Dvor depleted gas field in Serbia. Companies in Romania already are planning to add 2.15 Bcm of storage capacity by 2015 to the 2.85 Bcm now in operation. All of this storage capacity is in depleted fields. Bulgaria is planning to more than double the capacity of the Chiren storage facility by 2010, from 350 MMcm to 800 MMcm.

If there is greater availability of alternatives to underground gas storage on commercially attractive terms than has been assumed, it may be possible to get by with a little less storage capacity. Similarly, if the degree of flexibility in supply contracts is greater than has been assumed in the modeling and

Table 2.8 Key Parameters in Annual Load Modeling

Year type	Annual energy (Bcm/y)	Mean load (MMcm/d)	Peak load (MMcm/d)	Annual load factor (%)
Mean	8.0	21.9	43.8	45
1-in-20-years peak day	8.3	22.7	48.2	42
1-in-50-years annual energy	9.8	26.8	48.2	50

Source: Economic Consulting Associates' gas storage modeling.
Note: Bcm/y = billion cubic meters per year; MMcm/d = million cubic meters per day. Chart includes all markets of Southeast Europe, except Bulgaria and Romania.

if the capacity is available in the upstream transmission system, it may be possible to get by with a little less storage capacity. Conversely, if the contracts are less flexible than the modeling assumes or if the transmission capacity is more constrained, more storage capacity would be required.

If temperature-sensitive residential and commercial distribution-connected loads build up faster than assumed in the modeling, the storage capacity would be required more quickly than if those loads build up more slowly. Regional coordination, most likely with key roles for the donors, will be important in this respect, as the storage supply analysis in subsequent chapters indicates.

3.

SUPPLY-SIDE OPTIONS

The analysis of supply-side pipeline options initially sought to determine the costs of meeting the projected incremental demand via spur lines (regional branch lines) from the major transmission pipelines that are planned to cross the Southeast Europe (SEE) region and bring imports from new sources to the SEE markets and Western Europe. The analysis is complicated by uncertainty over which of these transmission options will materialize. This uncertainty results partly from related uncertainty about the relative prices of gas from the Russian Federation, the Caspian region, and other possible sources of supply.

The supply-side options include a number of potential new major import pipeline routes, liquefied natural gas (LNG) import options, and the branch transmission pipelines that will supply or interconnect each of the nine SEE markets. These are the steps in the supply-side analysis:

- comparing the supply costs and competitive prices of each new source (principally for Russian gas versus Caspian gas or LNG) to establish the potential competitive positions of new sources and their likely penetration of the market
- identifying and analyzing the gas import supply options—producer-country sources and routes of major transmission pipelines
- identifying the network nodes that will form the supply price reference points for comparing alternate gas supply costs
- adopting assumptions for pipeline design for the regional branch pipelines to supply each market from the major transmission lines, and defining the engineering costing methodology to estimate the cost of each pipeline segment

- configuring the regional branch pipelines for each market from each major transmission pipeline (where relevant)
- making an economic analysis of each regional branch pipeline, taking account of the incremental investment costs, gas price at the offtake from the major transmission pipeline, and the incremental demand
- comparing alternative regional branch pipelines, and identifying the most promising options for each market.

Analysis of Prices—Supply Side

The analysis of prices begins with consideration of the factors affecting future market prices. That discussion is followed by a review of prices for gas at the borders of Southeast Europe; and a review of transmission, distribution, and supply margins.

Factors Affecting Future Market Prices

The assumption made about the future price of Russian gas supplied to the nine SEE markets is crucial to the analysis. Caspian gas eventually will compete with Russian gas to supply European markets. Historically, Gazprom has practiced price discrimination through it its significant monopoly power and its strategic relationships with some countries in the region. The pricing formulas, or at least the parameters contained in the formulas, varied significantly among countries buying from Russia. Generally, Eastern and Southeast European countries paid lower prices than did Western European countries. Some countries that transit gas had transit agreements to receive payment for transit in gas rather than in cash (and, historically, received the most favorable gas prices)—in particular, Belarus and Ukraine. Domestic gas prices within Russia remain significantly lower than gas prices in Western Europe.

However, Russia has indicated its interest in selling gas to Europe at market prices. This simply may mean the withdrawal of special treatment in the form of discounts to favored buyers. Russia seems particularly keen to implement this principle for countries that are among the "frontline" transit partners; or those that are moving politically and economically away from their historic Soviet-era links with Russia and into the political and economic orbit of Europe, seeking to join the European Union (EU) and to set their energy sectors on a competitive market footing. Indeed, during the Russia-Ukraine gas price dispute in the winter of 2005/06, Gazprom cited the need to increase Ukraine's gas prices to bring them into line with market prices as justification for its interruption of gas supplies for several days while a resolution to the price dispute was negotiated. Similar themes were observed in Gazprom's winter 2006/07 oil price dispute with Belarus. Further discussion of the costs and supply policy for Russian gas prices is provided in appendix A.

Map 3.1 Key Existing and Potential Transmission Network Nodes for Southeast Europe

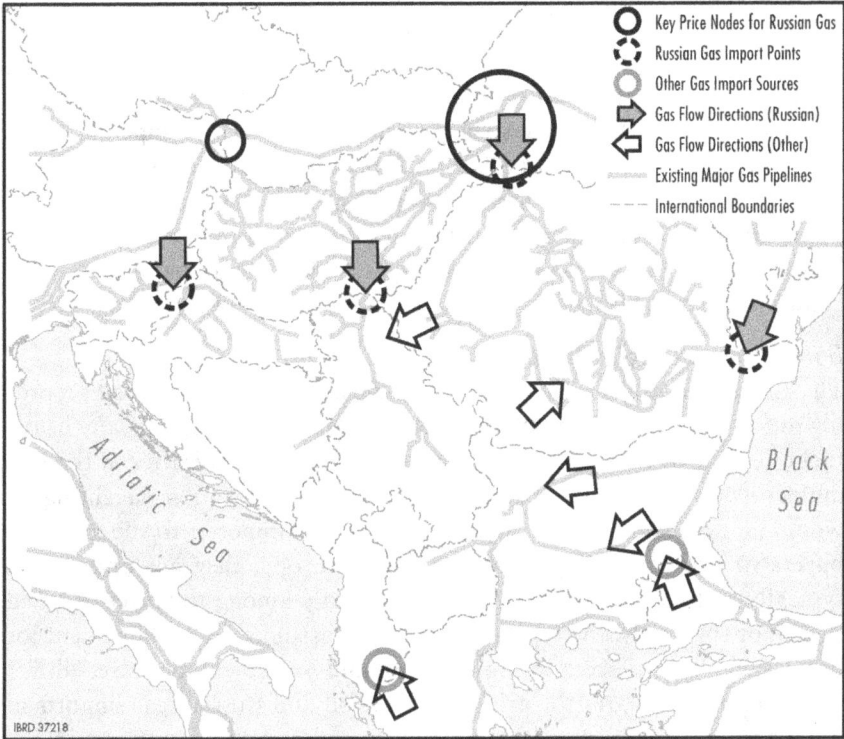

Sources: World Bank, compiled with reference to GIE, WinGas, and other published pipeline maps.

Map 3.1 shows key nodes for prices on the international gas transmission system:

- Baumgarten in Austria near the border with the Slovak Republic
- three import/transit points near Uzhgorod in Ukraine to
  - Velke Kapusany on the border with Slovakia
  - Beregdaróc on the border with Hungary
  - Mediesu Aurit on the border with Romania.

Also indicated are the four existing import points for Russian gas to the nine SEE markets:

- Rogatec on the Slovenian-Croatian border
- Kiskundorozsma on the Hungarian-Serbian border

- Mediesu Aurit on the Ukrainian-Romanian border
- Isaccea on the Ukrainian-Romanian border.

The potential future import point near Malkoclar on the Turkish-Bulgarian border for Caspian Sea gas delivered via Nabucco is indicated, as is an approximate point on the Greek-Albanian border for imports of either Caspian or Russian gas via the Turkey-Greece-Italy pipeline (TGI) or the trans-Adriatic pipeline (TAP). Branching flows from Nabucco to or through Bulgaria and Romania are indicated as well.

Comparison of recent historic Russian gas import prices to the SEE markets with European border price data suggests that any special prices or discounts to the nine SEE markets already may be a thing of the past.

Border Prices for Gas Imports

The gas imported from Russia to all of the SEE markets is priced according to formulas that use indexation to petroleum products, typically heavy fuel oil, light fuel oil, and No. 2 diesel. Although the specifics of the formulas—such as the base-year gas price and the indexation weightings—would be expected to differ somewhat from one importer to the next, for buyers in Central, Eastern and Southeast Europe, they are understood typically to be weighted approximately equally among the three indexed fuels. For this study, the typical weighting is assumed to be 35 percent for heavy fuel oil, 35 percent for light fuel oil and 30 percent for diesel oil.

Figure 3.1 compares the prices of crude oil and Russian gas imports at Baumgarten, Austria, for delivery to Italy and at Velke Kapusany on the Ukrainian-Slovak border for deliveries to Central and Southeast Europe since the beginning of 2000.

In addition to the indexation of gas prices to oil products, the pricing formulas contain other complexities, such as smoothing and time lags (which are inherent in the time-averaging approach), and may contain floors and/or ceilings on either the gas price or the indexed product prices. The effect of the time lags is clearly evident in figure 3.1. However, averaging, time lags and other complexities in actual pricing formulas is an unnecessary distraction for the purposes of the analysis in this study. The underlying relationships between crude oil prices and oil product prices, and between oil product prices and gas prices, allow a long-run equilibrium gas price to be inferred for any given long-run oil price assumption. The design of traditional long-term gas contract pricing smoothes out the volatility in oil spot prices, and investment decisions usually will be made with reference to an oil price level rather than to an arbitrary projection of fluctuating prices.

Figure 3.1 Historical Comparison of Crude Oil and Selected Estimated Gas Import Prices, 2000–09

Sources: U.S. Department of Energy, Energy Information Administration oil price data; ICIS Heren gas border price data analysis.
Note: FOB = free on board; Mcm = thousand cubic meters.

Transmission, Distribution, and Supply Margins

Table 3.1 shows the margins for transmission, distribution, and supply (and any local taxes on gas). These margins have been calculated by subtracting the estimated gas border prices shown at the top of the table from the competitive burner tip gas prices shown in table 2.7. The fuel-weighted values across the nine markets cover a large range.

There is a factor of about 1.5–2.0 between the lowest and highest oil price points presented (reading across each of the last three rows). This is large, but much smaller than the range of oil prices underlying it: $25 per barrel to $150 per barrel is a factor of 6.0. There is also a factor of about 1.5–2.0 between the minimum and maximum values across the nine markets at each of the oil price points.

Table 3.1   Margins for Transmission, Distribution, and Supply, Indicated by Netback Analysis

Market price	Western Ukraine border	Brent crude ($/bbl)					
		25	50	75	100	125	150
		Natural gas ($/Mcm)					
Weight	**Sector**	**90**	**170**	**250**	**330**	**410**	**490**
Transmission and distribution margin, by fuel							
(burner tip – border price, min~max in nine markets)							
Liquefied petroleum gas, 0%	Residential, some commercial	1,219 ~436	1,270 ~487	**1,321 ~537**	**1,371 ~588**	1,422 ~639	1,472 ~689
Diesel, 30%	Commercial, some industrial	799 ~575	911 ~687	**1,022 ~798**	**1,133 ~909**	1,245 ~1,021	1,356 ~1,132
Light fuel oil, 35%	Industrial, some commercial	693 ~171	715 ~193	**736 ~214**	**757 ~235**	779 ~257	800 ~278
Heavy fuel oil, 35%	Electricity, large industrial	200 ~15	223 ~38	**246 ~62**	**269 ~85**	293 ~108	316 ~131
Transmission and distribution margin, by country							
(burner tip – border price, weighted by fuel, rounded)							
Albania	All, weighted	270	320	**370**	**420**	470	520
Bosnia and Herzegovina	All, weighted	410	460	**510**	**560**	610	660
Bulgaria	All, weighted	400	450	**500**	**550**	590	640
Croatia	All, weighted	300	350	**400**	**450**	490	540
Kosovo	All, weighted	390	440	**480**	**530**	580	630
Macedonia, FYR	All, weighted	370	410	**460**	**510**	560	610
Montenegro	All, weighted	550	600	**650**	**700**	750	800
Romania	All, weighted	390	440	**480**	**530**	580	630
Serbia	All, weighted	390	440	**480**	**530**	580	630
Minimum		270	320	**370**	**420**	470	520
Midpoint		410	460	**510**	**560**	610	660
Maximum		550	600	**650**	**700**	750	800

Source: Economic Consulting Associates' analysis, using information on gas prices in Southeast Europe and Central and Eastern Europe and data from the Energy Information Administration.
Note: ~ = estimated range; bbl = barrel; Mcm = thousand cubic meters; Boldface type indicates the most likely scenarios; currently, the forward price curve is in this range, out to 2017.

The patterns are the same as those for the competitive burner tip netback prices in table 2.7. The margins potentially available to cover the transmission and distribution part of the value chain tend to be higher for liquefied petroleum gas (LPG) and diesel (the low-volume end of the natural gas market) and lower for the fuel oils (the high-volume end of the market). This is the expected relationship between margins and volume. The comparison of these margins with the estimated costs of transmission and distribution is presented in the section titled "Gas Value Chain."

Gas Sources of Potential Interest to Southeast Europe

The sources of gas that could supply Southeast Europe are reviewed in this section, followed by published data for the proven reserves of each country, and the supply availability and market dynamics.

Supply Options

Increased gasification requires increased supply. In assessing the economics of incremental new supplies, the study needs to consider both sources and delivery routes via pipeline or LNG. The gas sources taken into account in the study include fields in a vast arc centered on Central and Eastern Europe and sweeping clockwise from the Russian arctic all the way around to Algeria.[1] The sources and potential routes include

- Russian gas, transported along existing routes or via new routes
- Caspian gas, transported through new pipeline routes
- southern gas sources—Islamic Republic of Iran, Iraq, and Egypt
- LNG, most likely delivered within the Mediterranean basin from North African suppliers in Egypt, Libya, or Algeria.

Gas sources far to the northwest of the nine SEE markets (British, Dutch, and Norwegian North Sea gas) are not included in the list because the demand of Western European markets is, and is expected always to be, more than sufficient to absorb all of that production, so that gas never would flow as far as Southeast Europe.

Reserves

Table 3.2 shows the proved reserves and production for gas sources (by country) that are of potential interest to Southeast Europe. According to the *Statistical Review of World Energy* (BP 2006), the Russian Federation, the

---

[1] Geographically, North Sea gas may be closer to Southeast Europe than some of these other sources (or at least equidistant with them), but the large gas demands of Western Europe are in between the North Sea and Southeast Europe, so North Sea gas does not, and is not expected to, flow as far south and east as Southeast Europe.

Table 3.2 Proved Reserves and Production from Gas Sources of Interest to Southeast Europe, Various Years

Countries and regions	Proved reserves, end-2005 (Tcm)	Global share, end-2005 (%)	Production (Bcm) 1985	Production (Bcm) 1995	Production (Bcm) 2005	Change (%) 2004–05	Share of total (%) 2005	R/P (ratio) 2005
Azerbaijan	1.37	0.8	13.1	6.2	5.3	13.9	0.2	258.5
Kazakhstan	3.00	1.7	5.1	5.5	23.5	14.2	0.9	127.7
Romania	0.63	0.3	34.8	18.0	12.9	1.3	0.5	48.7
Russian Federation	47.82	26.6	431.0	555.4	598.0	1.5	21.6	80.0
Turkmenistan	2.90	1.6	77.6	30.1	58.8	7.9	2.1	49.3
Uzbekistan	1.85	1.0	32.3	45.3	55.7	a	2.0	33.2
Other	6.44	3.6	233.6	243.8	306.9	−3.0	11.1	21.0
Europe and Eurasia	64.01	35.6	827.5	904.3	1,061.1	0.8	38.4	60.3
Bahrain	0.09	0.1	4.5	7.2	9.9	1.3	0.4	9.1
Iran, Islamic Rep. of	26.74	14.9	14.6	35.3	87.0	2.8	3.1	307.4
Iraq	3.17	1.8	No data	No data	No data	No data	No data	>100.0
Kuwait	1.57	0.9	4.2	9.3	9.7	0.3	0.4	162.1
Oman	1.00	0.6	1.8	4.1	17.5	2.0	0.6	56.9
Qatar	25.78	14.3	5.5	13.5	43.5	11.4	1.6	592.7
Saudi Arabia	6.90	3.8	18.8	42.9	69.5	6.1	2.5	99.3
Syrian Arab Republic	0.31	0.2	0.1	1.9	5.4	3.0	0.2	57.4

Countries and regions	Proved reserves, end-2005 (Tcm)	Global share, end-2005 (%)	Production (Bcm) 1985	1995	2005	Change (%) 2004–05	Share of total (%) 2005	R/P (ratio) 2005
United Arab Emirates	6.04	3.4	13.2	31.3	46.6	0.9	1.7	129.5
Yemen, Rep. of	0.48	0.3	No data	No data	No data	No data	No data	>100.0
Middle East	72.13	40.1	63.6	148.9	292.5	4.6	10.6	246.6
Algeria	4.58	2.5	34.3	58.7	87.8	7.3	3.2	52.2
Egypt	1.89	1.1	4.1	11.0	34.7	29.4	1.3	54.5
Libya	1.49	0.8	4.7	5.8	11.7	79.5	0.4	127.4
Other, Africa	6.43	3.6	3.4	7.8	28.8	−0.3	1.0	223.3
Africa	14.39	8.0	46.5	83.3	163.0	13.3	5.9	88.3
World	179.83	100.0	1,676.3	2,142.4	2,763.0	2.5	100.0	65.1
Of which:								
EU25	2.57	1.4	164.0	195.4	199.7	−7.0	7.2	12.9
OECD	14.95	8.3	796.0	979.3	1,079.4	−1.3	39.1	13.8
FSU	58.32	32.4	599.8	659.8	760.3	2.2	27.5	76.7

Source: BP 2006.
Note: Bcm = billion cubic meters; EU25 = 25 members of the European Union; FSU = former Soviet Union; OECD = Organisation for Economic Co-operation and Development; R/P = reserves-to-production ratio (reserves divided by the most recent year's production); Tcm = trillion cubic meters.
a. Less than 0.05 percent.

current exclusive supplier of gas to SEE markets, had nearly 48 Tcm (trillion cubic meters; almost 1,700 Tcf [trillion cubic feet]) of proven gas reserves in 2005. And the countries of the former Soviet Union had 58 Tcm (more than 2,000 Tcf), about one third of the world's current proven gas reserves. Between them, the Islamic Republic of Iran and Qatar have more than 52 Tcm (in excess of 1,800 Tcf), which was just under 30 percent of the world's gas reserves.[2]

Availability of known gas reserves is not the main upstream issue for increased gasification of Southeast Europe. The key issues are whether there will be sufficient investment in the infrastructure to bring the gas to market, including production capacity at the fields and long-distance transmission pipelines, and the economics of those investments.

Map 3.2 shows the important gas basins of interest to the nine SEE markets (Albania, Bulgaria, Bosnia and Herzegovina, Croatia, Kosovo, FYR Macedonia, Montenegro, Romania, and Serbia). Major gas fields of key interest are indicated with triangles. Key routes for Russian gas are indicated in solid black lines; and routes from the Caspian, trans-Caspian, and Middle Eastern sources are in gray. The key nodes on the transmission network are at Baumgarten in Austria, Beregdaróc on the Ukraine-Hungary border, and near Ankara in Turkey.

Supplies of gas from Russia delivered via Ukraine to Europe originate from production at fields in the West Siberian Basin in the north. Future marginal production is expected to come from the Yamal Peninsula in the Arctic Circle.

Trans-Caspian gas from fields in Turkmenistan (the largest of which is Dauletabad), currently transits Uzbekistan, Kazakhstan, and Russia as it passes around the northern end of the Caspian Sea before transiting Ukraine and entering European markets. Because the routes to market for this gas currently pass through Russia, Russia effectively controls it; and this gas constitutes part of the mix of gas exported by Gazprom and its affiliated and subsidiary companies.

Caspian Sea gas from the potentially large Shah Deniz complex offshore from Azerbaijan will be able to be delivered to Europe when the Turkey-Bulgaria-Romania-Hungary-Austria Nabucco project is in place. The Nabucco pipeline also is planned to deliver gas from the Islamic Republic

---

[2] In more recent years, BP's published data on proven reserves have shown downward revisions for Russia (from just under 47.8 Tcm for 2005 in the 2006 edition of the *Statistical Review of World Energy*, to 43.3 Tcm for 2005 and 2008 in the 2009 edition); and an upward revision for some of the Central Asian states, most notably Turkmenistan (from 2.9 Tcm for 2005 in the 2006 edition, to 7.9 Tcm for 2008 in the 2009 edition). The Islamic Republic of Iran's proven reserve data also have been revised slightly upward.

Map 3.2   Gas Sources of Interest to the Nine SEE Markets

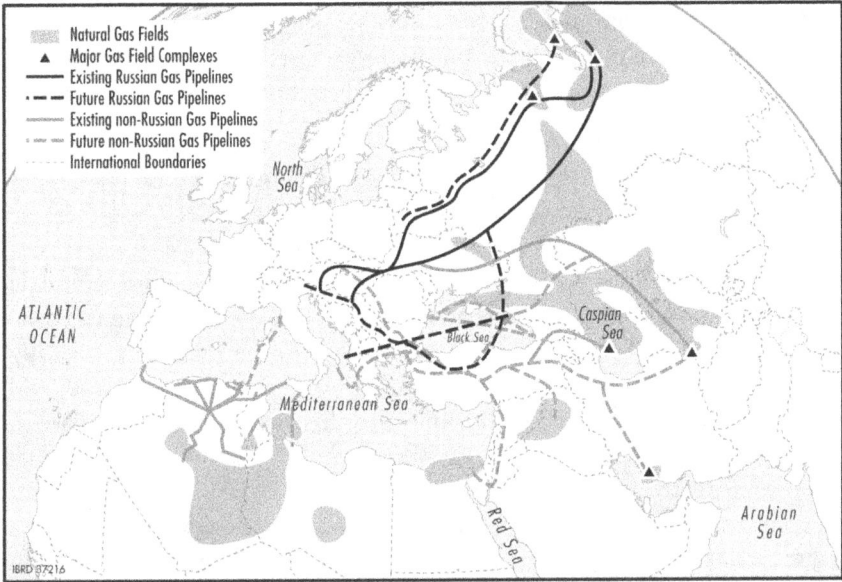

Legend:
- Natural Gas Fields
- ▲ Major Gas Field Complexes
- ── Existing Russian Gas Pipelines
- ·── Future Russian Gas Pipelines
- ── Existing non-Russian Gas Pipelines
- ·─· Future non-Russian Gas Pipelines
- International Boundaries

North Sea

ATLANTIC OCEAN

Caspian Sea

Black Sea

Mediterranean Sea

Red Sea

Arabian Sea

IBRD 37216

Sources: World Bank, compiled with reference to GIE, WinGas, and other published pipeline maps.

of Iran, or possibly from Turkmenistan via Iran. It also will be possible to deliver Iraqi gas along the same route—and potentially Egyptian gas, if and when the transmission pipeline infrastructure is in place.

Alternatively, Egyptian gas could be delivered as LNG because Egypt already has LNG liquefaction and export facilities. LNG exports to new receiving terminals on the Adriatic SEE coast also are possible, at least in theory. Croatia is probably the most likely location for such a terminal, and the Adria LNG consortium again is assessing such a development. Albania, Bosnia and Herzegovina, and Montenegro also have Adriatic coastlines.

It is expected that Caspian gas from Azerbaijan and the Islamic Republic of Iran and potentially from Turkmenistan, Iraq, and even Egypt will compete, in effect, at a point near Ankara where their pipeline routes converge with Russian gas delivered via Blue Stream. It is reasonable to assume that the price for SEE gas netted back to this point would be similar, regardless of the source. The transit and transmission price for delivering gas from this point to Turkey's western border also should be approximately equal across all the alternatives.

This observation removes the need to attempt to undertake a detailed study of marginal production costs for all of the potential new sources of gas to and through Southeast Europe to arrive at the price of gas from each of the various supply sources individually. This approach does not need to request confidential data from multiple countries that would be required to undertake economic analysis of upstream producer costs or the political factors influencing border pricing of the various supply options upstream of Turkey.

Supply Availability and Market Dynamics

The Organization of the Petroleum Exporting Countries (OPEC) and other oil-producing member-states, including Russia, have discovered that the present historically high oil price levels have not (or at least not yet) triggered global economic problems, such as the high inflation amid economic stagnation ("stagflation") that resulted from the two oil crises induced by the supply shocks of the 1970s. Oil prices have been pushed up steadily by relentlessly rising demand in China and, to a lesser extent, India; and they have been exacerbated by the unavailability of production capacity in Nigeria and elsewhere.

Most currently undeveloped oil reserves are under the control of national oil companies, and international oil companies increasingly are experiencing difficulty replacing their reserves. In this environment, governments in oil-producing countries appear reluctant to invest in large amounts of new production capacity. Possible explanations for this situation include (1) discipline within the members of the OPEC cartel combined with a parallel self-discipline by countries that are not members of the cartel, perhaps driven by a reluctance to risk undermining the currently high prices; (2) a belief that the current high prices will not persist sufficiently far into the future to justify new investment; (3) remaining reserves not being as large as previously reported (in accordance with the more bearish views of "peak oil" commentators); and (4) a general unwillingness or administrative inability within some governments to attract the necessary foreign investment to develop new reserves.

This situation in the oil market is relevant directly to the gas market because high oil prices underpin high gas prices, as a result of their substitutability at the margin, provided that ready access to large additional supplies of gas is not available. If investment in new gas production and transmission capacity from competing suppliers were relatively unconstrained, gas prices would experience downward pressure, more users would switch to gas, demand for oil products would fall, and upward pressure on oil prices would be relieved or even turn to downward pressure. This is the ideal scenario desired by the EU. (Note that in this scenario, oil and gas prices would not decouple until the point that all of the economic opportunities to substitute gas for oil had been exhausted.)

Given this background, there are indications that Russia's strategy in the gas market is to sustain high gas prices by limiting its investment in new gas production capacity for as long as possible, or at least for as long as needed to persuade European buyers to extend to at least 2030 their existing long-term contracts (which typically expire around 2015) while prices are high. This strategy is quite rational because it is in the commercial interests of Gazprom and in the fiscal interests of the Russian state. To be successful, the strategy also requires that Russia and Gazprom succeed in

- retaining transit control of trans-Caspian gas (from Kazakhstan, Turkmenistan, and Uzbekistan)
- keeping Caspian gas out of more direct routes to the European market (avoiding Russia)
- reducing the economic leverage of transit countries in general and, particularly, Ukraine and possibly Turkey in the future.

The Russian state and Gazprom aim to achieve the first objective by maintaining ambiguity over the status of the Caspian Sea under international law[3] and by maintaining strong political and economic relationships with the Islamic Republic of Iran, which provides an onshore alternative route for trans-Caspian gas to enter Turkey. The second objective is supported by a series of pipeline investments, such as Blue Stream; and preemptive announcements of projects, such as Blue Line and South Stream Nord and Sud. So far, they have been quite successful in achieving the third objective by such tactics as the combination of the Ukraine supply interruption and the project to build Nord Stream (the North-European Gas Pipeline) direct from Russia to Germany; Gazprom's strong position in Bulgaria with respect to the transit lines to Turkey and the joint announcement with ENI of Italy (in the presence of Russian and Italian ministers) of a feasibility study for the South Stream project that would pipe gas under the Black Sea directly from Russia to Bulgaria.

LNG Potential Supply
There is a possibility that some of the gas supplies for increased gasification in Southeast Europe could be sourced from LNG, rather than all of the necessary supplies of gas coming from Russia or the Caspian region.

---

[3] The future development of a trans-Caspian pipeline could not be blocked by Russia if the Caspian Sea is defined as a sea and, therefore, covered under the international maritime convention, the Law of the Sea Treaty.

This section examines the characteristics of LNG, identifies the options for its introduction to the markets of Southeast Europe and potential locations for LNG imports, and assesses the factors influencing the likelihood of new LNG imports to the area and its price competitiveness.

The potential future gas demand in Southeast Europe (or the apparent gas supply gap) is larger than the output of a typical LNG terminal. By 2025, there is a possibility that a third of the additional gas supply needed for Southeast Europe could come from LNG. Whether it actually will do so depends on many factors, including pricing, the prospects for transmission access to existing available receiving terminal capacity in the early years, the political will and resources to enable a new terminal to be built for the medium- to long-term, the availability of sufficiently large up-front demand (expected to require the parallel development of new gas-fired power stations within economic distance of the LNG regasification terminal), and the creditworthiness of the gas buyers. A key issue for Southeast Europe is that the potential volumes are relatively small in each of the countries, and flows would have to be aggregated to provide an anchor load to support the financing of such a terminal.

Successful development of a new terminal also would depend on such a new project not being competed away by an extension[4] (for example, a second or third LNG train) to an Italian LNG receiving terminal, such as the North Adriatic terminal.

The main approach to pricing used in this section is one of netbacks to determine the landed price. The regasified LNG would have to compete away pipeline gas and be attractive to LNG sellers, given the ease of transporting the gas to price-setting major markets elsewhere in Asia, Europe, and the United States.

International Market Fundamentals of LNG

Worldwide, total gas volumes delivered via LNG are much smaller than are volumes delivered by pipeline. However, the global LNG market continues to grow rapidly, at around 7 percent a year (approximately equivalent to doubling every 10 years). That is a significantly higher rate of growth than the pipeline gas market growth of 2–4 percent in most industrial countries. LNG often is described as being two separate markets (see figure 3.2):

---

[4] LNG projects commonly are referred to in the industry as "greenfield" for a project on a new location and as "brownfield" for an expansion project on an existing site. However, it seems slightly strange to describe an offshore terminal facility such as the Rovigo terminal as a brownfield.

1. the Atlantic market, where LNG coming mainly from the Middle East, North Africa, Norway (recently), and Trinidad is sent to Western Europe and North America
2. the Pacific market, where LNG from Alaska, Australia, Indonesia, Malaysia, and the Middle East is sent to Asian buyers, mainly in Japan, the Republic of Korea, and Taiwan (with China now emerging as a major buyer).

Middle East LNG can go either east to the Pacific market or west to the Atlantic market. Qatar is not only expected to be the swing producer for LNG into Europe because of its location and size; it also will be the producer that provides the supply-side price link between Atlantic and Pacific basin markets, because gas from Qatar can be delivered competitively through the Suez Canal into the Mediterranean market, via the Cape of Good Hope to the North American east coast market, or eastward to Asian markets.

When there are LNG receiving terminals on the west coast of the United States, that country will provide a demand-side price link between Atlantic and Pacific basin markets, in addition to the supply-side price link via Qatar. By that time, there will be one genuinely global LNG market characterized by liquid spot trading and with all prices almost certainly referenced to the Henry Hub.

The Atlantic Basin market has been growing faster than the Pacific market because it is a newer market, driven by U.S. demand to meet its gas shortage and driven in Europe by the decline of local production and the desire to diversify supply away from an overdependence on Russian gas.

LNG is characterized by very high fixed costs. In the past, those costs have tended to restrict the industry to a few of the major international and national oil companies. When compounded with geopolitical constraints, this has required long-term LNG supply contracts (20–25 years) to finance LNG development, a situation that has resulted in long investment cycles throughout the supply chain.

The LNG business is extremely capital intensive. As of April 2005, LNG was estimated to have $74 billion of net capital employed in just the midstream and downstream segments of the value chain (liquefaction, shipping, and regasification; see figure 3.3) (Kessler et al. 2005). A further $110 billion of capital will be employed by the end of 2008 (Kessler et al. 2005). In general, greenfield projects can cost up to 30 percent more than brownfield projects, both for liquefaction and regasification.

The rapid growth in the market has resulted in different utilization rates for liquefaction, shipping, and regasification (expressed in terms of actual

Figure 3.2   Overview of Atlantic and Pacific LNG Markets, 2000–15

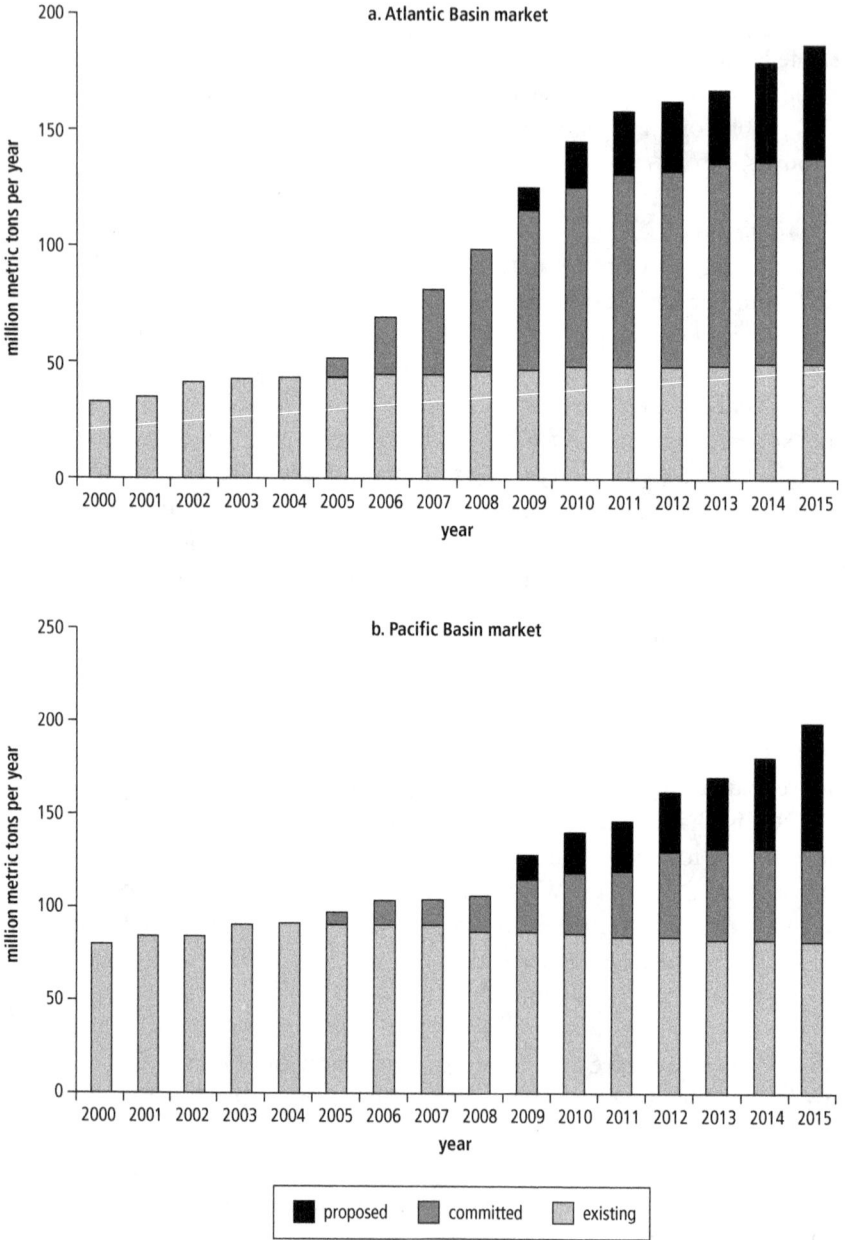

Source: Harris and Law 2007.
Note: LNG = liquefied natural gas.

Figure 3.3 Utilization of Liquefaction, Shipping, and Regasification Capacity, 2000–15

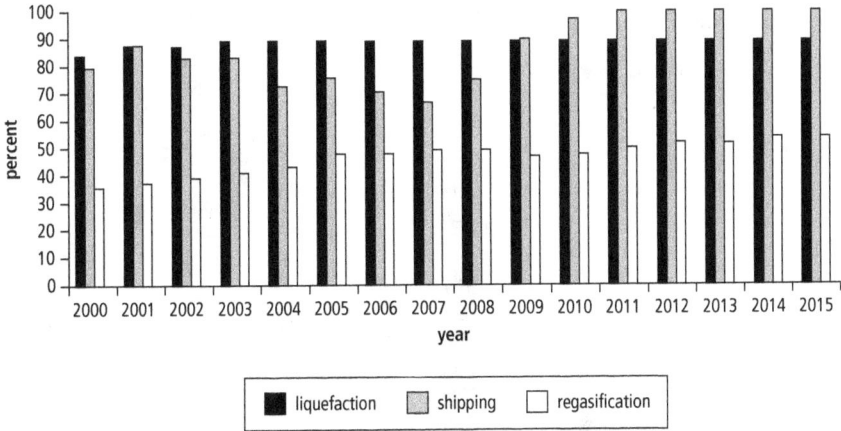

Source: Kessler et al. 2005.

throughput as a percentage of installed capacity). The limiting factor in the industry continues to be the liquefaction capacity. It can be seen in figure 3.3 that liquefaction capacity continues to be at approximately 90 percent, that shipping is underutilized (below 70 percent in 2007), and that regasification capacity utilization worldwide is less than 50 percent.

Each LNG trade route used to have dedicated, specialized LNG vessels usually owned and operated by the sellers and sized for the port and terminal facilities and the distance of travel. A trend has emerged in the last few years for independent shipping companies to enter the shipping market; and, in some cases, LNG shipping has been arranged by the buyers (either on an owned basis or chartered). Buying LNG under free on board (FOB) terms rather than under cost, insurance, and freight (CIF) terms changes the balance of risks between buyer and seller.[5] A small part of this trade

---

[5] Under FOB terms, title and risk pass to the buyer, who is responsible for paying all transportation and insurance costs, when the purchased commodity is delivered onboard the ship by the seller. Under CIF terms, title and risk pass to the buyer when the commodity is delivered onboard the ship by seller, but it is the seller who pays transportation and insurance costs to the destination port. Both sets of terms are used for sea or inland waterway transportation. Because the responsibility for forwarders' fees and freight shift rests with the seller under CIF, but with the buyer under FOB, according to international commercial terms, an LNG transaction between the seller and the buyer under CIF essentially is completed at the port of destination; under FOB, it essentially is completed at the port of shipment.

Figure 3.4 Typical Value Chain for LNG

Upstream LNG economics offer the highest returns, with regasification investments offering the lowest returns

- LNG is a capital-intensive business. A new project of 1 Bcfd requires more than $6 billion of capital investment from wellhead to regasification.

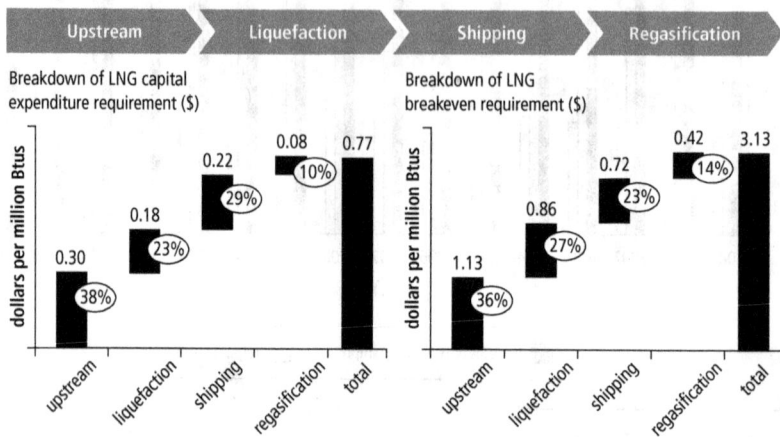

Based on a delivery project of 1 Bcfd, 6,500 nautical miles to market

Source: Analysis based on Kessler et al. (2005).
Note: Bcfd = billion cubic feet per day; Btu = British thermal unit; LNG = liquefied natural gas. Based on a 1-Bcfd delivery project, 6,500 nautical miles to market.

has been based on secondhand tankers as the industry moves into second-generation LNG projects.

Figure 3.4 shows that a typical new-build LNG chain with a capacity of 1 billion cubic feet per day (equivalent to 7.5 Mt/y [million tonnes per year] of LNG) and a 6,500-mile delivery distance has a breakeven price of $3.13 per million British thermal units (MMBtus). This assumes a minimum of 15 percent return on exploration and production and 8 percent on liquefaction, shipping, and regasification. (Many companies will require greater returns than this because of the inherent risks.)[6]

If the 7.5-Mt/y capacity described above is translated into a slightly smaller SEE project with capacity of 3–4 Mt/y (as discussed further below), the unit costs would be slightly higher, possibly around $3.5/MMBtu. However, shipping costs would reduce from $0.72/MMBtu (which is for a

---

[6] Note that the LNG chain costs from North Africa to the United States now probably are below $3/MMBtu for a new large project; and to Europe, they would be a little lower than that because of the shorter shipping distance.

distance of 6,500 nautical miles) to approximately $0.20/MMBtu, depending on the location of the LNG source. The conclusion is that the break-even cost for supply of LNG to Southeast Europe would be on the order of $3.0/MMBtu.[7] This estimated breakeven supply cost represents an absolute minimum to obtain financing, not the prices that actually would be achieved in the market. Suppliers will not offer buyers in Southeast Europe a price of $3.0/MMBtu when they can achieve more than that price elsewhere in the world marketplace (currently, two times that price).

Although further cost efficiencies undoubtedly will be achieved in the industry, it is difficult to assess how such efficiencies may affect the costs of a terminal for Southeast Europe. It would be prudent to forecast that the supply cost is likely to increase with inflation, although in practice the costs may decline in real terms. In the short term, costs in all parts of the oil and gas industry are being driven upward by the pressure on resources resulting from increases in the oil price affecting new LNG projects as well as oil and gas exploration and production. The link between oil prices and costs may be expected to work in reverse in a declining oil price scenario.

Average liquefaction train sizes have been increasing steadily. Early trains averaged little more than 1.0 Mt/y, whereas facilities built within the last five years average 3.0 Mt/y. Future trains are expected to average 4.6 Mt/y, with some of the largest trains (such as those in Qatar) reaching 7.8 Mt/y.

Capital costs per unit of capacity decline as train sizes increase, enabling liquefaction and regasification operators to realize economies of scale. Since the 1970s, unit construction costs of LNG liquefaction facilities have declined by an average 1.1 percent per year (Kessler et al. 2005). Further cost reductions are expected, particularly if train sizes continue to increase as expected. For example, the 7.8-Mt/y RasGas trains in Qatar (set for completion in 2009 and 2011) are expected to cost only $288 per tonne each year, $350 lower than Algeria's 1964 facility. LNG consultancies, such as Poten and Merlin, use a rule of thumb that each $100 capital cost savings per tonne of annual capacity translates to $0.20–$0.25/MMBtu in lower required LNG netback prices for delivery.[8]

The implication for Southeast Europe, which probably will be looking at terminal capacity with a single process train of 3–4 Mt/y, is that it is unlikely to be able to take advantage of some of the economies of scale open

---

[7] The cost of supply includes all cost chain elements from liquefaction to regasification and delivery into the transmission system, but excludes the cost of wellhead gas delivered to the liquefaction terminal.

[8] Costs are saved when projects are completed quickly. BG Group's Egyptian LNG project was the fastest ever, with 5 years occurring from contract award to market.

to the larger terminals. Also, unless there is a split sale of LNG to another buyer, the economies of scale at the liquefaction end will not be available.

Increases in steel costs and tightness in engineering capacity both for design and in vendors' factories over the last 18 months have caused a significant increase in costs: so much so that no new liquefaction capacity in producing countries came to financial close in 2006.

LNG Trading   An increasing volume of shorter-term trades has been occurring. In the mid-1990s as an attempt by sellers to sell individual cargoes to use any spare regasification capacity. (The large regasification plants often had been overdesigned to ensure that delivery capacity was not constrained.) The market, however, responded strongly to that attempt and the trend toward shorter-term trades has been increasing since that time. The rationale is straightforward: if a cargo is worth more when sold in North America than in Europe—even allowing for the different transportation costs and any other diversion costs—and if the contractual arrangements allow this to happen, the cargo can be sent instead to North America to make more money. The practice is a form of arbitrage. This arbitrage mechanism is a key reason for convergence of LNG prices around the world, and even Asian LNG and gas companies (both buyers and sellers) actively are considering the possibility of using the U.S. Henry Hub gas prices as an international marker for their own LNG and gas contract prices at some point in the future.

However, not all players are pursuing short-term arbitrage strategies. For example, there is little evidence that Qatar has been doing this to date. Many sellers and some buyers prefer more traditional arrangements to maintain reliable supply routes. The huge fixed costs and the consequent need to raise large loans where the banks still look to anchor loads and long-term contracts to underpin the repayments still limit the growth of shorter-term trades and spot markets in LNG. The likely evolution of such shorter-term contracting differs between the Atlantic market (where it has grown faster and nearly 15 percent of the market is now on a shorter-term basis) and the younger Pacific market (which is still dominated by traditional long-term contracts). The growth of short-term and spot trading is summarized in figure 3.5. The implications for Southeast Europe are that a new SEE terminal will have to compete for new supplies of LNG with terminals in Europe and farther afield; and that it will not be easy to obtain such supplies on a reliable basis, unless there is a long-term contract for the majority of the volumes required (Bros 2007).

LNG Pricing   The price of LNG in both the Pacific and Atlantic markets has been linked historically to oil prices. Figure 3.6 illustrates how pipeline gas, LNG, and oil prices have tended to move in tandem. In this sense Atlantic and

Figure 3.5 Growth of Shorter-Term LNG Trading, 1996–2020

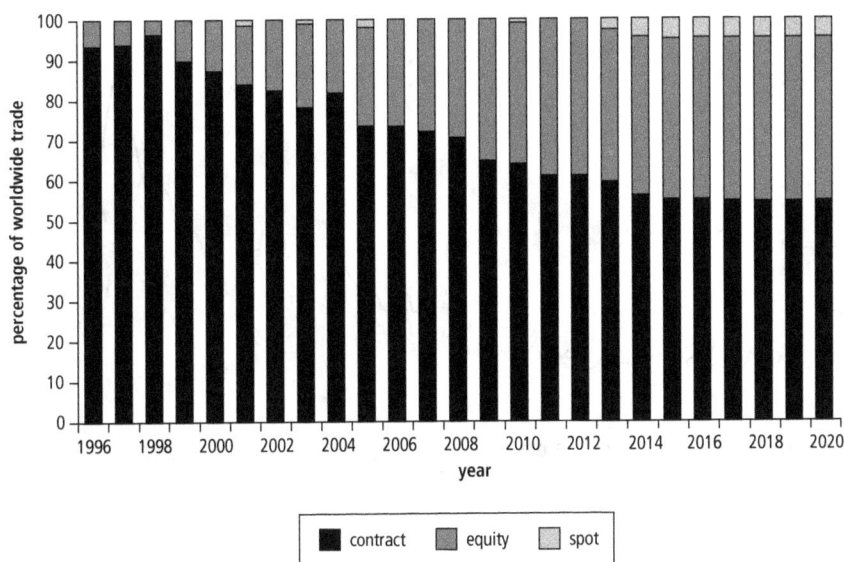

Source: Kessler et al. 2005.
Note: LNG = liquefied natural gas.

Pacific Basin prices are converging, although the volumes involved in LNG arbitrage sales are insufficient to guarantee complete price convergence.

Unlike pipeline gas—which has been indexed to a mixture of oil products (mainly fuel oil) and inflation in Europe and most countries outside North America and the United Kingdom—LNG pricing formulas since the mid-1970s have tended to have cap and collar mechanisms or an S-curve that protects sellers against very low oil prices (and ensures that interest on loans can be repaid)[9] and protects buyers against very high oil prices (see figure 3.7). Thus, if regasified LNG has to compete against pipeline gas (still largely indexed to oil product prices in continental Europe is) in these traditional but liberalizing markets, it may have a built-in price advantage in high oil price scenarios, if a similar collar does not apply to the pipeline gas contracts with which it is competing. In the process of negotiating for new contracts, however, pipeline gas suppliers may be expected to offer more favorable contract terms if such a scenario appears likely to prevail.

---

[9] The collar usually is designed as a minimum to cover the project financing.

Figure 3.6   Main Market Gas, LNG, and Oil Prices, 1996–2008

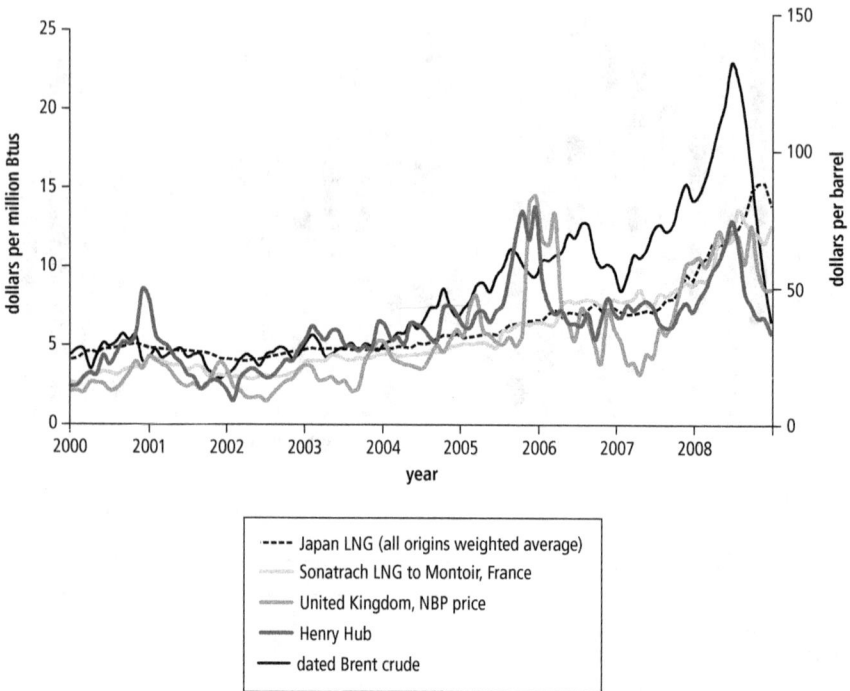

Source: Bloomberg.
Note: LNG = liquefied natural gas; NBP = National Balancing Point.

Figure 3.7   Market Developments in LNG Pricing

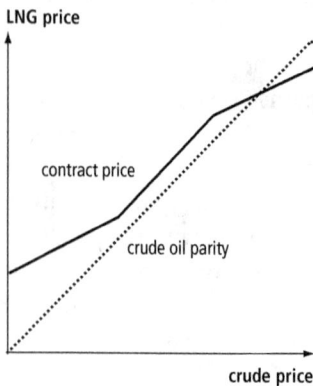

- Contracts traditionally are indexed to fuel oil prices.

- As a result of price volatility, new pricing arrangements were created to protect buyers and sellers of LNG.

- "S-curve" pricing protects the buyer from high oil prices and protects the seller from low oil prices.

- S-curves have an advantage over traditional gas contracts because they mitigate the risk of high oil prices.

- Recent tightness in the market has resulted in higher breakpoints in the S-curve, particularly in the Far East.

- Recently, there has been a move to indexing with wholesale gas prices (such as NBP or Henry Hub), which is effectively netback pricing.

Source: Authors' illustration.
Note: LNG = liquefied natural gas; NBP = National Balancing Point.

Pricing of LNG sold into the more liberalized gas markets in North America and, recently, the United Kingdom has been linked to prevailing gas prices rather than to oil prices.[10] In practice, under conditions of supply shortage over the past few years, those selling LNG into the United Kingdom have not assumed much price risk because U.K. wholesale gas prices have tended to be linked to equivalent fuel prices (mainly fuel oil). It could be argued that the reason for this link is that the U.K. spot market price[11] has shown a relatively high correlation with Norwegian gas (Troll) prices, plus or minus the costs of transportation from the continent, and that the Troll gas price is linked in turn to oil product prices. However, since the beginning of 2007, the United Kingdom has had excess import capacity, and gas prices have fallen—almost by a factor of two. This fall in gas prices has made the United Kingdom a less attractive place to sell LNG, and Qatar reportedly has switched some supplies destined for South Hook Train 2 to the United States (Harris and Law 2007). Historically, Henry Hub gas prices also have shown a strong correlation with fuel oil when supply and demand have been out of balance.

In the period just before oil prices spiraled upward in 2005, landmark deals were concluded for the sale of LNG to China and to India. The base prices quoted in the industry press (for example, in *World Gas Intelligence*) were on the order of $3.1/MMBtu and $3.2/MMBtu, respectively, fixed for five years. These deals were aimed at gaining a toehold in the emerging Chinese and Indian markets, and the prices were much lower than current LNG prices. Industry sources suggest that both contracts have since come under pressure for renegotiation, despite the fact that they contain no price reopener clauses.

It is not abnormal in the industry to find that important flagship gas and LNG projects on occasion have had advantageous terms. It is doubtful that Southeast Europe would be able to achieve similarly low initial prices, given that all the countries concerned already have a gas supply and sellers would not be attracted by the expected lower rate of growth and limited size of the SEE markets.

Current LNG Market Conditions and Medium-Term Outlook Despite large-capacity additions on the liquefaction side, maintenance delays and lack of available feedstock gas caused LNG production in the Atlantic Basin to grow at a much lower rate during 2006. Also, capacity utilization has lagged for a variety of reasons, such as delays in start-up of the new liquefaction

---

[10] Notable is the recent Qatargas III sale to the large South Hook terminal at Milford Haven in Wales.
[11] Prices are quoted at the national balancing point.

plants or maintenance needs. For example, difficulties acquiring feedstock supplies in countries such as Trinidad and Tobago and Nigeria were a primary factor that affected liquefaction operations during 2006.

In 2006 and 2007, LNG became very much a seller's market. In 2007, LNG sold consistently at $7–$10/MMBtu (CIF) in both the Pacific and Atlantic markets, and spot sales mainly were in the range of $5.8–$10.0/MMBtu throughout 2007. New buyers—such as the owners of the proposed terminal at Hong Kong (China), which has a notional start-up date of 2011, and others—found it extremely difficult to secure supplies, even on a long-term basis. Nor was it easy for buyers or traders to obtain cargoes at advantageous prices in the way they might have done only a year earlier. The utilization rates of shipping for companies like Excelerate (see "Infrastructure Options for Southeast Europe," below), which depends on a short-term trading strategy, were running at less than 50 percent in 2007. Three of Excelerate's ships had utilization rates of less than 40 percent. At the time, some industry analysts held the view that the shortage of liquefaction capacity would pertain until 2013 or even until 2015; but the combination of the global financial crisis and the development of shale gas in the United States more recently have led to relaxation of supply constraints and falling prices.

In tight market conditions, Southeast Europe could not have expected to secure LNG supplies for a new terminal on a short-term basis for a planned start-up before 2015. In any case, it would be difficult for any new terminal in Southeast Europe to access sufficient supplies to underpin investment before 2012–13; and a long-term deal will be necessary to secure a large proportion of the supplies.

LNG Supply Chain
The LNG supply chain requires consideration of LNG shipping costs and regasification terminals.

LNG Shipping Costs Figure 3.8 shows a detailed breakdown of shipping costs. This analysis is similar to recent information from various sources, including Poten and Partners Consultancy, Hurd (2005), and other commercially confidential reports. The breakeven CIF prices for LNG at a future SEE terminal would be determined by a netback formula equal to the price that could be obtained for that LNG in other markets (often taken to be the price at Henry Hub in the United States), with the difference in transport costs to the two locations netted off. As explained below in the section titled "Potential LNG Supply Sources for Southeast Europe," the most likely source of LNG supply to the area would be from North Africa—probably Egypt—or Qatar. The difference in shipping distances between those sources

Figure 3.8 LNG Shipping Costs and Carrier Size

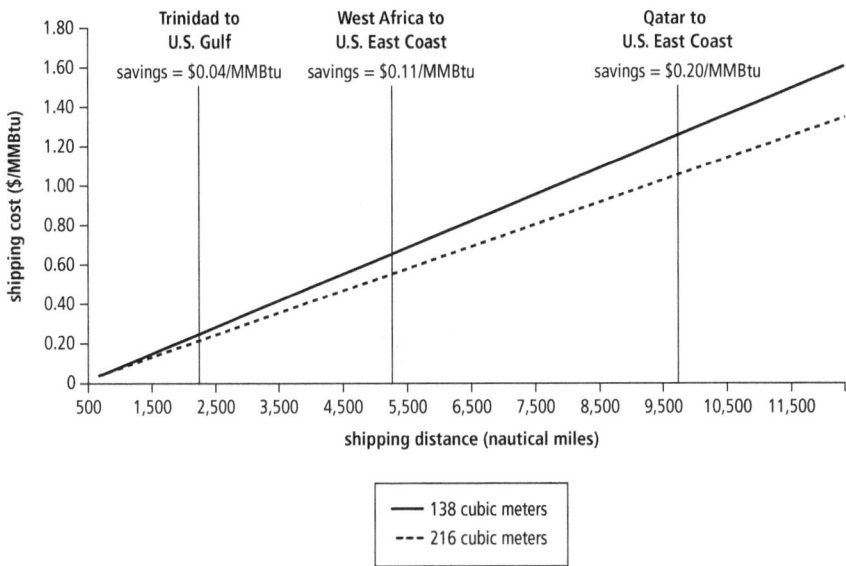

Source: Kessler et al. 2005.
Note: Btu = British thermal unit; LNG = liquefied natural gas; MMBtu = million Btus.

and Southeast Europe is approximately 1,500 miles, which is shown in figure 3.8 to equate to a difference in CIF price of $0.1–$0.2/MMBtu.

LNG prices currently are very much higher than the basic cost of supply, as analyzed above. The question then is to whom the excess rent passes— to the upstream consortium, to the liquefaction company, or to the shipping company (if this cost element is not included in the LNG price)? The economic rent almost invariably passes to the LNG seller (unless there is an integrated supply chain) in the current market because it is liquefaction capacity that is in short supply, not shipping or regasification terminals. In any event, this rent is far greater than the difference in shipping costs calculated above for supply from Qatar rather than from Egypt.

Regasification Terminals Experience suggests that obtaining approval for an LNG regasification terminal is not always easy. An LNG terminal is a large, industrial facility located on a coastline. If the heat in seawater is used to regasify the LNG, environmental impacts from cooling of the seawater ("thermal pollution") may be a concern. Across the other side of the Adriatic Sea, BG Group's proposed terminal at Brindisi in southern Italy has been met with environmental objections (in addition to other problems that have affected the project). There were objections on environmental grounds to the original proposal for an LNG terminal on the Island of Krk in Croatia. The revived proposal by the Adria LNG consortium has not yet obtained government approval, and environmental impact assessments of as many as five potential sites in Croatia are understood to have been commissioned by the Croatian government. Siting and obtaining the necessary permissions for an LNG terminal, therefore, is not necessarily a straightforward exercise.

An LNG receiving terminal consists of the following elements:

- LNG carrier berthing and unloading facilities
- LNG storage facilities
- a regasifying or vaporizing system
- facilities to handle boil-off gas
- high-pressure LNG pumps
- a metering and pressure regulation station
- a gas delivery pipeline.

Many different configurations are possible for the design of the receiving terminal. Figure 3.9 shows a typical arrangement.

Figure 3.9 Schematic of Typical LNG Regasification Terminal

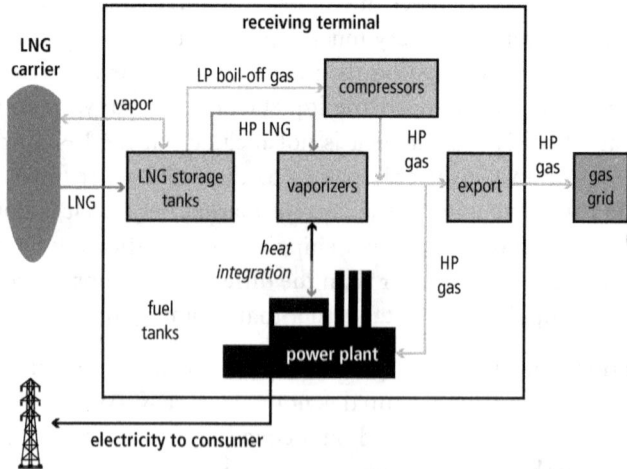

Source: Authors' illustration.
Note: HP = high-pressure; LNG = liquefied natural gas; LP = low-pressure.

Figure 3.10   LNG Regasification Capacity, 1990–2010

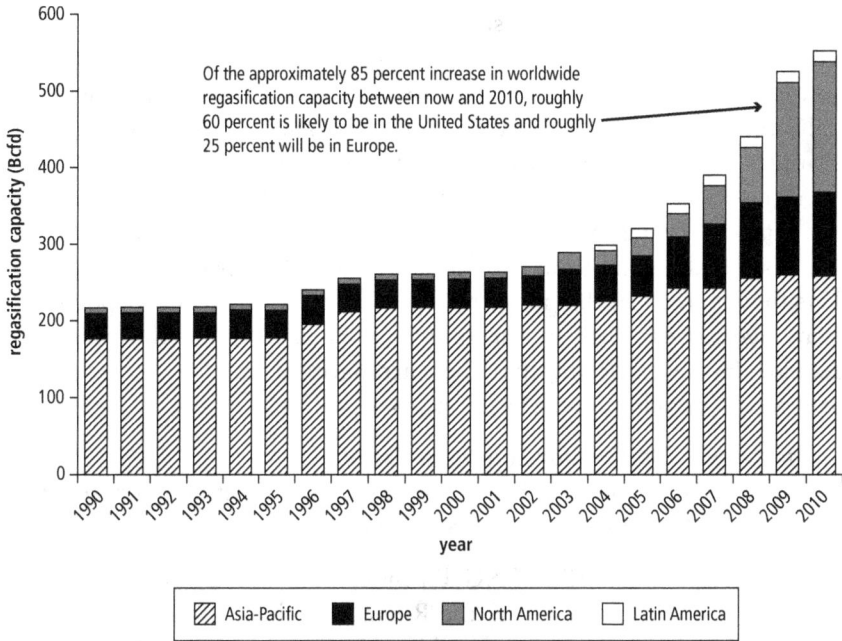

Of the approximately 85 percent increase in worldwide regasification capacity between now and 2010, roughly 60 percent is likely to be in the United States and roughly 25 percent will be in Europe.

Legend: Asia-Pacific | Europe | North America | Latin America

Source: Kessler et al. 2005.
Note: Bcfd = billion cubic feet per day; LNG = liquefied natural gas.

Regasification capacity (figure 3.10) has increased even more rapidly than has liquefaction capacity; indeed, as figure 3.3 shows, installed regasification capacity is now far greater than installed liquefaction capacity (that is, regasification utilization is far lower than liquefaction utilization). Regasification terminals used to be built to match the send-out capacity of the corresponding liquefaction plant on each dedicated trade route. However, more terminals are being built with excess capacity in the expectation of receiving LNG from a number of geographically diverse sources. This factor has exacerbated the low utilization rates for regasification terminals.

In most cases, it is necessary to dilute the regasified LNG with some nitrogen to meet local pipeline specifications (particularly Wobbe index) because LNG tends to be a little richer in higher hydrocarbons than is pipeline gas.

The likely extended period of excess supply conditions in regasification invariably will result in a period of consolidation, particularly among players with constrained balance sheets. This consolidation ultimately may be a concern to a developer of a terminal in Southeast Europe.

As noted above, LNG terminals face stiff opposition on environmental and safety grounds in many countries—particularly, the United States. Such opposition also has been the case at Krk in Croatia, where the original plans were shelved for several years. That proposed LNG regasification terminal now has been reactivated, and issues are being worked out by the new Adria LNG consortium of OMV (Austria), Total (France), INA (Croatia), RWE Transgas (the Czech Republic), and Geoplin (Slovenia).

A greenfield terminal is likely to take three-and-a-half years to design and build following the final investment decision; a brownfield extension, such as an additional train, would take slightly less, perhaps three years. This finding assumes that all preengineering, all consents, all supply agreements and all financing agreements are in place at the time of the investment decision. However, closing all of these arrangements can take an indeterminate period, possibly as long as five years.

Infrastructure Options for Southeast Europe
To bring LNG to Southeast Europe would require selecting a site, securing financing, and developing a new LNG terminal.

Development of a New SEE LNG Terminal   The first LNG regasification terminal in the Adriatic Sea is the Rovigo terminal offshore from Italy, installed in late 2008 and operational in 2009. New potential LNG terminal sites on the Adriatic coast in Southeast Europe include Krk, Ormisalj, Ploce, and several others being suggested by the Croatian government; and there is a potential site in Albania (Fier District) that the Albanian government is interested in developing as an LNG terminal. Having said that, it must be noted that initial feasibility and development studies are under way at Krk, and many of the issues found in the previous work on that site are starting to be explored with the authorities again. The earlier proposal failed because of environmental problems. The island is one of outstanding natural beauty, situated in a tourist area. Its new consortium's public presentations show potential for supplying markets in Austria, Croatia, Hungary, Italy, Romania, and Slovenia (Lewisch 2007). The terminal capacity far outstrips the needs of Croatia, which is a relatively small market and well served by domestic production, Russian gas, and gas via Hungary in the future. Therefore, the proposal is for the terminal to become a stepping-stone into the gas markets inland, particularly in Austria and the Baumgarten gas hub (see map 3.3). At present, there are no gas connections to Krk; and major reinforcement of transit lines from the coast would have to be carried out, thus adding to the costs.

Although a new SEE LNG terminal might take only three-and-a-half years to build after financial sanction, an indeterminate amount of time is required first to surmount all the hurdles to obtain consents as well as to

Map 3.3   Adria LNG, Krk, Croatia

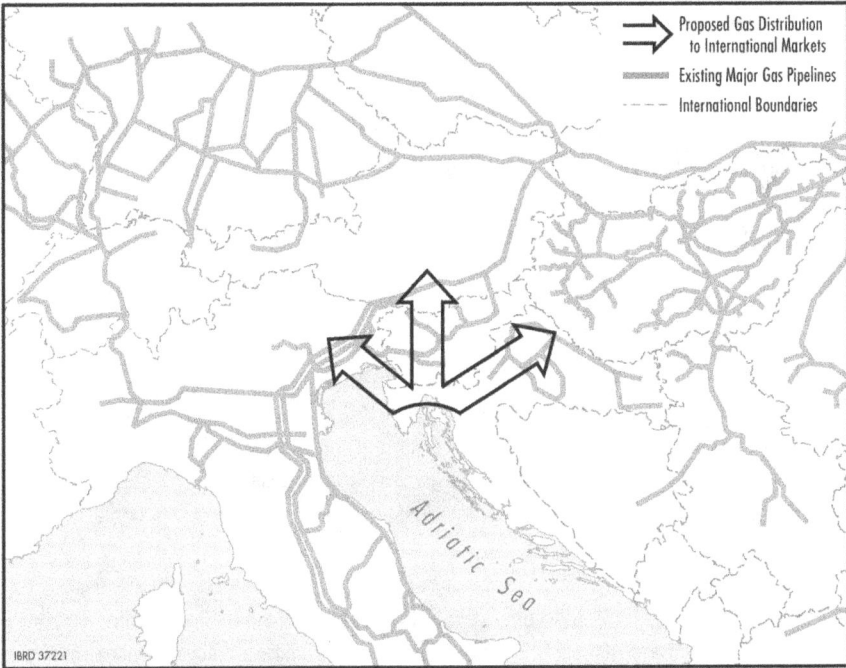

Sources: World Bank, based on information from Adria LNG, map compiled with reference to GIE, WinGas, and other published pipeline maps.
Note: LNG = liquefied natural gas.

arrange long-term LNG supplies; organize financing; and carry out the necessary engineering, commercial, and market studies.

If it proves difficult to obtain the necessary consents to develop a new terminal in SEE, then an "energy bridge" concept might be considered near Krk instead of an LNG terminal. In such an approach (described in box 3.1). LNG is regasified onboard a specially converted vessel. This possibility is supported by RWE's reported interest in Excelerate, its upstream position (as RWE A) in Egypt, its interest in Croatia, its energy-trading orientation, and its key interests in many Central and Western European gas and electricity markets. It would take only two years to install plus whatever time is needed to gain the necessary permits and to receive confirmation that sufficient entry capacity exists from the Croatian gas transmission system operator, Plinacro.

Criteria for Selecting a New Site   In selecting the site for an LNG terminal, the geology and topography of the area have to be studied both to ensure a

BOX 3.1

The "Energy Bridge" Model: An Alternative to a Regasification Terminal

The energy bridge concept may be an option for a would-be importer of liquefied natural gas (LNG) who faces difficulties getting a full regasification terminal approved or developed, as may turn out to be the case in Southeast Europe. Under this approach, LNG is regasified onboard a specially modified LNG vessel equipped to connect to a gas pipeline onshore. This alternative approach avoids possibly fatal delays in gaining approvals to build regasification terminals, and obviates the need to build very costly LNG terminals.

The concept has been developed for commercial application independently by Excelerate (originally part of El Paso, but sold to the Kaiser group) and Suez (which is not nearly as well advanced). These companies have been developing the technology for gasification onboard modified LNG vessels and for ship-to-ship LNG transfer systems. Shipboard gasification has enabled Excelerate to deliver LNG to multiple import facilities, both conventional terminals and three new "gas gateways."

The energy bridge concept requires converted LNG vessels of normal size and draft to be able to maneuver and tie up to an unloading facility. The reduced capital costs onshore can make this technology a viable option for more destinations, although marine facilities such as jetties and deep-water approaches are still necessary. Another attraction is where winter gas is needed rather than year-round baseload gas, and where the overall use of any regasification plant would be uneconomically low. Peak delivery rates of regasified LNG from energy bridge vessels can approach the delivery rates from standard LNG regasification terminals.

However, the energy bridge concept ties up more vessels on a given trade route than does conventional LNG delivery, and there is no storage in the supply chain (except by retaining the LNG onboard the vessel), effectively substituting vessel operating cost and demurrage charges for onshore tankage. The modified vessels also cost more than conventional vessels because they need additional process equipment and the ability to pick up submerged buoys and discharge when moored on single-point mooring systems (or jetties, where allowed by the authorities) for ship-to-ship transfer. There are special permitting issues for these gas gateways; and consent from the maritime authorities

(continued on next page)

in the United States, for example, have not been acquired without significant cost exposure.

Excelerate has a fleet of six LNG tankers under charter or dedicated ownership, two of which are still being built. With the necessary modifications, each costs as much as $30–$70 million more than conventional LNG vessels of the same size. They can be used as ordinary LNG vessels and let out on charter if no arbitrage opportunities can be found.

The cost of an energy bridge gateway depends very much on what infrastructure already exists in terms of both marine facilities like jetties and navigation channels, and on what pipeline facilities are available. Costs are very site specific. At Teesside in the United Kingdom, the additional onshore and marine facilities cost on the order of £75 million ($150 million). The U.S. Gulf gateway costs around $85 million. However, the North East gateway near Boston, Massachusetts, is estimated to have cost more than $230 million because it required subseas pipelines. (This cost may be compared with a conventional small LNG regasification terminal that might cost $350–$500 million.)

Energy bridge ships can discharge regasified LNG into normal high-pressure (75–80 bar) pipeline grids. Just as with conventional LNG terminals, however, nitrogen injection is almost always required to reduce the Wobbe index of the regasified gas to within local gas specification limits.

Permitting may be fast-tracked for energy bridge facilities, although Excelerate has found in the United States that doing so comes at a price.[1]

If the development of a full regasification terminal proves impossible in Southeast Europe, because of either environmental or commercial/financial constraints, then the energy bridge concept is an option that should be considered seriously. It would be prudent, however, not to rely on a short-term trading strategy to access LNG supplies in the way Excelerate's present business model operates.

Note

1. Mitigation for the North East gateway, for example, included substantial payments to the Massachusetts Lobstermen's Association, obligations for ongoing ocean floor mapping, installing an acoustic buoy program, remedies for the local harbor islands, compensation to local fishermen, and the conclusion of certain agreements on U.S. manning of vessels.

Source: Excelerate, http://www.excelerateenergy.com.

sound geographical base over which the plant foundations will be built and to take advantage of the topography during the design phase, if at all possible. Similarly, the basic weather patterns, climate, storm potential, and seismic conditions must be studied, together with the marine aspects of each site, such as navigational hazards, access to currents, tides, ease of approach, dredging required, sea traffic, and safe anchorage areas. Sites are selected on the criteria outlined in table 3.3.

The concerns relating to LNG terminals are not of continuous impact on the surrounding area (as with power stations or industrial emissions, for example), but relate to the assessment of risk of explosion or fire resulting from a catastrophic engineering failure or terrorist action. Such events have low probability but potentially severe consequences. The LNG industry has an excellent safety record. There has been no major fire involving an LNG tanker. Failures of LNG storage tanks are rare. The most serious LNG fires

Table 3.3 Criteria for LNG Receiving Terminal Site Selection

Category	Criteria
LNG carrier approach	Water depth, width, alignment, currents, navigational aids, other marine traffic, tugs, and pilots
Maneuvering basin	Water depth, wind, waves, currents, tugs, and so forth
Berth	Water depth, wind, waves, current, sterile zone, jetty length, mooring lines, tugs, pilots, and so forth
Site	Land availability, site preparation, onshore access, utilities, and emergency services
Pipelines	Route, geology, topography, depth and length, existing pipeline grids, and environmental issues associated with routes
Environment	Protected areas and current use of area; mitigation proposals for potential pollution, including chilling effects on seawater if open-rack vaporizers are used (a major issue in some parts of the world)
Safety	Separation from other marine traffic, industry, and populated areas
Cost	Total life cycle costs

Source: Authors' compilation.
Note: LNG = liquefied natural gas.

involving loss of life occurred in the 1940s, when tanks were poorly constructed, relative to today's standards, and when the safety and monitoring technologies used today were not available.

Therefore, LNG terminals generally have not been considered to pose a threat to surrounding communities. But the potential severity of a serious incident combined with communities' perceptions of the risk of such an incident, whether accurate or not, means that developers and governments usually prefer to locate terminals as far as possible from inhabited areas. In addition to the safety concerns, proximity to an industrial environment is more convenient and economic, in most cases.

A very important point is the availability of a local infrastructure with the proper utilities, transportation, road systems, and so forth. It also would be prudent to ensure that there is additional land adjacent to the terminal that is suitable for future expansion. These factors can make site selection difficult along the eastern coast of the Adriatic Sea, which is characterized by rocky mountains and slopes descending into the sea and a large number of small offshore islands that may constrain shipping access.

The Black Sea coast of Bulgaria and Romania is considered effectively off-limits to the development of LNG receiving terminals because safety concerns would make it impossible for LNG tankers to receive permission to navigate the Bosporus (which already is a highly congested shipping route).

Having sufficiently large anchor load for the regasified LNG, a stable regulatory system, and strong project sponsors who are capable of managing the complex backdrop of commercial, financing, and political issues all ultimately play a major part in whether a particular LNG terminal site is developed.

Financing Issues   Reaching financial closure on any new LNG receiving terminal requires confidence that all aspects of the project have been considered properly and that appropriate risk mitigation measures are in place. Equity providers usually are risk takers for a defined set of risks. For infrastructure projects, the challenge is to secure the debt portion with reasonable financial terms. Therefore, the project company or owner needs to make sure that the project design provides adequate security to the various lenders. Important elements in this financial design include

- involvement of international reputable management within the owner's organizational structure
- strong commitment to the equity investment by the sponsor, as a proof of risk taking
- economic importance of the project

- commercial viability of the project
- sound legal framework that substantially alleviates noncommercial risks and supports the commercial viability of the project
- appropriate contractual arrangements that underpin the robustness of the project
- strong completion and performance guarantees for the construction
- competence of the operator
- throughput guarantees that ensure commercial viability
- convertibility of revenues
- assurance of repayment.

In addition to the financing issues present in any LNG project, an SEE LNG project with multiple gas offtakers would face complications,[12] unless a single entity such as a large oil or gas company acted as the aggregator of demands. All of these factors will need to be considered by the developers of a new LNG terminal in Southeast Europe.

Existing and Proposed New Terminals in the Region

Existing LNG terminals nearest to the Adriatic Sea are ENI's Panigaglia terminal near Genoa (3.3 billion cubic meters per year [Bcm/y]) and the Revithoussa terminal near Athens. The latter terminal is 35 percent owned by Hellenic Petroleum SA and 65 percent owned by the Greek state, with 100 percent of the capacity reserved for DEPA. Neither of these existing terminals is expected to be in a position to supply Southeast Europe. Panigaglia is not in a suitable location to do so. The Revithoussa terminal send-out capacity currently is being expanded with a third storage tank, after which the site is understood to have no room for subsequent expansion. BOTAS Petroleum Pipeline Corporation, in Turkey, is making its excess summertime LNG available on the spot market.

Of the two terminals on the Italian side of the Adriatic expected to begin operating in 2008:

1. The North Adriatic LNG terminal (Isola di Porto Levante) will be a major import terminal positioned off the northeastern coast of Italy (17 kilometers offshore in 30 meters of water) between Venice and Punta della Maestra in Rovigo. It will have a nominal annual regasification capacity of 8 Bcm; and, from 2009, it will provide the Italian gas market with 6.4 Bcm/y for 25 years, supplied from RasGas II Train 4 in Qatar. The project sponsors are

---

[12] These complications might be analogous to those of the Nabucco project.

Qatargas, ExxonMobil, Edison, and Edison LNG Adriatico. The LNG supply contract is with Qatargas and ExxonMobil. Edison has signed a sale and purchase agreement with RasGas II that covers allocation of 80 percent of the terminal capacity (4.7 Mt/y of LNG) for 25 years. The remaining 20 percent of the capacity will be available to third-party users.[13]

2. The Brindisi LNG terminal in southern Italy had been planned as an import terminal on the "heel" of Italy. In 2003, the Economic Development Ministry authorized BG Group to build an LNG terminal with a nominal regasification capacity of 8 Bcm/y. In 2005, BG Group signed a sale and purchase agreement for the supply of 3.2 Bcm/y, (2.4 Mt/y of LNG) to Enel, beginning in 2008.[14] Supply is being sourced initially from Egyptian LNG Train 2, the output of which was sold in its entirety to BG Group's subsidiary, BG Gas Marketing. In April 2005, the Italian regulator granted a 20-year exemption from third-party access for 80 percent of the terminal. Start-up (originally planned for 2007) was delayed to 2010 because of local protests from environmental groups and politicians.

In March 2007, Italy's environment ministry announced that the government was seeking to annul the previous government authorization.[15] In the second quarter of 2007, the courts renounced the approvals, and it looks unlikely now that the terminal will be built in the next decade. This terminal would be relatively close to the likely landing point for the Greece-Italy section of the planned Turkey-Greece-Italy gas pipeline.

The Italian gas market is particularly attractive to many players. Although Italy is the third-largest natural gas market in Europe (approaching 80 Bcm/y), behind Germany and the United Kingdom, it has very high rates of return, and exports to countries in Southeast Europe would have to be priced attractively to compete gas away from the rapidly growing Italian market. However, there are indications from recent large take-or-pay deals that Italy has aspirations to become a regional gas market center and supplier. Access to Italian LNG terminals, including tariffs, is regulated by the Italian energy regulator (Autorità per l'Energi Electrica e il Gas) under Decision 120/01, as amended by Decision 127/02.

---

[13] For information about this terminal, visit http://www.hydrocarbons-technology.com/projects/adriatic/.

[14] For information about this terminal, visit http://www.bg-group.com/media/archive_2005/012405-sx.htm.

[15] For the news story concerning the ministry's efforts, visit http://uk.reuters.com/article/oilRpt/idUKL036154920070303 [accessed July 6, 2009].

There are many other proposed or possible LNG terminals in Italy, and many of those are at an early planning stage and may never be built. Included among these potential terminals are the following:

- Rosignano LNG Terminal (Livorno, Tuscany): developed by Edison, Solvay, and BP; 3-Bcm/y send-out capacity; 2008 proposed start-up
- Offshore Livorno Toscano Project (offshore Livorno): developed principally by Endesa and Amga Genova, 4 Bcm/y send-out capacity, fourth quarter of 2008 proposed start-up
- LNG MedGas Terminal (San Ferdinando, Calabria): developed by the Falck Group, at the permitting stage
- Gioia Tauro–San Ferdinando (Calabria): developed by Societa Petrolifera, Gioia Tauro, at permitting stage
- Taranto (Puglia): developed by Enel, appears to be on hold
- Vado Ligure (Liguria): developed by Enel, still at permitting stage
- Muggia (Friuli): developed by Enel, still at permitting stage, rejected by local authority
- Zaule (Trieste): developed by Gas Natural, still at permitting stage
- Priollo/Augusta/Melilli (Sicily): developed by Shell and ERG Power & Gas, still at pre-permitting stage
- Porto Empedocle (Sicily): developed by Nuove Energie, still at pre-permitting stage
- Offshore Trieste: developed by Endesa and Friulia (partially state owned), still at permitting stage (King and Spalding 2006).

If the Italian regulator were to deny exemption from third-party access to terminal expansions, that action might favor the development of an alternative new LNG receiving terminal in Southeast Europe.

Alternatives to a New LNG Receiving Terminal in Southeast Europe

Any developer of a new LNG receiving terminal in Southeast Europe would need to consider the potential competitive threat from other terminals, the economic and commercial opportunities for backhauling LNG via Revithoussa, and the economic and commercial opportunities from northern Italian LNG.

Potential Competitive Threat from Other Terminals   The possible development of other nearby terminals, especially in northern Italy, would present a competitive threat to the development of a new LNG terminal in Southeast Europe. Such terminals might compete away both supplies and the market for regasified gas and thereby prejudice the commercial viability of a new SEE terminal. The divergence of interests between the separate gas buyers in the SEE countries may make it difficult to aggregate sufficient volumes to underpin a new terminal, unless a major gas company (like ExxonMobil Gas Marketing) were to take on the volume and price risk and act as the primary buyer, on-selling to the local gas companies (or electricity generators, for new combined-cycle gas turbine [CCGT] plants) as required.

The competitive threat is especially evident at the proposed new Adria terminal in Croatia, which is close to an existing terminal in northern Italy, particularly if the costs of developing a greenfield LNG receiving terminal in Southeast Europe are higher than installing a second train at an existing site like Porto Levante.[16]

The existing LNG receiving terminal at Revithoussa in Greece is largely unused. That capacity could present a threat to a new LNG receiving terminal in Southeast Europe if gas could be delivered from it to the region. Turning the threat around, however, it becomes an economic and commercial opportunity for Southeast Europe: there is no need to incur the cost and risk of developing an LNG terminal in the short to medium term if SEE markets can access existing spare terminal capacity (Thomadakis and Avlonitis 2007).

Economic and Commercial Opportunities from LNG via Revithoussa   For present purposes, the Greek natural gas transmission system can be considered a "black box" containing sufficient capacity between the entry and exit points because the transmission owner, in effect, is required by the regulatory system to develop adequate capacity to avoid constraints within the system. The system has three entry points:

1. the original entry point on the Bulgaria-Greece border, through which most of Greece's contracted volumes are supplied from Russia
2. the Revithoussa LNG terminal
3. the new entry point on the Turkey-Greece border.

Currently, there are no exit points from Greece. When the Poseidon project (the submarine Greece-Italy section of the large Turkey-Greece-Italy project) is complete, there will be one exit point. For the present study, the possibility of a second exit point to supply Southeast Europe is of interest. This point could be either on the border of Greece and of the Former Yugoslav Republic of Macedonia or the Greece-Albania border. The situation is summarized in table 3.4.

---

[16] The costs of developing a greenfield site can be as much as 30 percent higher than the costs of a brownfield expansion, as noted above, but it is not clear how this economic cost comparison would translate to the case of the offshore Rovigo terminal in Italy.

Table 3.4 Greek Capacity and Potential for SEE Access to Revithoussa LNG

Border or network node	Yearly Capacity, 2007 *(Bcm)*	Future yearly capacity, 2010~15 *(Bcm)*
Entry points		
Bulgaria-Greece	5.475[a]	Bulgarian side uncertain
LNG-Greece	~3.000[b]	5.100[c]
Turkey-Greece	3.200	11.600[d]
Total	11.675	22.175
Exit points		
Greece, domestic	3.0	~7.000
Greece-Italy	No exit capacity at present	8.000–15.000[e]
Greece-FYR Macedonia or Greece-Albania	8.675[f]	0–7.175
Total	11.675	22.175

Source: Authors' compilation.
Note: ~ = approximately; Bcm = billion cubic meters; LNG = liquefied natural gas; Mcm = thousand cubic meters; MMcm = million cubic meters; SEE = Southeast Europe.
a. On a flat annual basis, this is the nominal capacity of the metering station on the entry to the Greek system. There may be more exit capacity on the Bulgarian side, but there is no information about that capacity.
b. The current utilization is 0.5 Bcm a year.
c. Requires installation of a third storage tank to increase the onsite storage from 130 Mcm to 220 Mcm.
d. This is the limit with maximum additional compression installed on the Turkish side, but with no new pipelines.
e. These are Economic Consulting Associates' estimates. The pipeline will be the deepest 32-inch-diameter pipeline in the world, at 1450 meters. The water pressure at that depth is more than 180 bar, so the operating pressure would be expected to be high. Blue Stream has 2 × 24-inch pipes at a depth of about 2,000 meters, each of which can deliver 8 Bcm a year. The capacity estimate of 15 Bcm shown here for the Greece-Italy pipeline probably is conservative. The Edison-DEPA consortium's published capacity figures refer to the 11.6-Bcm future capacity constraint upstream in Turkey.
f. There is no physical exit point from the Greek system to FYR Macedonia or to Albania today. This value represents the capacity that today is considered potentially available to such a future exit point.

According to this capacity balance analysis, more than 8.5 Bcm of unused entry capacity is available to new exit points from the Greek system today, and a little more than 7.0 Bcm would be available for delivery via new exit points at some time in the period between 2010 and 2015. Physically, much of this entry capacity is at the underused Revithoussa LNG terminal. Therefore, it should be possible for SEE markets to access 2.0–2.5 Bcm of capacity in the 2010–15 period for power station anchor demand. They would access this capacity by backhauling LNG from Revithoussa against the prevailing north-to-south flow in the Greek system, effectively reducing those flows by the amount of the LNG contract to Southeast Europe. Physically, the LNG would flow to Greek load near the demand center around Athens, while Russian (and possibly some Caspian) gas would flow from Russia via Bulgaria. It then would flow either through the Greek system and north into FYR Macedonia or Albania, or directly from Bulgaria to FYR Macedonia or to southern Serbia and into the nine SEE markets.

Because Greece still would be buying largely Russian gas (topped up by some LNG), Italy still would be buying Caspian gas, and Southeast Europe would be buying the LNG, these physical flows would be achieved by making a commercial swap. The main "if" regarding this possibility concerns the ability of buyers in the SEE markets to access LNG volumes (given that liquefaction capacity is currently very tight) and to do so at the right price.

Clearly, SEE buyers would be competing with buyers in the Italian market for LNG via Revithoussa, subject to the constraint of the headroom available to Edison above the 8.0 Bcm of capacity on the Poseidon Italy-Greece Interconnector pipeline that is exempt from third-party access.

There is no underground storage in Greece. Therefore, apart from the LNG storage tanks (only 130 Mcm [thousand cubic meters], expected to increase to 220 Mcm soon), swing is managed mainly using the entry points, suggesting firm entry capacity may be tighter than it would be for flat deliveries with underground gas storage (UGS) to match supply and demand. However, gas demand in Greece is dominated by the power sector, so seasonal swing is not as much of an issue as in markets dominated by residential and commercial gas-fired heating.

Economic and Commercial Opportunities from North Italian LNG   The costs of shipping LNG to a north Italian terminal will be much the same as shipping it to a SEE terminal. However, the regasified gas then would have to be transported from that terminal to SEE markets. Within Italy, this will be in the direction of most gas flows, so reinforcement of the pipeline system may be necessary.

From Trieste to SEE markets, flows would be effectively backhauling[17] against the main transit flows from Russia and the Caspian Sea; and although this undoubtedly will not be free of transmission fees, it may be

---

[17] Because the flow is in the opposite direction to the main flows, the trade of LNG from Italy to Croatia might not result in a net flow in that direction, but simply in a reduction in flow in the opposite direction.

possible to arrange commercial gas swaps that offset these physical flows. It is difficult to estimate the total costs that would have to be taken into account, but those costs are very unlikely to outweigh any advantage for a brownfield terminal development. Such an approach has obvious time advantages if compared with gaining approvals and designing and constructing a new greenfield terminal.

Potential LNG Supply Sources for Southeast Europe
The principal North Africa and Middle East sources of LNG are summarized in appendix B. The outlook for LNG supply is expected to remain tight around 2010, but may open up with further investment by around 2015 and should be less constrained by 2020. Other things being equal, LNG terminals serving the SSE market ideally would be supplied by LNG from the closest sources, especially North Africa (Algeria, Egypt, or Libya) to minimize shipping costs—both the number of ships required to be dedicated to the trade route and the number of days' sailing for each journey (the daily cost is made up of charter rates that take account of the capitalization).

A new SEE LNG regasification terminal would have to organize baseload LNG supplies. This need would be less pressing for use of capacity at an existing terminal, such as Revithoussa, but security of fuel supply for power stations would require some long-term contracts. There are several sources with which SEE buyers could negotiate for LNG supply:

- Egypt and Qatar are likely to have supplies available from about 2015 onward.
- The cost of supply of Qatar LNG might be approximately $0.1–$0.2/MMBtu more than that from Egypt because of additional shipping costs. However, this differential is likely to be swamped by differences in base price (ultimately, a matter for commercial negotiation) and differences in economic rent (resulting from the ability of sellers to price their LNG for sale to other markets). In other words, the difference in shipping costs would mean a difference in rent to the seller and the same price for the buyer.

As discussed in the "Study Methodology and Approach to Analysis" section of chapter 1, the underlying cost of supply (as distinct from the market price) of LNG from North Africa to Southeast Europe is likely to remain on the order of $3.0/MMBtu (plus inflation) over the plan period, with LNG from Qatar costing slightly more to transport than LNG from Egypt.

Even though the LNG market is likely to return to a more balanced position after 2013–15, the price of LNG in the European market is likely to be set by the price that could be achieved for the LNG in alternative destinations—particularly, the North American market—less the additional transport costs of perhaps $0.6/MMBtu. In turn, this LNG price will be determined by the price of local pipeline gas at Henry Hub. Given the increasing deficit in gas supply predicted for the North American region, the price of pipeline gas at Henry Hub is likely to continue to be related to the price of oil products as a substitute fuel. Therefore, if oil prices remain high ($60 a barrel or more), then gas prices at Henry Hub may continue to be $7–$10/MMBtu, which will set a marker for international LNG prices.

This means that the price of LNG in the international market—in particular, the netback to suppliers of LNG to Southeast Europe—is likely to continue to be substantially higher than the predicted breakeven cost of supply of LNG to Southeast Europe. This analysis uses the quite robust assumption that price convergence of LNG and pipeline gas around the world will continue, based on continuing oil price links either explicitly through contracts or implicitly resulting from substitute fuel values.

If European gas prices were to decouple from oil price over the plan period, as is the hope of the European Commission in its drive to liberalize the European gas markets, then European gas prices may start to fall,[18] relative to the prices that would have pertained under the present long-term contracts that are linked to oil products prices. In that scenario, European gas prices might not bear any relationship to prices in the United States (as was the case for certain periods in the 1980s and early 1990s). The problem with this scenario as far as LNG is concerned is that LNG suppliers might not find it as attractive to import LNG into Europe if they can achieve higher netback prices elsewhere (in the United States and East Asia, for example). If it appears that there still is higher market risk in Southeast Europe than in Western Europe, then it might make development of the SEE LNG market more difficult.

In either case, unless Southeast Europe is prepared to pay a small premium to gain geographical diversity of gas supplies, the price of LNG into the region is likely to be capped by the price of local pipeline gas. This could make LNG sales into the area unattractive, relative to sales elsewhere in the world.

One way to offset some of the price risk is to involve a powerful upstream sponsor in any SEE terminal project. Such vertical integration is a classic way to manage this type of risk. However, it seems unlikely that a new

---

[18]This is subject to any tendency toward increasing gas prices, relative to oil or coal resulting from future carbon emissions policies in Europe.

terminal in Southeast Europe would be regarded as a flagship project and given special terms because the rate of predicted economic growth and the relatively small market size would not make the region as attractive as, say, China or India for an LNG developer. That only reinforces the attractiveness of alternative LNG delivery options by contracting for available capacity at the existing Revithoussa terminal, backhauling from northern Italian terminals, and contracting for a share of future Adria LNG capacity.

Summary of the Prospects for LNG

Any new SEE terminal will have to compete with brownfield terminals in Italy. From the perspective of SEE markets, however, any cost advantage that the brownfield terminals would have might be offset by additional transport and transit costs to the SEE market.[19] The capital costs of terminals are very site specific; and without any concept engineering studies available in the public domain, it is difficult to estimate how much an SEE terminal might cost.

A conventional LNG terminal with a capacity of 3–4 Mt/y (typically, the cheapest option if the demand is sufficiently large) would deliver 4.0–5.5 Bcm of gas, which is about double the expected initial anchor load in the seven western SEE markets.[20] A 1.5–2.0-Mt/y LNG terminal sized to meet the anchor load would lose the economies-of-scale advantages, but would reduce exposure to supply contracts and match the potential anchor loads.

The most promising options in approximate descending order of likelihood are the following:

- Contract for LNG deliveries to Revithoussa in Greece to use its available capacity. This LNG would be well placed to meet demand in the southern markets of Southeast Europe (via backhauling and using commercial swaps for Russian and possibly some Caspian gas), particularly markets in southern Serbia, Kosovo, FYR Macedonia, Albania, Montenegro, and perhaps as far as southern Croatia.
- Backhaul LNG from terminals in northern Italy into the northern part of the nine SEE markets, particularly Croatia.
- Contract for a share of LNG delivered to the Krk Island Adria LNG terminal, if its development goes ahead.

---

[19] This is possible, unless the benefits of backhauling would keep these costs low.

[20] It seems extremely unlikely, given the terrain and current lack of pipeline infrastructure, that LNG landed on the eastern Adriatic coast could penetrate as far as the Romanian market, where the supply gap will be the largest.

Transmission Pipeline Supply Routes and Scenarios

Existing pipeline infrastructure and potential new routes are considered first in this section. Major new pipeline scenarios are outlined next, followed by an identification of their key characteristics and current status.

Existing Pipeline Infrastructure and Potential New Routes

Map 3.4 shows the projects of pan-European interest identified by INO-GATE (2006). The corridors, indicated in solid black lines, that are of most interest to the nine SEE markets all transit Turkey; they could transport Caspian gas from Azerbaijan or Turkmenistan, or gas from Egypt, the Islamic Republic of Iran, or Iraq. (The southern routes loosely indicated in map 3.4 are discussed in further detail below.)

At present, all gas imported to the nine SEE markets comes from (or at least through) Russia. Several markets also have indigenous gas. The country with the most significant amount of gas is Romania, where two thirds (11.6 Bcm out of 17.3 Bcm) of its gas was supplied from indigenous fields in 2005. Croatia was next, with more than half (1.57 Bcm out of 2.70 Bcm) of its gas supplied from its own sources in 2005. Serbia's gas reserves are

Map 3.4   European Gas Grid, Showing Potential New Pipelines to Europe

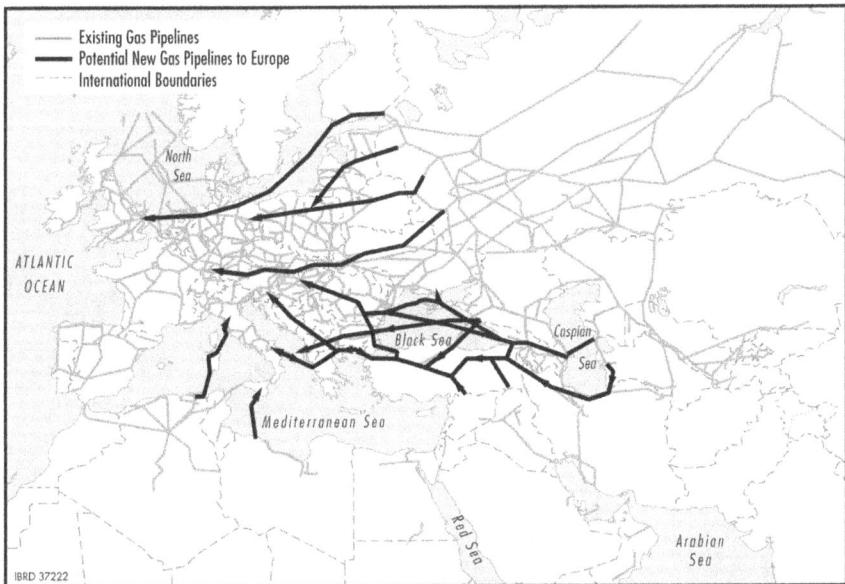

Sources: World Bank, based on EU information and compiled with reference to GIE, WinGas, and other published pipeline maps.

136

Table 3.5 Domestic Production, Import Volume, and Capacity in the SEE Markets
Billion cubic maters per year

	Northern markets		Central markets		Southern markets			Eastern markets	
	Croatia	Bosnia and Herzegovina	Serbia	Montenegro	Kosovo	Albania	FYR Macedonia	Romania	Bulgaria
Import capacity	1.84	0.74	6.10	—	—	—	0.80	38.3	27.6
− Available	0.71	0.36	3.57	—	—	—	0.72	10.9	5.9
= Import volume	1.13	0.38	2.53	—	—	—	0.08	27.4	21.7
− Export volume	—	—	0.38	—	—	—	—	21.7	18.5
= Russian gas	1.13	0.38	2.15	—	—	—	0.08	5.7	3.2
+ Indigenous gas	1.57	—	0.35	—	—	>0	—	11.6	0.3
= Total consumption	2.70	0.38	2.50	—	—	>0	0.08	17.3	3.2

Source: Economic Consulting Associates' research and analysis.
Note: — = absolute zero; SEE = Southeast Europe.

well into the production tail, supplying only a small quantity (0.35 Bcm out of 2.53 Bcm) in 2005. Table 3.5 shows the existing import capacities on an annual volume basis (for the case of a flat supply profile) and how much of those capacities was used in 2005. These data are shown on map 3.5.

To date, all gas imported from Russia flows in a southwesterly direction into the SEE markets, all of it transiting Ukraine. The major entry points to the nine markets are at the borders of Romania in the east; and in the north, via Hungary to Serbia and via the Slovak Republic, Austria. and Slovenia to Croatia. Much of the gas entering Romania at Isaccea near the Black Sea subsequently transits Romania. About 3 Bcm/y of it supplies Bulgaria; very small volumes (less than 0.1 Bcm/y) transit Bulgaria to supply FYR Macedonia; and the majority transits Bulgaria to supply Turkey. The Bosnia

Map 3.5   SEE Markets Domestic Production, Import Volume, and Capacity

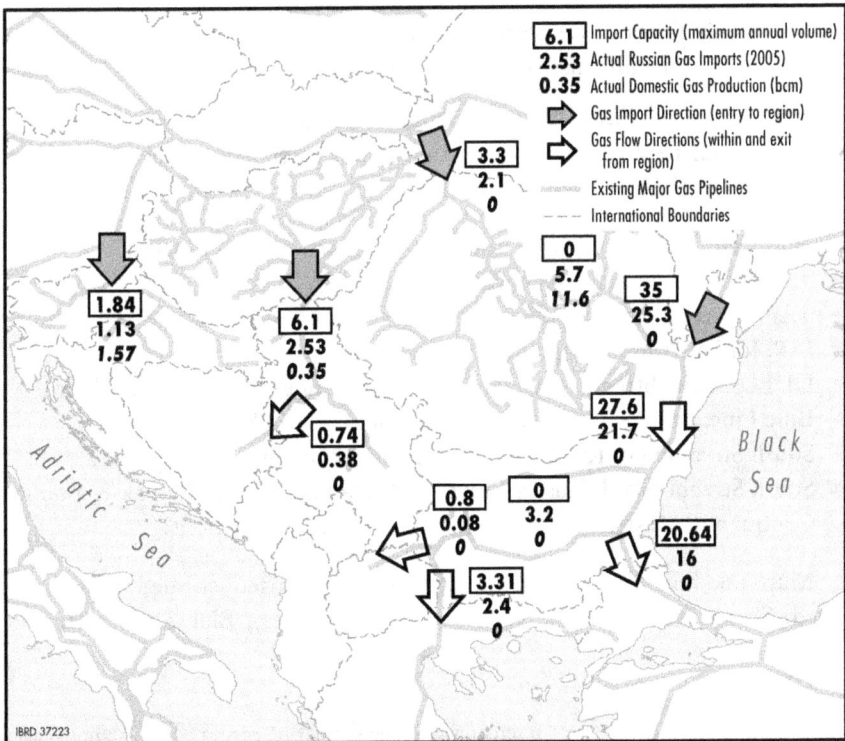

6.1	Import Capacity (maximum annual volume)
2.53	Actual Russian Gas Imports (2005)
0.35	Actual Domestic Gas Production (bcm)
→	Gas Import Direction (entry to region)
⇨	Gas Flow Directions (within and exit from region)
	Existing Major Gas Pipelines
----	International Boundaries

Sources: World Bank, based on GIE information and compiled with reference to GIE, WinGas, and other published pipeline maps.
Note: SEE = Southeast Europe.

and Herzegovina market has very limited supply via Serbia. The Albania, Kosovo, and Montenegro markets presently have no gas supply.

Table 3.6 summarizes the current import sources and routes to the nine SEE markets, and it indicates additional new routes and entry points in the development plans of the region's gas companies. There are two alternative development proposals for a second import point to Bosnia and Herzegovina:

- via Croatia at Bosanski Brod (developed by Plinacro and BH-Gas)
- via Serbia at Prnjavor (developed by Srbijagas and Republica Srpska).

Both of these proposals would move Russian gas through Beregdaróc on the Ukraine-Hungary border, which is the present point through which imports flow into Bosnia and Herzegovina. Croatia plans a new import point to deliver gas via Hungary at Donji Miholjac, and Serbia plans a new import point to deliver Russian gas via Romania and Bulgaria at Dimitrovgrad in the south.

This study takes those plans into account, and considers other possible new sources and transmission pipeline routes.

Identification of Major New Transmission Pipeline Scenarios

The potential new pipeline routes that could offer new supply options to some or all of the SEE markets are these:

- **Nabucco:** Turkey-Bulgaria-Romania-Hungary-Austria pipeline
- **TGI:** Turkey-Greece-Italy pipeline[21]
- **TAP:** trans-Adriatic pipeline
- **IAP:** Ionian-Adriatic pipeline[22]
- **GUEU-White Stream:** Caspian-Georgia-Ukraine-EU, via the Black Sea
- **Blue Line:** Russia-Turkey-Bulgaria-Serbia-Croatia-Slovenia-Italy[23]
- **South Stream Sud:** Russia-Bulgaria-FYR Macedonia-Albania-Italy
- **South Stream Nord:** Russia-Bulgaria-Romania-Hungary-Slovak Republic-Central and Western European markets, or other variations.

Map 3.6 shows the pipeline options being proposed, studied, and developed. South Stream (with Nord and Sud branches), Blue Stream II, and

---

[21] The DEPA-Edison Italy-Greece Interconnector, the submarine part of which is known also as the Poseidon project, is the last section of this pipeline route.

[22] This pipeline would be a branch from TAP, originating in Albania and passing through Montenegro up the Adriatic coast toward Croatia.

[23] Plans for this pipeline were announced with Srbijagas and the Serbian Ministry of Energy and Mining.

Table 3.6   Gas Import Sources and Routes to the Nine SEE Markets

Market	Source[a]	At	Border	Transit and transmission	Import BMS
Albania	—	—	—	—	—
Bosnia and Herzegovina	Gazprom/ Russia[b]	Beregdaróc[c]	UKR	HUN–SRB	Zvornik (Karakaj)
		Beregdaróc[c]	*UKR*	*HUN–CRO*	*Bosanski Brod[d]*
	Gazprom/ Russia[b]	*Beregdaróc[c]*	*UKR*	*HUN–SRB*	*Prnjavor[e]*
	Gazprom/ Russia[b]				
Bulgaria	Gazprom/ Russia[b]	Isaccea	UKR	ROM	Negru Voda
Croatia	Gazprom/ Russia[b,f]	Velke Kapusany	UKR	SVK–AUT– SLO	Rogatec
	Gazprom/ Russia[b]	*Beregdaróc[c]*	*UKR*	*HUN[g]*	*Donji Miholjac*
UNMIK	—	—	—	—	—
Macedonia, FYR	Gazprom/ Russia[b]	Isaccea	UKR	ROM–BUL	
Montenegro	—	—	—	—	—
Romania	Gazprom/ Russia[b]	Isaccea	UKR	—	Isaccea
	Gazprom/ Russia[b,h]	Mediesu Aurit	UKR	—	Mediesu Aurit
Serbia	Gazprom/ Russia[b,i]	Beregdaróc[c]	UKR	HUN	Horgos
	Gazprom/ Russia[b]	*Isaccea*	*UKR*	*ROM–BUL*	*Dimitrovgrad*

Sources: Economic Consulting Associates' research and country visits; GIE 2006.
Note: — = absolutely zero; AUT = Austria; BMS = border metering station; BUL = Bulgaria; CRO = Croatia; HUN = Hungary; ROM = Romania; SEE = Southeast Europe; SLO = Slovenia; SRB = Serbia; SVK = Slovak Republic; UNMIK = United Nations Interim Administration Mission in Kosovo. Additional new routes and entry points in the development plans of the region's gas companies are presented in italics.
a. Import sources set in italics are planned, not current.
b. Or the source may be a Gazprom-related trading company.
c. Measured at Beregovo metering station on the Ukraine side of the Ukraine-Hungary border.
d. Information from the development plans of BH-Gas Sarajevo and Plinacro.
e. Information from the development plans of Srbijagas and Republica Srpska.
f. Croatia also has domestic gas production.
g. Croatia plans to develop this interconnection to provide a new import point directly from Hungary.
h. Romania also has domestic gas production.
i. Serbia also has a very small proportion of domestic gas production.

Map 3.6   Regional Overview of Proposed Major Transmission Pipeline Projects

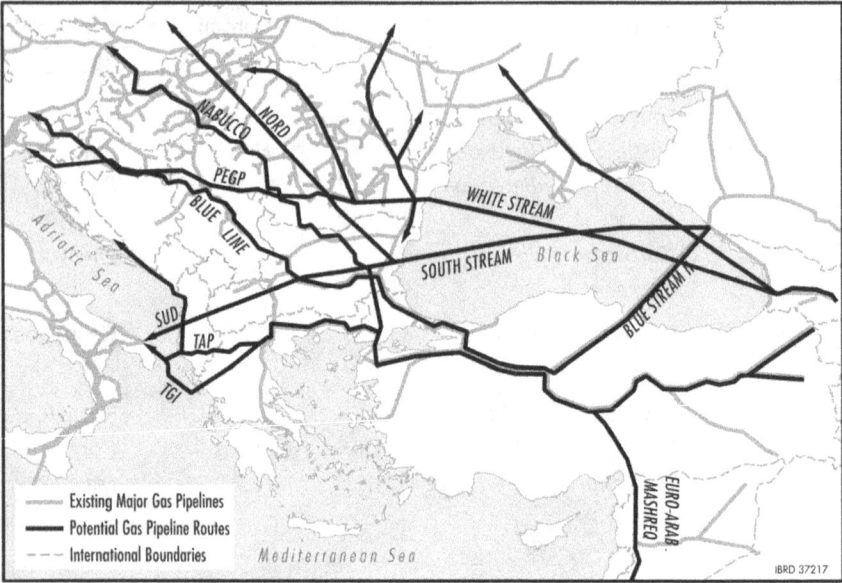

Sources: World Bank, compiled from pipeline companies' published information and with reference to GIE, WinGas, and other published pipeline maps.

Blue Line are Gazprom pipeline project proposals. Most of these pipelines would transport Caspian gas to Western European markets. The Euro-Arab Mashreq pipeline would transport Egyptian gas to or through Turkey. The Nabucco pipeline also could transport Iranian and Iraqi gas through Turkey to Europe.

Key Characteristics and Status of Major Pipeline Scenarios
Table 3.7 presents the transit countries, developers, and current status of the major regional pipeline projects identified; it includes the proposed source of gas for each project. The various potential major regional pipeline projects are of varying degrees of interest across the nine SEE markets, according to the distance and the difficulty of the terrain between the proposed route and each market.

The TGI project is being promoted by Edison of Italy (in collaboration with DEPA of Greece and BOTAS of Turkey) to bring gas for power generation into southern Italy. It would not pass through any of the nine markets, and the SEE countries would need transmission pipeline branches to deliver gas northward from a connection in the south. Turkey would be the key transit country; and either Albania or FYR Macedonia would be the front-line country of the nine SEE markets, if capacity were made available for any SEE market offtake from TGI.

The TAP project, being promoted by the Swiss-based energy trader EGL and new project partner StatoilHydro, is also an east-to-west route to deliver gas to Italy. It passes through Albania, which is a member of the Energy Community (EC). EGL, together with the Croatian gas transmission company Plinacro, also has proposed the IAP pipeline branch to deliver gas northward up the Adriatic coast to Croatia.

The Nabucco project is being undertaken by a consortium of gas companies from each of the five countries through which the project would pass: BOTAS, Bulgargaz, Transgaz, MOL, and OMV. It is a south-to-north route to Central and Western Europe, terminating at OMV's Baumgarten hub in Austria. The Lavant River valley in southern Austria accommodates the trans-Austria Gasleitung (TAG). This project comprises three pipelines of 38-, 40-, and 42-inch diameters and currently delivers gas originating in or transiting Russia from the Baumgarten hub to Tarvisio in northern Italy. The easement in this route has no room for additional pipelines, so Nabucco gas is not expected to be able to serve northern Italy as long as Italian buyers have contracts for Russian gas via Baumgarten. (Of course, it may be possible for traders to swap Caspian gas for Russian gas at Baumgarten; that would facilitate the physical flow of Caspian gas molecules along TAG to Italy.)

The GUEU pipeline is being proposed by an independent consortium.[24] In the GUEU-White Stream case, the SEE countries would take supply via Romania, with transmission branches delivering the gas westward into Southeast Europe. Gas either could be landed directly on the Romanian coast or be moved through Ukraine. Romania, rather than Bulgaria, would be the frontline country of the nine SEE markets. The GUEU route is potentially significant because it would provide both competition to Russian gas within Central and Eastern Europe and security of supply benefits. It may influence market prices in the region.

The pan-European gas pipeline (PEGP) is a proposal to parallel the Constanza-Trieste pan-European oil pipeline with a gas pipeline, thereby achieving economies of scale on the pipe-laying costs and making use of the route with topology giving rise to low (possibly the lowest) economic cost between the Black Sea and northeast Italy. The two possible options for gas at the entry point of the PEGP are compressed natural gas shuttled across the Black Sea from Georgia or Turkey or gas via a GUEU-White

---

[24] ECA has provided some initial economic analysis of the option to the consortium.

Table 3.7 Potential Major Regional Pipeline Projects

Pipeline	Gas	Transit countries	Developer (country)	Current status
Turkey-Greece–Italy pipeline	Caspian	Turkey, Greece, Italy	Edison (Italy), DEPA (Greece), in cooperation with BOTAS (Turkey)	Turkey-Greece: complete; Greece-Italy: finalizing gas supply agreements to reach Poseidon Final Investment Decision in late-2008
Trans-Adriatic pipeline (TAP)	Caspian, via Turkey	Turkey, Greece, **Albania,** Italy	EGL (Switzerland)	Front-end engineering design; in February 2008; EGL announced that StatoilHydro had joined TAP
Ionian-Adriatic pipeline	Caspian or Russian	Turkey, Greece, FYR **Macedonia, Kosovo, Montenegro, Bosnia and Herzegovina, Croatia,** Slovenia, Italy	EGL (Switzerland) and Plinacro Ltd. (Croatia)	On September 25, 2007, ministers from Albania, Croatia, and Montenegro signed an Intergovernmental Declaration and a Memorandum of Understanding on implementation[a]
Nabucco	Caspian and possibly some Russian, Iranian, and Middle Eastern	Turkey, **Bulgaria, Romania,** Hungary, Austria	BOTAS (Turkey), Bulgargaz (**Bulgaria**), Transgaz (**Romania**), MOL (Hungary), OMV (Austria)	Feasibility study completed; Nabucco International GmbH established; most of the five national Nabucco companies established; open season process; financial negotiations; appointment of engineers

Pipeline	Gas	Transit countries	Developer (country)	Current status
White Stream: Georgia-Ukraine-EU (GUEU) pipeline	Caspian, initially from Azerbaijan	Two route options: Georgia-[Black Sea]-Ukraine-**Romania** Georgia-[Black Sea]-Ukraine-Poland Georgia-[Black Sea]-**Romania-Serbia-Croatia**-Slovenia-Italy	GUEU, Inc. (private consortium registered in the United States)	Feasibility study
Pan-European gas pipeline	Caspian, initially from Azerbaijan	Constanza in **Romania**, via **Serbia, Croatia,** and Slovenia (or offshore) to Trieste in Italy	Transnafta (Serbia)	Proposal to parallel the Pan-European oil pipeline with a gas pipeline; Could offtake from GUEU-White Stream at Constanza
Blue Line (extension of Blue Stream/BS II)	Russian, and possibly Turkmen via Russia	Turkey, **Bulgaria, Serbia, Bosnia and Herzegovina** (possibly), **Croatia**, Slovenia, Italy	Gazprom (Russia)	Gazprom and MEM Serbia signed Memorandum of Understanding on December 20, 2006, in Belgrade
South Stream Nord	Russian, and possibly Turkmen via Russia	[Black Sea]-**Bulgaria-Romania**-Hungary-Slovenia-Italy or ... Hungary-Austria	Gazprom (Russia) and ENI (Italy)	Gazprom and ENI agreement signed on June 23, 2007, in the presence of ministers from Russia and Italy, quoting "preliminary cost studies" by Saipem
South Stream Sud	via Russia	[Black Sea]-**Bulgaria**-FYR **Macedonia-Albania**-Italy		

Sources: Economic Consulting Associates' research; developer presentations at the Energy Community Mini Gas Forum, Vienna, Austria, October 13, 2006.

Note: Shown in boldface are those studied SEE markets through which proposed projects transit.

a. Available at http://www.plinacro.hr/en_novosti.asp.

Stream pipeline from Georgia to Constanza in Romania, either directly or via Ukraine's Crimean Peninsula.

In contrast with Nabucco, the south-to-north Blue Line project would deliver gas through Blue Stream (and/or Blue Stream II) via Turkey, Bulgaria, Serbia, and Croatia to a point on the northeastern Italy-Slovenia border. One advantage of the Blue Line route is its avoidance of the constraint between Austria and northern Italy. At the time of writing, Blue Line's sponsor Gazprom has announced a Memorandum of Understanding with only one of the transit countries (Serbia).

Together with ENI of Italy, Gazprom also has announced its intention to study in detail the South Stream project for a submarine Black Sea pipeline from Russia directly to Bulgaria. This concept has two variants (or branches): Sud to the south via FYR Macedonia and Albania to Italy, and Nord to the north via Romania and Hungary toward Central and Western Europe.

All of the Gazprom proposals involve bypassing Ukraine and delivering gas through Bulgaria (either directly via the Black Sea or through Turkey). Bulgaria already is a transit country for Russian gas (with most of the volumes going to Turkey, some to Greece, and very small amounts to FYR Macedonia). Both Gazprom proposals clearly are strategies to preempt Caspian gas from gaining direct access to Western European markets (without the need to pass through Russia, as with Turkmen gas at present), via Nabucco, GUEU-White Stream, or future upgrades to capacity along the TGI corridor. With respect to the various Gazprom proposals, the key issues of interest to the SEE markets are the capacities that could become available to them; and the price, relative to Caspian gas and LNG.

The relative economics of gas from the various sources and routes outlined above will be affected by the economics of transmission to deliver that gas to European markets; by the upstream exploration, development, and production costs; and the competitive price in the destination markets.

Regional Gas Transmission Infrastructure

An integrated regional perspective on gas transmission infrastructure begins with an overview of the branch pipeline connections discussed above. This evolved into the EC Ring gas transmission concept. The benefits of the ring are discussed, and the method for analyzing it is explained in this section. The analysis considers the potential (or required) demand buildup, gas offtakes, and optimization of the EC Ring. The ring is compared with the separate branches considered in each scenario, and the potential for phased development and variations in development of the EC Ring is assessed. A summary and some conclusions on regional transmission complete the section.

Overview of Branch Pipeline Connections

The development of a regional transmission concept for increased gasification of the SEE markets began with a set of notional regional branch transmission pipelines that could deliver gas to the SEE markets from each of the major transmission pipeline scenarios under consideration. The details of these branches are presented in appendix D and are illustrated in the maps included in this section.

Map 3.7 shows the configurations of transmission branches that could deliver increased supplies of Russian gas from existing corridors to the markets of Southeast Europe.

Ungasified areas in Bulgaria can be served by spurs from the Bulgarian ring; and such areas in Romania can be served by spurs from the existing system and/or by rehabilitation of the existing Romanian transmission web.

Map 3.7   Branches with Offtakes for Russian Gas Supply from Existing Corridors

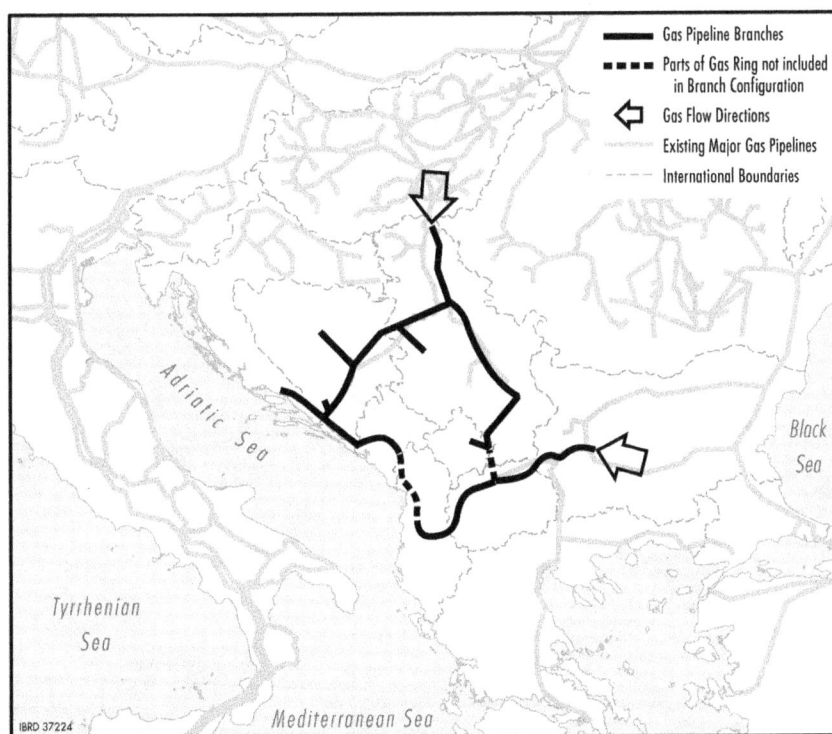

Sources: World Bank, compiled with reference to GIE, WinGas, and other published pipeline maps.

Albania and FYR Macedonia would be supplied via Bulgaria, requiring reinforcement back to the Bulgarian ring. Approximately following the flow of gas, Serbia, Bosnia and Herzegovina, southern Croatia, Montenegro, and the Kosovo markets would be supplied by reinforcement of the existing system via Hungary. An alternative to this strategy would be to supply the Kosovo market and southern Serbia via branches up to Nis and to Pristina from the new Bulgaria-Macedonia pipeline.

Map 3.8 shows a configuration of branches for offtake from the proposed Nabucco international pipeline project. These branches are almost identical to the configuration for offtake from existing Russian pipeline corridors. The exception is that the connection upstream of Belgrade comes from a point on the Nabucco pipeline near Timisoara, instead of from Hungary at the existing border station.

Map 3.8   Branches with Gas Offtake from the Proposed Nabucco Pipeline

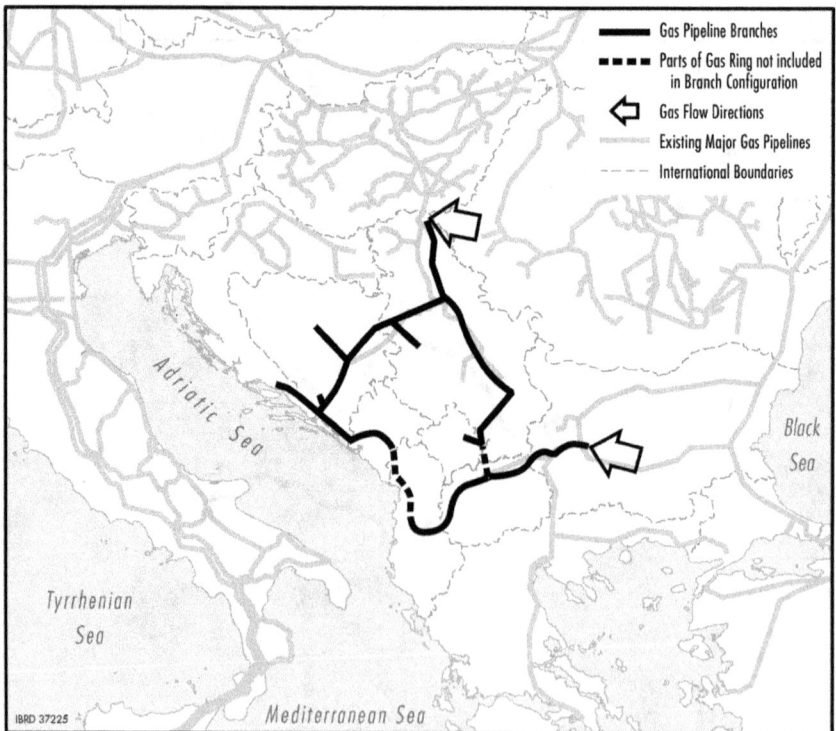

Sources: World Bank, compiled with reference to GIE, WinGas, and other published pipeline maps.

Map 3.9 shows a configuration of branches that could supply Albania, FYR Macedonia, and Kosovo, as well as Montenegro, Bosnia and Herzegovina, and southern Croatia from an offtake on the Greek transmission system. Parts of this route are similar to EGL's proposal for the trans-Adriatic pipeline and the IAP, running north along the coast toward Dubrovnik and Split.

This set of branches is focused very strongly on the completely nongasified markets of Albania, Kosovo, FYR Macedonia, and Montenegro, as well as the ungasified parts of southern Bosnia and Herzegovina and southern Croatia.

Map 3.10 shows a configuration of branches with offtakes from the proposed Blue Line project. This arrangement is quite similar to the configurations for offtake from existing Russian gas supply corridors and for offtake from Nabucco, except that the Blue Line pipeline itself would replace the

Map 3.9 Branches with Gas Offtake from the Greek Transmission System

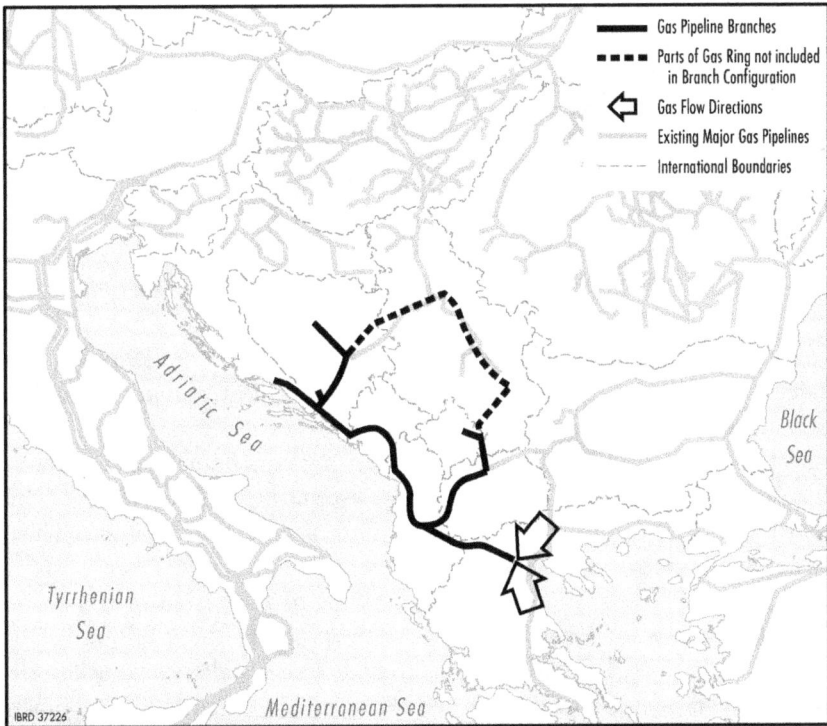

Sources: World Bank, compiled with reference to GIE, WinGas, and other published pipeline maps.

Map 3.10   Branches with Gas Offtake from the Proposed Blue Line Project

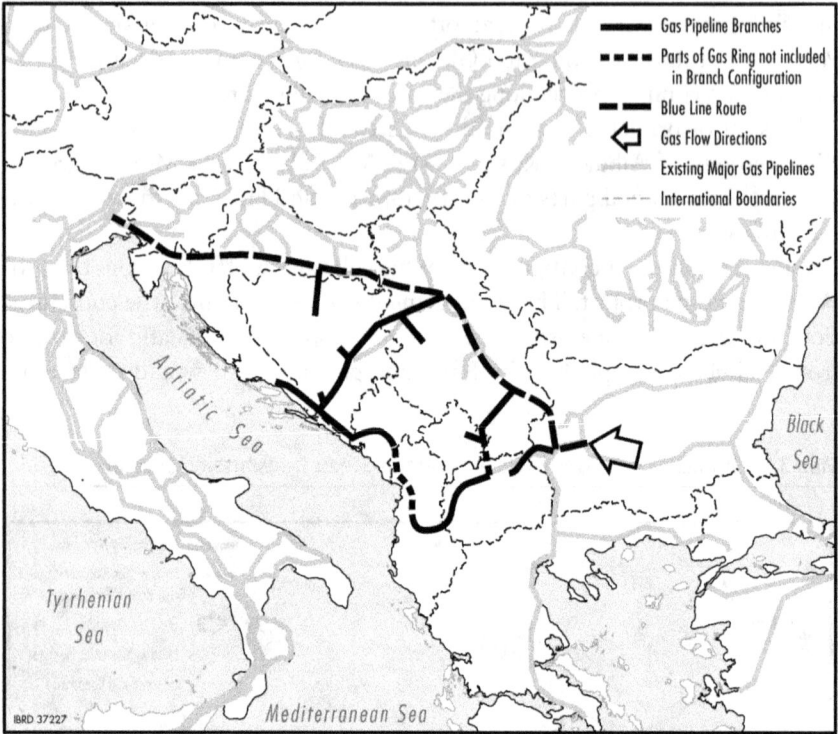

Legend:
- Gas Pipeline Branches
- Parts of Gas Ring not included in Branch Configuration
- Blue Line Route
- Gas Flow Directions
- Existing Major Gas Pipelines
- International Boundaries

Sources: World Bank, compiled with reference to GIE, WinGas, and other published pipeline maps.

need to build a section of branch pipeline between Nis and Belgrade; and Banja Luka would be supplied from an offtake via Croatia, rather than from the direction of Sarajevo.

When these maps of the regional transmission branch configuration offtakes under each major pipeline supply scenario are laid on top of one another, a number of common route alignments became apparent. Those common alignments reveal a ring configuration linking the seven western-most SEE markets, with external connections to the various major transmission pipeline scenarios. This naturally prompts the question, could proactive planning for development of such a regional ring be a key element of increased gasification in the region? This led to the development of the regional EC Gas Transmission Ring concept. Increased gasification of Southeast Europe is of particular interest to the members of the recently established EC; and it is of interest to the World Bank, KfW Entwicklungsbank, other donor organizations, and the European Commission.

The EC Gas Transmission Ring Concept

The EC Ring is a gas transmission pipeline that would link seven gas markets: Albania, Bosnia and Herzegovina, Croatia, Kosovo, FYR Macedonia, Montenegro, and Serbia. The ring concept emerged from consideration of the synergy between the notional regional transmission pipeline branches defined for the separate markets. It was first proposed by Economic Consulting Associates (ECA) at the Mini Gas Forum held in Vienna, Austria, in May 2007.

Map 3.11 shows the indicative route of the EC Ring (which is still a preliminary concept) in the context of the regional gas transmission pipeline infrastructure. Supply of gas to the ring could come from existing pipelines, from one or more of the possible new major transmission import pipelines, or from LNG imports. (Those options are discussed in greater detail in the section titled "Interaction with Western European Gas Markets," below.)

Map 3.11 Concept of the Energy Community Gas Ring in the Regional Context

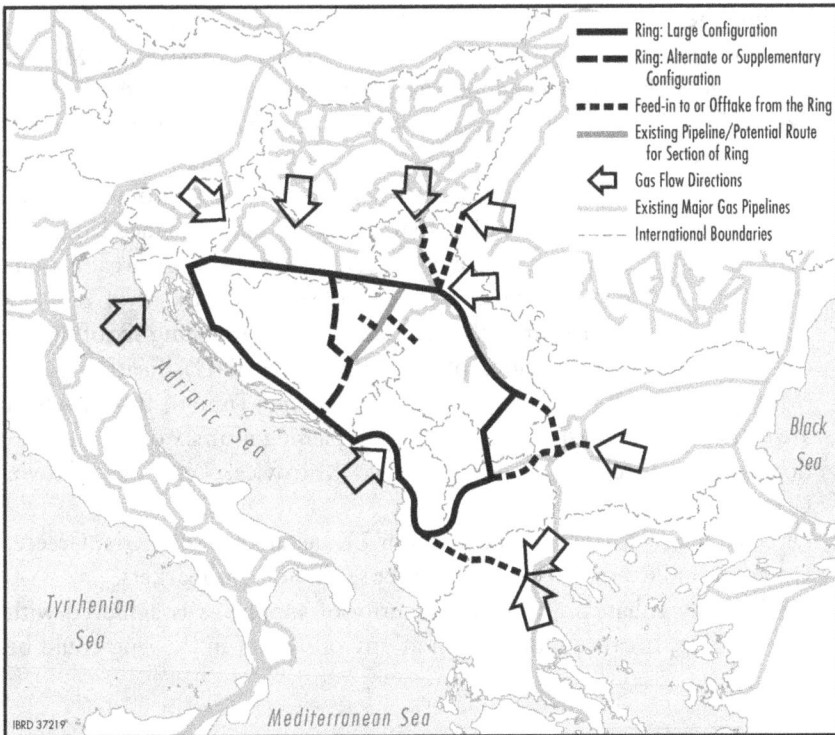

Sources: World Bank, compiled with reference to GIE, WinGas, and other published pipeline maps.

Description of the EC Ring's Benefits

The potential benefits available from development of such a gas ring would be numerous; they include the following economic, political, and technical features:

- Aligning naturally with the principles of the SEE Stability Pact.[25]
- Creating strong, practical economic incentives for countries to implement the terms of the Energy Charter Treaty with respect to gas, which otherwise may be seen as a "paper exercise" for those markets currently without gas.
- Facilitating increased supply diversity by allowing supply to the ring from almost any direction and from multiple directions, easing the connection of new sources by giving them access to a larger pool of demand than would be available via simple radial branches, and ensuring more secure access because of the technical security-of-supply benefits.
- Enabling gasification of the seven markets to proceed flexibly in relation to the development sequence of new major pipelines—such as GUEU-White Stream, Nabucco, PEGP, TAP, and TGI—bringing gas through or past the region.
- Linking the seven markets of the western part of Southeast Europe (Albania, Bosnia and Herzegovina, Croatia, Kosovo, FYR Macedonia, Montenegro, and Serbia) into a regional market configuration.
- Connecting six regional capitals (Belgrade, Sarajevo, Podgorica, Tirana, Skopje, and Pristina), three of which are ungasified at present.
- Fostering cooperation in the regional energy economy by promoting constructive interdependence (rather than complete independence from one another, on one hand, or dependence—as in reliance on upstream countries in the case of radial branch lines—on the other hand).
- Bringing gas deep into currently nongasified areas, touching six of the 20 distribution case study cities of the SEE Regional Gasification Study (Mostar, Niksic, Podgorica, Pristina, Skopje, and Tirana), five of which are completely nongasified at present; and passing near six other distribution case study cities (Elbasan, Kosovo Mitrovica, Leskovac, Tetovo, Uzice, and Zenica).
- Directly linking the gas markets of four EU neighbors—Bulgaria, Greece, Hungary, and Romania—with the other seven SEE gas markets.
- Significantly enhancing technical security of supply, as is achieved with any gas ring, because a disruption at any one point in the ring could be

---

[25] This pact has been replaced by the Regional Cooperation Council.

overcome by supply around the ring in the other direction. This configuration also would make the scheduling of any major maintenance work significantly easier.

- Allowing greater flexibility for balancing by the transmission system operator(s) in the region.
- Providing regionwide access to regional UGS for all seven westernmost SEE markets, which would increase security of supply via facilities being developed in the northeast corner (up to 0.8 Bcm at Banatski Dvor in Serbia); via other sites in central Serbia (3.0–5.0 Bcm); and possibly via additional potential storage sites nearby in Romania, Hungary, and Albania (0.5–2.0 Bcm) in the southwest corner on the opposite side of the EC Ring.
- Improving the commercial position of importers by allowing seasonal swing to be managed with regional storage contracts, rather than through import contracts.
- Diversifying the markets for importers both by increasing the access to alternate markets and by reducing importers' reliance on any one source of supply.
- Facilitating future development of meaningful regional gas trading, both from multiple sources of gas and multiple import points into the region, and between countries in the region.
- Realizing economies of scale over the long term as new injection points and UGS facilities are developed—points and facilities that would not result from the development of linear-radial branches.

Other key qualities of the EC Ring include the following:

- It could be developed incrementally.
- Transmission capacity around the ring would increase simply by the future addition of each new injection point.
- It may be able to complement and build on existing infrastructure in some places. For example, the eastern side of the ring initially could be formed by the existing Belgrade-Nis transmission pipeline.
- It could complement the development of future major infrastructure to transport gas through the region, subject to cooperation with the developers of such projects. For example, the eastern and western sides of the ring are on the same alignment as the Blue Line and Ionian-Adriatic transmission pipelines, respectively, so the ring might be considered as two lateral links between those two pipelines.
- It would enable development of gas-fired power stations (CCGT) in Albania, western Croatia, FYR Macedonia, and Montenegro, with such "anchor" loads also underpinning the development of the ring.

In an effort to ensure that regional benefits including both the difficult-to-quantify and the qualitative benefits described above, donors may wish to assist in funding the total or incremental cost of the ring, relative to the cost of radial branch transmission pipelines that otherwise may be built in the absence of the ring. By building the ring and indicating availability of funds, the chances that the regional branches will develop into the surrounding markets would be enhanced greatly. Therefore, full funding of the ring would be a major initiative to promote gasification of the seven markets.

Methodology for Analyzing the EC Ring

The steps in analyzing the conceptual design and cost of the ring are summarized below and discussed in more detail thereafter:

1. identifying anchor loads for the initial gas demand (using the updated GIS [SEE Consultants 2007])
2. determining the simultaneous maximum demand on the ring at various stages of its development: from the initial injection point to buildup of demand with additional injection points
3. determining the limiting case of maximum demand
4. sizing the pipelines and compressors
5. calculating the capital costs
6. comparing the cost of the ring with the costs of separate branch lines to each market from the most favorable major transmission pipeline for each market
7. calculating the incremental cost of the ring, compared with the investment required for each separate market.

Demand Buildup, Offtakes, and Optimization of the EC Ring

To optimize the diameter of the ring pipeline, it is necessary to consider the buildup of projected future demand, the peak flows at the offtake points, the locations of injection points, the seasonality of projected demand, and the locations of potential UGS facilities. One of the benefits of a ring is that the capacity may increase as each new separate injection point is added: the ring facilitates balancing. This principle is illustrated in figure 3.11. The greatest benefits of a ring come from the addition of the second injection point, and they diminish with each additional injection point. Referring to the example shown in figure 3.11, the capital expenditure saving for two injection points versus one point would be more than 30 percent; then more than 20 percent for three points, relative to two; and just over 10 percent for four points, relative to three (based on calculations using appendix table C.1). If UGS facilities were located at points on the ring different from the injection points, they also could be used to

Figure 3.11 Effect of Adding Injection Points on the Capacity of a Ring

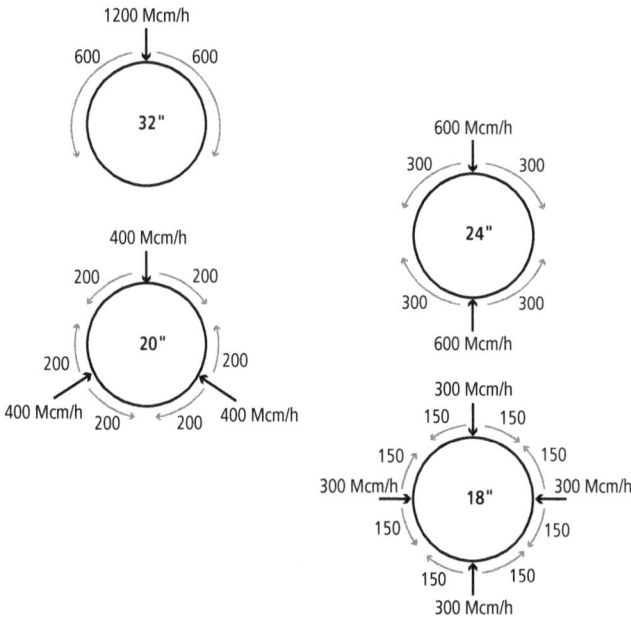

Source: Economic Consulting Associates.
Note: Mcm/h = thousand cubic meters per hour.

flatten the seasonal variation in flows on the ring, and thereby effectively expand its peak capacity for a given number of injection points.

The small number of large initial anchor loads would be expected to have a higher annual load factor than the large number of relatively small heating-driven commercial and residential distribution customer loads that would be added later as distribution networks develop. Therefore, one potential development approach would be first to size the ring with sufficient capacity to enable delivery of peak flows to the initial anchor loads from a single injection point (which is the worst-case and perhaps most likely scenario), and then to add injection points and storage capacity when appropriate, as required by the buildup of both annual load and loads with greater seasonal swing.

These results and the peak hourly flows are summarized in table 3.8. The gas demand peak flow values (given as thousand cubic meters per hour) in the last column of the table are based on all the instantaneous demands of all of the capacity operating at full load, with the assumption of 53 percent thermal efficiency for CCGT plants (which is the same assumption used for the estimation of annual demand values in the second-last column), and

38 percent thermal efficiency for open-cycle gas turbine plants. It is important to note that CCGT plants would need to be located on or near the ring to anchor the development of the EC Ring.[26] Given the relative need for new capacity, the location of lignite resources in the region, and the benefits of generation in strengthening transmission grids, the most likely candidate locations for those plants would be Albania, southern Croatia, FYR Macedonia, and Montenegro.

The loads would build up over time, so the full capacity would not be needed in the first year; and as gas from a new injection point became available, the maximum flows on the ring would be reduced. Therefore, as an example, a ring could be designed to deliver the flows required for anchor loads and then could have its delivery capacity increased to handle the long-term loads by the addition of a second and a third injection point spaced around the ring. Referring to the updated GIS results (SEE Consultants 2007) and ECA's demand projections, the following demand buildup and offtake points have been assumed to determine the ring capacity requirements:

- **initial anchor demand** of 2.2–2.5 Bcm/y (notionally, in 2011), supplied from a single injection point serving a total of 2,100 megawatts of CCGT capacity comprising two 300-megawatt power stations (notionally located in western Croatia near Dubrovnik and in Montenegro near Niksic) and three 500-megawatt power stations (notionally located in western Croatia near Ploce or Split, in Albania, and in FYR Macedonia)
- **long-term demand** of 7 Bcm/y (after 15 years; notionally, in 2025), supplied from as many injection points and UGS facilities as required by their physical locations around the ring; and serving all sectors, including seasonal commercial and residential distribution loads, which would be expected to build up as the city distribution networks develop.

In the initial anchor demand assumption (described in the "Anchor Loads" section of chapter 2), the maximum hourly flow required into the ring if all 2,100 megawatts of CCGT power plants were operating at full load would be 370 Mcm, as indicated in table 3.8. The annual consumption range of 2.2–2.5 Bcm is equivalent to an annual load factor of 70–80 percent. If this peak flow could be delivered equally around the two sides of the ring, from any given single injection point, the maximum flow required on any section of the ring would be 185 Mcm/h. Appendix table C.1 shows

---

[26] The integrated development of the ring and the associated initial anchor power station loads likely would lead to an earlier development of one or more CCGTs. It also is possible that the locations of those plants would be different if the ring did not exist, given the cost advantages of siting the plants close to the ring.

Table 3.8   Source of Anchor Demand Assumptions

Original GIS		Updated GIS			
OCGT (MW)	CCGT (MW)	OCGT (MW)	CCGT (MW)	Estimated gas demand (Bcm/y)	(Mcm/h)
Original GIS Scenario B/Case 2A2: "Fully interconnected power system without any transmission constraints and partial environmental compliance" (gas at $275/Mcm, decreasing to $195/Mcm)					
	5 × 300		1 × 300		230
	+ 3 × 500	1 × 100	+ 2 × 500		+25
None	= 3,000	= 100	= 1,300	1.35 ~ 1.55	= 255
Removing economically unjustified rehabilitation from the official programme:					
			2 × 300		
			+ 3 × 500		
None	1,300	None	= 2,100	2.20 ~ 2.50	370
High fuel prices (gas at $368/Mcm, increasing to $392/Mcm):					
			1 × 300		230
		1 × 100	+ 2 × 500		+25
None	2,100	= 100	= 1,300	1.35 ~ 1.55	= 255
Low fuel prices (gas at $250/Mcm, decreasing to $120/Mcm):					
			5 × 300		705
		2 × 100	+ 5 × 500		+50
None	2,100	= 200	= 4,000	4.15 ~ 4.75	= 755
Carbon $27/t CO₂:					
			3 × 300		
			+ 14 × 500		
None	2,100	None	= 7,900[a]	8.20 ~ 9.40	1,395

Source: Updated Southeast Europe Generation Investment Study.
Note: ~ = approximately; Bcm/y = billion cubic meters per year; CCGT = combined-cycle gas turbine; GIS = Southeast Europe Generation Investment Study ; Mcm/h = thousand cubic meters per hour; MW = megawatt; OCGT = open-cycle gas turbine.
a. Maximum capacity constraint in the model.

the maximum hourly flows that are assumed to be delivered by each pipeline diameter. Delivering peak flows of 185 Mcm/h would require a 20-inch pipeline, which can deliver up to 200 Mcm/h.

In the case of long-term demand, the power sector demand is modeled as growing by 50 percent in 10 years, to about 3.6 Bcm/y; and the 4.4 Bcm/y balance of the 8.0-Bcm annual demand is modeled as coming from highly seasonal commercial and residential customers, with an assumed annual load factor of less than 50 percent. In this case, the maximum flow for the power plants (assumed in the worst case to be 100 percent coincident with the smaller loads) would be 650 Mcm/h, and the other loads would be 525 Mcm/y. Assuming conservatively (worst case) that the smaller loads would be coincident with the power station peak demand implies a peak demand of 1,235 Mcm/h, which is equivalent to 65 percent weighted average annual load factor.

In practice, power demand from the CCGT stations may not peak in winter, and thus may be noncoincident with commercial and residential heating loads. This would be the case if the power stations in question were located on the Adriatic coast, primarily serving tourist-driven summer peak loads, with the heating demand serving the needs of local households and businesses. The Adriatic coast of western Croatia and Montenegro is considered the most promising location for power stations to anchor the ring (together with sites in Albania and FYR Macedonia) because of the electricity transmission system reinforcement benefits that this location would provide; and because power stations in that area would anchor the development of the western part of the ring, which is farthest from the existing gas infrastructure.

Delivering 1,235 Mcm/h though a 20-inch ring (maximum flow, 200 Mcm/h) would require a minimum of four injection points, assuming optimum distribution of those points with respect to the offtakes. (The limit that could be delivered around a ring through three optimally spaced injection points is 1,200 Mcm/h). Four may be an unrealistically large number of injection points, given the neighboring systems' configuration and the potential upstream transmission pipelines that could supply the ring. Therefore, it is clear that the limiting case is the long-term demand, not the initial anchor demand; and a larger diameter pipeline would be required.

Two injection points implies peak flows of 309 Mcm/h (assuming they were optimally distributed around the ring with respect to the offtake points and volumes), which correspond to a 24-inch pipeline diameter.

The annual average (that is, "flat") flow needed to deliver annual volumes of 7 Bcm is just 800 Mcm/h. But a 24-inch ring could deliver up to 1,240 Mcm/h from two injection points (310 Mcm/h flowing in each of two directions from each of two injection points, assuming their optimal distribution around the ring with respect to the offtake points and volumes). This information suggests that it would be possible to serve more than 7 Bcm of annual gas demand from two injection points, if UGS facilities located near the ring had adequate seasonal storage capacity and sufficient maximum deliverability to meet the winter peak demand. The UGS facilities' connections to the ring and the injection points would have to be relatively favorable to the volumes and locations of offtakes from the ring. Such considerations should be taken into account in the detailed planning and engineering design of the ring.

Comparison of the EC Ring with the Branches in Each Scenario
Table 3.9 compares the diameters for each section of transmission pipeline in each of the regional branch transmission scenarios defined in appendix D with those of the proposed EC Ring. Table 3.10 corresponds to table 3.9, comparing the capital cost estimates for each section of transmission pipeline in each of the regional branch transmission scenarios with those of the proposed ring. The values include the capital cost of the pipelines and compression and other facilities for each branch. Comparing the ring with the branches shows how the attributes of a ring offer the prospect of optimizing the diameters and costs. Completion of the ring would involve building a slightly longer pipeline length than would be used for branches, at a diameter that would be smaller in parts and larger in parts than the branches (which are telescoped down toward the final offtake).

Given the design rule of thumb that a compressor station is needed every 200 kilometers, a ring approximately 1,200 kilometers long would require the first injection point and at least five compressor stations to move gas around the ring. If the gas pressure were not high enough at the injection point, then a sixth compressor station would be needed there. It would be advisable to locate the other five compressor stations at anticipated future injection points, if possible, in case it is necessary in the future to raise the pressure of gas injected onto the ring at those new injection points.

The capital cost of a 1,264-kilometer, 24-inch ring over the combination of easy and hard terrain around the route of the seven SEE markets would be approximately $775 million. Five compressor stations, 14 offtake stations (an average of two in each market), and eight border metering stations would add another $177 million. The estimated total cost would be $952 million. The capital cost of 2,100 megawatts of CCGT capacity would be on the order of $1.00–$1.25 billion.

The capital cost of the pipeline connection from the major transmission infrastructure down to the ring would be additional to the costs shown in table 3.10, and would depend on the particular scenario in question. Table 3.11 shows the capital cost estimates for the various scenarios. A 24-inch pipeline would not be adequate to supply the peak flow for the initial anchor loads; 26-inch pipelines would be capable of delivering up to 390 Mcm/h, more than enough for the initial anchor loads peak flow of 355 Mcm/h.

Table 3.9 Diameters for Each Section of Each Branch Along the Ring Alignment

Section	Length (km)	Market	Russian (in)	Nabucco (in)	Blue Line (in)	WBC (in)	Ionian-Adriatic	TAP (in)	TGI (in)	GUEU-PEGP (in)	Ring (in)
KSV|SRB-Nis	71	SRB	18 and 20	18 and 20	30	n.a.	TBC	n.a.	n.a.	18 and 20	24
Nis-Belgrade	215	SRB	22	22	Main pipeline	n.a.	TBC	n.a.	n.a.	22	24
Belgrade-SRB|BH	117	SRB	28	28	24	n.a.	TBC	n.a.	n.a.	28	24
SRB|BH-Sarajevo	94	BH	28	28	24	16	TBC	n.a.	n.a.	28	24
Sarajevo-Mostar	83	BH	20	20	20	20	TBC	20	20	20	24
Mostar-CRO|BH[a]	34	BH	18	18	18	18	TBC	20	20	18	24
CRO|BH-BH|CRO[b]	20	BH	16	16	16	16	TBC	24	24	16	24
BH|CRO-BH-CRO|MTG	90	CRO	16	16	16	16	TBC	24	24	16	24
CRO|MTG-Niksic	60	MTG	16	16	16	16	TBC	24	24	16	24
Niksic-Podgorica	50	MTG	12	12	12	12	TBC	24	24	12	24

Section	Length (km)	Market	Russian (in)	Nabucco (in)	Blue Line (in)	WBC (in)	Ionian-Adriatic (in)	TAP (in)	TGI (in)	GUEU-PEGP (in)	Ring (in)
Podgorica-MTG|ALB	22	MTG	n.a.	n.a.	n.a.	n.a.	TBC	28	28	n.a.	24
MTG|ALB-Tirana	121	ALB	n.a.	n.a.	n.a.	n.a.	TBC	28	28	n.a.	24
Tirana-ALB|MAC	75	ALB	20	20	20	20	TBC	28	28	20	24
ALB|MAC-Skopje	94	MAC	20	20	20	20	TBC	28	28	20	24
Skopje-MAC|KSV	22	MAC	n.a.	n.a.	28	n.a.	TBC	18	18	n.a.	24
MAC|KSV-Pristina	63	KSV	n.a.	n.a.	28	n.a.	TBC	18	18	n.a.	24
Pristina-KSV|SRB	33	KSV	18	18	30	n.a.	TBC	n.a.	n.a.	18	24
Total	1,264	All 7	12–28	12–28	12–34	12–20	TBC	18–28	18–28	12–28	24

Source: Authors' compilation.

Note: ALB = Albania; BH = Bosnia and Herzegovina; CRO = Croatia; GUEU = Georgia-Ukraine-European Union; in = inches; km = kilometers; KSV = Kosovo; MAC = FYR Macedonia; MTG = Montenegro; n.a. = not applicable; PEGP = pan-European gas pipeline; TAP = trans-Adriatic pipeline; TBC = to be confirmed; SRB = Serbia; TGI = Turkey-Greece-Italy; km = kilometer; WBC = Western Balkan Corridor.

a. Border of Bosnia and Herzegovina with Croatia, near Dracevo and Metkovic, for offtake northward toward Split in Croatia.

b. Border of Bosnia and Herzegovina with Croatia, on the western side of the Bosnia and Herzegovina section of coastline.

Table 3.10 Capital Cost Matrix for Each Section of Each Branch on the Ring Alignment

Section	Length (km)	Market	Russian ($ million)	Nabucco ($ million)	Blue Line ($ million)	WBC ($ million)	Ionian-Adriatic ($ million)	TAP ($ million)	TGI ($ million)	GUEU-PEGP ($ million)	RING ($ million)
KSV|SRB-Nis	71	SRB	28	28	50	n.a.	TBA	n.a.	n.a.	28	38
Nis-Belgrade	215	SRB	118	118	Main pipeline[a]	n.a.	TBA	n.a.	n.a.	118	114[b]
Belgrade-SRB|BH	117	SRB	99	99	62	n.a.	TBA	n.a.	n.a.	99	62
SRB|BH-Sarajevo	94	BH	95	95	86	41	TBA	n.a.	n.a.	95	67
Sarajevo-Mostar	83	BH	47	47	47	54	TBA	47	47	47	59
Mostar-CRO|BH[c]	34	BH	20	20	20	20	TBA	23	23	20	24
CRO|BH-BH|CRO[d]	20	BH	9	9	9	Main pipeline[a]	Main pipeline[a]	14	14	9	14[b]
BH|CRO-BH-CRO|MTG	90	CRO	32	32	32	Main pipeline[a]	Main pipeline[a]	52	52	32	49[b]
CRO|MTG-Niksic	60	MTG	26	26	26	Main pipeline[a]	Main pipeline[a]	43	43	26	43[b]
Niksic-Podgorica	50	MTG	12	12	12	Main pipeline[a]	Main pipeline[a]	27	27	12	27[b]

Section	Length (km)	Market	Russian ($ million)	Nabucco ($ million)	Blue Line ($ million)	WBC ($ million)	Ionian-Adriatic ($ million)	TAP ($ million)	TGI ($ million)	GUEU-PEGP ($ million)	RING ($ million)
Podgorica-MTG|ALB	22	MTG	n.a.	n.a.	n.a.	Main pipeline[a]	Main pipeline[a]	14	14	n.a.	12[b]
MTG|ALB-Tirana	121	ALB	n.a.	n.a.	n.a.	Main pipeline[c]	Main pipeline[c]	99	99	n.a.	79[b]
Tirana-ALB|MAC	75	ALB	42	42	42	42	TBA	68	68	42	53
ALB|MAC-Skopje	94	MAC	55	55	55	55	TBA	66	66	55	62
Skopje-MAC|KSV	22	MAC	n.a.	n.a.	23	n.a.	TBA	18	18	n.a.	12
MAC|KSV-Pristina	63	KSV	n.a.	n.a.	43	n.a.	TBA	27	27	n.a.	38
Pristina-KSV|SRB	33	KSV	17	17	35	n.a.	TBA	n.a.	n.a.	17	23
Total	1,264	All 7	600	600	542	212	TBA	498	498	600	775

Source: Authors' compilation.

Note: ALB = Albania; BH = Bosnia and Herzegovina; CRO = Croatia; GUEU = Georgia-Ukraine-European Union; KSV = Kosovo; MAC = FYR Macedonia; MTG = Montenegro; n.a. = not applicable; PEGP = Pan-European Gas Pipeline; TAP = trans-Adriatic pipeline; TBA = to be announced; SRB = Serbia; TGI = Turkey-Greece-Italy; km = kilometer; Western Balkan Corridor.

a. This is contingent on the main pipeline being financed separately. If applied to the ring, this could save $114 million for 215 kilometers of 24-inch pipeline in the case of the Blue Line and $224 million for 363 kilometers of 24-inch pipeline in the case of WBC or the Ionian-Adriatic pipeline.

b. These costs are associated with note a.

c. Border of Bosnia and Herzegovina with Croatia, near Dracevo and Metkovic, for offtake northward toward Split in Croatia.

d. Border of Bosnia and Herzegovina with Croatia, on the western side of the Bosnia and Herzegovina section of coastline.

Table 3.11 Estimate of Capital Cost of First New Pipeline to Injection Point

Scenario	Gas	Via	From–to	Diameter (in)	Length (km)	Capital expenditure ($ million)
Gazprom	Russian	Ukraine	Kekskemet–Belgrade	26	270	~195
Nabucco	Caspian	Turkey	Tomisoara–Belgrade	26	132	~100
Nabucco	Caspian	Turkey	Doupnitsa–Nis	26	160	~130
Gazprom	Russian	Bulgaria	Doupnitsa–Skopje	24	139	~100
Blue Line	Russian	Turkey	Delivered at Nis	n.a.	0	0
Greece (TAP)	Unspecified	Greece	Berat–Tirana	26	141	~135
Greece (IGI)	Unspecified	Turkey	Grevana–Tirana	26	212	~190

Source: Penspen.
Note: ~ = approximately; IGI = Italy-Greece Interconnector; in = inches; km = kilometers; n.a. = not applicable; TAP = trans-Adriatic pipeline. In the case of the IGI and TAP scenarios, the connection would be at the Greek border, with all of the capital cost in the Greek system covered by the Greek transmission system operator. In practice, therefore, the capital cost "seen" by Southeast Europe would be lower than what is shown here, but the Greek transmission tariff would need to be added. The same would apply to an LNG backhaul scenario.

The capital cost of transmission branches from the ring down to load centers in each market would be additional to the costs in tables 3.10 and 3.11, as would the costs of distribution networks in each newly gasified city. However, those costs would be the same for a ring as for the various branch pipeline scenarios, and so have no bearing on the comparison between the two approaches.

The increment (in each country, and for the region as a whole) of the capital cost of the ring, compared with the branch transmission line alternatives to supply each market, can be thought of as the premium required to obtain the difficult-to-quantify and qualitative benefits of the ring. These incremental costs are shown in table 3.12. The capital costs for the branch scenarios are different from those shown in table 3.10 because that table includes only the sections of the branches that overlap with the route

Table 3.12 Estimated Incremental Capital Costs for the Ring, Relative to Alternatives

Scenario	Gas	Via	Delivered at	Capital expenditure		
				Branches[a] ($ million)	Ring ($ million)	Incremental cost ($ million)
Blue Line	Russian	Turkey	Nis and Belgrade	~800	~985	~185+
Nabucco	Caspian	Turkey	Nis	~1,040	~1,100	~60+
Nabucco	Caspian	Turkey	Belgrade	~905	~1,060	~155+
Gazprom	Russian	Ukraine	Belgrade	~995	~1,140	~145+
Gazprom	Russian	Turkey	Skopje	~995	~1,055	~60+
WBC	Unspecified	Unspecified	Skopje-Sarajevo	~945	~1,050	~105+

Source: Economic Consulting Associates' calculations, based on Penspen analysis.

Note: ~ = approximately; WBC = Western Balkan Corridor. Plus signs following each figure in the last column remind the reader that these capital cost estimates do not include the discounted present value of the second, third, and possibly fourth connections; nor do they include the development of new underground gas storage facilities for managing seasonal swing.

a. Excludes supply to northern Croatia and spur lines to cities in Bulgaria and Romania.

of the ring. The capital costs of the ring in table 3.12 include the capital cost of the initial connection to the ring from the relevant major transmission pipeline scenario. It must be noted that the initial capital cost estimates for the ring shown in table 3.12 do not include the discounted present value of the second, third, and possibly fourth connections; nor do they include the development of new UGS facilities for managing seasonal swing. Some combination of new connections and UGS would be required to deliver all of the 8 Bcm of annual long-term demand that is projected.

The incremental capital costs range from $60 million for supply of gas at Nis or Skopje (by Gazprom or Nabucco via Turkey and Bulgaria) to $185 million for the Blue Line. In the case of an alternative coastal route for western Balkan corridor (which is similar to the IAP route proposed by the EGL consortium that is promoting the TAP project), initial capital cost savings could be made on the western coastal section of the ring.

It is important to note that the notional branches for the TGI and TAP scenarios do not extend up into Serbia. Therefore, the capital costs for those branches really are not comparable with the ring because they do not serve the seven markets to the extent that the ring would serve them. Therefore, TGI and TAP have not been shown because such comparisons would not be like-with-like comparisons. However, supply from either TGI or TAP would be very favorable for the ring because the injection point near Tirana would be close to the expected locations of the power station anchor loads in Albania, western Croatia, FYR Macedonia, and Montenegro.

Potential for Phased Development and Variations of the EC Ring

There is strong potential for the EC Ring to be developed in phases, rather than all at once. If the initial phases were underpinned by sufficient anchor loads, the development would be similar to that of the branches. However, instead of building pipelines with a large diameter at the offtake (approximately 750 millimeters [30 inches] or more) and that telescoped down to a small diameter at the end (approximately 400 millimeters [16 inches] or less), the entire length would be developed at a constant diameter of probably 600 millimeters (24 inches). Such a design would make the pipeline suitable for later connection with other sections to form the EC Ring. Building at a constant diameter of roughly 600 millimeters would be sufficient for the anchor loads, but growth (including buildup of load on distribution networks) would require additional capacity from completion of the ring and supply from more than one injection point.

If new gas-fired power stations in the ungasified markets of Albania, southern Croatia, FYR Macedonia, and Montenegro were able to contract for LNG delivered via the currently unused capacity at Revithoussa, for

Caspian gas delivered via Turkey and Greece, and/or Russian gas delivered via Bulgaria or via Bulgaria and Greece, then the branch configuration shown in map 3.9 could form the first phase of the EC Ring's development.

Summary and Conclusions on Regional Transmission

The EC Ring is a flexible concept designed to link seven gas markets and facilitate integration of existing and new supply sources. It offers many advantages for regional gasification, such as potential diversity of supply, incremental development possibilities, and independence from any one particular new supply route. Key features of its development include the following:

1. Initial demand from gas-fired combined-cycle power stations would be necessary to anchor the development of the ring. The first phase of development would involve constructing the power stations, the ring, and the infrastructure from the first new injection point upstream to the offtake point from the relevant major transmission pipeline. Demand from other large, non-power sector loads (for example, industrial sites) also would help in financing the ring.
2. A 24-inch ring should be able to serve the gas demand of five new CCGT power stations, totaling 2,100 megawatts (notionally, 2 × 300 megawatts plus 3 × 500 megawatts) with a coincident maximum gas demand of 355 Mcm/h, from a single new injection point anywhere on the ring. Some additional capacity could be made available for other large loads outside the power sector.
3. The addition of new injection points as the upstream infrastructure capacity becomes available would expand the peak flow delivery capacity of the ring in proportion to the capacity and relative locations of the new injection points. Two well-spaced injection points could deliver 7 Bcm/y of gas with a 65 percent load factor (1,235 Mcm/h peak flow). One or more UGS facilities would allow for larger long-term volumes to be served at the same load factor, or for the same long-term volume to be served at a lower load factor.

The capital cost of a 1,264-kilometer, 24-inch ring over the combination of easy and hard terrain around the route of the seven SEE markets would be about $775 million. Five compressor stations, 14 offtake stations (an average of two in each market), and eight border metering stations would add another $177 million, bringing the estimated total cost to $952 million. The capital cost of 2,100 megawatts of CCGT capacity would be approximately $1.00–$1.25 billion.

In addition, there would be the capital cost of the pipeline connection from the major transmission infrastructure to the ring. The cost would be specific to a particular scenario. The estimates for 26-inch pipelines capable of delivering as much as 390 Mcm/h (more than enough for the initial anchor loads) range from $100 million to $195 million. The capital cost of transmission branches from the ring to load centers in each market would be added to that amount, as would the costs of distribution networks in each newly gasified city; but these costs would be the same as the costs for the branch transmission alternatives in the various scenarios.

If it proved possible, initially, to use the existing pipeline infrastructure between Nis and Belgrade and between Belgrade and Sarajevo, doing so would save (or defer) as much as $243 million of the initial capital investment. The ability to use that infrastructure would depend on the flows required and on the condition of the pipelines concerned, particularly their maximum operating pressure. That, in turn, would depend on the locations of the initial injection point (and any supporting injection points) and on the locations and volumes of the offtake points to the power stations supplied by the ring.

Connecting the ring to the existing transmission system infrastructure near Belgrade in central Serbia and near Skopje in FYR Macedonia would provide a modest amount of redundancy to support the single new injection point, thus improving the reliability and flexibility of the ring. The ring also could improve the reliability and flexibility of the tied-in systems.

The incremental capital costs for the ring (in the range of $60–$185 million) appear reasonable, in light of the list of difficult-to-quantify and qualitative benefits outlined above.

An EC Ring with a capital cost of $952 million, and with throughput building up from an anchor load of 2.5 Bcm/y to 8.0 Bcm/y over a period of 15 years (and allowing slow buildup to just 3 Bcm in the first 5 years while new distribution network development is in the early stages) would require a levelized transmission tariff equivalent to $25/Mcm, plus about $1/Mcm to cover the operating costs of compression (assuming 0.5 percent of throughput is required for compression gas).

Regional Underground Gas Storage

Underground storage is expected to be the method with the largest potential for meeting seasonal and peak daily and hourly demands. However, it is not the only option. The amount of storage that is economic to provide is indicated by an analysis of the opportunity costs of storage. The economic rationale is that storage should not be developed beyond its economic opportunity cost, which is given by the marginal cost of the cheapest alternative method. Analyzing all of the available options enables us to define the limit of economic storage and the most economic combination of alternatives for meeting each level of demand (seasonal swing, daily peaks, the 1-in-20-years peak day and the 1-in-50-years energy). The available options, sorted in descending order of expected cost, are

- customer interruption (non-firm supply contracts)
- additional line-pack (for example, by building the EC Ring to a larger diameter)
- peak or seasonal LNG supply
- higher maximum daily contract quantities and larger pipeline capacity
- salt cavern underground gas storage facilities
- depleted field underground gas storage facilities
- alternate secondary or backup fuels for power and industry
- seasonal dispatch of gas-fired power plants.

There is some uncertainty over the relative costs; and the order may vary, depending on the specific circumstances of the system in question. This section reviews the potential UGS sites identified in Southeast Europe, in terms of their geologic characteristics and the estimated costs of developing them. It then looks at the costs of the alternatives. With this information in hand, the section offers an analysis of the economics of underground storage.

Existing UGS Facilities
Map 3.12 shows the 10 existing and many potential UGS sites in the nine SEE markets, relative to the position of the existing and potential transmission infrastructure. The existing facilities have a total working capacity of 3.78 Bcm. Most of this capacity (3.20 Bcm) is in Bulgaria and Romania, with the remaining 0.58 Bcm all at one facility in Croatia. Banatski Dvor in Serbia soon will have working capacity, as it is filled with cushion and working gas over the years to 2017 (see figure 3.12). Table 3.13 shows the known details about existing and potential UGS facilities in the nine SEE markets.

Potential UGS Sites and Their Geologic Characteristics
As the demand analysis in chapter 2's "Storage Demand" section reveals, there clearly will be a need to develop more UGS capacity in the seven western SEE markets as the region is gasified. Many sites throughout Southeast Europe have development or redevelopment potential as UGS facilities. Most of them are depleted gas or oil fields (reservoirs), although there are some salt formations in which caverns could be formed for gas storage. Among the potential sites described in table 3.13, Banatski Dvor in Serbia is already under development: the reservoir is to be filled progressively to its 0.8-Bcm working capacity (plus cushion gas) over the coming years. Seven sites planned for UGS development will yield a total capacity of just

Map 3.12 Existing and Potential UGS Sites in Southeast Europe

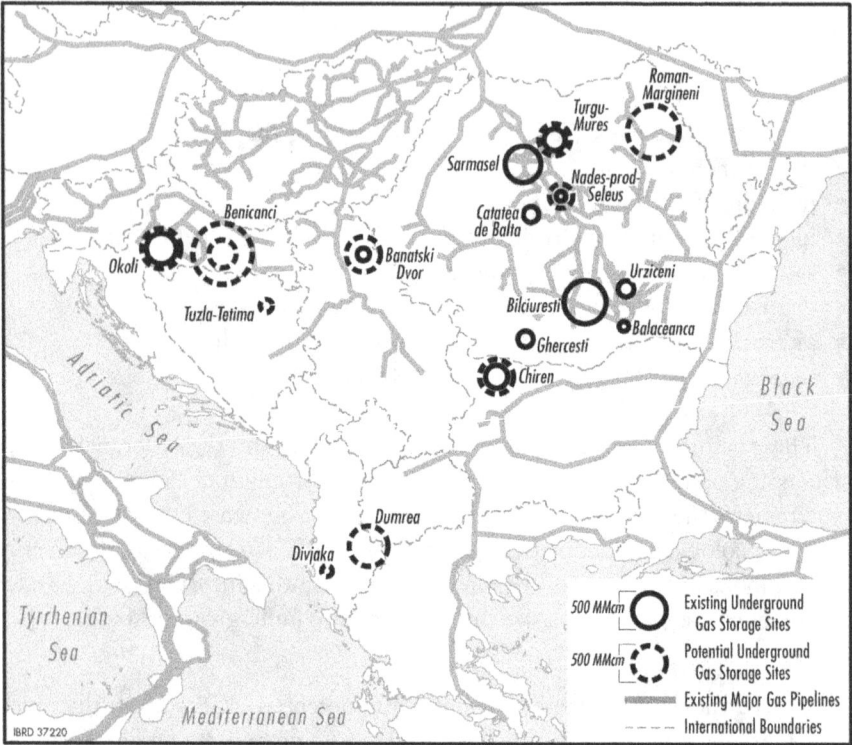

Sources: World Bank, compiled with reference to GIE, WinGas, and other published pipeline maps.
Note: UGS = underground gas storage.

over 3.5 Bcm. Of this total, 2.6 Bcm of capacity is in Bulgaria and Romania with just 0.9 Bcm in the other seven markets. In addition, there are concepts for an additional estimated 6.1 Bcm of UGS capacity in the seven westernmost SEE markets.

Because most of the need for storage to support further gasification will be in the seven westernmost markets, and because Bulgaria and Romania have more developed and mature gas markets, this study's analytical effort on potential new UGS facilities focused on possible sites in Albania, Bosnia and Herzegovina, Croatia, and Serbia. Table 3.14 summarizes the various potential UGS sites, and indicates in bold the six sites for which sufficient descriptive information and numerical data were available to allow quantitative analysis. Arranged in approximate order of likely commercial development and attractiveness from a regional perspective, those sites are

Figure 3.12   Capacity Development Plan for Banatski Dvor UGS, 2008–17

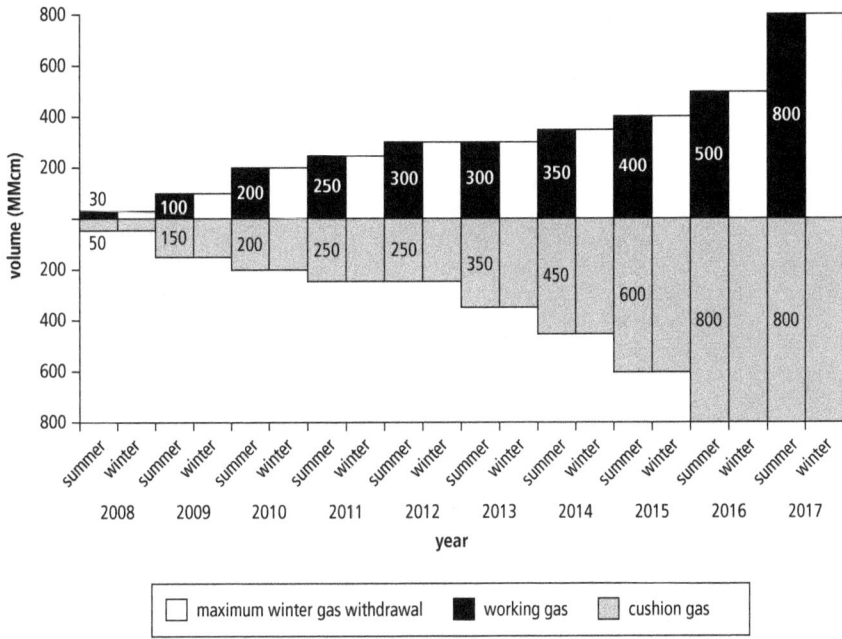

Source: Srbijagas.
Note: UGS = underground gas storage.

- **Banatski Dvor,** depleted gas field in Serbia
- **Benicanci,** depleted oil field redevelopment in Croatia
- **Tuzla-Tetima,** working salt mines in Bosnia and Herzegovina
- **Dumrea,** undeveloped salt formation in Albania
- **Okoli 2b,** depleted oil field UGS expansion in Croatia
- **Divjaka,** depleted gas field in Albania.

Banatski Dvor is under development now; and the first withdrawals began, at least on a small scale, in the winter 2008/09.

In Croatia, no decision has been made about which of the two options is preferred. INA plans a pilot project encompassing two wells with injection of 200 MMcm over two years to investigate the injection and withdrawal behavior of the structure at Benicanci.

In Bosnia and Herzegovina, the concept of leaching the storage caverns is based strongly on the assumption that the brine coming out would be processed by the salt mine operator. The start of the storage project is

Table 3.13 Existing and Potential UGS Facilities in Southeast Europe

Country/Company	Facility		Status	Working gas volume (MMcm)	Peak capacity		TPA[a]	Facility Type[b]	By year
					Withdrawal (MMcm/d)	Injection (MMcm/d)			
Southeast Europe									
Subtotal	10		Existing	3,780	12.17	9.87			
	4	Expansion } of which:		1,400	4.40	3.00			
	10	New		9,640	42.20	25.85			
	1		Under construction	800	9.00	7.00			
	0		Committed	0	0	0			
	7		Planned	3,560	12.50	7.50			
	0		Proposed	0					
	6		Concept	6,680	25.10	14.35			
Subtotal	14		Potential	11,040	46.60	28.85			
Total	24		All	14,820	58.77	38.72			

Country/Company	Facility		Status	Working gas volume (MMcm)	Peak capacity		TPA[a]	Facility Type[b]	By year
					Withdrawal (MMcm/d)	Injection (MMcm/d)			
Albania									
Not specified	Divjaka	New	Concept	60	0.50	0.35		R	
Not specified	Dumrea–regional / transit	New	Concept	240	1.29	0.43		S	
Not specified	Dumrea–national	New	Concept	1,120	6.00	2.00		S	
Bosnia and Herzegovina									
BH-Gas	Tuzla-Tetima	New	Planned	60	1.90	0.50		S	
Bulgaria				350	3.30	3.00			
BulgarTransGaz	Chiren	Existing	Operating	350	3.30	3.00		R	
BulgarTransGaz	Chiren	Expansion	Planned	450				R	2010

(continued on next page)

Table 3.13 Existing and Potential UGS Facilities in Southeast Europe *(Continued)*

| Country/ Company | Facility | Status | Working gas volume (MMcm) | Peak capacity | | TPA[a] | Facility Type[b] | By year |
				Withdrawal (MMcm/d)	Injection (MMcm/d)			
Croatia			580	5.80	3.80			
INA	Okoli	Existing	Operating	580	5.80	3.80	R	R
INA	Okoli 2b	Expansion	Planned	400	4.40	3.00		R
INA	Benicanci–stage 1	New	Planned	500	6.20	4.00		R
INA	Benicanci–later stages	New	Concept	1,500	18.60	12.00		R
Romania			2,850					
Romgaz	Sarmasel	Existing	Operating	700				R
Romgaz	Gherceati	Existing	Operating	150				R
Romgaz	Urziceni	Existing	Operating	200				R
Romgaz	Balaceanca	Existing	Operating	50				R
Romgaz	Bilciuresti	Existing	Operating	1,250				R

Country/Company	Facility	Status		Working gas volume (MMcm)	Peak capacity				By year
					Withdrawal (MMcm/d)	Injection (MMcm/d)	TPA[a]	Facility Type[b]	
Romgaz	Cetatea de Balta	Existing	Operating	150				R	
Amgaz	Nades-Prod-Seleus	Existing	Operating	50	0.27	0.27		R	
Depomures	Târgu Mures	Existing	Operating	300	2.80	2.80		R	
Amgaz	Nades-Prod-Seleus	Expansion	Planned	250				R	2010
Depomures	Târgu Mures	Expansion	Planned	300				R	2013
Romgaz	Roman-Margineni	New	Planned	1,600				R	2015

(continued on next page)

Table 3.13   Existing and Potential UGS Facilities in Southeast Europe (Continued)

Country/ Company	Facility		Status	Working gas volume (MMcm)	Peak capacity		TPA[a]	Facility Type[b]	By year
					Withdrawal (MMcm/d)	Injection (MMcm/d)			
Serbia									
Srbijagas	Banatski Dvor	New	Under construction[c]	800	9.00	7.00		R	2018
Srbijagas	Srbobran Tilva Begejci Medja	New	Concept	1,000				R	
Srbijagas	Mokrin	New	Concept	3,000				R	
Srbijagas	Ostrovo Staro Selo	New	Concept	Unknown				R	

Sources: GSE storage map and dataset, February 2008, and GSE storage projects database, June 2008 (both available at http://www.gie.eu), supplemented by regional knowledge from other sources.

Note: LNG = liquefied natural gas; MMcm/d = millions of cubic meters per day; TPA = third-party access; R = regulated; S = salt cavern; UGS = underground gas storage.
a. Types of TPA are none, regulated, and hybrid.
b. Types of storage facilities are aquifer, salt cavern, LNG peak shaving, and depleted reservoir.
c. Working volume ramping up to 800 MMcm, as the facility is filled by winter 2017/18.

Table 3.14   Summary of Potential UGS Sites Identified

Market	Site	Type	Comments
Albania	**Dumrea**	Salt formation	Potentially very large
	Divjaka	Depleted field	Structure appears "tight"
	Frakulla	Depleted field	Too small for use as UGS
Bosnia and Herzegovina	**Tuzla-Tetima**	Salt formation	Some small potential
Bulgaria	Chiren	Depleted field	Expansion planned
Croatia	**Okoli 2b**	Depleted field	Some expansion potential
	Benicanci	Depleted field	Potentially large, challenging
Kosovo	None	None	None identified
Macedonia, FYR	None	None	None identified
Montenegro	None	None	None identified
Romania	Nades-Prod-Seleus	Depleted field	Planned expansion
	Târgu Mures	Depleted field	Planned expansion
	Roman-Margineni	Depleted field	Planned new project
Serbia	**Banatski Dvor**	Depleted field	Already under development
	Srbobran Tilva Begejci Medja Mokrin Ostrovo Staro Selo	Depleted fields	Future possibilities; no data; not yet studied

Sources: GIE (2008a, 2008b), supplemented by regional knowledge from other sources.
Note: UGS = underground gas storage. Boldface type indicates the six sites for which sufficient descriptive information and numerical data were available to allow quantitative analysis.

pending because privatization of the salt mining company has not been decided, and that has given rise to uncertainties regarding a reliable execution of the leaching operation.

In Albania, the development of both Dumrea and Divjaka as UGS facilities is at the conceptual stage.

The detailed technical analysis providing the input for the economic analysis is presented in appendix E.

Development Cost Estimates

The development costs for storage have been estimated, using the following systematic method: Interviews were conducted with underground storage experts and regulators in each of the markets identified as having sites of potential interest as UGS facilities. The ECA/UGS team was able to meet with representatives of

- the Energy Agency of the Republic of Serbia, in Belgrade
- INA, in Zagreb
- BH-Gas, in Sarajevo
- The Ministry of Energy and Mining and Albpetrol, in Tirana.

The discussions in these meetings allowed the team's technical specialist from Untergrundspeicher und Geotechnologie System in Germany to use the geologic data and correlative explanations available to establish an understanding, the most likely optimum engineering specifications for future UGS facilities at the potential sites. The parameters estimated in the technical specifications are shown in table 3.15. Some of the parameters are common between the two categories of sites, and others are unique to either salt formations or depleted fields.

The details of the estimated values for each parameter at each site are shown in appendix E. The sites are discussed below in approximate order of the maturity of their development plans.

Banatski Dvor Depleted Gas Field, Serbia Because of commercial sensitivities and ongoing discussions about the sale of Serbian gas industry assets at the time of the study, representatives of Srbijagas explained that they were unable to meet with consultants from ECA and Untergrundspeicher und Geotechnologie System to discuss underground gas storage in Serbia. However, the consultants were able to meet with staff from the Energy Agency of the Republic of Serbia. With their responses to the consultants' questions and with publicly available information, it was possible to form a suitably detailed picture of the storage site's development.

Banatski Dvor is a depleted gas field in Serbia, northeast of Belgrade. It already is under redevelopment as a UGS site. The first phase of surface facil-

Table 3.15 Parameters for UGS Facilities' Engineering Specifications

Salt formations (caverns)	Depleted oil and gas fields
Cavern diameter (m)	n.a.
Cavern height (m)	n.a.
Cavern net volume (m³)	n.a.
Maximum pressure (bar)	n.a.
Minimum pressure (bar)	n.a.
Working gas volume (MMcm)	Working gas volume (MMcm)
Cushion gas volume (MMcm)	Cushion gas volume (MMcm)
	Maximum withdrawal rate (MMscm/d)
Number of production wells (n)	Number of production wells (n)
Average well depth (m)	Average well depth (m)
Taking into account (if known):	
Caverns simultaneously leaching (n)	n.a.
Leaching water flow rates (m³/h)	n.a.
Time for cavern creation (mo)	n.a.
	Porosity (%)
	Permeability (mDarcy)

Source: Authors' compilation.
Note: m = meters; mDarcy = milliDarcy; MMcm = million cubic meters; MMscm/d = million standard cubic meters per day; mo = months; m³/h = cubic meters per hour; n.a. = not applicable; UGS = underground gas storage.

ities is in place, and gas injection began in 2008. The development plan calls for cushion gas to be reestablished progressively each summer (along with working gas), allowing gradually increasing withdrawals to be made each winter, until the facility reaches its working capacity of 800 MMcm, supported by 800 MMcm of cushion gas. This plan is illustrated in figure 3.12, showing the intended cushion gas and working gas levels at the end of each summer/beginning of each winter season. In each summer throughout the development period, additional cushion gas will be injected and working gas available for withdrawal in the following winter will be increased. Increasing injection capacity more rapidly than currently planned (by bringing forward the drilling of new wells and installation of additional compressors in the surface facilities) may enable the development schedule to be advanced, relative to that shown in the figure.

When the cushion gas reaches its final level of 800 MMcm, the maximum daily injection rate is estimated to be 5–7 MMcm, and the maximum daily withdrawal rate is expected to be 7–11 MMcm. The capital costs of wells and surface facilities at Banatski Dvor are estimated to have a present value of approximately €155 million. It should be noted that much of this investment already has been made.

Tuzla-Tetima Salt Caverns, Bosnia and Herzegovina   The consultants met with engineering staff from BH-Gas in Sarajevo and received access to earlier feasibility studies on the future underground storage development of Tuzla-Tetima. The BH-Gas staff answered all of the questions necessary to assess the technical and economic potential of the site.

Construction of salt caverns in the Tuzla-Tetima salt formation is the only UGS opportunity identified so far in Bosnia and Herzegovina. A 2002 study[27] indicated the possibility of four caverns, each with a net geometrical volume of 120,000 square meters and a total working gas storage capacity of 60 MMcm.

Technically, it would be possible to construct several more caverns in the salt formation; but the government has reserved the remaining salt resources for industrial salt production.

A total cushion gas requirement of 12 MMcm is estimated to support the 50-MMcm total working capacity in four caverns. Minimum and maximum pressures would be 2.5 megapascals, and 12.5 megapascals, respectively, with respective maximum daily injection and withdrawal rates of 0.5 and 1.9 MMcm.

It is noted that there are difficult hydrogeologic conditions in the overburden, and that recompression of the outcoming gas in the final withdrawal phase might be necessary.

The present value of capital costs is estimated at approximately €50 million.

Benicanci Depleted Oil Field, Croatia   Detailed feasibility studies of Benicanci's potential for redevelopment as an underground storage facility have been carried out by or on behalf of INA. These studies are commercially confidential and were not available for review by the study team. However, senior technical INA personnel with a thorough technical knowledge of the site met with the consultants in Zagreb, and were able to provide enough information for the study team to make independent engineering cost estimates and to assess the technical and economic potential of the site.

---

[27] The specific study was the 2002 Tuzla-Tetima Underground Storage Pre-feasibility Study, conducted by Rudarski Institute, Tuzla.

Benicanci is a depleted oil field with active water drive. The reservoir is characterized by several bulges in which gas storage "bubbles" can be injected. The particular conditions are somewhat complex (a two-phase flow [gas and liquid], with three different media: oil, natural gas, and water), requiring that development of the storage reservoir be done very gradually over a period of approximately 15 years.

It is estimated that a working gas volume of 500 MMcm in the first phase and as much as 2,000 MMcm over the long term could be established. The initial phase would require 450 MMcm of cushion gas. Maximum daily withdrawal capacity is estimated at 6.2 MMcm from eight production wells, with an average depth of 1,080 meters. The field is characterized by combined porous and fissured brecciated rock material from limestone and dolomite. The porosity of the field is about 8 percent, and the permeability roughly 300 millidarcies.

Okoli 2b Depleted Oil Field, Croatia   INA personnel provided information about Okoli, a depleted gas field in which there a UGS facility is operating (580 MMcm working capacity). Okoli 2b is a separate reservoir in the same field. Because the potential storage horizon is significantly deeper and completely separated from the facility already in use, the development of Okoli 2b technically would be the construction of a completely new storage facility, not an extension of the existing one.

The estimated working gas volume of Okoli 2b would be 400 MMcm, with a cushion gas requirement of 350 MMcm. The maximum daily withdrawal capacity would be approximately 4 MMcm from 13 production wells that have an average depth of 2,100 meters.

The potential to use existing infrastructure and the presence of a connection to the pipeline grid are advantages to developing this site. The disadvantages include very low reservoir pressure (a large volume of cushion gas would be required, and the low pressure hampers the drilling of new wells), and the low permeability of the structure.

Dumrea Salt Formation, Albania   With the assistance of the Ministry of Economy, Trade, and Energy, the consultants met with a large team from the Ministry of Petroleum in Tirana and with engineers and geologists from Albpetrol. Earlier feasibility study documents were not available for review, but the experts present provided technical information on the potential underground gas storage sites in Albania.

The salt dome of Dumrea is a large diapir covering a surface area of approximately 250 square kilometers. The salt mirror is mostly at a depth of about 2,000 meters. The overburden is largely karstic, and it consists of gypsum and anhydrite. The salt reaches down to 6,000 meters. The salt volume is estimated at 1,400 square kilometers.

Several exploratory wells have been drilled into the salt. From these wells, the salt quality seems not to be ideal for solution mining because it contains 15 percent insoluble material with the occurrence of potash salt. The other potential problem is that significant parts of the salt formation are at depths too great to be useful for the formation of UGS caverns. It is expected that the salt dome may outcrop closer to the surface in some locations, although this is uncertain. Presumably based on that assumption, a feasibility study undertaken in the 1990s proposed storage caverns operated in the pressure range 80–200 bar. That pressure range implies that the caverns have been planned in the depth interval of approximately 1,150–1,500 meters. That feasibility study was not available to the consulting team, so the team relied on information from in-person discussions with experts in Albania who are familiar with the earlier study.

Proceeding on the assumption that a sufficiently extensive part of the very large salt formation is suitably close to the surface to be useful for UGS development, there are two possible approaches to its development:

- development on a small scale, suitable for the expected small future needs of the Albanian gas market
- development on a large scale, suitable for providing gas storage services to the regional and transit markets.

These are considered to be mutually exclusive options because of the presence or absence of economic synergies with commercial salt production. In the smaller-scale case, the quantities of salt would be too small to be of interest to a salt mining investor, so the costs of leaching and brine disposal would need to be recovered from the UGS operation. In the larger-scale case, it is assumed that a salt producer would be interested, and the incremental costs for gas storage would be proportionately lower.

The first scenario is for two caverns, each 55–60 meters in diameter and 200 meters high. Each would store 65–75 MMcm (with roughly 50 MMcm of cushion gas), for a total of 130–150 MMcm of working gas, using a pressure range of 90–215 bar. Leaching these two caverns in parallel would take about four years. The present value of capital costs for the smaller-scale case, discounted at 10 percent per year, is estimated to be about €68 million.

The larger-scale scenario is for eight caverns, each 70–80 meters in diameter and 200–300 meters high Each cavern would store 130–150 MMcm (with about 100 MMcm of cushion gas), for a total of 1,200 MMcm of working gas, using a pressure range of 90–215 bar. Leaching four such caverns in parallel would take about eight years, and a second stage to leach the other four caverns would take another eight years. The present value of capital costs for this larger-scale case, discounted at 10 percent a year, is estimated to be about €73 million.

It is clear that the larger-scale option is more attractive, if a salt mining company can be attracted to the development.

Divjaka Depleted Gas Field, Albania   The Albanian experts who met with the consultants also provided information on depleted field potential. Divjaka was exploited between 1960 and 1980, and it is practically empty. During that time, about 1.3 Bcm of natural gas was produced. The Divjaka field consists of 25 different reservoir layers, each 4–6 meters thick in the depth interval from 2,000 to 2,600 meters, with no water drive.

The possibility of gas storage in the Divjaka field had been investigated by a feasibility study, and, although the study itself was not available, information from it was offered by the Albanian experts. The field productivity data provided are somewhat difficult to reconcile. On the one hand, a porosity value of 16–20 percent and a permeability value of 153 millidarcies were given, indicating rather good reservoir performance. On the other hand, it was said that the field had been exploited by 70 production wells, corresponding to an average daily productivity rate of 2.65 Mcm per well, which is very low. This ambiguity in the limited information available means that the optimum approach for redeveloping Divjaka as a UGS facility is unclear.

It is known that new wells drilled in Divjaka would have to be quite deep (2,000–2,600 meters)—and therefore expensive. The low reservoir pressure would require specific measures to keep the mud column stable while drilling (even after loading with cushion gas), which would prompt additional costs of as much as 50 percent. The large number of production wells would mean high maintenance costs. The incremental contribution of new wells to the overall performance of the storage facility would be rather small, even if new horizontal wells were considered. For these reasons, a rather high cushion gas volume and rather low working gas volume development concept is assumed for the purposes of this report, as explained in appendix E.

A UGS facility at Divjaka would have an estimated working gas volume of about 60 MMcm, with cushion gas of 170 MMcm and a fairly narrow operating pressure range of 110–130 bar. The maximum daily withdrawal capacity would be approximately 0.5 MMcm from 70 (existing) production wells, and the maximum daily injection rate would be about 0.35 MMcm.

The present value of capital expenditures for this development concept, discounted at 10 percent a year, is estimated to be roughly €39 million.

Summary of Cost Estimates   Table 3.16 summarizes the estimated economic costs of providing gas storage at each of the six potential sites studied.

Table 3.16   Summary of Economic Costs for Six Potential UGS Facilities

Present values[a]	Albania site Divjaka	Dumrea (national case)	Dumrea (regional case)	Bosnia and Herzegovina site Tuzla-Tetima	Croatia site Okoli 2b	Benicanci (phase 1 case)	Serbia site Banatski Dvor
Capital expenditure (€ million)	39.0	67.6	73.1	49.9	155.1	83.0	101.6
Capital expenditure ($ million)	54.6	94.6	102.4	69.9	217.1	116.2	142.3
Cushion gas (MMcm)	170	100	800	12	350	400	800
One-off injection[b] ($ million)	0.9	0.4	1.0	0.1	2.0	2.0	2.4
Holding cost ($ million)	39.3	16.5	41.0	2.4	76.6	78.6	101.0
Final working capacity (MMcm)	60	240	1,120	60	400	500	800
Present value (working capacity) (MMcm)	383.8	1,269.9	1,765.1	379.1	2 735.2	2,371.2	3,317.5
Unit costs							
Working capacity[c] ($/Mcm)	246.9	87.8	81.8	190.8	108.1	83.0	74.0
Holding cost[d] ($/Mcm)	12.5	12.5	12.5	12.5	12.5	12.5	12.5
Subtotal unit cost[e] ($/Mcm)	259.4	100.3	94.3	203.3	120.6	95.5	86.5
Injection costs[f] ($/Mcm)	6.3	9.4	12.5	12.5	7.8	7.8	7.8

Present values[a]	Albania site			Bosnia and Herzegovina site	Croatia site		Serbia site
	Divjaka	Dumrea (national case)	Dumrea (regional case)	Tuzla-Tetima	Okoli 2b	Benicanci (phase 1 case)	Banatski Dvor
Cost per unit ($/Mcm) for ...[g]	265.7	76.2	59.7	114.1	104.3	84.2	77.0
Number of equivalent cycles[h] per year	1.00	1.50	2.00	2.00	1.25	1.25	1.25

Source: Authors' compilation.

Note: Mcm = thousand cubic meters; MMcm = million cubic meters; UGS = underground gas storage. Input assumptions: Brent crude oil price level, $75 a barrel; corresponding gas price level, $250/Mcm; foreign exchange rate, $1.40/euro; discount rate, 10 percent per annum.

a. All of the values shown are present values over 20 years (except for the "working capacity" where the final value is shown in the table); whereas the working capacity of most of the facilities is not 100 percent of its final value in the first year, but is built up to the final value over several years as caverns are leached (in the case of salt formations), as cushion gas is injected, as new wells are drilled, and as surface facilities developed, with operation typically commencing a year or two after the first capital expenditure. The discounted presented values in the analysis take all of these time effects into account.

b. This is the one-off injection cost for the cushion gas. This cost would be borne by the storage owner or operator.

c. This is the level required to recover, from working capacity charges, over 20 years of operation, the present value of the capital costs and cushion gas injection and holding costs at the given discount rate. This would be the *minimum* amount payable by storage users for access to the capacity for the facility to be viable.

d. This is the cost of holding the stored gas for six months (that is, from injection to withdrawal on a single-cycle, simple seasonal basis). This economic cost would be borne by storage users as owners of the gas. From a financial point of view, an up-front outlay for the cushion gas is required. Only the holding cost enters the analysis from an economic point of view, as the cushion gas is a recoverable resource, should the storage facility ever be decommissioned in the future. Because only holding costs are included, it is not necessary to deduct the final value of the cushion gas from the economic costs. In practice, only the holding cost of the cushion gas should be charged to storage users.

e. This is the subtotal of the unit costs on a capacity basis, excluding operating costs.

f. This is the cost of injecting the working gas. This would be incurred by the storage operator, and charged to the users as part of the storage fees.

g. This is the cost per unit of stored gas, taking into account the assumed number of equivalent cycles per year. This represents the total economic cost of storage under the given assumptions.

h. The assumptions in this row represent the consultants' judgment of realistic levels of cycling, based on the likely level of market demand constrained by an understanding of the technical characteristics of each site.

From the estimated parameters at each site, engineering capital costs were estimated (in euros), with reference to similar UGS projects in Europe in the period 2007 through early-2008, adjusting the costs for the physical and market conditions in Southeast Europe. Euro-denominated capital costs were converted to U.S. dollars at an assumed exchange rate, and discounted to present values. Costs related to gas prices, such as the cost of injecting cushion and working gas (with the working assumption of gas compressors), the annual costs of holding cushion gas, and the six-month cost of holding working gas all were linked to the relevant dollar oil price scenario, using the same method as used in the other parts of this study. Gas injection costs and cushion gas holding costs were discounted to present values, and those values were then summed and divided by the present value of the annual stream of future working gas capacity available in each year to give the economic cost of that working gas storage capacity, on the assumption of a constant charge over the economic life of the facility (assumed to be 20 years).

Finally, the economic costs were estimated on a per-unit volume of stored gas basis, taking into account the likely number of storage cycles per year at each potential facility. A greater number of cycles increases the total cost of injecting the stored gas, but spreads the cost of the working gas capacity over a greater volume of stored gas.

As a result of demand volatility (and changes in supply conditions), typically it is desirable both economically and commercially to be able to reinject some gas to storage in winter and to withdraw some gas from storage in summer. If some storage users need to inject while others are withdrawing (and vice versa), and they have not been able to trade directly, then they effectively can trade through the storage facility (to the profit of the storage owner or operator). In such cases, the net direction of flow may not change. However, it is possible on unseasonably warm winter days or unseasonably cold summer days, or when a large customer is forced to suspend operations and reduce or suspend gas deliveries, that the market as a whole will need to inject in the winter or withdraw in the summer. This leads to cycling, increasing above one the number of injection and withdrawal cycles per year.

Salt caverns, which typically have high maximum withdrawal rates, may be cycled quite frequently. Depleted fields are not so flexible. This fact is reflected in the cycling assumptions at the bottom of table 3.16. The Dumrea salt caverns under the national variant (serving only Albania's market) are assumed to be cycled less than they would be under a regional variant (serving transit demand).

Economically Preferred Potential UGS Facilities Based on the preceding analysis, the economically preferred UGS facilities in Southeast Europe, from a regional perspective, are Banatski Dvor, Benicanci, and Dumrea. In the long run, these sites would provide well over 2 Bcm of working gas storage capacity, which would be sufficient for the expected requirements of the SEE gas market until 2025. Table 3.17 summarizes the key results of the economic cost analysis for these three UGS facilities.

It is important to note that the preference for these sites assumes that the EC Gas Ring is in place, connecting all of the relevant markets, as are the necessary market and institutional arrangements to ease regional cross-border gas flows to and from the storage facilities. If that is not the case, then the Dumrea facility in Albania would not be able to provide modulation services for gas demand in markets distant from it. Instead, it would be able to serve only the Albanian market (in which case the smaller national variant would be selected); or it could serve the Albanian market plus transit, if the trans-Adriatic pipeline were in place and needing storage services.

Figure 3.13 shows the supply and demand outlook for regional storage in Southeast Europe (not including Bulgaria and Romania), with the three preferred options indicated. Banatski Dvor UGS in Serbia (already

Table 3.17 Preferred Near- and Medium-Term UGS Options in Western Southeast Europe

Factor	Banatski Dvor	Benicanci	Dumrea	Total
Geological type	Field	Field	Salt formation	n.a.
Capital cost ($ million, discounted at 10% per annum)	142	116	102	360
Capacity (MMcm)	800	500	1,120	2,420
Withdrawal rate (MMcm/d)	9.0	6.2	6.0	21.2
Capacity cost ($/Mcm)	74	83	82	n.a.
Number of cycles per year	1.25	1.25	2.00	n.a.
Volume cost ($/Mcm)	77	84	60	n.a.

Source: Economic Consulting Associates' storage model, using underground gas storage engineering cost estimates that are based on data from national experts.
Note: Mcm = thousand cubic meters; MMcm = million cubic meters; n.a. = not applicable; UGS = underground gas storage.

Figure 3.13 Storage Demand Outlook and Supply Options in Non-EU Southeast Europe

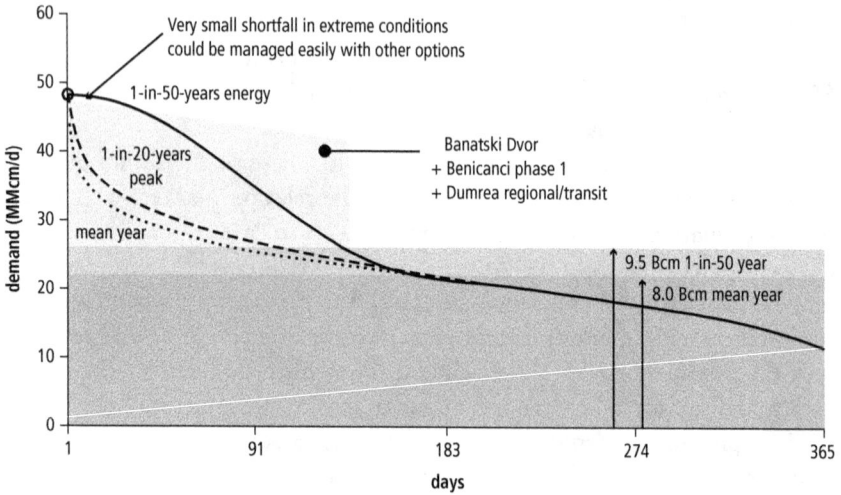

Source: Economic Consulting Associates' storage model.
Note: EU = European Union; MMcm/d = million cubic meters per day.

under development), plus Benicanci phase 1 and the large version of Dumrea development (suitable for providing modulation services on a regional basis and support for transit flows) would be sufficient to meet the storage demand for gasification on the EC Ring.

Developing some of the sites identified in the region will involve quite long lead times. This is especially true for leaching salt caverns at Dumrea; but it also applies to the development of Benicanci, where the geologic characteristics demand particular care. Therefore, careful coordination of storage development with distribution development as part of the regional gasification initiative will be crucial. The World Bank and KfW could play a valuable role in such coordination among the parties involved in the region and between storage and distribution developments.

Cost of Alternatives to UGS

It would not make sense to incur the cost of underground gas storage if there were an alternative way to match demand with supply at a lower economic cost. Therefore, the economics of UGS is determined by the cost of alternatives—that is, the opportunity cost. Theoretically, there are many ways to match gas demand with supply. Those ways identified for analysis in this study are the following:

- entering into interruptible (nonfirm) contracts with large customers
- storing in line-pack from building the EC Ring with a larger diameter
- importing LNG to meet peak demand and the seasonal swing
- expanding physical pipeline capacity and gas supply contract terms
- using alternate secondary or backup fuels for power and industry
- dispatching gas-fired power plants on a counterseasonal basis.

Each of those methods is discussed in greater detail below.

Interruptible (Non-Firm) Contracts with Customers   One alternative to storage is having interruptible contracts with large (usually industrial) customers. The prices of such contracts will depend on the economic value of interruptions to those customers. There is a high degree of uncertainty around estimates of these values, partly as a result of the complexity of defining supply interruptions. The dimensions of the interruptions include their frequency, their duration, and how much advance notification customers are able to receive.

Despite the uncertainty, the economic cost of interruption (or the value of lost load) is known to be quite high. The issue was addressed in a 2006 study for the U.K. Department of Trade and Industry (now termed the Department of Business, Enterprise, and Regulatory Reform):

> It is not straightforward to calculate as the costs of energy interruptions depend on a number of. . . . This, inevitably, leads to controversy as to the best way to estimate value of lost load, and a wide range of estimates have been proposed by various academics, consultants and market participants. However, these estimates tend to be within the same order of magnitude (e.g., for gas, we are aware of estimates in the range of £5/therm to £30/therm) (Ilex 2006, p. 12).

Using an exchange rate of 1.6 U.S. dollars to the British pound, this range is equivalent to about $2,800 for16,000/Mcm. The same study mentions using "estimates of the direct and indirect economic loss resulting from companies in specific sectors ceasing production due to interruptions to their gas supplies . . ." estimated the average cost of "unserved gas" to energy-intensive industrial users at around £12/therm, which is equivalent to nearly $7,000/Mcm on the above assumption (Ilex 2006, p. 12).

That study describes a method for using the gross value added by industry as the basis for estimating the sector's cost of interruption. Table 3.18 shows this approach for a selection of markets in Southeast Europe. These values fall in the bottom half of the range mentioned above. These numbers clearly are quite approximate, first-order estimates. Some of the industries may not be using gas, which would reduce the denominator and increase the result. Furthermore, this is an average method, and the value of gas at the margin would be expected to be higher.

It is clear from the results that the economic cost of storage is well below the expected cost of customer interruptions. Such interruptions should be interpreted as frequent interruptions with no notification, from which the adverse economic and commercial effects can be quite high. Therefore, it makes economic sense to invest in storage to the extent necessary to keep such interruptions very infrequent.

However, it is well known that interruptible contracts are common in many industries, with customers choosing to accept non-firm gas characterized by contractually agreed occasional interruptions of an agreed maximum duration and with an agreed period of notice in exchange for a lower price than would be available for firm or contractually guaranteed continuous gas supply. This willingness implies that pre-agreed costs are much lower than the values for unexpected interruptions with no warning, as in table 3.18. For example, a factory may be prepared to accept interruption in exchange for compensation equal to its forgone marginal profits on the lost production. This would yield figures considerably lower than those in table 3.18. The willingness to contract on an interruptible basis will vary from industry to industry, and it will depend on the relationship between fixed and variable costs and the significance of gas costs in each firm's production cost function.

Table 3.18 Estimates of the Value of Lost Load, Selected Gas Markets in the Region, 2006

Market	Manufacturing GVA ($ billion)	Total annual gas consumption (Bcm)	Industrial annual gas consumption (Bcm)	Value of lost load ($/Mcm)
Croatia	7.36	2.7	0.9	~ 8,300
Bulgaria	4.76	3.0	1.0	~4,800
Romania	2.51	16.4	5.4	~ 4,600
Serbia	4.63	2.5	1.6	~ 2,900

Sources: BP (2008) and other sources; United Nations GDP statistics.
Note: ~ = approximately; Bcm = billion cubic meters; GVA = gross value added; Mcm = thousand cubic meters.

Non-firm supply arrangements have the potential to reduce the amount of storage capacity that is required. This point is related closely to the discussions below. The discussion of alternate secondary or backup fuels for power and industry explains that gas interruption can be relatively low in cost where a backup fuel is being carried anyway. The discussion of counterseasonal dispatch of gas-fired power plants concerns the power sector, where there is large potential for interruption.

Line-Pack from a Larger EC Ring The quantity of gas in a gas pipeline transmission system at any moment in time depends on the system's physical internal volume and the pressure and temperature of the gas. Transmission systems are operated between maximum and minimum operating pressure specifications. At any given temperature level, the difference between these pressure levels represents a quantity of gas known as the maximum possible "line-pack." This line-pack is used to manage the hourly or intraday variations in load.

The question is whether it would make economic sense to build the EC Ring at a larger diameter (to accommodate long-term growth) and to use the additional volume as storage in the short to medium term (either instead of UGS or as a way to defer underground storage development). Table 3.19 shows the calculation of line-pack for the 24-inch-diameter base case and the incremental line-pack and costs for three larger pipe diameters.

The incremental capital cost of enlarging the EC Ring is very high, ranging from $278 million to increase the small version of the ring from 24 inches to a 30-inch diameter, up to more than $1.3 billion to increase the large version of the ring from 24 inches to 42 inches in diameter. Using the additional volume of stored gas from these diameter enlargements for a single annual storage cycle would cost about $8,000/Mcm-roughly 100 times the cost of underground storage capacity. However, when the same volume is used to cycle gas to meet daily peaks, using 135 equivalent full cycles over the course of a year, the incremental cost falls to approximately $60/Mcm. (The cost of line-pack on the base 24-inch diameter, with the same pressure range assumption, suggests a cost just over $100/Mcm.)

When these costs are spread over all distribution-connected volumes (on the basis that line-pack provides an intraday balancing service required by all distribution-connected customers), the unit cost falls to between $0.05/Mcm and $0.25/Mcm, compared with a line-pack cost in the base case of about $0.20/Mcm.

At the equivalent of 135 full cycles per year, the incremental cost of line-pack becomes comparable with UGS. But serving the few peak days each year involves far fewer than 135 cycles. Therefore, the analysis confirms

Table 3.19   Line-Pack in the EC Ring

Dimension	Base		Incremental	
Diameter, nominal (in)	24	30	36	42
Diameter, nominal (mm)	600	750	900	1,050
Cross-sectional area (m³)	0.283	0.442	0.636	0.866
Physical volume of the EC Ring:				
Small version ('000 m³)	357	558	804	1,094
Medium version ('000 m³)	414	647	931	1,268
Large version ('000 m³)	485	758	1,092	1,486
Pressure range (barg)	20	20	20	20
Gas volume (ideal gas law approximation):				
Small version (MMcm)	7.1	11.2	16.1	21.9
Medium version (MMcm)	8.3	12.9	18.6	25.4
Large version (MMcm)	9.7	15.2	21.8	29.7
Incremental line-pack (relative to 24-inch-diameter EC Ring):				
Small version (MMcm)	n.a.	4.0	8.9	14.7
Medium version (MMcm)	n.a.	4.7	10.3	17.1
Large version (MMcm)	n.a.	5.5	12.1	20.0
Unit cost:				
Easy ($ million/km)	0.593	0.789	1.020	1.305
Hard ($ million/km)	0.794	1.041	1.322	1.657
Pipeline capital expenditure:				
Small version ($ million)	866	1,145	1,466	1,855
Medium version ($ million)	1,005	1,328	1,700	2,151
Large version ($ million)	1,145	1,514	1,943	2,463
Cost per unit of incremental line-pack, based on a single annual cycle:				
Small version ($ million)	n.a.	8,124	7,878	7,874
Medium version ($ million)	n.a.	8,134	7,887	7,882
Large version ($ million)	n.a.	7,954	7,725	7,735

(continued on next page)

Table 3.19 Line-Pack in the EC Ring (Continued)

Dimension	Base		Incremental	
Cost per unit of incremental line-pack based on 135 equivalent full cycles per year:				
Small version ($/Mcm)	105	60	58	58
Medium version ($/Mcm)	106	60	58	58
Large version ($/Mcm)	103	59	57	57
Incremental unit cost spread, based on 135 cycles spread over all distribution-connected volumes:				
Small version ($/Mcm)	0.17	0.05	0.11	0.19
Medium version ($/Mcm)	0.19	0.06	0.13	0.22
Large version ($/Mcm)	0.22	0.07	0.15	0.25
EC Ring lengths:	Small version: 680 easy + 584 hard = 1,264 km total			
	Medium version: 780 easy + 684 hard = 1,464 km total			
	Large version: 1,080 easy + 636 hard = 1,716 km total			

Source: Authors' compilation.
Note: barg = bar gauge; EC = Energy Community; in = inches; km = kilometers; m³ = cubic meters; Mcm = thousand cubic meters; mm = millimeters; MMcm = million cubic meters.

that line-pack storage in transmission systems is economic for intraday balancing (which is what it is used for in all gas systems), but that it cannot compete economically with UGS for low-cycle balancing requirements.

Imported Peak or Seasonal LNG Supply Seasonal LNG supply might be another way to manage seasonal variation in load. Under this approach, SEE wholesale gas buyers would contract for winter LNG deliveries to an LNG receiving terminal on the Adriatic coast, with the intention of avoiding the cost of developing the equivalent amount of UGS capacity.

A first-order estimate of the costs of such a strategy can be made with reference to market price data for LNG and futures prices on hubs with liquid trading. Data from Nymex and the U.S. Department of Energy for the period September 2007 to July 2008 confirm that weighted-average LNG import prices in the United States track Henry Hub prices very closely.

The long-run difference between summer and winter natural gas futures contracts in the United Kingdom in early October 2008 was about 12 pence/therm or £1.20/MMBtu. Using the exchange rate at that time, this is equivalent to a winter-summer seasonal price spread of about $2.10/MMBtu, which is equivalent to about $74/Mcm. The spread between U.S. winter and summer futures prices is considerably narrower: about $0.80/MMBtu or roughly $28/Mcm. These price differences can be seen in figure 3.14.

It would be reasonable to conclude that if Southeast Europe were to purchase winter gas for seasonal swing management, it would need to pay at least the U.K. winter price minus the difference in shipping costs from the producer's port of origin, if one takes the following facts into account:

- The United Kingdom is closer geographically to Southeast Europe than the United States is to Southeast Europe
- U.K. gas price levels are higher than U.S. gas price levels.
- The winter-summer price difference in the United Kingdom is greater than it is in the United States.
- The price differential is likely to be fairly stable as gas prices move up and down with oil prices.

In early October 2008, the LNG shipping cost from North Africa to Barcelona was less than $0.20/MMBtu; and from North Africa to the Isle of Grain in the United Kingdom or to Zeebrugge in Belgium, the cost was approximately $0.40/MMBtu. From the Middle East to Barcelona, the cost was about $1.25/MMBtu. Therefore, from the Middle East to a port on the Adriatic coast would be expected to be about $1.00/MMBtu. From the Middle East to the Isle of Grain or Zeebrugge, the cost was more than $1.50/MMBtu (ICIS Heren, *Global LNG Markets,* September 26, 2008, p. 5).

Therefore, to provide the same netback price to a North African producer (such as Sonatrach), SEE LNG buyers would need to pay no less than $0.20/MMBtu ($7/Mcm) below the U.K. National Balancing Point (NBP) price. To provide the same netback to a Middle East producer, SEE buyers would have to pay no less than $0.50/MMBtu ($18/Mcm) below the U.K. NBP price. This analysis is consistent with the observation that Italy's Rovigo LNG terminal in the northern Adriatic is to be supplied with gas from Qatar. If available, Middle East gas likely would be the most attractive to Southeast Europe. Egyptian gas probably would be more attractive, but availability would be the issue.

After adjusting the producer country's netback for the difference between shipping costs to the next-best port and an Adriatic port, the costs of regasification would need to be added. These costs are about $0.45/MMBtu ($16/Mcm), doubled to allow for the half-yearly seasonal utilization for a total of $0.90/MMBtu ($32/Mcm). Adding $37/Mcm to this (that is, adding half of the $74/Mcm winter-summer NBP spread, which is the difference between a flat annual "strip" of gas and a winter strip of gas) gives an incremental cost of $69/Mcm.

Figure 3.14 Comparison of U.K. and U.S. Gas Price Forward Curves, Early October 2008

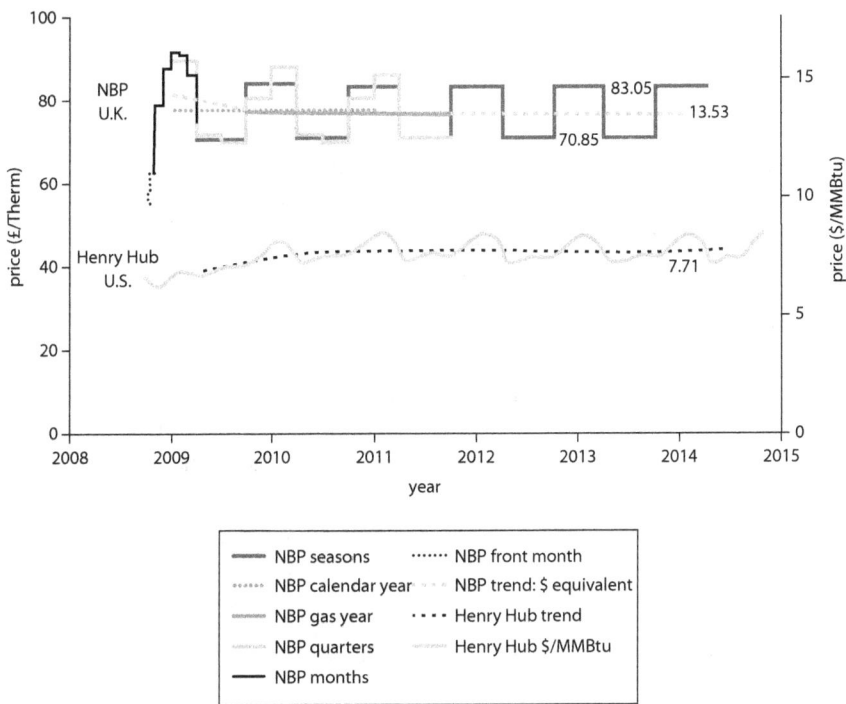

Sources: U.K. data, ICIS Heren, from the International Petroleum Exchange, London; U.S. data from the *Wall Street Journal online market data.*
Note: Btu = British thermal unit; MMBtu = million Btus; NBP = National Balancing Point.

On face value, this costs seems competitive: it is somewhat less than the estimated cost of storage at Banatski Dvor and Benicanci, and somewhat more expensive than the estimated cost of storage at Dumrea. However, there are several important factors that mean the comparison is not strictly like-with-like:

1. Any difference between the underlying costs of LNG and pipeline gas into Southeast Europe would have to be added to the above incremental cost to yield the overall cost of using LNG instead of seasonal storage.
2. The strategy would rely on the ability to purchase spot cargoes, which may not always be available when needed. Even if contracting ahead on a seasonal basis were possible, it would be very unlikely to be able to contract as far

ahead as can be done for pipeline delivery; and doing so would offer none of the flexibility that pipeline delivery provides in the timing of volumes.

3. Related to the second point, the purchasers would have significant price exposure to the LNG spot market for significant proportions of total annual volumes (particularly as high swing distribution-connected loads build up).

4. LNG would not provide any of the additional operational flexibility so valuable for system balancing. The LNG storage tanks onsite at the unloading and regasification facility are quite small. Furthermore, it is not possible to inject gas into the onshore LNG storage tanks (regasification is a one-way process: there is no liquefaction capacity in a regasification terminal, nor would it ever be economic to have such capacity).

When all of these considerations are taken into account, it is clear that the commercial and supply security risks of seasonal LNG deliveries (even if it were possible to contract for them) are far too great to justify any small price advantage that might appear to exist from the simple calculation above. Therefore, LNG therefore not considered an economic alternative to UGS. In practice, when supply contingencies occur as a result of the problems outlined above, the opportunity cost would not be the apparently reasonable cost of seasonal LNG supply, but rather the value of lost load described in table 3.18.

Gas Supply Contract Flexibility and Expanded Pipeline Gas Supply Capacity The terms in gas supply contracts allow the buyer a degree of flexibility in the profile on which gas is taken at the contract price. If the limits of that flexibility are exceeded, the buyer will incur penalties. Important terms in gas supply contracts usually include

- annual contract quantity (ACQ)
- maximum daily quantity (MDQ)
- maximum demand penalty (MDP)
- take-or-pay quantity (TPQ)
- take-or-pay penalty (TPP).

The MDP is an uplift on the contract price that must be paid for gas taken in excess of the MDQ. The TPP is the fraction of the contract price that must be paid for any untaken part of the TPQ.[28]

---

[28] Gas sales and purchase agreements often allow for some or all of the untaken TPQ to be rolled forward to subsequent periods (but paid for up front). Contracts also have a range of differences in the period over which the TPQ is specified—annually, quarterly, or monthly. The contract terms modeled have been idealized and simplified for the purposes of estimating the range of opportunity costs of storage that would be expected from using the possibilities of flexibility in sales and purchase agreements.

When initially contracting for gas supply, the buyer will have in mind an expected future demand for gas. The amount of gas actually taken in a given year is the actual annual quantity (AAQ). This quantity normally will vary from year to year, (for example, as a result of different temperature conditions from one year to the next, unexpectedly high or low rates of demand growth, or other factors.[29]

The degree of flexibility in contract terms means that the buyer does not need to completely flatten the annual profile at the contract delivery point, using storage; rather, the purchaser can have a certain amount of seasonal swing and daily variability, at no additional cost. Beyond this, the buyer may consider contracting for more gas than the expected demand, and incur TPPs if they are less costly than developing UGS facilities or buying storage services from a third party. This section considers just such a strategy as one of the opportunity costs for UGS.

Analyzing this strategy is done by modeling the incremental costs (from TPPs incurred) per unit of avoided storage working volume, under varying contract terms and different oil and gas price scenarios. The modeling assumes that untaken volumes from the TPQ cannot be rolled forward for use in a future period.[30]

The modeling is based on an AAQ of 8 Bcm, equivalent to the projected SEE long-run demand, which is equivalent to an annual average daily quantity of 21.92 MMcm. This is the load profile that is presented in figures 2.17 and 2.18 on seasonal swing in storage demand. The contract terms and price scenarios modeled are

- an MDQ of 105 percent, 110 percent, 115 percent, 120 percent, and 125 percent
- an MDP of 5 percent, 10 percent, and 20 percent
- a TPQ of 80 percent, 85 percent, and 90 percent
- a TPP of 70 percent, 80 percent, and 90 percent
- barrel of oil (thousand cubic meters of gas) price scenarios of $50 ($170), $75 ($250), and $100 ($330).

---

[29] Typical contracts, especially for newly gasified regions, might include provision for demand to build up over a number of years. To make the analysis manageable, constant year-to-year quantities are assumed.

[30] This is a reasonable assumption because, if the contracting strategies modeled were deployed indefinitely, the untaken gas also would be rolled forward indefinitely. In that case, its future value to the buyer (offsetting the up-front payment for it) would be discounted to zero, which has the same financial effect as the modeling assumption. Usually, TPQ volumes not taken by the end of the contract period are forfeited, which also has the same financial effect as the modeling assumption.

Volumes above the ACQ are at the standard contract price, provided that the MDQ is not exceeded on any day. If the MDQ is exceeded, the MDP applies to the excess volumes.

One strategy would be to contract for the expected demand in an average year (ACQ = AAQ). Under this strategy, TPPs would not be incurred, but the MDQ would be exceeded and penalties would be paid for the excess volumes. The opportunity cost of storage arising from the gas supply contract would be the gas price multiplied by the MDP, as shown for various gas price scenarios in table 3.20.

Table 3.21 shows that, for various contracted MDQ percentages, 2.0–2.5 Bcm of storage working capacity theoretically could be avoided (based on meeting the requirement in a 1-in-50 cold year, provided that 21–26 MMcm/d of peak deliverability beyond the MDQ upstream of the supply point was available.

Any cost for that additional pipeline capacity would be added to the values shown in table 3.20. Although the storage working volume avoided by such a strategy is small, it can be seen that the additional deliverability required to meet the peak days (in the 1-in-20 peak year) would be greater than the MDQ. This capacity would be required all the way upstream from the contract delivery point, and it has to be said that all of this capacity would be extremely unlikely to be available at the same penalty charged for small increments above the MDQ. As a first-order approximation, this at least double would transmission costs between the wellhead and the offtake from the transmission system in Southeast Europe. Given that these costs are approximately $70/Mcm plus roughly $35/Mcm for the EC Ring, that would add at least $100/Mcm to the costs in table 3.20, before adding any higher penalties to allow for the additional wellhead capacity implicit in such a strategy.

Table 3.20 Opportunity Cost of Storage, Gas Supply Contract Strategy ACQ = AAQ

Price scenario		Maximum demand penalty		
Oil ($/bbl)	Gas ($/Mcm)	5% ($/Mcm)	10% ($/Mcm)	20% ($/Mcm)
100	330	16.50	33	66
75	250	12.50	25	50
50	170	8.50	17	34

Source: Economic Consulting Associates' calculations.
Note: AAQ = actual annual quantity; ACQ = annual contract quantity; bbl = barrel; Mcm = thousand cubic meters.

Table 3.21 Avoided Storage Capacity, ACQ = AAQ Strategy

Maximum daily quantity		Storage working capacity avoided[a]	Extra deliverability still required[b]
(Percent of ACQ)	(MMcm/d)	(Bcm)	(MMcm/d)
105	23.0	2.64	35.4
110	24.1	2.47	34.1
115	**25.2**	**2.32**	**33.2**
120	26.3	2.16	32.1
125	27.4	2.02	31.0

Source: Economic Consulting Associates' storage simulation model.
Note: AAQ = actual annual quantity; ACQ = annual contract quantity; Bcm = billion cubic meters;
MMcm/d = million cubic meters per day. Midpoint or typical values are presented in bold type.
a. To meet 1-in-50-cold-years winter needs.
b To meet 1-in-20-years cold day demand.

Therefore, the opportunity costs of paying MDPs plus additional transmission costs, instead of investing in storage, would be expected to be at least $120/Mcm and perhaps more than $150/Mcm in the oil price scenario that puts oil at $75 a barrel. This cost is well in excess of the estimated costs of UGS in Southeast Europe.

A related strategy to reduce or avoid the need for storage would be to contract for more than the expected demand in an average year, such that the expected demand equals the TPQ. Such a strategy would reduce slightly the storage working capacity avoided and the additional deliverability required beyond the contract MDQ, as described immediately above. There would be a risk of incurring TPPs in below-average years, but the ability to roll over volumes should cancel out those penalties in above-average years. The costs of such a strategy would not be significantly lower than those described above, and similar peak deliverability problems still would be present.

Another strategy to reduce or avoid the need for storage would be to contract for more than the expected demand in an average year, such that the average demand in the peak month is equal to the MDQ in the contract. Depending on the value of the MDQ in the contract, this strategy could mean incurring TPPs in average years, as well as penalties for exceeding the MDQ on peak days.

Table 3.22 shows the contract opportunity cost for this strategy. The annual contract quantity required varies inversely with the MDQ in the contract, as does the contract opportunity cost. The lower the MDQ as

Table 3.22   Avoided Storage Capacity, Peak Month Average Day = MDQ Strategy

Maximum daily quantity		With 8 Bcm/y expected AAQ, contract for ACQ	Storage working capacity avoided[a]	Contract opportunity cost	Extra deliverability still required[b]
(Percent of ACQ)	*(MMcm/d)*	*(Bcm/y)*	*(Bcm)*	*($/Mcm)*	*(MMcm/d)*
Oil $100/bbl, Gas $330/Mcm:					
105	23.0	11.10	1.48	262	26.5
110	24.1	10.59	1.48	186	26.5
115	**25.2**	**10.14**	**1.48**	**116**	**26.5**
120	26.3	9.71	1.48	52	26.5
125	27.4	9.32	1.48	7	26.5
Oil $75/bbl, Gas $250/Mcm:					
105	23.0	11.10	1.48	199	26.5
110	24.1	10.59	1.48	141	26.5
115	**25.2**	**10.14**	**1.48**	**88**	**26.5**
120	26.3	9.71	1.48	39	26.5
125	27.4	9.32	1.48	5	26.5
Oil $50/bbl, Gas $170/Mcm:					
105	23.0	11.10	1.48	135	26.5
110	24.1	10.59	1.48	96	26.5
115	**25.2**	**10.14**	**1.48**	**60**	**26.5**
120	26.3	9.71	1.48	27	26.5
125	27.4	9.32	1.48	3	26.5

Source: Economic Consulting Associates' storage simulation model.
Note: ACQ = annual contract quantity; bbl = barrel; Bcm/y = billion cubic meters per year;
Mcm = thousand cubic meters; MDQ = maximum daily quantity;
MMcm/d = million cubic meters per day. Midpoint or typical values are presented in bold type.
a. To meet 1-in-50-cold-years winter needs.
b. To meet 1-in-20-years cold day demand.

a percentage of the average daily contract quantity, the higher the ACQ needs to be set to make the MDQ equal to the average daily demand in the peak month. This increases the TPPs incurred in the average year. (There also would be some MDPs for exceeding the MDQ on peak days; but they would be very small, compared with the TPPs in an average year.)

With a typical MDQ of approximately 15 percent above average contract quantity, the contract opportunity cost is just under $90/Mcm in the $75-a-barrel oil price scenario. This amount is above the estimated cost of UGS in Southeast Europe, before accounting for the cost of the extra peak deliverability required through the transmission system downstream of the wellhead. With additional peak deliverability approximately equal to the MDQ in the contract (which approximately would double transmission costs between the wellhead and the offtake form the transmission system in Southeast Europe) adding at least another $100/Mcm to the opportunity costs in table 3.22.

In practice, the avoided storage costs and peak deliverability would be met by some other storage facilities between the producing-country's wellheads and Southeast Europe. It is clear from the above analysis that the opportunity costs of storage arising from using contract flexibility to avoid storage are greater than the costs of developing storage. Even if very flexible contract terms can be negotiated at low cost (which is unlikely), the additional costs of upstream transmission capacity will drive up the opportunity cost well beyond the cost of storage.

Alternate Secondary or Backup Fuels for Power and Industry   It is normal for power stations and large industries using gas as a primary fuel to have tanks onsite, with a backup liquid fuel like distillate or light fuel oil. Where such backup fuel is present, the opportunity exists to call on it instead of gas storage. The willingness of plant operators to have a backup fuel will depend on the amount of fuel stored and their preparedness to draw down stocks that are likely to be viewed as an emergency backup fuel.

Because gas is priced against petroleum products, with a small discount, the continual movement of gas prices with oil product prices underpins much of the economic analysis in this study; and means that using backup fuels (thereby reducing the need for storage capacity) can reduce to very low levels the cost of managing gas supply interruptions.

Many industrial gas users decide to have backup fuel tanks whether or not they enter into an interruptible gas supply contract. In these cases, it could be argued that there is no incremental capital cost associated with the backup fuel. But this could be considered double-counting (for emergencies and notified interruptions) the backup fuel tank capacity. In practical terms, applying a "no double-counting" condition describes plant operators who are unwilling to draw down backup fuel stocks in cases of contractually notified gas supply interruption. In such cases, entering into an interruptible gas supply contract would require capital investment in additional fuel storage tanks, along with the holding cost (interest) on the stored fuel. This additional cost would reduce the economic cost advantage of the backup fuel, relative to gas storage. The cost of UGS versus the cost of storing liquid backup fuels in tanks at industrial sites then would become the key comparison (plus any incremental maintenance costs associated with using a less clean-burning fuel than gas).

Referring to the very high economic cost of unexpected customer interruption, the facts that gas and liquid fuels are price linked and that liquid fuel storage tanks usually would be cheaper than underground gas storage on a like-with-like basis, it is clear why large industrial customers to normally have some backup fuel capability. The economic potential of backup fuels should be maximized with cost-reflective pricing of interruptible gas contracts.

Counterseasonal Dispatch of Gas-Fired Power Plants   The modeling of future demand for gas storage in Southeast Europe, discussed in the "Seasonal Swing" section of chapter 2, is based on the conservative assumption that peaks in power sector demand for gas will coincide with peaks in other (mainly distribution-connected) customers' demand for gas. Managing power sector gas demand to be counterseasonal creates the potential to reduce the need for storage capacity.

The power systems in Croatia and Serbia (two of the larger systems on the western side of Southeast Europe) peak in the winter. However, the growth in electricity demand on the Adriatic coast is driven increasingly by the summer tourist season. The Adriatic coast is where the need for new generation capacity is most needed, and it is the region where gas-fired generation with a low environmental impact is most valuable.

It is possible that a counterseasonal (summer-peaking) dispatch regime for gas-fired power plants is more economic than is proseasonal (winter-peaking) regime. If so, it would reduce the amount of storage capacity required by flattening the seasonal swing on the distribution-connected gas demand. Even if regional demand and transmission constraints do not favor counterseasonal dispatch of gas-fired power plants on the Adriatic coastal part of Southeast Europe, counterseasonal dispatch could be economically and commercially attractive.

Counterseasonal dispatch would be achieved in practice by dispatching other plants in preference to gas-fired plants in the winter and dispatching gas-fired plants in preference to other plants in the summer. Contributions to such a strategy could include scheduling annual maintenance of CCGT plants in winter; and maximizing summer hydroelectric dispatch and minimizing winter hydroelectric dispatch, to the extent allowed by storage capacity and inflows.

These strategies are consistent with the economic value of gas, which is higher in winter and lower in summer. If power generators were exposed to a wholesale market reflecting seasonal fluctuations in the gas price, they would tend to pursue such strategies to the extent that they maximized their returns—or at least minimized the annual cost of generation.

The value of gas to a gas-fired power station on any given day is the price at which it could sell that gas back into the gas market, not the average annual price in the power station's gas contract. Because the power station will have a contractual obligation to take gas in any case, the decision on any given day is whether to use that gas to generate electricity or to sell it to other users in the gas market. Therefore, as long as the market value of the gas on a given day is greater than the cost of purchasing electricity from other generators (or generating it from other power stations owned by the same company) to meet contractual obligations in the power market, then it will be both economic and profitable to do so, promoting counterseasonal dispatch and minimizing the amount of storage required to meet the region's gas demand.

Some fairly detailed modeling of the regional power system would be required to identify the economic cost of counterseasonal dispatch of future gas-fired power stations; but the preceding qualitative analysis prompts us to expect that there would be some potential for this strategy to be more economic than UGS at the margin. The strategy would not have value until distribution-connected gas loads started to grow.

Relative Economics of Underground Storage

The analysis in this section shows that underground storage in Southeast Europe is more economic than

- allowing customers to be interrupted
- building a larger EC Ring, and using the incremental line-pack for longer-than-intraday storage
- using LNG for seasonal and peak supply
- implementing strategies designed to use contract flexibility instead of storage.

The opportunity costs of these alternatives are higher than the cost of UGS under reasonable assumptions and for the provision of comparable balancing services.

Using alternative or secondary backup fuels in industry and power stations is likely to be more attractive than underground storage, particularly for low-frequency use on the coldest days and where these backup facilities need to be maintained anyway. Dispatching gas-fired plants in a counterseasonal manner when distribution loads build up also is likely to be economically attractive. Although these options cannot be expected to have sufficient potential to replace the need for UGS capacity in Southeast Europe, their potential to reduce the amount of UGS capacity required in the region should be explored thoroughly.

The marginal economic value of seasonal storage sets the opportunity cost for strategic storage capacity, because seasonal storage is the alternative use for such long-term storage. Large customers are at liberty to carry strategic storage stocks (which they may do simply by contracting for additional storage in seasonal storage facilities). For smaller customers, the need for strategic storage is a policy decision that is discussed further in the "Security of Supply" section of chapter 4.

Economics of Gas Distribution Networks

The aims of the analysis of gas distribution in the sample cities were to examine the typical conditions for gas distribution development in each market, to test the assumptions on demand and price competitiveness of gas, and to estimate the cost of transmission and supply to sample cities requiring new gas connections or major expansion of networks. Because it was not possible to carry out comprehensive city distribution studies in each market, the approach was to base the analysis on a small sample of cities.

The scope of the study provides for 20 case study cities selected from among the nine SEE markets, with at least one city in each market. The list of cities was agreed in consultation with energy ministry representatives from each market. The final list of 20 cities is included in table 3.23. In markets with no gas supply at present, the list includes the capital city and one other city.

Methodology for Distribution Case Studies

The case studies involved estimating the potential annual gas demand from demand connected to a future gas distribution system—including demand of residential, commercial, and small industrial customers; demand in the peak hour; and, hence, the notional distribution network design, capital costs, service costs, and connection installation costs. The costs of converting or replacing customers' appliances also were taken into account.

Estimation of Annual Potential Gas Demand   For most of the towns and cities considered in this study, there is little or no available official data concerning energy consumption. Therefore, it has been necessary to adopt a top-down approach in assessing potential gas demand, supported by local market research that identified the overall market structure and, where possible, provided information on demographics and the size and type of large industrial and commercial loads.

In towns where inadequate data were available, demand estimates were constructed using a number of assumptions based on overall industry experience.

Residential Sector   The demand estimates are built up from the residential side, starting with the population of each city, the number of residential dwellings, and an assumption of the mean annual gas consumption potential per dwelling. The commercial and industrial demands are inferred, with reference to the estimated residential demand using typical sectoral shares.

Potential residential annual demand has been estimated by applying an assumed annual consumption figure per household to the number of households within the study area. Based on European and regional experience, overall residential demand has been modeled using average annual gas consumption of just over 1,000 cubic meters (1 Mcm) for a typical apartment or small house.[31]

Where available, actual data from the region show the mean number of occupants per dwelling to be 2.9–4.9, with anticipation that this statistic will fall over time. The proportion of apartments for case study cities where actual data are available varies between 71 percent and 80 percent. Where data on the number and type of households are not available, it has been assumed that each household has four occupants, and that 75 percent of households are apartments and 25 percent are houses.

---

[31] This consumption level is equivalent to just under 10,000 kilowatt hours, 340 therms, 34 MMBtus, or 36 gigajoules. Data gathered during an earlier ECA study for Serbia indicated a range from 746 cubic meters a year for typical modern flats in Belgrade's climate conditions (design temperature –15°C, 2,520 heating degree-days) and up to 1,270 cubic meters a year for poor-quality, pre-1970 flats in Novi Sad's climate conditions (design temperature –20°C, 2,680 heating degree-days). The Serbian data suggest that the quality of building design and construction (insulation) is a more important variable than climatic range within the region. There certainly is variation in climatic conditions between the Adriatic coast and the inland regions. However, most of the case study cities are inland, and most of the potential residential heating demand for gas will be inland. The average annual household consumption assumption is considered conservative. The regulator in Ireland accepts 1,500 cubic meters as the annual average for small residential dwellings. Anecdotal evidence from gas industry managers in the region indicates that it is common for householders to heat only parts of a house or apartment, and not to heat them to very warm temperatures to keep costs down. This fact supports the view that gas consumption for heating is likely to have high income elasticities. The assumptions about the growth in number of households and penetration rate also are conservative.

Table 3.23 Distribution Case Study Cities

Market	Candidate city	Distribution	Population	Comments
Albania	Tirana[a]	No	700,000	Far from existing transmission
	Elbasan	No	123,200	Far from existing transmission
Bosnia and Herzegovina	Banja Luka	No	173,700	Far from existing transmission
	Zenica	No	85,600	Connected to end of existing transmission; main customer is Mittal Steel mill
	Mostar	No	64,300	Far from existing transmission
Bulgaria	Vidin	No	69,400	Moderately far from existing transmission
	Smolyan	No	69,300	Moderately far from existing transmission
	Krjali	No	65,000	Moderately far from existing transmission
Croatia	Split	No	175,100	Far from existing transmission, coastal
	Rijeka	LPG	163,700	Moderately far from existing transmission, near proposed LNG terminal, coastal
Kosovo	Pristina[a]	No	550,000	Moderately far from existing transmission
	Kosovska Mitrovica	No	120,000	Moderately far from existing transmission

Market	Candidate city	Distribution	Population	Comments
Macedonia, FYR	Skopje[a]	No	467,300	Connected to transmission; only 0.08 Bcm/y of 0.8 Bcm/y capacity is used
	Tetovo	No	50,400	Near existing transmission
Montenegro	Podgorica	No	136,500	Far from existing transmission
	Niksic	No	90,000	Far from existing transmission
Romania	Dobreta Turnu-Severin	No	106,000	On Nabucco route
	Horezu	No	7,000	Very near transmission, but has tiny population; case study of limit of viability?
Serbia	Leskovac	No	78,000	Moderately far from existing transmission
	Uzice	No	55,000	Moderately far from existing transmission; distribution in early development

Source: Authors' compilation.

Note: Bcm/y = billion cubic meters per year; LNG = liquefied natural gas.

a. Capital city.

The above assumptions and estimates of population make it possible to estimate potential long-run residential gas demand. This assumption has been done on the basis of current population (that is, not increased to allow for growth over the period during which residential distribution networks are developed and residential gas demand builds up), and without allowing for projected declines in the mean number of occupants per dwelling (which will tend to increase the number of dwellings for a given population level). Those assumptions are conservative, tending to underestimate the long-run demand.

Commercial and Industrial Sectors Full feasibility studies for distribution investments involve on-the-ground, street-by-street surveys of the types of businesses, their size, their current fuel use, and their potential for switching to gas. Such detailed bottom-up data were not available for the present study, so the potential commercial and industrial sector annual gas demand had to be estimated, using a top-down approach. This was done in proportion to the population of each case study city. Drawing on the experience of EIHP, the Energy Institute of Croatia, in carrying out in-depth distribution prefeasibility and feasibility studies on other cities in the region, it has been assumed that the following will be the sectoral breakdown of total annual demand:

- 60 percent residential demand
- 25 percent commercial demand
- 15 percent industrial demand.

This method of estimating demand means that demand results will tend to be underestimates for cities that have more energy-intensive industries and overestimates for cities that have fewer such industries. The results are not considered to be highly sensitive to this problem for two reasons: first, none of the cities is understood to be heavily industrial; and, second, very large industries will be transmission connected, not distribution connected, so they will not have any effect on the distribution economics.

Peak Hour Demand An estimate of peak hour demand is required to calculate the size and cost of the spur line from the transmission system to each city distribution network, the cost of the distribution mains system, and the cost of customer connections.

For residential customers, a peak hourly demand of 3 cubic meters has been used, consistent with the typical requirements of a medium-size central heating unit and a cooker. This peak hour flow is conservative (that is, it is on the high end of expectations for peak demand), meaning that the cost estimates are more likely overestimated than underestimated. The actual requirement would depend on the pattern of use, the type of controls, the weather patterns, and the standard of insulation in buildings.

Peak hour demands for the commercial and industrial sectors have been calculated from the annual volumes estimated, using the above method, by applying the following estimated load factors:

- 25 percent for commercial load
- 30 percent for industrial load.

The 25 percent load factor applied to the commercial sector is typical of small and medium-size commercial enterprises. Whereas the load factor for industry could exceed 80 percent for large-scale, energy-intensive continuous manufacturing processes (which may be transmission connected), the figure of 30 percent assumes that the distribution-connected industrial sector customers comprise mainly light industries operating on a single-shift basis.

Distribution System Design   Consistent with current European practice, it is assumed that bulk supply of gas within urban areas is achieved via steel distribution pipelines operating at pressures of up to 16 bar. Notional designs for the high-pressure (HP) steel distribution system have been developed to serve demand centers that have been identified from satellite images of each of the cities.

These steel systems have been sized to cater to total peak flow, while maintaining a minimum pressure of 7 bar and a maximum velocity of 20 meters a second. A diversity factor of 75 percent has been applied to the peak residential demand component when calculating pipe sizes for the HP distribution system.

In line with industry practice, it is assumed that the majority of the gas distribution network will be constructed from polyethylene pipes and fittings, will be supplied from the HP distribution system via a number of district pressure-reducing installations, and will operate at medium pressure. An operating pressure of 4 bar has been assumed for the purposes of this study.

To calculate distribution system cost, a generic model has been constructed, based on the design of a section of actual network covering an area of 1.74 square kilometers in a densely occupied urban area. That particular network serves 1,233 properties. Of those properties, 83 percent are apartment blocks with 4–12 apartments per block, 7 percent are individual houses, and 10 percent are small commercial properties.

For the purposes of this study, the generic distribution system model uses the same geographic layout as the real network design; but a number of scenarios covering different levels of demand have been developed, in line with the energy demand density calculated for each of the case study cities.

The reference network was designed with a maximum pressure of 4 bar, minimum pressure of 2 bar, and maximum velocity of 20 meters per second, using modern hydraulic modeling software.

The three scenarios investigated covered customer densities in the range of 3,800–7,400 customers per square kilometer, with equivalent peak hourly demand of 20.0–38.4 Mcm—approximately 11.5–22.0 Mcm an hour per square kilometer. The total length of the network was 14.6 kilometers and remained the same for each scenario; diameters changed as necessary to meet the required conditions of flow, maximum pressure, minimum pressure, and maximum gas velocity. Each scenario considered the network being supplied via two district regulator stations.

Distribution Network Costs Estimates of unit construction costs, derived from a number of recent projects undertaken by Penspen, were applied to the three network designs. Total network costs per customer are shown in table 3.24.

It has been assumed that both residential and commercial customers will be served from a common network because, in many cases, both property types are mixed within the same area. Such an assumption is thought valid for dispersed small and medium-size commercial premises, which often are similar in size and character to large residential customers. Although commercial premises, such as university campuses and hospitals, can be similar to small and medium-size industrial undertakings, market research and the advice of EIHP and the other local consultants suggests that faculty buildings and clinics often are dispersed throughout the towns. Therefore, the assumption of dispersed small and medium-size commercial premises is considered reasonably robust for the case study cities.

A review of satellite imagery and maps of the towns shows that industrial areas occupy approximately 10 percent of the land area. This figure has

Table 3.24 Reference Cases for Typical Distribution Costs

Case	Number of customers	Customer density (no./km²)	Peak demand (Mcm/h)	Network cost ($ million)	Cost per customer ($)
Case 1	6,667	3,800	20.0	1.7	260
Case 2	12,800	7,400	38.4	2.3	178
Case 3	11,300	6,500	33.9	2.0	180

Source: Penspen.
Note: Mcm = thousand cubic meters; no./km² = number per square kilometer.

been assumed to apply in all cases. It also has been assumed that the cost of gas distribution networks serving industry is the same per unit of area as the cost of those supplying residential and commercial areas.

Service Costs   Penspen's inhouse cost data have been used to derive cost estimates for services connecting customers' properties to the distribution mains system. The service cost covers mains connection, service pipe, pressure regulator, meter, fittings, and meter cabinet. Costs vary, depending on the type and size of the premises served. Residential service costs per customer are calculated from the weighted average of costs of a service supplying an apartment block and the cost of service for an individual house.

Service/connection costs for industrial and commercial customers have been calculated on a global basis for each town, and are based on an estimate of connection cost for typical customer types, expressed as dollars per cubic meter per hour. A hourly value of $266 per cubic meter has been used in developing industrial and commercial connection costs. This value has been derived from inhouse project data for a network with a high proportion of small commercial loads, resulting in an average peak hourly load of 12 cubic meters. This cost could fall significantly in networks serving large-scale customers.

The total cost of connection for each of these sectors thus is the product of the unit cost and the estimated peak hourly flow for each sector (table 3.25).

Installation Costs   Customers face an additional capital cost in connecting to a gas supply. The cost of the internal installation pipe-work between the outlet of the gas meter and the appliances needs to be taken into consideration when evaluating economic feasibility. It has been assumed that each residential customer in a house will require an average of 10 meters of internal pipe-work at an installed cost of $20 per meter, costing $200 per house

Table 3.25   Cost of Service Connections to Distribution Mains

Service	Weighting (%)	Number of customers	Cost per service ($ million)	Cost per customer ($)
Apartment service	75	4	3,000	750
House service	25	1	1,100	1,100
Weighted average	n.a.	n.a.	n.a.	812

Source: Penspen.
Note: n.a. = not applicable.

in total; and that each residential customer in an apartment will require 7.5 meters at the same price, costing $150 in total.

Appliance Conversion Costs   It is estimated that the cost of converting a residential LPG cooker or water heater could be approximately $35, if conversion were carried out on a large scale. Conversion of a residential oil-fired central heating boiler could be approximately $800, making the purchase of a new wall-mounted combination heating and hot water boiler ("combiboiler") with balanced flue an attractive alternative.

Economic Results of Distribution Case Studies

Regional transmission costs of about $25/Mcm (downstream of the offtake points from a major transmission pipeline, such as the TGI, TAP, or Nabucco). Adding local distribution costs for most of the cities brings the total to $100–$200/Mcm. Adding residential connection and installation costs raises the total to $250–$350/Mcm.

Table 3.26 shows the estimated costs of transmission and distribution for each of the 20 case study cities. The three largest cities—Tirana, Pristina, and Skopje—have the lowest estimated distribution costs (roughly $40/Mcm, and approximately $215/Mcm when residential connection and installation costs are included). The smallest town—Horezu, Romania—has the highest distribution costs ($750/Mcm, approaching $1,000/Mcm for residential customers when connection and installation costs are added). This cost level would be unlikely to be economic with oil prices below $70 a barrel.

All of these values are based on discounting 20 years of projected volumes building up linearly from zero to the long-run demand over 10 years, at a discount rate of 10 percent a year. Comparison of the values in table 3.26 with those in table 3.1 suggest that there is sufficient margin for most distribution costs around these levels. In a number of cities, however, the transmission and distribution costs exceed the margin for heavy fuel oil; but transmission-connected customers using heavy fuel oil could be converted to gas in some cities.

Changing the buildup to 15 years, and discounting just 15 years of revenues at 15 percent a year, more than doubles the transmission and distribution charges necessary to recover the investment. The margins appear large enough for this in many cities. Figure 3.15 plots the transmission plus distribution cost results from table 3.26 against the population of each city.

Box 3.2 provides a case study of some of the commercial strategies that can be used to build a successful gas distribution business, while ensuring that the financial incentives for customers to switch to gas and continue using it align with the economics of gas.

Table 3.26 Estimated Costs of Transmission and Distribution
$/Mcm

Market/city	Population	Transmission	Distribution	Transmission and distribution for nonresidential use	Connection and installation	Transmission and distribution for residential use
Albania						
Tirana	700,000	26	39	64	175	240
Elbasan	123,200	26	96	122	175	297
Bosnia and Herzegovina						
Banja Luka	173,700	26	113	139	176	314
Zenica	85,600	26	168	193	175	368
Mostar	64,300	26	106	132	175	307
Bulgaria						
Krjali	65,000	26	112	138	175	313
Vidin	69,400	26	148	173	175	349
Smolyan	69,300	26	103	129	175	304
Croatia						
Split	175,100	26	170	195	175	371
Rijeka	163,700	26	148	174	175	349

(continued on next page)

Table 3.26 Estimated Costs of Transmission and Distribution (Continued)
$/Mcm

Market/city	Population	Transmission	Distribution	Transmission and distribution for nonresidential use	Connection and installation	Transmission and distribution for residential use
Kosovo						
Pristina	550,000	26	35	61	175	236
Kosovska Mitrovica	120,000	26	106	131	175	307
Macedonia, FYR						
Skopje	467,300	26	41	67	175	242
Tetovo	50,400	26	162	188	175	363
Montenegro						
Podgorica	136,500	26	61	87	175	262
Niksic	90,000	26	125	151	175	326
Romania						
Drobeta Turnu Severin	106,000	26	133	159	176	334
Horezu	7,000	26	751	777	180	957
Serbia						
Leskovac	78,000	26	143	169	175	344
Uzice	55,000	26	246	272	175	447

Source: Economic Consulting Associates' analysis, using Penspen cost estimates.
Note: Mcm = thousand cubic meters.

Figure 3.15 Estimated City Distribution Costs Versus Population

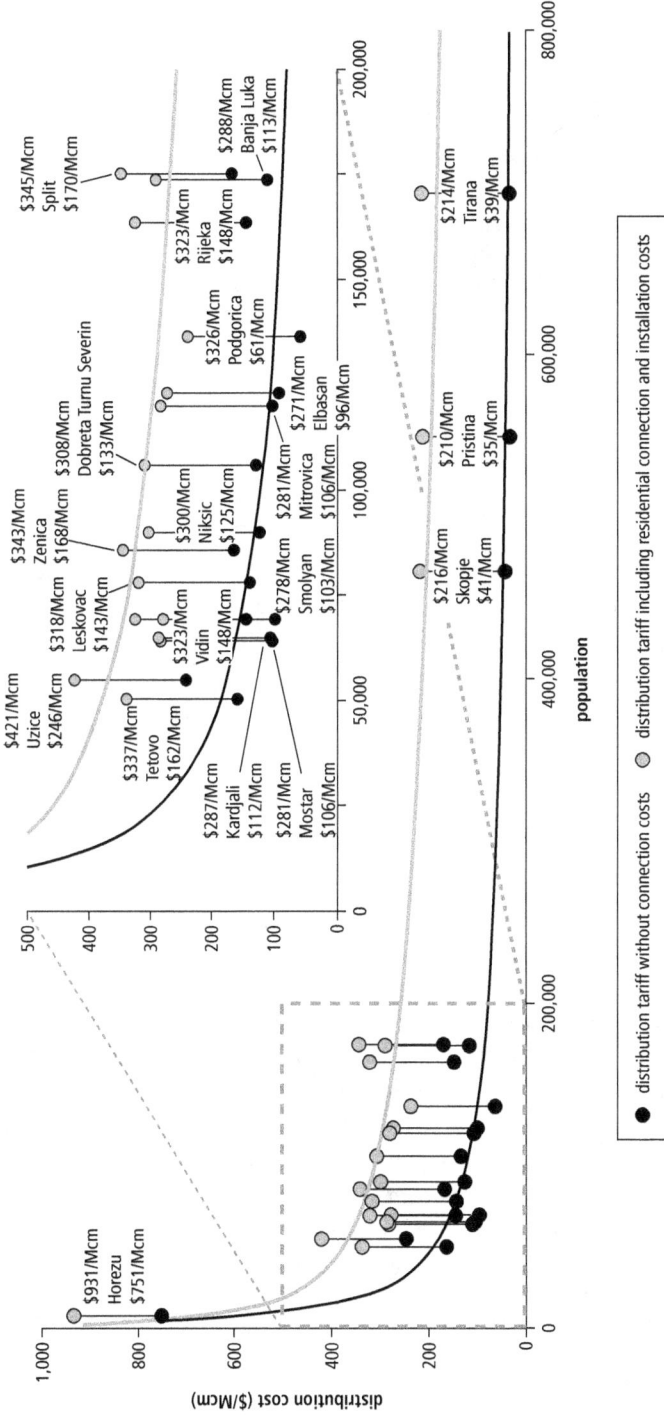

Source: Authors' illustration.
Note: Mcm = thousand cubic meters.

Case Study: Building a Distribution Business in Nigeria

To make the gas price attractive over time, and to remove foreign exchange risk, Shell offered Nigerian industrial and commercial gas customers a price based on a formula linked to a U.S. dollar-denominated fuel price index for each customer's present fuel, with a 10 percent discount to the price of that fuel.

To provide customers with an incentive to connect to the new gas network, Shell offered introductory price discounts, in addition to the 10 percent discount against the indexed price of their present fuel. The level of the introductory discount was calculated to be sufficient for each customer to recover, on a three-year simple payback basis, the costs within its premises ("downstream of the meter") for the installation of pipe-work and equipment changeover.

Shell declined offers of financing from the African Development Bank for financing customers' internal installation and conversion costs. Shell, of course, could have financed those costs itself, if it had wanted to do so. The reason it chose not to finance them was its desire for customers to make those investments and to have a financial incentive in actually using gas to realize the savings to recover those investments. Customers willing and able to finance their internal installation and conversion costs were more likely to be creditworthy, so Shell's approach also acted as a useful filter in reducing its commercial risk as the gas network developer.

In practice, customers realized additional benefits from changing to gas, such as reduced fuel storage costs, reduced maintenance costs, the opportunity to install new processes, and increased revenues from higher product quality. Those types of benefits were so significant in some cases that some customers were able to recover their up-front gas conversion investments in as little as six months. Allowing the customers to reap those benefits proved to be a good way to build the gas distribution business.

The general business environment in Nigeria is very difficult in almost every respect. Shell's success in developing a gas distribution business there suggests that, with the right commercial approach, it should be possible to develop gas distribution businesses in currently ungasified SEE markets. However, one key factor in this case study does differ from the situation in South-

(continued on next page)

east Europe: the gas supplied to customers was from Shell's oil and gas fields in Nigeria, where much gas produced in association with oil is flared.

In Southeast Europe, retail supply should be unbundled from distribution network services, according to the Energy Community Treaty. In that context, offering large customers a gas price linked to oil products would reflect the upstream price of gas and (if designed correctly) would ensure that customers have a financial incentive to keep using gas. Ensuring that customers continue to use gas is likely to be as important in Southeast Europe as in Nigeria to reduce the financial risk to the revenue stream required to recover the up-front investment in transmission and distribution network infrastructure.

Source: Penspen.

Application of the Distribution Case Study Results to the Region

The 20 case study cities have just over 3.3 million inhabitants, out of an urban population in the region of almost 31.0 million and a total population of 55.0 million. Of those 3.3 million people, some 3.0 million are in case study cities in the seven non-EU member markets in the region, out of an urban population of 13.6 million and a total population of just over 25.0 million (table 3.27).

The cities and towns are more likely to be economic and the small towns less likely to be economic. A conservative assumption is that 50 percent of the urban population of the seven non-EU countries could be provided with access to gas. If 50 percent of them take it up, that would account for about 3.4 million people using gas. That number is slightly higher than the total population of the 20 case study cities. It would be equivalent to about 1 million households, plus commercial and industrial users. Higher or lower coverage, and higher or lower gas take-up would lead to correspondingly higher or lower levels of demand.

Gas Value Chain

Russia has been, and still is, the dominant gas supplier to Southeast Europe. In this role, it has been able to determine and implement its gas pricing policy in conjunction with its overall strategy for gas development and trade, and in furtherance of its relationships with neighboring and gas-importing countries. Now that there is the near-future prospect of some gas supply competition in Southeast Europe, with the expected establishment of

Table 3.27 Case Study Cities in the Context of the Region

Market	Total population (million)	Urban population (million/percent of total) (million)	Case study city population (thousand)	50% coverage (million)	50% penetration (thousand)
Romania	21.8	11.9/54	113	Largely gasified	
Bulgaria	7.8	5.4/70	204	Partially gasified	
Serbia	9.9	5.3/54	133	2.65	1,325
Croatia	4.5	2.5/56	339	1.25	625
Bosnia and Herzegovina	3.9	1.8/45	324	0.90	450
Macedonia, FYR	2.0	1.4/68	518	0.70	350
Albania	3.1	1.4/45	823	0.70	350
Kosovo	2.0	0.8/40	670	0.40	200
Montenegro	0.6	0.3/54	226	0.15	75
SEE 7 subtotal	25.5	13.5/52	3,000	6.75	3,375
Total/weighted average	55.1	30.8/55	3,350	n.a.	n.a.

Sources: UNDP (2006), tables 1, 5, and 14, supplemented with International Monetary Fund and World Bank data for Kosovo, Montenegro, and Serbia.
Note: n.a. = not applicable. Differing national definitions of "urban" apply, so cross-country comparisons should be made with caution.

import routes for Caspian gas, it becomes more important to examine the costs of Russian gas supply along the value chain. Doing so will enable us to compare Russian, Caspian, and other gas sources; and to determine the competitive advantage any of them might have.

Methodology

In chapter 2, the section titled "Fuel Price Scenarios" describes the estimation of import prices at the western Ukraine border, based on the typical price indexation of long-term Russian gas contracts for SEE markets, as well as the price relationships between international marker prices for key petroleum products and crude oil, inferred from historical prices. The analysis suggests Russian gas prices at the western Ukraine border could be $230/Mcm when crude oil is at $65 a barrel, $165/Mcm with crude at $45 a barrel, and $100/Mcm with crude at $25 a barrel.

Map 3.1 shows existing and potential key nodes on the transmission network around the nine SEE markets. The large black circle indicates the node (or nodes) on the western Ukraine border near Uzhgorod. There are three international border stations near this point: at Velke Kapusany on the Slovak border, at Beregdaróc on the Hungarian border, and at Mediesu Aurit on the Romanian border. The price at the western Ukraine border is a key point in the value chain for Russian gas because all of the major Russian pipelines converge at this point, and it is commonly the delivery point for Russian gas contracts to Western Europe.[32] For the SEE markets, the value chain downstream of this point includes steps for

- transit and transmission across the Slovak Republic, Austria, and Slovenia, to Rogatec on the Croatian border
- transit and transmission across Hungary to Kiskundorozsma on the Serbian border
- transmission via national systems in Southeast Europe (and transit to neighboring SEE markets), at present from Serbia to Bosnia and Herzegovina
- distribution
- any taxes.

---

[32] Gas can be delivered to this point from the West Siberian Basin (and in future the Yamal Peninsula) and from as far south as the huge Dauletabad field in Turkmenistan. For contracts delivered at the western Ukraine border, the seller (Gazprom) pays Ukraine for transmission and transit, and the buyer in Central or Western Europe pays for transmission and transit to the countries downstream of that point. The western Ukraine border is the former Soviet border.

Of these steps in the value chain, distribution (and probably taxes) will be the same, regardless of the source of the gas and the import point. The first two steps—transit and transmission—may vary somewhat, according to the source of the gas and the import point.

Russian Gas Value Chain

The value chain for Russian gas upstream of Uzhgorod is shown in figure 3.16, with Brent crude oil selling at $65 a barrel; in figure 3.17, with Brent crude oil at $45 a barrel; and in figure 3.18 with Brent crude oil at $25 a barrel.

The following observations can be made about those figures:

- With Brent crude prices at $65 a barrel, there is substantial producer rent of close to $70/Mcm, even with upper limit wellhead costs of $45/Mcm and Russian transmission costs of $45/Mcm. These are the estimated costs for Yamal Peninsula gas.
- With a barrel of Brent crude selling for $45, producer rent is just under $20 a barrel, and the same wellhead and transmission cost assumptions as in the bullet point above. Lower wellhead and transmission costs would increase the producer rent by a corresponding amount.
- With Brent crude oil selling at $25 a barrel, there would be no producer rent, and only the lowest-cost fields ($13/Mcm at the wellhead) would be

Figure 3.16   Value Chain for Russian Gas with Brent Crude Oil at $65 a Barrel

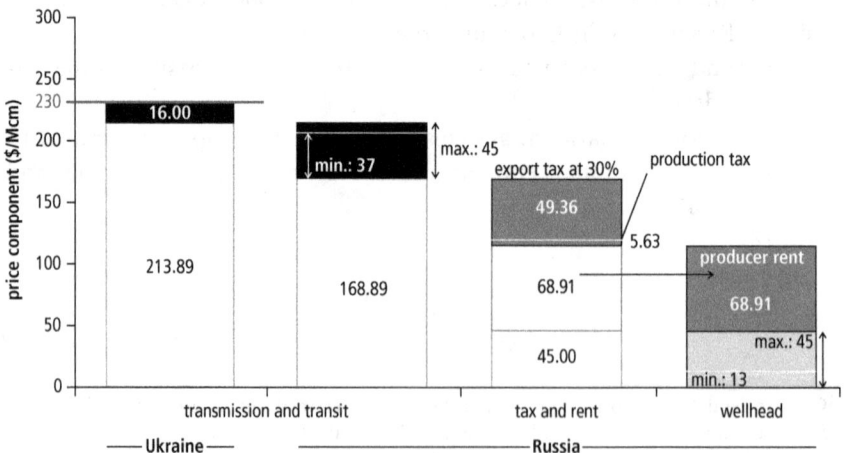

Source: Economic Consulting Associates' analysis, using data from Energywise Consultants.
Note: bbl = barrel; max = maximum; Mcm = thousand cubic meters; min = minimum.

economic. Reducing export and/or production taxes (the government's share of the rent) would increase the level of economic wellhead costs, but only to just under $38/Mcm—still somewhat less than the estimated $45/Mcm for marginal fields on the Yamal Peninsula.

Figure 3.17 Value Chain for Russian Gas with Brent Crude Oil at $45 a Barrel

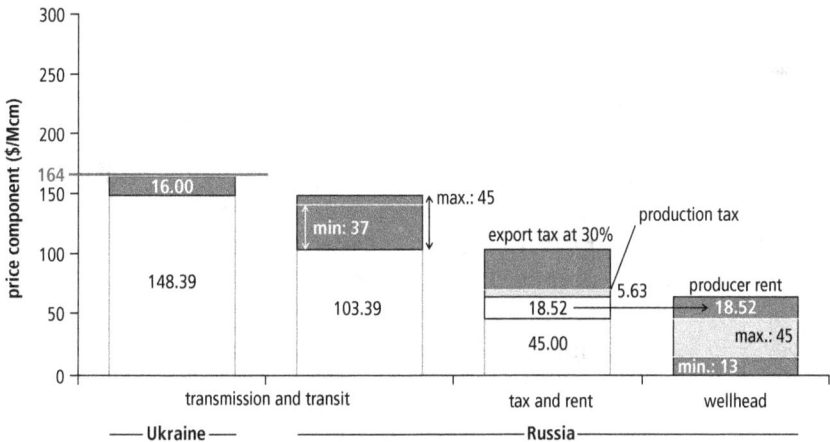

Source: Economic Consulting Associates' analysis, using data from Energywise Consultants.
Note: bbl = barrel; max = maximum; Mcm = thousand cubic meters; min = minimum.

Figure 3.18 Value Chain for Russian Gas with Brent Crude Oil at $25 a Barrel

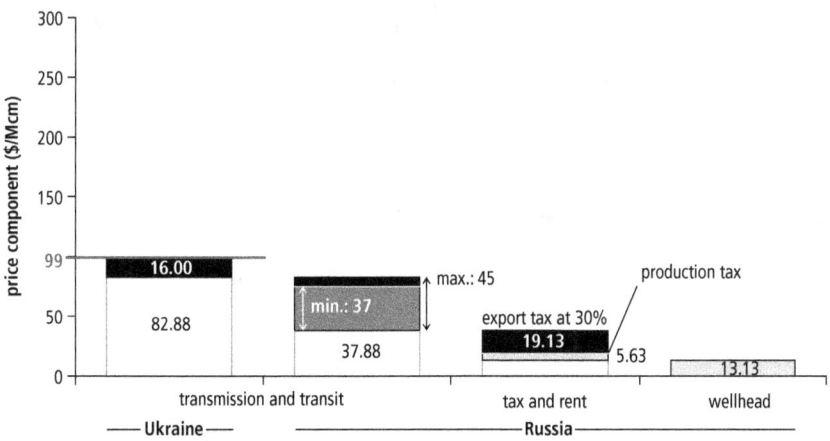

Source: Economic Consulting Associates' analysis, using data from Energywise Consultants.
Note: bbl = barrel; max = maximum; Mcm = thousand cubic meters; min = minimum.

With production tax for Russian gas fixed at its current level of $5.63/Mcm, gas export tax at its present level of 30 percent, a marginal cost at the wellhead of $45/Mcm, and Russian transmission cost at $45/Mcm, it is estimated that producer rent would fall to zero with crude oil prices at $37.65 a barrel. With no export tax and all other assumptions the same, the producer rent would fall to zero with crude oil prices at $28.89 a barrel. With no export tax and no production tax, producer rent would fall to zero at $27.17 a barrel.

Upstream Costs

Estimates of the long-run marginal cost of Russian gas production have been made on the basis of available project-by-project data. The projected costs include value added tax on capital expenditure (because of the difficulties of recovering it), and they reflect a 12 percent real rate of return on investment. Generally, development in Russia is becoming ever more expensive.

Because the commissioning dates for specific gas fields are uncertain, the information on the long-run marginal production cost has been grouped by categories of fields, location, and geology. Table 3.28 shows future peak gas production in Russia with an estimated cost.

Table 3.28   Future Russian Gas Production

Gas fields group	Peak gas production (Bcm/y)	LRMC ex-field gas production cost ($/Mcm)	Brent crude price above which production is estimated to be economical[a] ($/bbl)
Ob-Tazovsky Guba fields	80–85	13–18	22–24
Achimovian suite reserves, East Urengoi zone	100	20–25	24–27
Bolshekhetskaya depression fields (Yamal Nenets autonomous district)	30–40	26–32	27–29
Yamal Peninsula fields	250	40–45	35–38

Source: Economic Consulting Associates' analysis, using data from Energywise Consultants.
Note: bbl = barrel; Bcm/y = billion cubic meters per year; LRMC = long-run marginal cost; Mcm = thousand cubic meters.
a. Assuming production tax of Rub 147/Mcm, equivalent to $ 5.63/Mcm at an exchange rate of 26.124008 Rub per U.S. dollar and export tax of 30 percent of the customs value. Lower taxes would mean these fields were economic to develop at lower crude oil prices, and vice versa.

Comparison of the Upstream Value Chains
for Russian and Caspian Gas

It is helpful to compare the value chain for Caspian gas delivered via the proposed Nabucco pipeline with the above picture of the value chain for Russian gas upstream of the western Ukraine border near Uzhgorod. Table 3.29 makes this comparison.

The values in the right-hand half of the table are based on modeling of the economic cost at the beachhead of gas from Shah Deniz, using data from publicly available sources. Shah Deniz is an enormous complex of fields, estimated to contain as much as 625 Bcm (22 Tcf) of gas. The Phase 1 development is expected to recover about 175 Bcm of gas (about 6 Tcf). The gas field is wet, and quite rich in condensates. It is estimated that there are sufficient condensates to cover the development costs; and that the marginal cost of the gas is close to zero, or probably negative, depending on the oil price.

This result, combined with estimates of the cost of transmission (even using higher, more conservative capital cost estimates for the pipeline than those published by the Nabucco consortium), suggests that Caspian gas delivered via Nabucco will be highly competitive with Russian gas. Even when the Russian government export tax and production tax are added to the estimate of producer rent to make a direct like-with-like comparison with Caspian gas, the values in table 3.29 suggest that Caspian gas will have an economic advantage over Russian gas.

This economic advantage will not necessarily translate into lower import prices for importers in the nine SEE markets. The rent is probably more likely to flow upstream to transit countries and producers than downstream to consumers. (Bulgaria and Romania may be able to capture some of the available rent via participation in the Nabucco project.) However, it suggests that gas should be in a strong position to displace petroleum products in the nine SEE markets, even in a low oil price scenario.

The Nabucco International Pipeline Company publicly has stated that it is open to a proportion of the gas (perhaps 20–30 percent) being injected by Russia. However, the extent to which Gazprom might be prepared to reduce prices—relative to the current pricing formulas—to retain future contract volumes that might otherwise be met by Caspian gas remains to be seen.

Also remaining to be seen is how Gazprom's future pricing behavior might change in response to gas from the Caspian Sea region competing with Russian gas in the markets of Southeast Europe. Gazprom has proposed Blue Stream II to transport additional gas to Turkey and to compete directly with Caspian gas injected into the Nabucco pipeline. More recently, Gazprom and ENI of Italy signed an agreement for the South Stream project, a proposed pipeline from Dzhubga on Russia's Black Sea coast (the start

Table 3.29 Upstream Value Chains for Russian and Caspian Gas

Price elements	Brent crude ($/bbl)					
	Price for gas from Russia[a] ($/Mcm)			Price for gas from the Caspian Sea[b] ($/Mcm)		
	25	45	65	25	45	65
Ukraine, near Uzhgorod	100	165	230	n.a.	n.a.	n.a.
Romania, near Timisoara	n.a.	n.a.	n.a.	100	165	230
Netting back:						
Transit and transmission[c]	16	16	16	33+	33+	33+
	Russia–Ukraine border			Georgia–Turkey border		
Export tax (at 30%)	19.13	34.24	49.36	n.a.	n.a.	n.a.
Transmission (minimum to maximum)[d]	37 to 45	37 to 45	37 to 45	8~10	8~10	8~10
Production tax	5.63	5.63	5.63	n.a.	n.a.	n.a.
Producer rent[e]	–32 to 8	20 to 60	70 to 110	>56 to 58	>122 to 166	>187 to 263
Beachhead price	n.a.	n.a.	n.a.	Approximately 0	–42 to 0	–74 to 0
Wellhead (maximum to minimum)	13 to 45	13 to 45	13 to 45	n.a.	n.a.	n.a.

Source: Economic Consulting Associates' analysis and modeling, using publicly available data from various sources.
Note: Mcm = thousand cubic meters; n.a. = not applicable.
a. West Siberian Basin and Yamal Peninsula.
b. Based on the Shah Deniz field in Azerbaijan.
c. This is the transmission and transit cost within Ukraine up to the western border near Uzhgorod, compared with an estimate of the transmission and transit cost on Nabucco up to a point near Timisoara, plus a branch to the Romania-Serbia border.
d. This is the transmission cost within Russia, compared with an estimate of the transmission and transit cost on the South Caucasus Pipeline to the Georgia-Turkey border.
e. In the case of Caspian gas, where the Azeri production and export taxes are unknown and where the transmission and transit fees on Nabucco are unknown, the producer rent would be divided among the producers, the governments of Azerbaijan, Georgia, Turkey, Bulgaria, Romania, and Hungary and the shareholders of the Nabucco International Pipeline company.

of the existing Blue Stream pipeline) via a 900-kilometer submarine pipeline straight across the Black Sea to the Bulgarian coast, presumably landing near Burgas or possibly near Varna. According to the public announcement, two overland routes are being studied from there: a southern route toward the heel of Italy, and a northern route in the general direction of the Baumgarten hub. Blue Stream establishes Turkey as a transit competitor to Ukraine. South Stream would bypass both Ukraine and Turkey, reducing Turkey's position as a transit country.

All available information suggests that the era of special below-market prices for former eastern bloc countries is over, and that Russian gas exports will be sold at market prices to all buyers. But the implication of the value chain analysis is that Gazprom's marginal costs of production and transmission (particularly from development of the large Yamal Peninsula reserves) mean that it will have less flexibility at the margin to reduce prices than will the developers of Caspian gas (for example, to deal with a lower oil price environment, or to compete with other sources).

Interaction with Western European Gas Markets

The aim of this section is to show the expected influences of Western European gas markets on price formation and on future gas prices in the SEE markets.

Supply-Demand Balance in Western Europe

Gas demand in the EU25 in 2006 was just under 470 Bcm. Growth from just less than 380 Bcm in 1996 has been very close to linear. A straight-line extrapolation backward from the past decade also fits very well to the smooth S-curve from 1965 to 1980, and to the more uneven growth between 1980 and 1995. Projecting forward, using this line, would see annual demand reach 600 Bcm between 2015 and 2020, and 700 Bcm between 2025 and 2030.

Demand in Western Europe[33] in 2006 was just under 425 Bcm. The pattern of growth is identical to that of the EU25; and the same projection method would see demand reach 500 Bcm between 2010 and 2015, 600 Bcm between 2020 and 2025, and about 650 Bcm by 2030. These results are shown in figure 3.19.

Production in Western Europe was just over 265 Bcm in 2006, leaving an import requirement of just under 160 Bcm. If Western Europe's gas production declines as expected and demand grows as expected, the import

---

[33] Western Europe here includes Austria, Belgium, Denmark, Finland, France, Germany, Ireland, Italy, Luxembourg, the Netherlands, Norway, Portugal, Spain, Sweden, Switzerland, and the United Kingdom.

Figure 3.19 Historical and Projected Gas Demand in Western Europe, 1960–2030

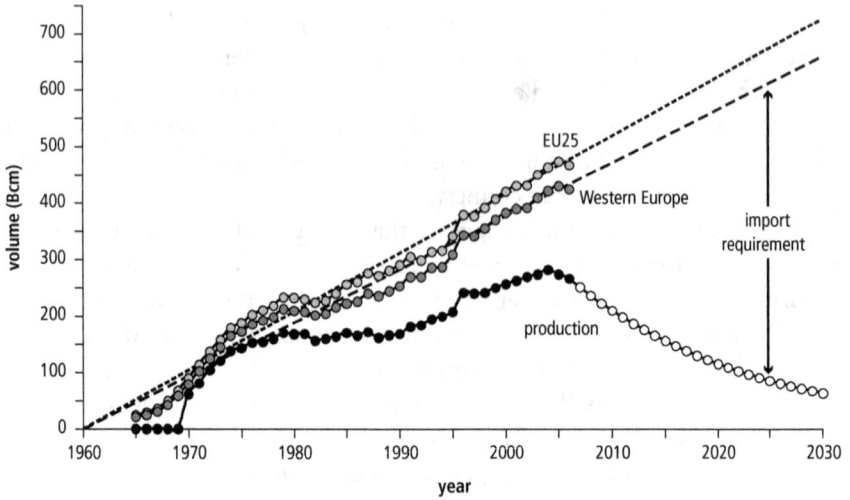

Source: BP's 2007 projection of Western European production
Note: Bcm = billion cubic meters.

requirement will expand to about 250 Bcm by 2010, to more than 450 Bcm by 2020, and to roughly 600 Bcm by 2030. A less rapid decline in Western European indigenous production and/or slower demand growth would result in a smaller import requirement. Nevertheless, it seems clear that Western Europe will be looking to all of the gas sources in the vast arc sweeping from the North Sea to the Russian Arctic, through western Siberia, to the trans-Caspian states, the Caspian Sea, and the Middle East (including the Islamic Republic of Iran and Iraq), through Egypt, across North Africa, and down to West Africa to meet demand. Both new pipelines and LNG developments will be required to close the supply gap.

Overview of Neighboring Markets
Table 3.30 shows natural gas trade movements by pipeline and LNG from sources around Europe to markets within Europe in 2006. Four of the nine SEE markets appear in the table: Bulgaria, Croatia, Romania, and Serbia. The gas imports of Bosnia and Herzegovina and of FYR Macedonia are very small, so they are included among "Others." The analysis in table 3.29, comparing the value chain for Caspian gas delivered via the proposed Nabucco pipeline to Baumgarten with the value chain for delivery of Russian gas to the western Ukraine border near Uzhgorod and from there to Baumgarten, suggests the importance of the Baumgarten hub in price formation for the SEE region.

Table 3.30 Selected Natural Gas Trade Movements by Pipeline and LNG, 2006

Bcm

From \ To	North Sea					Russia	Caspian			North Africa		LNG				Total
	Denmark	Germany	Netherlands	Norway	U.K.		Turkmenistan	Iran, Islamic Rep. of	Others	Algeria	Libya	Algeria	Libya	Egypt	Nigeria	
To																
Austria	—	1.10	—	0.78	—	6.85	—	—	—	—	—	—	—	—	—	**8.73**
Bulgaria	—	—	—	—	—	2.85	—	—	—	—	—	—	—	—	—	2.85
Croatia	—	—	—	—	—	0.75	—	—	0.40	—	—	—	—	—	—	1.15
Czech Republic	—	—	—	2.35	—	7.13	—	—	—	—	—	—	—	—	—	**9.48**
Germany	1.92	—	21.30	26.80	3.08	36.54	—	—	1.20	—	—	—	—	—	—	**90.84**
Greece	—	—	—	—	—	2.40	—	—	—	—	—	0.45	—	0.04	—	2.89
Hungary	—	0.83	—	—	—	8.32	—	—	1.80	—	—	—	—	—	—	**10.95**
Italy	—	2.50	8.70	7.20	0.80	22.92	—	—	—	24.46	7.69	3.00	—	0.10	—	**77.37**
Netherlands	2.24	4.50	—	7.00	1.82	2.97	—	—	2.52	—	—	—	—	—	—	**18.53**
Poland	—	0.35	—	0.49	—	7.00	0.21	—	—	—	—	—	—	—	—	**10.57**
Romania	—	1.30	—	—	—	3.95	—	—	1.00	—	—	—	—	—	—	**6.25**
Serbia	—	—	—	—	—	2.15	—	—	—	—	—	—	—	—	—	**2.15**
Slovak Rep.	—	—	—	—	—	6.30	—	—	—	—	—	—	—	—	—	**6.30**
Slovenia	—	—	—	—	—	0.56	—	—	0.10	0.44	—	—	—	—	—	**1.10**
Turkey	—	—	—	—	—	19.65	—	5.69	—	—	—	4.60	—	—	1.12	**31.06**
Others	0.93	4.15	18.60	39.38	4.24	21.12	5.80	—	—	12.02	—	16.63	0.72	14.83	16.46	**32.01**
Total	5.09	14.73	48.60	84.00	9.94	151.46	6.01	5.69	7.02	36.92	7.69	24.68	0.72	14.97	17.58	311.11

Source: BP's *Statistical Review of World Energy, 2007.*
Note: — = no movement; LNG = liquefied natural gas.

The Italian gas market is expected to exert an equally strong or stronger influence on price formation in the SEE markets. Italy currently imports gas from

- the North Sea, at Griespass on Italy's northern border with Switzerland
- Russia, via the TAG pipeline at Tarvisio on Italy's northeastern border with Austria
- Algeria, via the trans-Mediterranean (TransMed) pipeline landed at Mazara del Vallo on Italy's southwestern coastal tip in Sicily
- Libya, via the Green Stream pipeline landed at Gela on the southern Sicilian coast.

In the future, Italy is expected to import additional gas from

- Qatar, via LNG to the Rovigo terminal at Porto Levante on Italy's northern Adriatic sea coast (from 2009)
- the Caspian Sea (and/or Russia), via Turkey, Greece, and a submarine pipeline landed on the heel of Italy at its easternmost point at Otranto
- Algeria, via Sardinia and landed on Italy's western coast
- other North African countries (possibly including Egypt), and even West African countries (such as Nigeria), via LNG to proposed terminals around the coast.

This means that, at the margin, physical flows of gas from sources in all of five supply regions in the vast arc around Europe will be entering Italy: from the North Sea, Russia, the Caspian Sea, the Middle East, and North Africa.[34] Therefore, all producers in those counties selling gas to buyers in Italy will be expected to face the same price in the Italian market. The price terms in long-term contracts will reflect the market conditions at the time they are negotiated.

This principle would be expected to apply to both piped gas and LNG, and it suggests that Italy's virtual hub for gas trading—the Punto di Scambio Virtuale—is likely to emerge as a key location in Europe as the LNG and European gas markets mature and trading becomes more liquid.

In fact, given the full set of supply sources to which the Italian market will be exposed, and the size of the Italian domestic market (at 77.1 Bcm in 2006, the third-largest in Western Europe after the United Kingdom [90.8 Bcm] and Germany [87.2 Bcm], and more than eight times the size of the Austrian market [9.4 Bcm]), the Punto di Scambio Virtuale is expected to be a more significant location for price formation than Baumgarten. The latter currently has

---

[34] This would increase to six sources, including West Africa if Nigerian LNG is sold into the Italian market in the future. As table 3.30 shows, Turkey was the only European or Mediterranean market that bought Nigerian LNG in 2006.

only Russian gas passing through it and in the future will have gas from only two or three sources (Caspian gas via Nabucco and possibly LNG via Krk, although the LNG probably will be via swaps rather than physical flows).

Therefore, price netbacks from Italy and the SEE markets to a common point on the common upstream supply route should be equal. This effect is particularly strong for the seven westernmost SEE markets, but also will be relevant for Bulgaria and Romania, although they may be more directly influenced by price netbacks from the Austrian hub at Baumgarten when Nabucco is operational.

Supply-Demand Balance in Italy

Figure 3.20 shows the historical production and consumption of gas in Italy, as well as projected contract deliveries of gas from Russia, North Africa (mainly Algeria), and the North Sea. Gas demand in Italy will be determined largely by the rate of growth of power sector demand, which is expected to saturate (in terms of fuel market share) at some stage, depending on the competitive position of gas relative to the other fuel options. Two projections of Italian gas demand are shown in the figure:

- an optimistic one, reaching 84 Bcm in 2008, 88 Bcm in 2010, 100 Bcm in 2015, 110 Bcm in 2020, and 120 Bcm by 2030

Figure 3.20   Projected Maximum Capacity and Annual Gas Demand in Italy, 1970–2030

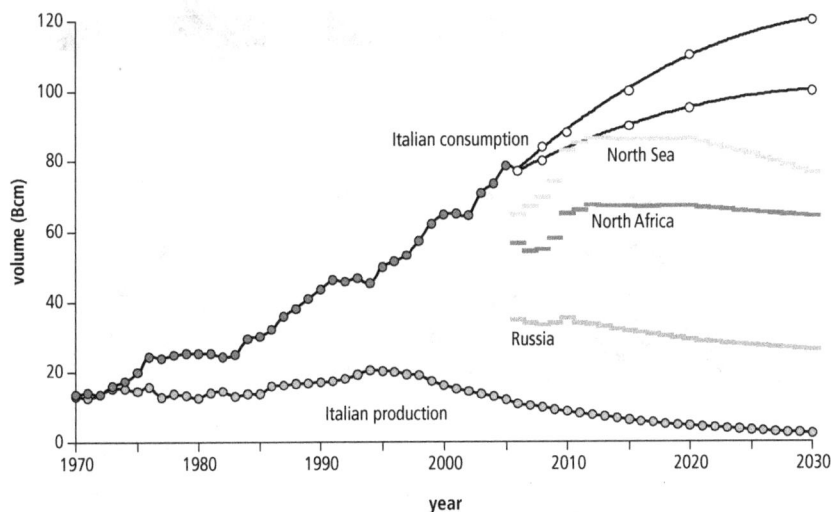

Sources: BP's *Statistical Review of World Energy*, 2002, 2003, 2004, 2005, 2006, and 2007.
Note: Bcm = billion cubic meters.

- a pessimistic one, reaching 80 Bcm in 2008, 90 Bcm in 2015, 95 Bcm in 2020, and 100 Bcm by 2030.

Most projections by Italian industry players that ECA has seen fall within this range: 90–100 Bcm by 2015 and 95–110 Bcm by 2020. Italy is a mature gas province: indigenous production peaked in the mid-1990s, and the gas fields are now in decline.

Figure 3.21 shows the indigenous production in Italy, plus entry capacity for current pipelines and LNG terminals, for projects under development and for planned and possible projects. The optimistic and pessimistic demand projections from figure 3.20 are superimposed. Italian entry capacity needs to exceed projected demand for two reasons: to allow for contingencies and to allow for any seasonal demand swing that cannot be managed by storage. Nevertheless, it is clear that not all of the new capacity will be required at the planned dates; and some projects will slip back, particularly the various LNG projects toward the top of the figure. The TAP project (not shown on this figure) may be able to displace some of those LNG projects, if it can access gas volumes from the east more competitively.

Figure 3.21   Projected Maximum Capacity and Annual Gas Demand in Italy, 2005–30

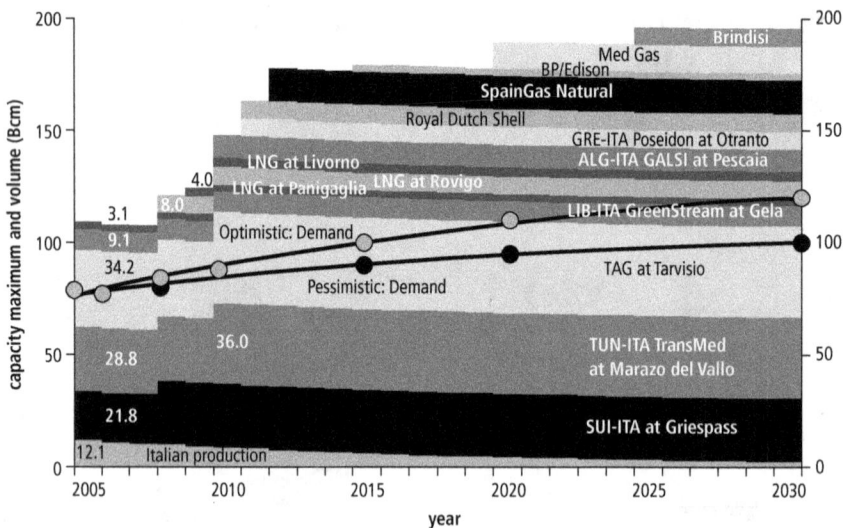

Sources: Economic Consulting Associates' research.
Note: ALG-ITA GALSI = Algeria-Italy-GALSI; Bcm = billion cubic meters; GRE-ITA = Greece-Italy; LIB-ITA = Libya-Italy; LNG = liquefied natural gas; SUI-ITA = Switzerland-Italy; TAG = trans-Austria pipeline; TUN-ITA = Tunisia-Italy.

The capacity-demand situation in Italy is relatively tight in the period up to about 2010; then it is likely to open up considerably, depending on the date that capacity from the various new projects becomes operational.

Historical and Projected Prices into Italy
Figure 3.22 shows historical gas prices for supply to the Italian market at

- Blaregnies, on the Belgium-France border, for North Sea gas
- Baumgarten, inside the Austria-Slovak Republic border, for Russian gas
- the Tunisian border, for North African (Algerian) gas.

The Brent crude oil spot price and ECA's estimate of typical SEE gas prices are superimposed. Transmission fees to Griespass on the Switzerland-Italy border would be added to the Blaregnies price, and transmission fees for transport via TAG from Baumgarten to Tarvisio on the Austria-Italy

Figure 3.22 Historical Prices for Gas from Various Sources to the Italian Market, 2000–09

Europe Brent spot price FOB (left axis)
North Sea at Blaregnies (right axis)
Russian at Blaumgarten (right axis)
North African at Tunisian border

Sources: U.S. Department of Energy, Energy Information Administration oil price data; ICIS Heren gas border price data.
Note: FOB = free on board; Mcm = thousand cubic meters.

border are added to the Baumgarten price. The TAG fees are calculated to be €5.53/Mcm, which is equivalent to $7.74/Mcm at an exchange rate of 1.4 U.S. dollar per euro. On a distance basis, that is just over S$2/Mcm per 100 kilometers. Adding the TransMed transmission fees to the Tunisian border price would give the landed price at Mazara del Vallo on the Sicilian coast. The Algerian gas price is somewhat lower than the North Sea and Russian gas prices.

Implications of SEE Interaction with Western European Markets

The proximity to and the present and future degree of transmission interconnections with the neighboring Western European gas market will influence the outlook for Southeast Europe. The configuration of major new transmission pipelines to Europe is the first factor to be considered. Then the implications of specific options are summarized: backhauling LNG from Revithoussa with a Russian gas swap, backhauling gas from Italy with a Russian gas swap, and direct offtake of Caspian gas from Nabucco or the PEGP.

Overview of the Options for Gas Supply to Southeast Europe   Map 3.13 summarizes the options for gas supply to various entry points on the EC Ring. In addition to the physical flow options shown in map 3.13, the planned expansion of the TransMed capacity from 28.8 Bcm/y to 36 Bcm/y in 2010 (shown in figure 3.21), makes the prospect of backhauling Algerian gas through the Greece-Italy Interconnector (for which there will be full third-party access) potentially attractive from a commercial and economic point of view.

Table 3.31 summarizes all of the gas supply options for the EC Ring, organized by the source of contracted gas; the infrastructure required and the transmission delivery mode; the contract arrangements required outside of the SEE destination markets; the market exposure associated with the option; and comments on each option's characteristics, such as its prerequisites, advantages, and disadvantages.

LNG Backhauling from Revithoussa, with Russian Gas Swap   A connection from the Greek grid to the EC Ring would provide access to LNG delivered via Revithoussa (giving Southeast Europe direct commercial exposure to Mediterranean LNG prices), to Caspian gas delivered via Turkey, or to Russian gas delivered via Bulgaria. The connection would make economic use of existing available capacity on the Greek gas transmission system and at the Revithoussa LNG terminal entry point, possibly supplemented by capacity on the Turkey-Greece border. In practice, buyers in Southeast Europe could contract for LNG delivered via Revithoussa, with a commercial swap for Russian gas flowing either directly though Bulgaria to FYR Macedonia or less directly though Bulgaria and Greece to FYR Macedonia or Albania. Such arrange-

Map 3.13 Options for Gas Supply to the Seven Westernmost SEE Markets

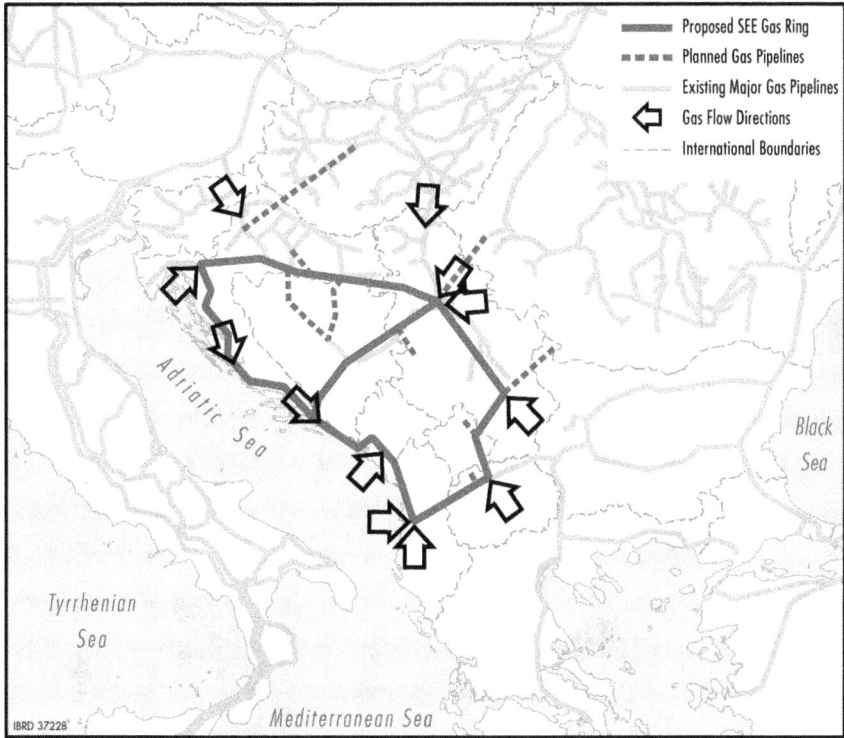

Sources: World Bank, compiled with reference to GIE, WinGas, and other published pipeline maps.
Note: SEE = Southeast Europe.

ments would release economic value through reductions in transmission costs. The "ifs" in this scenario are access to liquefaction (and shipping) capacity, and access to LNG volumes in a very tight market and at prices that buyers in the region would be willing to pay. Electricity tariff levels and bill collection rates in the SEE countries will underpin the creditworthiness of offtakers, which (together with the supply-demand balance and market arrangements in each market and in the region as a whole) will underpin the creditworthiness of power plant developers as gas buyers.

Backhauling of Gas from Italy, with Russian Gas Swap When a pipeline to the heel of Italy is in place (either the Poseidon submarine section of the larger TGI string or TAP), the possibility would open up for backhauling of North African gas or a mix of Italian gas sources against the flow of Caspian (and/or Russian) gas to Italy, facilitated by commercial swaps, so that SEE

Table 3.31 Supply Options for the EC Ring in Southeast Europe

Contract source	Infrastructure and delivery mode	Contract arrangements required outside Southeast Europe	Market exposure	Comments
LNG: Algeria, Egypt, others	Revithoussa LNG terminal, Greece; backhaul north through the Greek grid to the border of FYR Macedonia or Albania; new transmission pipeline connecting to EC Ring	• LNG delivery contract(s) • Transmission capacity in Greece • Swap contract(s) for physical Russian gas via Bulgaria onto EC Ring	Mediterranean LNG prevailing long-term contract prices	No need to invest up front in new LNG receiving terminal capacity on Adriatic coast.
Algeria or Italian mix of sources	Backhaul west-to-east through the IGI from Italy (full third-party access exists for this)	• Contract(s) with sources supplying Italian market (for example, Algerian gas or LNG) • Transmission capacity in Greece • Swap contract(s) for physical Russian gas via Bulgaria onto EC Ring	Italian market/ Punto di Scambio Virtuale prices, or long-term contracts reflective of Italian market outlook	Requires sufficient physical entry capacity into the Italian market from the other directions (south, northwest, northeast, and LNG). It appears from data in figure 3.33 that this will not be a problem.
Azeri or other Caspian sources	New pipeline connection to Serbia from (future) Nabucco pipeline, via Bulgaria or Romania	• Contract with gas marketers for delivery into Nabucco entry point on Turkish border • Transmission capacity from Nabucco Pipeline International to offtake • Transmission capacity in Bulgaria or Romania	Caspian gas long-term contracts in competition with Russian gas and other sources	This is contingent on Nabucco proceeding.

Contract source	Infrastructure and delivery mode	Contract arrangements required outside Southeast Europe	Market exposure	Comments
Azeri or other Caspian sources	Offtake from PEGP in Serbia, near Belgrade	• Contract for delivery of gas into PEGP entry point at Constanza, Romania • Contract with PEGP transmission owner for delivery to offtake point near Belgrade	Caspian gas long-term contracts in competition with Russian gas and other sources	This is contingent on PEGP proceeding and on infrastructure upstream of Constanza (such as GUEU-White Stream).
Russia	New pipeline connection to EC Ring, via Bulgaria or Romania or along existing corridor via Hungary from existing or reinforced pipeline infrastructure	• Contract(s) with Gazprom/Gazexport (including transit contract via Ukraine) • Transmission capacity in Hungary or Romania and Bulgaria	Gazprom pricing and contract terms	Upstream transmission reinforcement may be needed. Extends current exposure; no diversity or new price exposure. Possible fallback option or candidate for second entry point to the EC Ring.

(continued on next page)

Table 3.31 Supply Options for the EC Ring in Southeast Europe *(Continued)*

Contract source	Infrastructure and delivery mode	Contract arrangements required outside Southeast Europe	Market exposure	Comments
Russia	Offtake from Blue Line to an entry point on the EC Ring near Nis or Belgrade	• Contract(s) with Gazprom/Gazexport • Transit arrangements with Turkey • *Note:* EU-member Bulgaria is under the transmission arrangements of EU Directive 2003/55.	Gazprom pricing and contract terms	Could provide two injection points to the ring—at Nis and Belgrade—pressurizing the northern and southern halves and possibly making the eastern section redundant.
Russia	Offtake from the proposed South Stream pipeline (from Nord branch via Bulgarian system, or from Sud branch) to an entry point near Belgrade, Nis, Skopje, or Tirana	• Contract(s) with Gazprom/Gazexport • *Note:* EU-member Bulgaria is under the transmission arrangements of EU Directive 2003/55	Gazprom pricing and contract terms	With Bulgaria in the EU, it provides direct supply from Russia to the EU with no transit, bypassing Ukraine and Turkey (as does Nord Stream from Russia to Germany, bypassing Ukraine and Belarus).

Source: Authors' compilation.
Note: EC = Energy Community; EU = European Union; GUEU = Georgia-Ukraine-EU; IGI = Italy-Greece Interconnector; LNG = liquefied natural gas; PEGP = pan-European gas pipeline.

buyers would receive Caspian (and/or Russian) gas molecules contracted by buyers in Italy who would receive gas molecules from other sources (LNG, North Africa, North Sea, or Russia) contracted by SEE buyers. This would link the future SEE gas market to Italian long-term contract prices and to traded prices on the Punto di Scambio Virtuale hub.

Direct Offtake of Caspian Gas from Nabucco or the PEGP   Connection of the ring to an offtake point on Nabucco would provide the SEE markets on the EC Ring with direct access to Caspian gas (and potentially Iranian and Iraqi gas in the future), at prices netted back from the Baumgarten hub. Connection of the ring to an offtake point on the PEGP may provide the SEE markets with direct access to Caspian gas via the GUEU-White Stream project.

Implications of Supply Analysis for Each SEE Market
In addition to the regional perspective provided above, the particular circumstances of each market in the region are considered in this section.

Albania
In the 1980s, Albania had a significant gas industry (1 Bcm a year), but domestic production has dwindled to practically nothing (0.03 Bcm/y) now; and most of the pipeline infrastructure has deteriorated beyond use. The prospects for increased domestic production are very slim. The Albanian energy strategy foresees a major role for gas from imports of piped natural gas or of LNG. A gas law is being drafted; and it is intended that, in due course, the existing electricity regulator will be expanded to regulate the gas sector as well as power.

The primary and urgent need is in the electricity sector because Albania currently is about 600 megawatts short of capacity in the power sector. There is a number of CCGT projects in progress or in the planning stages. Other large potential customers are the cement industry in Elbasan and a brick factory near Tirana. Households increasingly are using LPG for heating and other domestic purposes. With the rebuilding of transmission and distribution systems, potential annual demand could reach 1 Bcm by 2025.

The need for power generation capacity increases the prospects for gas development in Albania. Probably the most attractive initial plan would be to bring supply via an offtake point on the Greek border, from the Greek or Bulgarian systems via FYR Macedonia. The numerous supply possibilities are summarized table 3.32. Albania also could transit northward to Montenegro gas delivered via the Greek system (and/or the FYR Macedonia system). Such a pipeline should be sized at constant diameter along its length, with a view to it subsequently forming part of the EC Ring.

Table 3.32 Supply Options of Immediate Interest to Albania

Transmission connection	Contract source(s)	Delivery and physical flows	Physical source and swaps
Greek border	Contract for LNG via Revithoussa	Backhaul through Greek system. Physical molecules flow to Athens. Russian gas flows to Albania through the Greek transmission system.	Swap LNG delivered at Revithoussa for Russian gas contracted to Greece at the Greece-Bulgaria border, and pay Greek transmission fees. Yields transmission cost savings in Greece.
FYR Macedonian border	Contract for LNG via Revithoussa	Backhaul through Greek system. Physical molecules flow to Athens. Russian gas flows to Albania, directed from Bulgaria via FYR Macedonia.	Swap LNG at Revithoussa for Russian gas contracted to Greece on the Bulgarian system, and pay Bulgarian exit fees and FYR Macedonian transmission fees. Yields transmission cost savings in Greece and Bulgaria.
Greek border	Contract for Algerian gas via TransMed	Backhaul through Greece-Italy Poseidon pipeline and Greek system. Physical molecules flow up into Italian system. Russian and/or Caspian gas flows to Albania through the Greek system, reducing Greece-Italy flows.	Swap Algerian gas at Mazara del Vallo for Caspian gas at the Greece-Albania border (or at the Turkey-Greece border, and pay Greek transmission fees). Yields transmission cost savings on Poseidon, and may yield some transmission cost savings in Greece.

Transmission connection	Contract source(s)	Delivery and physical flows	Physical source and swaps
FYR Macedonian border	Contract for Algerian gas via TransMed	Backhaul through Greece-Italy Poseidon pipeline and Greek system. Physical molecules flow up into Italian system. Russian and/or Caspian gas flows to Albania through the Greek system and via FYR Macedonia, reducing Greece-Italy flows.	Swap Algerian gas at Mazara del Vallo for Caspian gas at the FYR Macedonia-Albania border (or at the Greece-FYR Macedonia border, and pay Macedonian transmission fees; or at the Turkey-Greece border, and pay the Greek and FYR Macedonian transmission fees). Yields transmission cost savings on Poseidon, and may yield some transmission cost savings in Greece.
TAP	Contract for Russian and/ or Caspian gas	Conventional delivery via the Greek system and through Albania, with offtake in Albania.	Russian and/or Caspian gas. No swaps required.
TAP	Contract for Algerian gas via TransMed	Backhaul through TAP direct to Albania. Physical molecules flow up into Italian system. Russian and/or Caspian gas flows to Albania through the Greek system, reducing Greece-Italy flows on TAP.	Swap Algerian gas at Mazara del Vallo for Caspian and/or Russian gas at the Greece-Albania border, and pay Greek transmission fees. Yields transmission cost savings on TAP, and may yield some transmission cost savings in Greece.

Source: Authors' compilation.
Note: LNG = liquefied natural gas; TAP = trans-Adriatic pipeline; TransMed = trans-Mediterranean pipeline.

Bosnia and Herzegovina

Bosnia and Herzegovina has no indigenous production of gas, and imports all current gas supplies from Russia. At the policy level, the intention is to bring the gas industry into line with European Union Directive 55 on gas. A gas law has been drafted at the state level; but agreement has not been reached at the entity level, where responsibility for energy ultimately rests under the Dayton Accords.

The largest single customer on the Bosnia and Herzegovina system is the Bihac alumina plant. Other large customers include the Mittal steel plant in Zenica, a brick factory in Visoko, and a cement factory in Kakanj. Natural gas is the main source of energy for households in Sarajevo. Current annual demand of approximately 0.3 Bcm has the potential to grow to 1.4 Bcm by 2025. To achieve this level of growth, gas will have to compete effectively with cheap heavy fuel oil, produced, for example, at the Slavonski Brod refinery (3.5 percent sulfur).

Investment in storage (in the potential UGS facility, using a salt cavern at Tuzla and having a capacity of 0.06–0.10 Bcm) could be used to help manage seasonal swing, and it would reduce the investment requirements for transmission pipelines or allow greater capacity from a pipeline of a given size.

Increased demand in Bosnia and Herzegovina could be met from the east, via an upgraded branch from Belgrade toward Sarajevo, branching at Sarajevo northwest to Zenica and Banja Luka, and southeast to Mostar, with connection to the future southern Serbian system. Such a system could be supplied by increased flows of Russian gas into Serbia, southward via Hungary or northward via Bulgaria, or by Caspian gas from an offtake point in Romania (or perhaps in Bulgaria).

Alternatively, increased gas demand could be met from the south, via a pipeline northwards from the Greek system through Albania and Montenegro along the Adriatic coast. and the previous discussion of Albania, and especially table 3.32, describe the supply possibilities for this transmission option. These pipelines should be sized at constant diameters along their lengths, with a view to their ultimately forming part of the EC Gas Transmission Ring.

Bulgaria

Bulgaria is a key gas transit country. Approximately 16 Bcm of Russian gas currently pass through the Bulgarian system to Turkey, smaller flows pass to Greece, and tiny flows pass to FYR Macedonia. It is expected that the flows from Bulgaria to Turkey will reverse in the future, as Russian gas via Blue Stream plus Caspian gas plus Iranian and possibly Iraqi and Egyptian gas flow toward Europe in excess of Turkey's demand. The major transit flows through Bulgaria then would be Caspian (and possibly some Russian) gas in the Nabucco pipeline from Turkey to Romania toward Central Europe, and Russian gas flows via Serbia toward northeast Italy.

Bulgaria's own consumption of gas is met primarily from imports (approximately 2.9 Bcm a year). Domestic production, mainly from the Black Sea, contributes the remainder (0.3 Bcm/y). For added security of supply, Bulgaria has 0.45 Bcm of storage in its natural gas system at a UGS facility at Chiren. The Bulgarian transmission ring has a capacity of 6–7 Bcm/y, only half of which is used at present.

Energy sector reforms resulted in a new Energy Act being passed in 2003, and an energy regulator established in 1999 was expanded in 2005 to include water (the State Energy and Water Regulatory Commission). The commission licenses gas market players and sets tariffs, which are aligned to international prices.

Present annual demand is approximately 3.2 Bcm, and it is forecast to grow to 6.3 Bcm by 2025. This demand could be higher if gas is used for power generation, in place of the presently anticipated investments in hydroelectric and nuclear generation being made. Gas demand now is rather evenly divided among district heating, the chemicals industry (principally fertilizers), and households.

Bulgaria is concerned about diversifying sources of supply. It is a participant in the Nabucco project through the 20 percent shareholding of Bulgar-TransGaz. Landing LNG on Bulgaria's Black Sea coast is not considered feasible because of the constraints on shipping through the Bosporus.

Croatia

Croatia is a significant producer of gas (1.6 Bcm/y), relative to the size of its market. The remainder of its current annual requirements (1.1 Bcm) are imported from Russia. A new pipeline connection with Hungary is being developed by Plinacro (in coordination with MOL) to increase imports from Russia, via Ukraine, by as much as 1.5 Bcm/y. Annual demand is projected to rise in the next 20 years from 2.7 Bcm to 4.2 Bcm; so, in principle, the expanded gas import arrangements with Russia should provide adequate supplies until 2025.

In practice, growth well could be higher than expected in the main areas of gas consumption: power plants, refineries, and urban gas distribution. The section titled "LNG Potential Supply," earlier in this chapter, describes the Adria LNG receiving terminal proposed at Krk Island. The bulk of its 10–15 Bcm/y would be destined for larger markets, such as Italy, but such a development clearly would supplement and diversify Croatia's gas supply.

There is an existing UGS facility at Okoli, a depleted field with 0.5 Bcm of seasonal storage. Upgrading and expansion would give another 0.4–0.5 Bcm.

The transmission system extensions from Karlovac to Split are under development by Plinacro, with later extension planned farther south along the Adriatic coast. Such development down the Dalmatian coast would depend on the development of a large, new, gas-fired power plant, possibly close to Split. The connection of this part of the Croatian system to a pipeline delivering gas northward from the Greek system, via Albania and Montenegro, greatly would strengthen this long radial branch of the Croatian system; and it would provide access to a wide diversity of sources. The earlier discussion focused on Albania, and especially table 3.32, describe in detail the supply possibilities for this transmission option.

Kosovo

Currently, there is no gas market in Kosovo. Industrial, district heating, and household energy needs are met by electricity (from lignite) and heavy fuel oil. Besides electricity, fuel wood and LPG are used by households, mainly in the small towns and villages. Future energy plans, however, do include gas, with the replacement of heavy fuel oil by gas in district heating plants being a particular target. The other potential large consumption would be in cofiring the lignite power station with some quantities of gas to improve air emissions. Such a technique has proved successful at the Longannet power station in Scotland.

The Energy Regulatory Office is responsible for regulating electricity and heating, but is yet to have its mandate expanded to include gas. The Ministry of Energy and Mining is preparing a gas law.

Annual demand in Kosovo is projected to grow to 0.9 Bcm by 2025.

The supply options for Kosovo include a branch supplying Russian gas from the east, via Nis in southern Serbia; and a branch via FYR Macedonia supplying gas, via the Bulgarian or Greek systems. Gas via the Greek system would open up a large number of possibilities (described in detail in the section on Albania and especially in table 3.32).

FYR Macedonia

FYR Macedonia has an Energy Market Law that covers both electricity and gas. The sector is regulated by the Energy Regulatory Commission, which has published a methodology for gas transmission, distribution, and supply pricing.

With no indigenous supplies, consumption of gas in the country is met entirely from imports. Only about 10 percent of the annual capacity of the small 0.8-Bcm/y transmission pipeline from Bulgaria to FYR Macedonia is used at present. Most (approximately 80 percent) of that gas is used for electricity generation in small plants. Other large customers are steel plants and district heating companies. It is government policy for gas transmission to be extended to all major towns where combined heat-and-power facilities will replace nongas district heating plants. With power, industry, and other end uses also projected to grow, it is possible that annual demand for gas will expand rapidly from 0.1 Bcm to 1.2 Bcm by 2025 (an average annual growth of 13 percent).

Such growth would require significant anchor loads to underpin the initial transmission investment. Power stations are the main candidates. A 500-megawatt CCGT power station, for example, would require about 0.6 Bcm of gas each year (running in the base load).

The transmission connections options for FYR Macedonia include a connection to the Greek system in the south, reinforcement of the connection with the Bulgarian system in the east, a connection with Albania in the west, and a connection via Kosovo in the north. A pipeline providing connections with Albania and Kosovo should be sized at constant diameter along the entire length, with a view to subsequently being connected from Pristina to Nis and extended from Albania northward through Montenegro, forming the EC Ring. The supply possibilities are summarized in table 3.33.

Montenegro

Currently, there is no gas usage in Montenegro. The main component of energy supply is the electric power system. This is based on hydropower from indigenous sources and imports of electricity from Serbia. The country has abundant reserves of lignite and thermal coal. The aluminium smelter and products plant uses 100 kilotons of heavy fuel oil a year, and is a candidate for switching to gas. Households widely use wood for heating and other purposes, and gas is unlikely to displace wood in this setting.

An energy law was passed in 2003, a regulatory agency was established in 2004, and an Energy Action Plan was formulated in 2006. With only 17 percent of its hydro potential presently developed, future expansion of power generation will be based primarily on hydro resources; but a gas-fired plant is expected to be built, probably near the Podgorica load center. Industrial uses also are expected to grow. By 2025, total annual demand is projected to reach 0.3 Bcm.

A 500-megawatt CCGT power station—requiring about 0.6 Bcm of gas a year (running in the base load)—would anchor investment in a pipeline northward from the Greek system, via Albania, and connecting to the Croatian coastal extension southward from Split. The supply possibilities for this option include all of those sources previously described for Albania

Table 3.33 Supply Options of Immediate Interest to FYR Macedonia

Transmission connection	Contract source(s)	Delivery and physical flows	Physical source and swaps
Bulgarian border	Contract for increased Russian gas supplies	Via Bulgaria, as with present contracts.[a]	Swap LNG at Revithoussa for Russian gas contracted to Greece on the Bulgarian system, and pay Bulgarian exit fees and Macedonian transmission fees. Yields transmission cost savings in Greece and Bulgaria.
Bulgarian border	Contract for LNG via Revithoussa	Backhaul through Greek system. Physical molecules flow to Athens. Russian gas flows to FYR Macedonia via Bulgaria.	Swap LNG at Revithoussa for Russian gas contracted to Greece on the Bulgarian system, and pay Bulgarian exit fees and Macedonian transmission fees. Yields transmission cost savings in Greece and Bulgaria.
Greek border	Contract for LNG via Revithoussa	Backhaul through Greek system. Physical molecules flow to Athens. Russian gas flows to FYR Macedonia through the Greek transmission system.	Swap LNG delivered at Revithoussa for Russian gas contracted to Greece at the Greece-Bulgaria border, and pay Greek transmission fees. Yields transmission cost savings in Greece.
Greek border	Contract for Algerian gas via TransMed	Backhaul through Greece-Italy Poseidon pipeline or TAP and the Greek system. Physical molecules flow up into Italian system. Russian and/or Caspian gas flows through the Greek system. Reduces Greece-Italy flows.	Swap Algerian gas at Mazara del Vallo for Caspian gas at the Greece-FYR Macedonia border (or at the Turkey-Greece border, and pay Greek transmission fees). Yields transmission cost savings on Poseidon, and may yield some transmission cost savings in Greece.

Table 3.33 Supply Options of Immediate Interest to FYR Macedonia *(Continued)*

Transmission connection	Contract source(s)	Delivery and physical flows	Physical source and swaps
Albanian and Bulgarian or Greek borders	Contract for Algerian gas via TransMed	Backhaul through Greece-Italy Poseidon pipeline or TAP and the Greek system. Russian and/or Caspian gas flows to FYR Macedonia either though the Greek system or via Bulgaria, reducing Greece-Italy flows on Poseidon or TAP.	Swap Algerian gas at Mazara del Vallo for Caspian gas at the Greek border (or at the Turkey-Greece border, and pay the Greek transmission fees) or swap for Russian gas at the Bulgarian border. Yields transmission cost savings on Poseidon, and may yield some transmission cost savings in Greece or Bulgaria.
UNMIK border	Transit gas delivered via the Greek system to Kosovo	Via Skopje or via Nis	Direct contracting for offtake of Russian or Caspian gas or backhaul LNG or Algerian gas through Greece and swap for Caspian or Russian gas.

Source: Authors' compilation.
Notes: LNG = liquefied natural gas; TAP = trans-Adriatic pipeline; TransMed = trans-Mediterranean pipeline; UNMIK = United Nations Interim Administration Mission in Kosovo.
a. Unusual in the region, FYR Macedonia contracts for Russian gas at the Bulgaria-Macedonia border, not at Ukraine's western border, so Gazexport pays the transmission fees to the Macedonian border.

(especially those presented in table 3.32); and the mix of supply options for Croatia, when the pipeline reaches the Croatian system. Such a branch pipeline should be sized at constant diameter along its length, with a view to subsequent connection across Bosnia and Herzegovina to the north of Montenegro to form the EG Ring.

Romania

Romania, by far, has the largest indigenous gas production of the markets in this study, supplying two thirds of national requirements; and it has an established import system for the balance of its demand. However, the country is a mature gas province, and indigenous gas production is expected to decrease by 2–3 percent a year, thereby increasing the need to import gas.

Underground storage is used to improve security of supply and make it possible to deal with the seasonal demand swing. At present, meeting daily peaks is a problem, and some customers have been put on interruptible tariff agreements. There have been extensive reforms in Romania's well-developed gas sector in recent years, overseen since 2001 by an independent gas regulator. Gas prices have been increased toward import parity; but international prices also have increased, and domestic prices remain well below international levels. With Romania's accession to the EU, further liberalization and privatization of the gas market is planned.

Present annual gas consumption is approximately 17 Bcm. Industry consumes more than half of the gas, with the remainder split between power generation and residential or commercial uses. With the closure or restructuring of inefficient industries, no growth in industrial demand for gas is expected. Despite higher prices than consumers are used to paying, growth is anticipated in district heating (in competition with coal-fired systems) and in domestic demand. Although there are no current gas-fired power projects, there will be increased demand from the electricity sector over time as new CCGT plants are developed.

The future import supply options for Romania include increased supplies of Russian gas; offtake of Caspian gas from Nabucco, in which Transgaz is a 20 percent shareholder; and direct import of Caspian (Azeri) gas, via the proposed GUEU-White Stream pipeline under the Black Sea from Georgia.

Serbia

Serbia has been producing its own gas for half a century, but always has been a net importer of gas. Northern Serbia is fully gasified; western and central Serbia are only partly gasified; and the southern region has hardly any gas. To remedy these disparities, there is a National Action Plan for Gasification, with investment resources for gas projects channeled through the National Infrastructure Development Fund. Investment also is taking place in the import supply network, notably the Dimitrovgrad-Nis project (referred to as MG10). The gas sector is regulated by the Energy Agency of the Republic of Serbia.

In gasified areas, most large industries (notably, fertilizer and synthetic rubber) use gas. There are no immediate plans for gas-fired power stations, but some CCGT plants may be built when the low-cost hydro projects have been implemented. Increased demand from households and district heating is expected. Annual gas demand is forecast to grow modestly, from 2.5 Bcm in 2005 to 3.6 Bcm in 2025.

The main future supply options for Serbia are

- increased supply of Russian gas, via Hungary in the north, which would require either increased capacity from the border all the way through Hungary to Ukraine
- increased supply of Russian gas, via the new MG10 connection from Bulgaria in the south
- offtake from Nabucco at the nearest point in Romania (near Timisoara) to an entry point to the Srbijagas transmission system near Belgrade.

Reinforcement of the Belgrade-Sarajevo pipeline would make possible increased deliveries of gas to Bosnia and Herzegovina. A pipeline connection from Nis to Pristina would make possible the transportation of gas to Kosovo. When developed, both of those pipeline connections should be built at constant diameters along their lengths, with a view to their eventually forming a part of the EC Ring. Such a ring would make possible the regional trading of gas among Albania, Bosnia and Herzegovina, Croatia, Greece, FYR Macedonia, Montenegro, and Serbia.

4.

INSTITUTIONAL FRAMEWORK

This chapter addresses Task 9 of the study terms of reference, which calls for the elaboration of broad principles of a regional institutional framework to support market development and mobilization of finance for investments. The detailed framework is to be consistent with the 2003 European Union (EU) Gas Directive. Each of the nine markets is to be benchmarked against the detailed framework, and reform challenges to gas market development are to be discussed on a case-by-case basis. With regard to the framework itself, the terms of reference make specific mention of regulatory requirements, unbundling of gas markets, tariff reforms, and payment discipline. Other pertinent elements are to be added as appropriate.

The Gas Market in Southeast Europe
As the Southeast Europe (SEE) gasification project has evolved, the key institutional issues that have emerged are centered around the following question: What is needed to make regional gas projects happen? This question needs to be considered in relation to projects of different size and scope:

- What are the requirements for bilateral and relatively small regional gas projects?
- What institutional structure will be required for large regional gas projects—in particular, for the Energy Community (EC) Gas Transmission Ring concept—to be financed and implemented?

The problem this chapter seeks to address is that complex regional gas infrastructure projects often are difficult to bring to fruition. Strong economic fundamentals and clear strategic advantages, both of which lead to firm political backing, are not sufficient in themselves to overcome the very real difficulties of securing financing and executing the projects.

As is discussed in more detail later in the chapter, these difficulties arise from the existence of significant risks (such as the risk that demand projections will not be met, thus causing revenues not to be realized and loans not to be repaid), and from factors such as the lack of a harmonized framework for gas trade. Even in a purely national gas transmission project, there are many risks to be dealt with and institutional obstacles to be overcome. Moving from national to bilateral and then to multicountry, cross-border projects adds significantly to the risks, and makes it far more difficult and complex to reach financial closure and project implementation.

The obstacles and time required to bring cross-border gas projects to fruition will be minimized in situations where favorable conditions exist in three key areas:

1. **National gas markets**—The markets involved have well-developed gas policies and stable, predictable regulatory frameworks.
2. **Cross-border framework**—Harmonized mechanisms for investment in and operation of cross-border gas pipeline projects have been agreed,
3. **Financing**—There is a strategy to minimize and/or mitigate financing risks.

These areas clearly overlap, particularly in project financing: a sound national gas sector and harmonized cross-border arrangement would mean that the major specific project risks have been attenuated, leaving more generic items (such as country risk) to be catered for in the negotiations over the financing package. Nonetheless, these three areas provide a convenient way in which to categorize and discuss the issues at stake. The subsections of this chapter address the following topics:

- national gas markets
- necessary elements of the cross-border institutional framework
- risks and financing
- concluding observations.

The remainder of this section provides an overview of existing regional initiatives introduces lessons from some international case studies, which are referred to later in the chapter.

Existing Regional Initiatives
Within the long-term goal of moving toward a single, competitive, secure market for gas throughout Europe, various regional initiatives systematically

are addressing each of the areas identified above. In Southeast Europe, this is a vigorous, ongoing process. A great deal has been achieved already, with further strengthening of key aspects being expected in the near future. Much of the momentum comes from the support of the European Commission and the Energy Community, with many of the technical aspects being elaborated through the Madrid Forum.

There are many different components, the details of which are given later in the chapter; but here we provide a summary of key regional institutions and sample programs relating to the three areas highlighted above—national gas market environment, cross-border framework, and regional gas project financing:

- EC—All the SEE markets are signatories to the EC Treaty, which includes, in particular, a strong commitment to conform to the European Union Gas Directive (2003/55/EC). The following points are relevant to the treaty:
  - The EC Secretariat is assisting countries in the implementation of their action plans, which have been established for each country to ensure rapid conformity with the Gas Directive and advancement of related EC goals.
  - The EC's Gas Regulatory Group has drafted the New Gas Infrastructure Investment Regulations (NGIIR), which currently are under discussion.
- European Regulator's Group for Electricity and Gas (ERGEG)—This is an EU institution, but produces materials that are relevant for all SEE countries—notably, with respect to achieving conformity with the EU Gas Transmission Access Regulation (1775/2005):
  - guidelines covering best practices in areas such as gas balancing, storage, and third-party access to liquefied natural gas (LNG) terminals
  - guidelines of good practice on open season procedures, which are particularly relevant to proposed SEE pipeline projects.
- Energy Charter—Six SEE countries are members, and one is an observer. Two of the main areas of focus for the Energy Charter are these:
  - trade and transit: useful documents include *Model Intergovernmental and Host Government Agreements for Cross-Border Pipelines,* which provides a neutral and nonprescriptive starting point for negotiations on trade and transit arrangements
  - investment promotion: various strategies being pursued to facilitate investment and speed up the investment process. The dispute settlement mechanisms offered under the Charter have proved useful in this regard in a number of infrastructure projects.

Lessons from International Examples

To illustrate how cross-border harmonization has been achieved in other regions, reference is made in the following sections to several projects that have reached or are expected soon to reach financial closure. These cases indicate both the difficulties of and some successful approaches to multi-country gas infrastructure projects. As already mentioned, moving from bilateral to multicountry projects significantly increases the degree of complexity and difficulty of implementation.

Bilateral projects usually are structured so that national responsibility is assumed for infrastructure within each territory. Simple agreements providing for the development, financing, construction, ownership, and operation of the gas infrastructure suffice, but often are replaced quickly by more ambitious arrangements.

An example of a bilateral gas project in Europe is the Balgzand-Bacton Line This is a 235-kilometer undersea pipeline with a capacity of 15 billion cubic meters (Bcm). It runs between Balgzand in the Netherlands and Bacton in the United Kingdom. The operating company is a joint venture of E.ON Ruhrgas, Fluxys, and Gasunie (the state-owned transmission system operator in the Netherlands). The procedure for obtaining a third-party access waiver for the €500 million project is described in box 4.1.

An example of a three-country gas pipeline project that is even closer to the SEE region is the South Caucasus Pipeline (SCP) project, which can be contrasted with the West African Gas Pipeline. The SCP project is delivering Caspian gas from Azerbaijan through Georgia to Turkey, via a 692-kilometer, 8-Bcm pipeline financed and built by private companies. This $1 billion project required a more complex structure of agreements than was the case for the West Africa Gas Pipeline. These agreements are described in box 4.2.

More ambitious still is the five-country Nabucco project. Its institutional structure is of particular interest for the proposed EC Gas Ring. Nabucco, costed at €5 billion, is to provide a 3,300-kilometer pipeline capable of delivering up to 31 Bcm of gas a year from the Caspian area and other sources to Austria, via Turkey, Bulgaria, Romania, and Hungary. The project is yet to reach financial closure. Its corporate structure is of particular interest in this report and is discussed in the section titled "EC Ring Corporate Structure," later in this chapter.

The Balgzand-Bacton, SCP, and Nabucco project routes are illustrated in map 4.1.

Conditions in Africa may seem remote from those in the SEE region, but two recent gas pipeline projects have involved innovative guarantee and risk mitigation structures that are applicable in other regions. These are the

The Balgzand-Bacton Line

The Balgzand-Bacton Line provides a good example of a project that entailed a significant level of investment (€500 million) and a correspondingly high level of risk. To go forward, it required secure, long-term transport contracts in a well-defined regulatory environment. It took several years for the commercial aspects to be put in place. In 2003, an application for exemption from third-party access requirements, under Article 22 of the European Union (EU) Gas Directive, was made to both the Dutch and British regulators (DTe and the Office of Gas and Electricity Markets [Ofgem], respectively). In the British case at that time, Ofgem did not have the necessary powers, but acted nonetheless as though the subsequent provisions of the 2004 Energy Act were in place.

Ofgem recommended a definitive unbundling of the infrastructure operator—at the time, GTS (the Belgian network operator, a subsidiary of Gasunie)—going even beyond EU requirements. The sponsors also were required to undertake an "open-season" procedure. This procedure was to enable informed decision making by the regulators with respect to capacity requirements. The stipulations arising from these regulatory decisions and the subsequent process were that

- capacity be reserved for holders of long-term contracts
- unused capacity be made available to other operators on the basis of the use-it-or-lose-it principle.

For this project, a 16-year waiver of third-party access finally was granted in 2005. A coordination agreement also was signed between the Dutch and British authorities.

Source: Ghiosso 2006.

Southern Africa Regional Gas Pipeline and the West African Gas Pipeline projects (map 4.2):

- **Southern Africa Regional Gas Project**—Commissioned in 2004, this is an 865-kilometer overland pipeline with an initial delivery capacity of 3 Bcm and a final capacity of 6 Bcm. It delivers gas from Mozambique to a petrochemical plant (Sasol) in South Africa. The project was started on the basis of a simple cross-border treaty; later, however, a bilateral

BOX 4.2

South Caucasus Pipeline Project

The recently implemented South Caucasus Pipeline (SCP) project, which supplies Caspian gas from Azerbaijan to Turkey via Georgia, provides a relevant SEE region case study of how a carefully constructed set of agreements can form a sufficient basis of risk mitigation for a gas transmission project. In this case, the seller is a joint-venture company of public and private enterprises, and the transmission line has been financed and built by private companies. The key agreements for the project were these:

- host government agreements (HGA), between SCP (the transmission company) and Azerbaijan and between SCP and Georgia (including transit fees for Georgia, which may be claimed in the form of gas)
- intergovernmental agreements (IGA), between Azerbaijan and Georgia and between Azerbaijan and Turkey
- production-sharing agreement (PSA), between the Azerbaijan government and the seven Shah Deniz consortium partners
- pipeline construction and operation agreements, between SCP and contractors
- transportation agreement, between SCP (as pipeline owners/operators) and Shah Deniz (SD) partners (as gas shippers)
- sale and purchase agreements (SPAs), between SCP/Shah Deniz shippers and both Georgia and Turkey.

The key agreements are illustrated in figure included here.

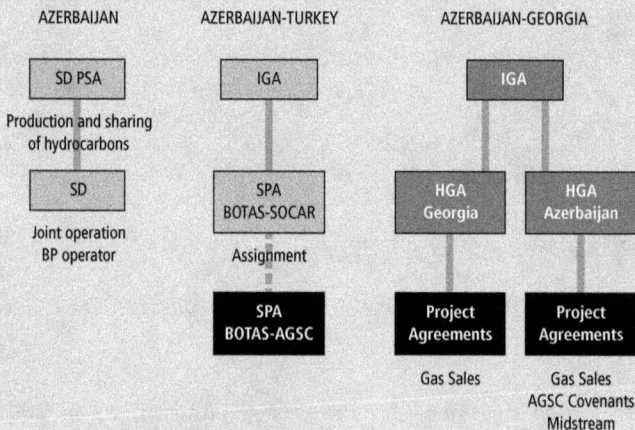

Note: AGSC = Azerbaijan Gas Supply Company; SOCAR = State Oil Company of the Azerbaijan Republic.

(continued on next page)

The agreements were negotiated on a back-to-back basis, and they provided an interlocking framework that enabled a complex project across three countries with significant private financing to go ahead without any overarching institutional structure or political agreements. The internationally enforceable agreements among the three governments and between each government and the project developers, complemented by agreements securing the supply (PSA) and offtake (SPA), were negotiated over a two-year period. The use of international arbitration and dispute resolution provisions was a key part of the agreements and a critical element for the private parties. The intergovernmental agreements made use of the Energy Charter dispute resolution procedures, a precedent that could be adopted for similar projects in Southeast Europe.

Source: Economic Consulting Associates.

Map 4.1   European and SEE Gas Projects

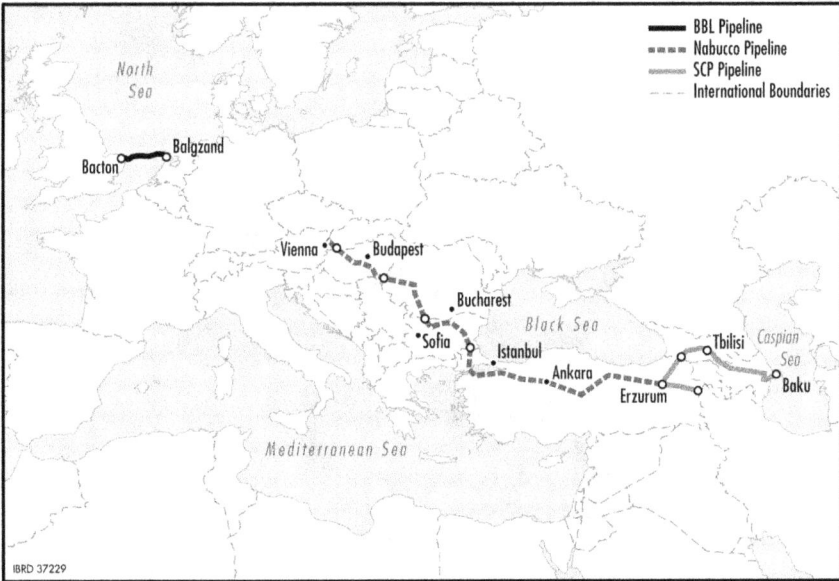

Source: World Bank.

Map 4.2 European and SEE Gas Projects

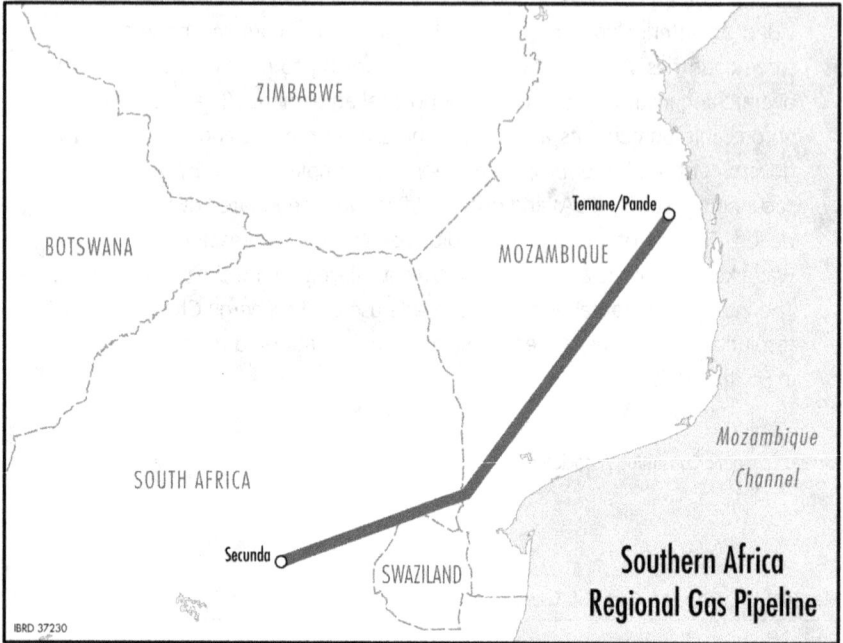

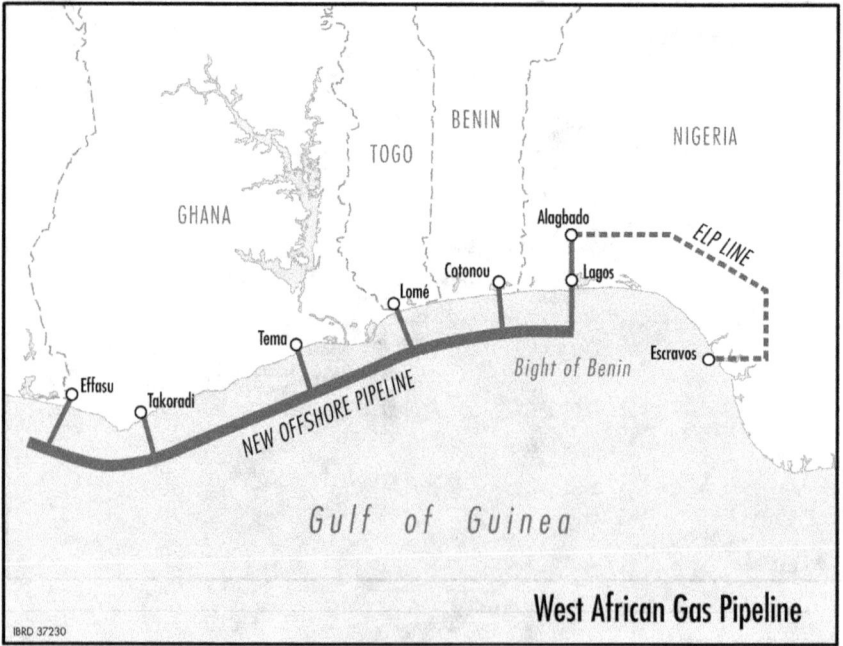

Southern Africa
Regional Gas Pipeline

West African Gas Pipeline

Source: World Bank.

agreement on natural gas trade was reached, with the broad objective of developing Mozambique gas for the markets in both countries. A gas commission was established to oversee trade and to harmonize regulatory requirements.

- **West African Gas Pipeline**—This $500 million project consists of a 1,033-kilometer pipeline with capacity of 2 Bcm (expandable to 6 Bcm), delivering gas from Nigeria to small national markets in Benin, Togo, and Ghana. The project promoters are a mix of state-owned entities and private oil companies, so the structure is a public-private partnership. By building the pipeline offshore in international waters, problems of transit rights were avoided and the resulting structure of agreements was simplified. The support of the World Bank and other international financial institutions was important in mitigating risks and reaching closure.

In the remainder of the chapter, different case studies are used to discuss various specific issues. The Balgzand-Bacton project is used to illustrate open-season and third-party access waiver requirements in a regional context. The SCP exemplifies the range of legal agreements required for a regional gas project. Nabucco's institutional structure is presented as a possible option for the EC Gas Ring; and the two projects from environments with high commercial risk outside the region (in Africa, in these examples) are used to illustrate how risk mitigation instruments can be used to achieve financial closure.

National Gas Markets
This section considers the requirements in individual markets, the commitment to the EU policy framework for the gas sector, and the EC Secretariat's monitoring of attainment of the agreed provisions.

Requirements in Individual Markets
To facilitate rapid growth of the gas sector, including providing the basis for cooperation in cross-border trade, individual markets need to create a stable and predictable environment that encourages investment in the sector. To a large extent, what is needed is a conducive business environment—that is, one where the rule of law is certain; bureaucratic procedures for starting, operating, and terminating a business are straightforward; there is currency convertibility with stable and predictable exchange and interest rates; and there is access to local and international finance.

Such concerns apply to all types of investments. The specific requirements in the gas sector relate to having well-defined energy policies and a predictable regulatory framework. Ideally, the following need to be clearly defined and institutionalized:

- an independent regulator
- transparent cost-based tariff rules
- designation and licensing of transmission and distribution systems operators, or of combined operators
- unbundling and transparency requirements
- rules of access to transmission and to storage
- operational rules, including management and allocation of interconnection capacity, balancing procedures, mechanisms to deal with congestion, and access conditions to storage and line-pack
- public service obligation and customer protection
- monitoring of security of supply
- technical safety and other technical rules
- competitive market opening so that some, and eventually all, customers are able to choose their gas supplier
- restricted possibility of limiting third-party access in order to secure new investment
- open season to determine capacity requirements and to invest to ensure adequacy of capacity
- a cross-border trade mechanism
- dispute resolution mechanisms

Commitment to the EU Framework for Gas

The above requirements are best met through adhering to a recognized standard that precisely codifies the standards in each of the areas listed. This is provided by European Union Gas Directive 2003/55/EC. Members of the EC committed themselves to being in compliance with the directive within one year of accession to the EC Treaty. In practice, the requirements of the directive are difficult to meet, and the process has been extended over a longer period. With regard to competition, the agreed timetable for customers to have access to competitive gas suppliers is

- from January 1, 2008, all nonhousehold customers
- from January 1, 2015, all customers.

As mentioned above, an important item in the approved work program of the EC Secretariat is to assist members in achieving these target dates. Road maps have been established and action plans drawn up for both gas and electricity. The structure of the road maps and action plans is shown in figure 4.1.

Figure 4.1   Road Map and Action Plan Structure

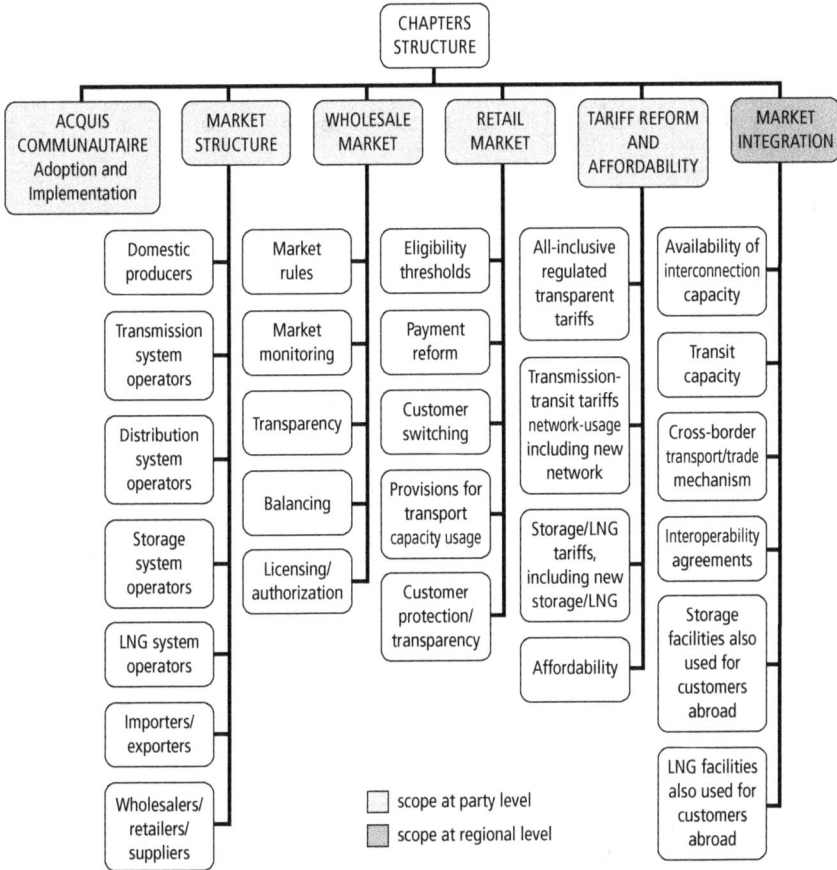

Source: Energy Community Secretariat.
Note: LNG = liquefied natural gas.

EC Secretariat's Monitoring of Attainment of Agreed Provisions

The EC Secretariat has provided guidelines and checklists for each item in figure 4.1. This also facilitates the collection of data for monitoring purposes across the region. A quarterly system of monitoring, starting in November 2006, has been established. Table 4.1 shows the results as of late 2008. Implementation actions for the governments in each market are grouped under eight categories:

- third-party access
- monitoring of security of supply

Table 4.1 Progress on Implementation of EC Treaty Provisions in the Nine SEE Markets, Late 2008

Market	Third-party access	Security of supply	Unbundling provisions and access to accounts	Technical rules	Public service obligations and consumer protection	Market opening	New infrastructure and exemptions	Cross-border trade mechanism	Progress (%)
EC markets already in the EU and currently served by gas:									
Bulgaria	■	■	■	■	○	○	◆	●	70
Romania	■	■	○	■	○	■	■	●	80
EC markets currently served by gas:									
Croatia	■	■	■	■	■	■	■	◆	90
Serbia	■	■	○	■	○	■	●	●	65
EC markets with limited gas import and capacity:									
Bosnia and Herzegovina	●	●	●	●	●	●	●	●	0
Macedonia, FYR	○	◆	◆	◆	◆	◆	◆	●	33
EC markets currently without any gas infrastructure:									
Albania	○	○	○	◆	○	◆	○	●	50
Kosovo	○	◆	○	◆	○	◆	■	●	50
Montenegro	●	●	●	●	●	●	●	●	0
Progress (%)	65	60	55	55	55	55	55	0	50

Source: Analysis by Economic Consulting Associates, using data from the Energy Community Secretariat, presented in Ljubljana, Slovenia, on October 10, 2008.
Note: ● = getting started; ◆ = some provisions available; ○ = some provisions missing; ■ = all provisions available; EC = Energy Community; EU = European Union.

- unbundling provisions and access to accounts
- technical rules
- public service obligation and customer protection
- market opening
- new infrastructure and exemptions
- cross-border trade mechanism.

Major differences exist between countries at different stages of gas market development. In this regard, it is convenient to distinguish between three groups of countries:

1. Relatively mature gas markets—Bulgaria, Romania, and Serbia
   - completing the unbundling of incumbent companies
   - accelerating privatization
   - monitoring market development progress (including full market opening and customer switching in Bulgaria and Romania)
   - promoting new gas infrastructure (implementation of projects).
2. Rapidly growing gas markets—Croatia and the former Yugoslav Republic of Macedonia
   - completing secondary legislation
   - opening the market
   - promoting the new gas infrastructure.
3. Small and/or underdeveloped gas markets—Albania, Bosnia and Herzegovina, Kosovo, and Montenegro
   - completing primary legislation (gas act)
   - developing secondary legislation
   - promoting new gas infrastructure.

It is notable that, outside of the first group of countries, there are very few instances in the matrix presented in table 4.1 where the Gas Directive provisions have been achieved. In this regard, the EC Secretariat has identified the following general problems in the opening of the SEE gas markets:

- persistence of regulated prices, making new market entry difficult and delaying the arrival of competition
- lack of legal unbundling and insufficient managerial separation of transmission and distribution system operators to ensure their independence
- persistent discrimination in third-party access to networks and lack of transparency in network tariffs

- insufficient power of regulators, particularly in setting tariffs for access to networks
- insufficient capacity of regulators, especially in the management and allocation of interconnection capacity.

Despite the prevalence of these problems, the rigorous approach to tackling the commitments that have been made has produced the following results:

- *by the fourth quarter of 2007*—harmonized and stable regulation for a common energy market (implementation of the Acquis Communautaire)
- *by the beginning of 2008*—cost-reflective tariffs, transparent, and nondiscriminatory access to the system.

Cross-Border Framework

The challenge of the cross-border environment is first to create a unified operational approach and then to create mechanisms to facilitate investment in new interconnectors. Each of these challenges has a number of dimensions, and some of the key aspects are these:

- harmonization of operations
  - access and allocation
  - interoperability
  - transparency
  - balancing
  - gas storage
  - LNG
- agreement on cross-border investments
  - tariff treatment
  - open-season procedures
  - regulatory treatment of cross-border, domestic, and nondomestic investment
  - need for a standardized approach to exemptions from third-party access requirements.

A third-party access waiver often is crucial to provide the ensured revenue streams required for the projects to attract financing. Creating new capacity is part of the objective of ensuring security of supply and laying the basis for future competition, but the immediate effect of restricting third-party access is clearly anticompetitive in the short run. However, the anticompetitive effects can be blunted prior to the granting of the waiver by the regulators imposing measures that favor new entrants:

- widen participation in the project to players in addition to the initial project sponsors
- require a properly managed open season (among other things, to reserve capacity for long-term contracts before project finalization)
- reserve part of capacity for third parties and/or short-term contracts
- define rules to allow reallocation, thereby avoiding contractual congestion and making maximum use of physical capacity (such as the use-it-or-lose-it principle)
- require and facilitate exchange of capacities on a secondary market.

Harmonization of Operations across Borders

Reference has already been made to the EC's New Gas Infrastructure Investment Regulation. Building on the experience of successful cross-border pipeline projects elsewhere, the starting point of the NGIIR is the recognition of the need for a seamless cross-border operational regime. To achieve this regime, the NGIIR envisages a single transmission operator required to establish and implement a unified operational methodology for capacity booking, allocation, gas balancing, capacity transfer, and any other matters of relevance to shippers.

The NGIIR approach is grounded in two key concepts:

1. The transmission project operator (TPO) is to be the single transmission system operator responsible for negotiating, implementing, and operating an international pipeline project.
2. The TPO is to offer a one-stop-shop facility so that shippers of gas need deal with only one entity, with the assurance that there will be uniform operational arrangements despite the fact that the gas may be transported over several different legal jurisdictions.

The NGIIR is neither retroactive nor mandatory. Nevertheless, it is an approach that is well received in Southeast Europe, and the idea of a single TPO responsible for implementing the NGIIR is thus expected to become the norm for transborder pipeline projects and for shared storage and LNG facilities in the region. Indeed, in the NGIIR, a "regional project" is defined as one that is being operated by a TPO.[1]

---

[1] Other components of the definition of a regional project are that it is subject to two or more jurisdictions and provides a new gas supply to the region.

The central concerns of the NGIIR revolve around third-party access and capacity allocation. The default regulatory regime is one in which a third-party access exemption has not been granted. As laid out in Annex 1 of the NGIIR, the main rules that are to apply for the regulated third-party access regime are as follows:

- Network customers will have only one contractual relationship for gas transport services, for all sections of the pipeline system in question.
- The TPO will design the entry/exit regime (including tariff methodology), with sufficient entry/exit points to ensure increased competition/security of supply in countries through which the infrastructure passes.
- A regulated tariff methodology, based on a cost-reflective approach, is to be agreed by the TPO and the EC Regulatory Board before the project commences.
- TPOs will offer both long-term and short-term firm capacity, including firm backhauling services.
- The TPO will conduct an open season to inform potential users about the services to be offered, to ensure that adequate capacity is being provided and to make well-informed initial allocations.
- TPOs will implement standardized nomination procedures.
- To manage congestion, TPOs will facilitate and encourage trade on the secondary market.
- Through contractual requirements and/or fines, hoarding will not be permitted or will be penalized: contracted but unused capacity normally will be made available to the primary market, according to the use-it-or-lose-it principle.
- EU best practice will apply to issues, such as transparency, secondary market trading of allocations, use-it-or-lose-it, open season, and interoperability.

In practice, all new cross-border investment projects have required a waiver from the third-party access requirements. The experience of the Balgzand-Bacton Line project exemplifies this, and is described in box 4.1. The SCP, the Southern Africa Regional Gas Project, and the West African Gas Pipeline are based, at least initially, on privileged access by the foundation offtakers.

Facilitating Cross-Border Pipeline Investments

The NGIIR anticipates that exemptions from the regulated third-party access regime may be required to ensure that investment projects go ahead. Annex 2 of the NGIIR lays out "Regulations for Exemptions," which offer guidelines to standardize the approach to applying the provision of the Gas Directive that allows for exemptions (Article 22). It goes on to discuss such issues as determining the level of exemptions in different countries with varying gas demands along the pipeline route. The main components are these:

- For regional projects, exemptions under Article 22 are to be submitted by the TPO to the EC Regulatory Board, which will consult with EC
- Decisions will be made on a case-by-case basis, applying the Article 22 objectives of ensuring that the investment enhances competition in gas supply and security of supply.
- Particular aspects to be systematically considered are the legal unbundling and ownership structure of the TPO, the allocation of long-term and short-term capacity, proposals for handling congestion, and a harmonized basis for transmission tariffs.
- Detailed requirements for open-season procedures are laid out.
- Exemptions are only to be granted if the level of risk is such that the project would not go ahead without an exemption.

An example of a recent project in which the open-season requirements were an important pre-requisite for the granting of a third-party access exemption is provided in box 4.1.

The NGIIR Article 22 guidelines do not emphasize the fact that when the decision in principle to grant an exemption has been made, the regulatory authorities still have a considerable degree of discretion to exercise. In keeping with the case-by-case philosophy, the *extent* (full or partial) and *duration* of exemption should be tailored to the specific project.

The guidelines offered in the NGIIR are sound, but the implied bipolar approach (standard regulated third-party access or partial/total exemption) is an unnecessary narrowing of possible approaches. In the context of examining regulatory options for encouraging new investment, the 2005 Council of European Energy Regulators' document on "Investments in Gas Infrastructure and the Role of the EU National Regulatory Authorities" offers a somewhat richer menu of possible regulatory approaches:

- standard regulated third-party access (default regime, as in Spain)
- regulated third-party access with an enhanced rate of return to compensate for higher risks and, in some cases, multiannual tariffs (the enhanced rate of return may be considered on a case-by-case basis)
- a specific third-party access regime, detailing a level of reserved capacity for the sponsors and the remainder for other users (as in Italy)
- a partial or total third-party access exemption through Article 22.

Table 4.2 gives examples of the application of these approaches in recent EU investment projects. Although the NGIIR presumption of Article 22 exemption does apply in most cases, there are examples of the other approaches

Table 4.2 Selected EU Cross-Border Gas Supply Investments

Country	Project	Status	Annual capacity	Regulatory regime	Capacity allocation
Belgium/ United Kingdom	Enhancement of the IUK reverse capacity (from Belgium to U.K.)	Approved	+8 Bcm in December 2005; +7 Bcm in December 2006	Negotiated TPA	Open season
Belgium	Zeebrugge LNG terminal extension	Approved	Extension of capacity from 4.5 Bcm to 9 Bcm	Regulated TPA enhanced rate of return with multiannual tariffs	Open season long-term reservations
France	Fos-Cavaou LNG terminal	Approved	8.25 Bcm	Regulated TPA rate of return to be decided	90% reserved for sponsors; 10% reg. TPA (FCFS) for other shippers
Italy	Rovigo LNG facility	Administration authorizations granted	4.8 Bcm, with possible extension to 8.0 Bcm	Exemption under Article 22	80% of capacity reserved for sponsors for 25 years; 20% for other shippers
Italy	Brindisi LNG facility	Administration authorizations granted	8 Bcm	Exemption under Article 22 requested	80% of capacity reserved for sponsors for 20 years; 20% for other shippers
Netherlands	Balgzand-Bacton (interconnection from Netherlands to United Kingdom)	Approved	Approximately 16 Bcm	Exemption under Article 22	Open season long-term reservations, possibility to trade capacity on the secondary market, UIOLI mechanism
Spain	Barcelona LNG terminal	Various projects at various stages (from under construction to planned)	5-Bcm increase of capacity	Regulated TPA default regime	FCFS 25% for short-term contracts

Country	Project	Status	Annual capacity	Regulatory regime	Capacity allocation
Spain	Cartagena LNG terminal	Various projects at various stages (from under construction to planned)	5-Bcm increase of capacity	Regulated TPA default regime	FCFS 25% for short-term contracts
Spain	Huelva LNG terminal	Various projects at various stages (from under construction to planned)	7-Bcm increase of capacity	Regulated TPA default regime	FCFS 25% for short-term contracts
Spain	Mugardos LNG plant	Administrative authorizations	7-Bcm increase of capacity	Regulated TPA default regime	FCFS 25% for short-term contracts
Spain	Sagunto LNG plant	Under construction	6.5 Bcm	Regulated TPA default regime	FCFS 25% for short-term contracts
United Kingdom	Isle of Grain LNG facility	Under construction	5 Bcm for the first phase	Exemption under Article 22	Open season long-term reservations; full TPA exemption (UIOLI)
United Kingdom	Milford Haven Dragon LNG facility	Planning permission	6 Bcm for the first phase	Exemption under Article 22	Open season long-term reservations; full TPA exemption (UIOLI)
United Kingdom	Milford Haven South Hook LNG facility	Planning permission and regulatory approval	10.5 Bcm for the first phase + 10.5 Bcm	Exemption under Article 22	Long-term reservations; full TPA exemption (UIOLI)

Source: CEER 2005, table 6.
Note: Bcm = billion cubic meters; EU = European Union; FCFS = first come/first served; IUK = Interconnector UK Ltd.; LNG = liquefied natural gas; TPA = third-party access; UIOLI = use it or lose it.

from EU countries. In Spain, the regulated third-party access default regime applies to all of its LNG projects, with 75 percent of capacity being allocated on a first-come/first-served basis and 25 percent being reserved for short-term contracts. In the case of the LNG terminals in Belgium and France, the investment incentive is in the form of enhanced rates of return rather than the regulatory norm for gas assets in those jurisdictions. In Italy, 80 percent of the capacity is reserved for the sponsors for 20 years, with the balance of 20 percent being available for other shippers.

A prerequisite for investment is that there is a stable framework in place for the gas sector. This can be achieved either through a series of interlocking contracts (as in the example of the SCP; see box 4.2) or through a credible and reliable regulatory regime that extends across international boundaries. Incentives that are specific to the project (such as an enhanced rate of return or restrictions on third-party access) also may be crucial for a project to reach financial closure, but these need to be added to an underlying framework that minimizes policy and institutional risks for investors. (These issues are taken up in more detail in the next section.)

Underground Gas Storage

A number of regulatory issues need to be considered for underground gas storage (UGS). Although UGS is a category of gas infrastructure distinct from LNG, transmission and distribution, the regulatory issues relevant to storage tend to have themes that overlap somewhat with those for transmission.

Directive 2003/55/EC includes a number of articles related to storage. As EU member-states, Bulgaria and Romania are bound by the directive; and as contracting parties to the EC Treaty, the other markets in Southeast Europe also are bound to implement the terms of the directive. One of the key areas in which some latitude is available to governments and regulators in implementing the terms of the directive is in the basis for access to storage.

Not all of the markets of Southeast Europe have existing UGS facilities or the potential for further UGS development. This uneven geological endowment is to be expected. Therefore, successful regional gas market development will require regulatory arrangements that facilitate the optimum economic use of storage resources among the countries in the region, subject to the physical configuration of the interconnected transmission pipeline system. Both open access to storage on transparent, nondiscriminatory terms and cross-border trading arrangements will be required to make this work.

The Gas Directive mentions security of supply in several places. It notes that storage is essential for security of supply, which is defined as a public service requirement and a customer protection obligation. Such security is supposed to be monitored in terms of the supply-demand balance and capacity. Enhancing security of supply is a requirement for exemption from the provisions of Article 18 on third-party access, Article 19 on Access to Storage, Article 20 on access to upstream pipeline networks, and Article 25 on the requirements placed on regulatory authorities.

In the Gas Directive, a "storage facility" is defined as

> a facility used for the stocking of natural gas and owned and/or operated by a natural gas undertaking, including the part of LNG facilities used for storage but excluding the portion used for production operations, and excluding facilities reserved exclusively for transmission system operators in carrying out their functions.

A "storage system operator" is

> a natural or legal person who carries out the function of storage and is responsible for operating a storage facility.

And "ancillary services" are

> all services necessary for access to and the operation of transmission and/or distribution networks and/or LNG facilities and/or storage facilities including load balancing and blending, but excluding facilities reserved exclusively for transmission system operators carrying out their functions.

Regulatory Issues

Regulators will have an interest in a number of principles regarding UGS. Efficient development and use of storage needs to be encouraged, relative to other options available for balancing supply and demand. The intention is that just enough storage capacity be developed to avoid higher-cost alternatives. Prices (or expected future prices) for storage services need to be sufficiently high to encourage investment in new storage facilities. At the same time, it should not be possible for storage owners to sustain prices above economic levels. Cost-reflective pricing (whether market determined or regulated) and the absence of barriers to new storage investment are the key principles for achieving these twin regulatory objectives.

It is important that the owner of storage facilities is not able to abuse its market position—for example, to favor a subsidiary or related company. Therefore, the regulatory arrangements need to allow nondiscriminatory access to storage.

Because geological storage potential is unevenly distributed among countries (as is true with hydrocarbon resources), the regional regulatory environment needs to ensure that economically feasible storage potential is developed to meet the needs of the region for storage services, and not just the needs of the individual market in which the geological structure happens to be located.

Transparency is another important regulatory principle. This can be achieved through the timely provision to the market of information about storage operations. Gas Infrastructure Europe (GIE) publishes a weekly "Aggregated Storage Inventory."[2] Figure 4.2 plots the published data for the geographic areas shown.

The data set contains data on historical and current aggregated weekly storage levels, the percentage full, and the accuracy level of the data. The

---

[2] The inventory is available at the GIE Web site, http://www.gie.eu.com/maps_data/index.html.

Figure 4.2 Aggregated Gas Storage Inventory Data Published by Gas Infrastructure Europe, 2007 and 2008

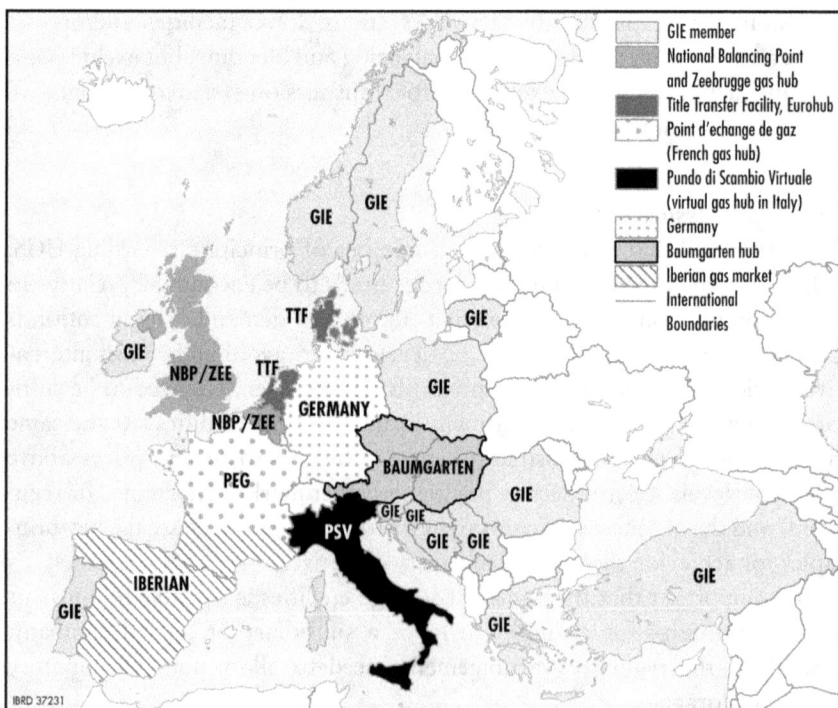

(continued)

Figure 4.2 Aggregated Gas Storage Inventory Data Published by Gas Infrastructure Europe, 2007 and 2008 *(Continued)*

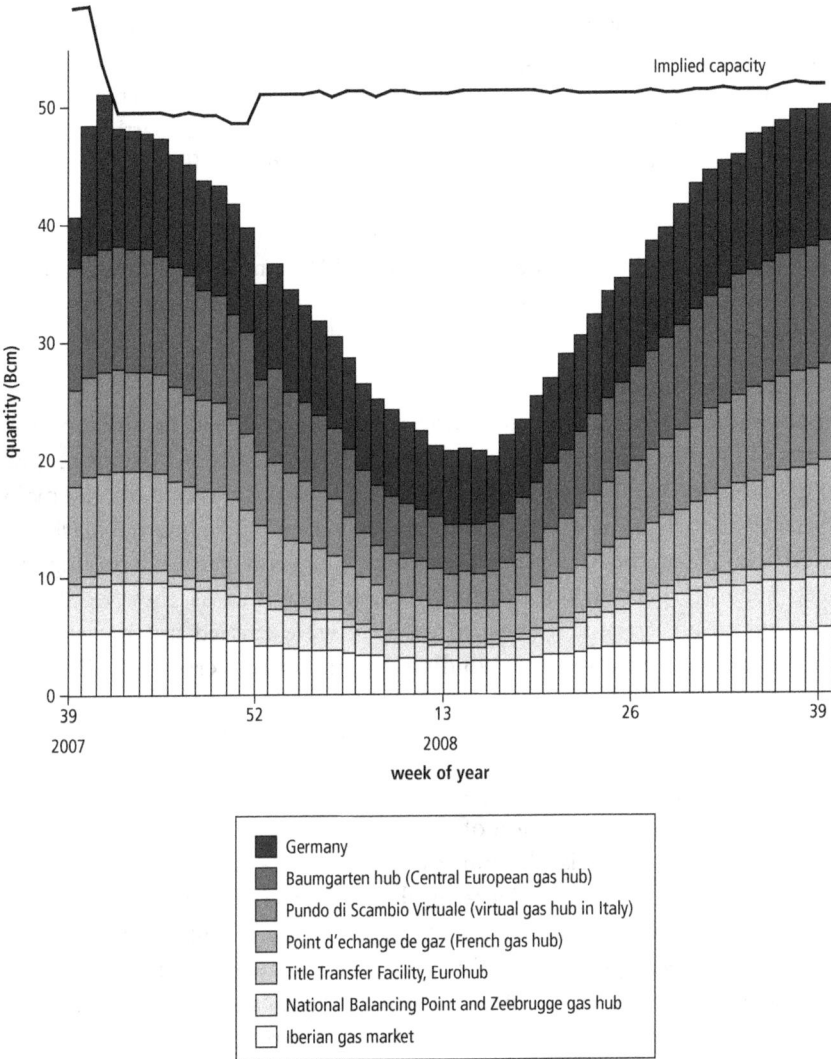

Source: Gas Infrastructure Europe, http://www.gie.eu.com/maps_data/index.html.
Note: Bcm = billion cubic meters.

publication of these data through GIE has been agreed voluntarily by the members as per Regional Energy Market project areas (hub areas). GIE notes that this initiative goes beyond that required by the Guidelines for Good Practice by Storage System Operators and the Gas Directive. The information provided helps the market operate efficiently and effectively. Publishing the data in an aggregated format through GIE guarantees that commercially sensitive information is not disclosed. GIE also provides links to the Web sites of storage operators for information on current and future available (unbooked) capacity.

A number of companies in the SEE markets already are GIE members, so it should be possible for storage operators in Southeast Europe to participate very easily in the publication of aggregate storage data through GIE in the future.

In addition to its benefits in balancing national and regional markets, UGS is beneficial for supporting gas transit. It increases reliability and technical security for downstream markets. It enables supply to continue if there is any form of interruption or disruption in the pipeline system upstream of the storage facility.

Requirements under the EC Treaty

Under the EC Treaty, the contracting parties have agreed to abide by the terms of Directive 2003/55/EC. This directive has several provisions related to gas storage. The Preamble includes access to storage as one of "the main obstacles in arriving at a fully operational and competitive internal market."

Article 17 of the Gas Directive requires natural gas undertakings to keep separate accounts for their "storage activities as they would be required to do if the activities in question were carried out by separate undertakings, with a view to avoiding discrimination, cross-subsidisation and distortion of competition."

Article 18 requires member-states (and therefore contracting parties to the EC Treaty) to

> ensure the implementation of a system of third party access to the transmission and distribution system, and LNG facilities based on published tariffs, applicable to all eligible customers, including supply undertakings, and applied objectively and without discrimination between system users. Member States shall ensure that these tariffs, or the methodologies underlying their calculation shall be approved prior to their entry into force by a regulatory authority referred to in Article 25(1) and that these tariffs—and the methodologies, where only methodologies are approved—are published prior to their entry into force.

Although Article 18 does not mention storage, third-party access to transmission (and cross-border trading arrangements) will be particularly important in Southeast Europe because some of the markets do not have UGS facilities and (at least according to current knowledge) are not endowed with geological potential for UGS.

Article 19 does deal specifically with access to storage.[3] The member-states and contracting parties to the EC Treaty are given a choice of two procedures, provided that they "shall operate in accordance with objective, transparent and non-discriminatory criteria":

1. Under negotiated access, member-states are required to "take the necessary measures for natural gas undertakings and eligible customers either inside or outside the territory covered by the interconnected system to be able to negotiate access to storage and linepack, when technically and/or economically necessary for providing efficient access to the system . . . and the [commercial] parties are obliged to negotiate access to storage, linepack and other ancillary services in good faith." Storage system operators and natural gas undertakings are to publish their main commercial conditions for the use of storage, linepack and other ancillary services annually.
2. Under regulated access, member-states also are required to enable access from outside the territory covered by the interconnected system, on the basis of published tariffs and/or other terms and obligations. In a competitive market, this right of access to storage for eligible customers may be given by enabling them to enter into supply contracts with competing natural gas undertakings other than the owner or operator of the system or a related undertaking.

Article 22 on new infrastructure provides for exemption (on request) from the provisions of articles 18 (third-party access); 19 (access to storage); 20 (access to upstream pipeline networks); and 25 (regulatory authorities), part 2 (methodologies to calculate tariffs and charges for balancing services), part 3 (member-state approval and rejection), and pare 4 (regulatory authority to require nondiscriminatory terms and conditions), subject to the following five conditions:

1. **Competition and security of supply**—"the investment must enhance competition in gas supply and enhance security of supply"
2. **Necessity**—"the level of risk attached to the investment is such that the investment would not take place unless an exemption was granted"

---

[3] The provisions of Article 19 exclude "ancillary services and temporary storage that are related to LNG facilities and are necessary for the re-gasification process and subsequent delivery to the transmission system."

3. **Legal separation**—"the infrastructure must be owned by a natural or legal person which is separate at least in terms of its legal form from the system operators in whose systems that infrastructure will be built"
4. **The user-pays principle**—"charges are levied on users of that infrastructure"
5. **No adverse effects**—the exemption is not detrimental to competition or the effective functioning of the internal gas market, or to the efficient functioning of the regulated system to which the infrastructure is connected.

It should be noted that, in addition to completely new infrastructure, the Article 22 exemption also may be requested for significant increases of capacity in existing infrastructure and to modifications of such infrastructure that enable the development of new sources of gas supply.

Regional Storage

All of the markets in Southeast Europe that develop increased demand for natural gas (some of them for the first time) will require gas storage services for managing seasonal swing, daily peaks, and security of supply. However, as chapter 3's discussion of existing and potential UGS facilities in SE Europe shows, a number of the individual markets in Southeast Europe do not have UGS facilities, nor do they currently have known geological potential to develop such facilities. Therefore, to match storage services to regional storage demands, it will be necessary to implement operational arrangements in the SEE gas market that are open to cross-border flows.

Under the EC Treaty, contracting parties are required to abide by Regulation 1775/2005/EC on conditions for access to the natural gas transmission networks. Article 3.2 of this regulation (on tariffs for access to networks) requires that

> Tariffs for network access shall not restrict market liquidity nor distort trade across borders of different transmission systems. Where differences in tariff structures or balancing mechanisms would hamper trade across transmission systems, and notwithstanding Article 25(2) of Directive 2003/55/EC, transmission system operators shall, in close cooperation with the relevant national authorities, actively pursue convergence of tariff structures and charging principles including in relation to balancing.

With third-party access to transmission systems and undistorted trade across borders within Southeast Europe, there should be no nontechnical barriers to gas companies and their customers in markets without UGS accessing storage services in neighboring markets.

Regulated Versus Market-Based Storage

A regulatory policy choice exists as to whether gas storage services are to be a regulated or a market-based activity. In paragraph 22 of its Preamble, the Gas Directive keeps the two alternatives open:

> Further measures should be taken in order to ensure transparent and non-discriminatory tariffs for access to transportation. Those tariffs should be applicable to all users on a non-discriminatory basis. Where a storage facility, linepack or ancillary service operates in a sufficiently competitive market, access could be allowed on the basis of transparent and non-discriminatory market-based mechanisms.

Given the need for governments in Southeast Europe to make a policy choice on this issue within the framework of the EC Treaty and the Gas Directive, the question that arises is, what is most appropriate in the context of the development of a robust regional market that will best promote increased gasification in Southeast Europe? Considerations to take into account in arriving at this policy choice include the following:

- Underground storage is one capacity resource in balancing variations in demand with available supply capacity.
- Opportunity cost sets the economic value of storage.
- Where prices are unregulated, the market should not be able to charge a price above the opportunity cost of storage (at least in the long run).
- Market pricing should attract investment up to the economic level.
- Regulating the storage price to below its opportunity cost would be expected to result in underdevelopment of storage capacity.
- A balancing market that sends clear, economically cost-reflective price signals is the key to the financial attractiveness of storage.

Security of Supply

Security of supply recently has become a central policy consideration for the gas sector in Europe; and storage is an integral part of the debate on the optimum level of security and on how best to ensure it is achieved in practice. There is no directive specifying storage or security-of-supply requirements, although the issues have been discussed at the EU level. Policy makers in Southeast Europe should see their markets and storage needs as part of the immediate region and in the wider European context.

The European Policy Context and Debate   Energy security of supply, and the role of gas in this effort, has been discussed at length in Europe in recent years. This discussion is part of the increasingly widespread international recognition of the importance of energy security in general. More recently, the topic has moved up the policy and regulatory agenda in response to several brief, but high-profile, interruptions to European pipeline energy supply. Security of gas supply became prominent as a public policy concern in Europe during the Russia-Ukraine gas dispute in January 2006, when supply was interrupted briefly.

In November 2000, the European Commission adopted the Green Paper "Towards a European Strategy for the Security of Energy Supply."[4] Covering all energy sources, this paper acknowledged "the impossibility of energy self-sufficiency" for the EU; and it discussed nuclear energy, coal, oil, and natural gas as "less than perfect energy options." It discussed the challenge of climate change and the gradual integration of energy markets. In the final part, it outlined an energy strategy to secure future supply, discussing weaknesses in current energy supply and tomorrow's priorities. The weaknesses assessed included four hurdles to security of supply: physical, economic, social, and environmental risks. Mention of political risk was notable by its absence. ·

First priority was given to actions to limiting demand; and second priority was given to managing supply dependence by developing renewable energy and reexamining nuclear energy, maintaining competition in the oil industry, and ensuring external supplies by establishing ongoing dialogue with producer-countries and strengthening supply networks. A growing dependence on gas (including in power generation) was acknowledged, as was the apparent inevitability of growing dependence on Russia for gas supplies. The "continuity of supplies from the former Soviet Union, and then Russia, over the last 25 years" was noted as "testimony to an exemplary stability." Nevertheless, the paper stated that a "long term strategy in the framework of a partnership with Russia would be an important step to the benefit of supply security." The Green Paper mentioned the U.S. strategic petroleum reserve (for oil), but did not contain any references to UGS.

The EU Gas Security of Supply Directive The issue of gas storage did arise in the subsequent public debate on the Green Paper. Council Directive 2004/67/EC concerning measures to safeguard security of natural gas supply was adopted on April 26, 2004.[5] This five-page directive does not require member-states to establish strategic gas storages and maintain strategic gas reserves for security-of-supply reasons. All of the provisions are quite gen-

---

[4] The paper can be found at the following Web site: http://ec.europa.eu/energy/green-paper-energy-supply/doc/green_paper_energy_supply_en.pdf.
[5] The directive is available at the following Web site: http://energy.eu/directives/l_12720040429en00920096.pdf.

eral, and specific policies on strategic storage are left to the governments of individual member-states:

> Indicative minimum targets for gas storage could be set either at national level or by the industry. It is understood that this should not create any additional investment obligations. (Preamble, para. 7)
>
> Member States, having due regard to the geological conditions of their territory and the economic and technical feasibility, may also take the necessary measures to ensure that gas storage facilities located within their territory contribute to an appropriate degree to achieving the security of supply standards. (Article 4.4)
>
> If an adequate level of interconnection is available, Member States may take the appropriate measures in cooperation with another Member State, including bilateral agreements, to achieve the security of supply standards using gas storage facilities located within that other Member State. These measures, in particular bilateral agreements, shall not impede the proper functioning of the internal gas market. (Article 4.5)
>
> Member States may set or require the industry to set indicative minimum targets for a possible future contribution of storage, either located within or outside the Member State, to security of supply. These targets shall be published. (Article 4.6)

Reporting the levels of storage capacity (Article 5.1b); and monitoring the levels of working gas, of the withdrawal capacity of gas storage, and of interconnection of the national gas systems of member-states are required (Article 6.1c, d).

Implications for Governments in Southeast Europe Just as it remains a matter for each EU member-state to decide on its own national policy on security of supply in general and on strategic gas storage in particular, so there is no requirement in the EC Treaty for the contracting parties to maintain strategic gas reserves. We are aware of two European countries that have decided to maintain such reserves for security-of-supply purposes: Italy and Hungary. These examples are likely to be of interest to governments in Southeast Europe that are considering the gas security-of-supply issue.

In the case of Italy, the government requires strategic storage reserves equal to 10 percent of the annual imports from non-EU countries. Currently, this is 5.1 Bcm/y (Carnevalini 2008). Italy consumed 77.8 Bcm of gas in 2007, and the country's total imports (consumption minus production) were 68.9 Bcm (BP 2008).

In Hungary the energy sector is highly gas dependent (45 percent and increasing), the gas sector is highly import dependent (80 percent and increasing), and 100 percent of the imports come from Russia. Unlike the Czech Republic and the Slovak Republic, Hungary is not on a main transit route. It was not surprising that Hungary's vulnerability to gas import supply disruption became clearly evident during the Russia-Ukraine gas price dispute of January 2006. Act #26 of 2006 establishes a legal requirement to store 1.2 Bcm of strategic reserves. The obligation (and exclusive rights) to secure these reserves rests with the Hungarian Hydrocarbon Stockpiling Association, which has established a special-purpose vehicle, MMBF Zrt (in which a 67 percent ownership share was acquired by MOL). The strategic reserves currently are being established in a newly developed storage facility, and 1.2 Bcm represents 10 percent of Hungary's 2005 import volume. This percentage is declining as demand grows and domestic production declines.

The Preamble to the Gas Directive notes that

> Storage facilities are essential means, amongst other things, of implementing public service obligations such as security of supply. This should not lead to distortion of competition or discrimination in the access to storage. (para. 21)

There are economic and financial costs to carrying strategic reserves. Observation of markets suggests that strategic reserves will not be carried without a legal obligation to do so. The cost of carrying strategic reserves needs to be allocated equitably across customers, according to their benefit from it. If a government decides on a policy of requiring strategic reserves, the legal obligation to do so most naturally rests with suppliers. Large consumers, such as factories and power stations, can be left to decide whether to bear the cost of carrying strategic reserves or to bear the risk of interruption.

If a legal requirement to carry strategic reserves (for example, one placed on suppliers) is established, it is necessary to define the circumstances in which the strategic reserve can be drawn down. The authority to make the decision usually would be vested in the minister of energy.

Not only is storage most effective when it is situated closest to the demand it serves (even for managing seasonal swing and daily peaks), but each country also will naturally prefer to have strategic storage within its borders. However, it must be remembered that a number of the individual markets in Southeast Europe do not have UGS facilities and currently do not have known geological potential to develop such facilities. Therefore, it is expected that regional cooperation of the kind described in Article 4.5 of the

Gas Security of Supply Directive (quoted above) will be necessary for security of supply in Southeast Europe.

Financing of Regional Gas Investments

Financing gas investments in the region without placing undue strain on national budgets, meeting the requirements for financing, and mitigating risk are significant challenges.

Minimizing of National Budget Subventions

Gas sector investments in pipelines or LNG facilities are highly capital intensive. In the past, such investments were undertaken by the public sector, either through direct investments from the state budget or through budgetary subventions to support the investment programs of state enterprises. Where loans were supplied by commercial banks or development finance institutions, they generally were subject to sovereign guarantees. Such guarantees are contingent liabilities in the national accounts.

Increasingly, governments are seeking to reduce the demands of infrastructure financing on the national budget. An ideal situation would be one in which private investors finance and implement infrastructure projects, or one whereby a public-private partnership arrangement is structured to attract a competent technical partner supplying both expertise and a significant portion of the capital. Those options would be "ideal" in the sense that they would enable a government to direct scarce public resources to other pressing needs while being confident that infrastructural services would be provided efficiently. Another ideal precondition would be to have a competent regulator in place to ensure that the interests of consumers and investors are protected properly. As already highlighted in the case of regional projects, the regulatory framework has to be harmonized and operational in all the markets involved.

Even in the absence of private sector investment, a government can reduce the national budget impact of traditional forms of gas sector financing by structuring a large infrastructure project in a way that makes it suitable for project financing. This is a specialized funding structure that typically involves the bulk of the financing being provided as debt (loans) while minimizing the risks to the project sponsor (in this case, the government or a state-owned enterprise).

In a typical project-financing structure, the sponsors set up a project company to own or operate the assets. The sponsors inject, say, 10–20 percent of the project construction costs and initial working capital into this "special-purpose vehicle" as equity, with the remainder of the financing being provided as international and domestic debt. The debt of the vehicle does not appear on the balance sheet of the state-owned enterprise. The vehicle is expected to finance its debt payments from the project's future cash flows. This is referred to as "nonrecourse finance" because lenders have no recourse to the sponsors or shareholders of the project company for repayment of the loan. (A modified structure that retains some degree of risk for the sponsors is "limited recourse financing.")

In practice, it is rare that large regional infrastructure projects can be financed in a way that does not involve national budgets to some degree. Where there is private sector interest, some form of sovereign guarantees invariably will be needed. Similarly, special-purpose vehicle structures are more likely to offer limited recourse rather than truly nonrecourse financing, leaving the national fiscus exposed to some degree. Risk mitigation instruments, including various forms of guarantees and insurance, can reduce the extent of that exposure significantly.

In current circumstances, these considerations clearly apply in the SEE region. As the region continues to develop and becomes more closely allied with the EU, it will offer stronger economies and more robust institutions. Investor and financier perceptions of risks will decline, and it will become easier to attract private investors and to establish nonrecourse financing of projects. At this point, however, SEE countries have rather adverse country risk and commercial credit ratings (see figure 4.3 and tables 4.3 and 4.4).

Requirements for Gas Project Financing

Obtaining the necessary finance for a large regional gas project is difficult and challenging. The process brings into focus all the main elements of the project. Ideally, the principal requirements for financial closure that should be in place are as follows:

- **Good project design**—The project must be designed to match supply with demand in an efficient and cost-effective manner. Tariffs should be cost reflective, and projected revenues should be adequate to cover all costs, including financing requirements.
- **A properly structured contractual framework**—Commercial risk, especially volume risk, is of particular concern for gas projects.[6] Requiring offtakers to commit to take-or-pay contracts is one of the basic ways to reduce this risk. In the case of regional projects, a complex set of interlocking contractual arrangements is likely to be necessary. (Box 4.2 provides a brief discussion of the contracts associated with the SCP project.)

---

[6] For a detailed categorization and description of risks associated with gas projects, see the section titled "Risk and Risk Mitigation Instruments," later in this chapter.

Figure 4.3   Rule of Law Indicators: Percentile Ranks for Southeast Europe

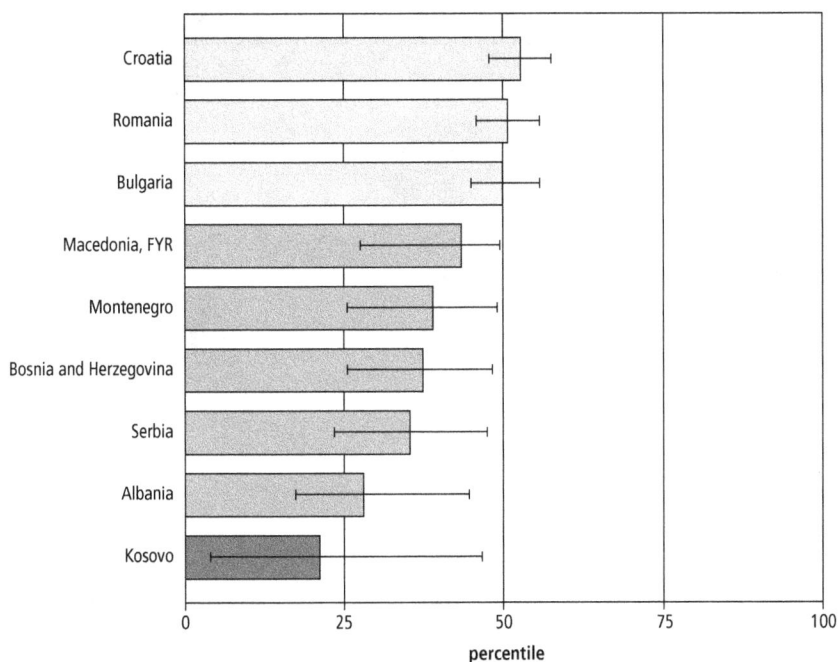

Source: Kaufmann, Kraay, and Mastruzzi 2007.

Table 4.3   Country Risk Ratings

Market	Country risk 1	Country risk 2
Albania	Medium high	High
Bosnia and Herzegovina	Medium high	Medium high
Bulgaria	Medium	Low
Croatia	Medium	Medium low
Kosovo	High	—
Macedonia, FYR	Medium high	Medium high
Montenegro	Medium high	Medium high
Romania	Medium	Low
Serbia	Medium high	Medium high

Sources: Country risk 1—ranking of countries according to rule-of-law indicators (Kaufmann, Kraay, and Mastruzzi 2007); country risk 2—Oxford Analytica/Aon Political Risk Service, 2007 Political Risk Map 2007. *Note:* — = not available. The main differences (Bulgaria and Romania) probably reflect the different dates of the ratings and the fact that those two countries have since become members of the European Union.

Table 4.4   Commercial Credit Ratings

Market	Standard & Poor's rating	Fitch rating
Albania	—	—
Bosnia and Herzegovina	—	—
Bulgaria	BBB+	BBB
Croatia	BBB+	BBB–
Kosovo	—	—
Macedonia, FYR	BB+	BB+
Montenegro	—	—
Romania	BBB–	BBB
Serbia	—	BB–

Source: Rating agency Web sites.
Note: — = not available.

- **A predictable gas sector regulatory environment**—A coherent framework for the gas sector has to be in place to ensure that tariffs and operating conditions are predictable. In principle, regulation can be achieved through contractual arrangements; but, in practice, all the SEE countries either already have established or intend to establish fully fledged regulatory institutions and are furthermore committed to the harmonization needed to facilitate and accommodate regional projects.
- **A transmission project operator in place (for a regional project)**—Having a TPO with a one-stop-shop mandate is not just a convenience for users of a cross-border facility; it also enhances the transparency and predictability of arrangements from the viewpoint of investors and financiers.
- **Legal recourse in the event of disputes**—If there is a breach of contract, it is important that agreed dispute resolution procedures and mechanisms be in place. As noted in the discussion of the SCP project in box 4.2, the key agreements incorporated internationally enforceable versions of the Energy Charter dispute resolution provisions. Future regional gas projects within Southeast Europe can take advantage of this precedent. The EC Secretariat's *Model Intergovernmental and Host Government Agreements for Cross-Border Pipelines* provides a neutral and nonprescriptive starting point for negotiations on trade and transit arrangements, and the EC's dispute settlement mechanisms usefully can be incorporated in regional gas project agreements.
- **Risk mitigation instruments in place**—Most of the main project risks would be catered for if all of the above requirements were met in full. In

practice, significant remaining elements of risk (as well as others not yet described) can be ameliorated to some degree by risk mitigation instruments (RMIs). Including RMIs in the negotiations often can tip the balance, making it possible to finalize a complete financing package.

A more detailed discussion of risk and risk management instruments is given in the next section. It is important at the outset to observe that RMIs are not a panacea. They cannot make poorly structured projects bankable or turn unreliable borrowers into good credit risks. RMIs are a complement to, not a substitute for, a well-designed project, properly structured contracts, and a supportive policy and regulatory environment.

Risk and Risk Mitigation Instruments

There is a high level of risk associated with regional gas projects. Risks arise at all stages of the project (planning, design, construction, and operation); and from sources that are internal to the project (such as the risk that gas demand will fall short of projections), as well as external factors (such as a breakdown of law and order leading to sabotage of gas pipelines). For analytic convenience, the risks can be considered to fall into two categories: political and commercial.

As outlined in the previous section, there are two approaches to risk mitigation. The first approach is to structure the project and the contracts so as to minimize the risks. This effort is spelled out in table 4.5, which lists the main elements of political and commercial risk and the associated structural and contractual approaches to risk mitigation.

The second approach to risk mitigation is to cover risks with guarantees or various forms of insurance. The "default" for this approach is a sovereign guarantee; but, as discussed previously, it is desirable from several viewpoints for governments to limit sovereign guarantee exposure. The second approach thus focuses on obtaining the support of agencies able to provide RMIs.

The two approaches to risk mitigation are strongly interrelated because the terms and conditions on which RMIs are made available are greatly influenced by the quality of project design and contractual arrangements. The description so far implies a sequenced approach—contracts first, RMIs second. In practice, the two aspects very often are finalized simultaneously, after an iterative negotiation process.

Regarding RMIs, figure 4.4 illustrates the two types of project participants seeking RMIs. These are the equity investors (project sponsors, exposed to investment risk) and the providers of loans (debt holders, exposed to credit risk).

Table 4.5   Categories of Project Risk and Contractual Approaches to Risk Mitigation

Risk type	Structural and contractual risk mitigation
Political risk mitigation matrix	
Expropriation risk	• Reputational impact of government expropriation • Diplomatic ramifications • Contract specifies compensation from government for loss of earnings • Involve international financial institutions
Security risk	• Law and order and military action • Private security force • Address underlying cause
Breach of contract risk	• Carefully structure contracts to ensure fairness • Support contracts with investment treaties (for example the Energy Charter Treaty) • Involve international financial institutions
Legal and regulatory risk	• Establish clear, comprehensive legal framework and strong judiciary • Form agreement with government to freeze current legal environment • Allow pass-through of costs arising from change in regulations • Host government takes a financial stake
Currency transfer restrictions risk	• Payment in commonly traded currency • Establish open financial system and independent monetary authority • Political risk insurance • Involve international financial institutions
Dispute resolution risk	• Strengthen regulatory regime and independence of judiciary • Arbitrate in neutral third country or use third-country law as substantive law of contract and to govern arbitral proceedings • Ensure project is economically viable and contract terms are fair and agreed transparently • Use International Center for Settlement of Investment Disputes arbitration

(continued)

Table 4.5 Categories of Project Risk and Contractual Approaches to Risk Mitigation
(Continued)

Risk type	Structural and contractual risk mitigation
Commercial risk mitigation matrix	
Planning risk	• Perform careful due diligence onsite • Make project agreements and financing contingent on planning approval • Government assists fast-track approval, coordinates planning authorities, and provides a streamlined planning process • Include government as joint-venture partner
Design risk	• Pass cost overruns to contractor through an engineering procurement and construction contract
Construction risk	• Pass cost overruns to contractor through an engineering procurement and construction contract
Volume risk	• Establish long-term, firm offtake guarantees or take-or-pay agreements
Supply risk	• Perform routine maintenance • Law enforcement, military protection against sabotage
Payment risk	• Collateral security • Escrow account, advance payment
Exchange rate risk	• Index payment to commonly traded currency • Use domestically sourced components and labor, where possible
Interest rate risk	• Use fixed-interest loans

Source: Economic Consulting Associates.

The ultimate objective in securing RMIs is to obtain full risk coverage, but a more common outcome is partial risk coverage. Through a syndication of RMIs from different agencies, a high degree of risk coverage can be attained. However, it is difficult, time consuming, and costly to negotiate a complex financing package that involves many different players providing a mix of equity, loans, and RMIs. As a result, some balance has to be struck between complexity and the amount of risk exposure left uncovered.

Figure 4.4 Risk Coverage Typology

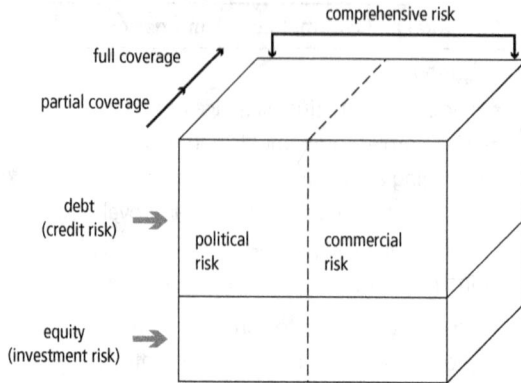

Source: Matsukawa and Habeck 2007.

An example of syndicated guarantees in a regional gas project is provided by the $1 billion Southern Africa Regional Gas Pipeline. This project was financed by a hybrid of corporate debt and project financing, much of it originating from South Africa. To reach financial closure, it was important to have RMI coverage of the political risks associated with the Mozambique components of the project.

As illustrated in figure 4.5, approximately $230 million of the debt contracted by the producing company (Sasol Petroleum) and the transporting company (Republic of Mozambique Pipeline Investment Company) were covered by a mix of political RMIs from the World Bank (International Bank for Reconstruction and Development [IBRD] enclave partial risk guarantee), the Export Credit Insurance Corporation of South Africa, and the Multilateral Investment Guarantee Agency (MIGA; part of the World Bank Group). A proportion of the MIGA guarantee was reinsured by SACE of Italy and by the Export Finance and Insurance Corporation of Australia.

The main RMIs to be considered for regional infrastructure projects fall into three categories:

- political risk RMIs (covering political but not commercial risks):
  - partial risk guarantee
  - partial risk insurance
- comprehensive RMIs (covering both political and commercial risks):
  - partial credit guarantee
  - export credit guarantee

Figure 4.5 Sample Gas Project Guarantee Structure

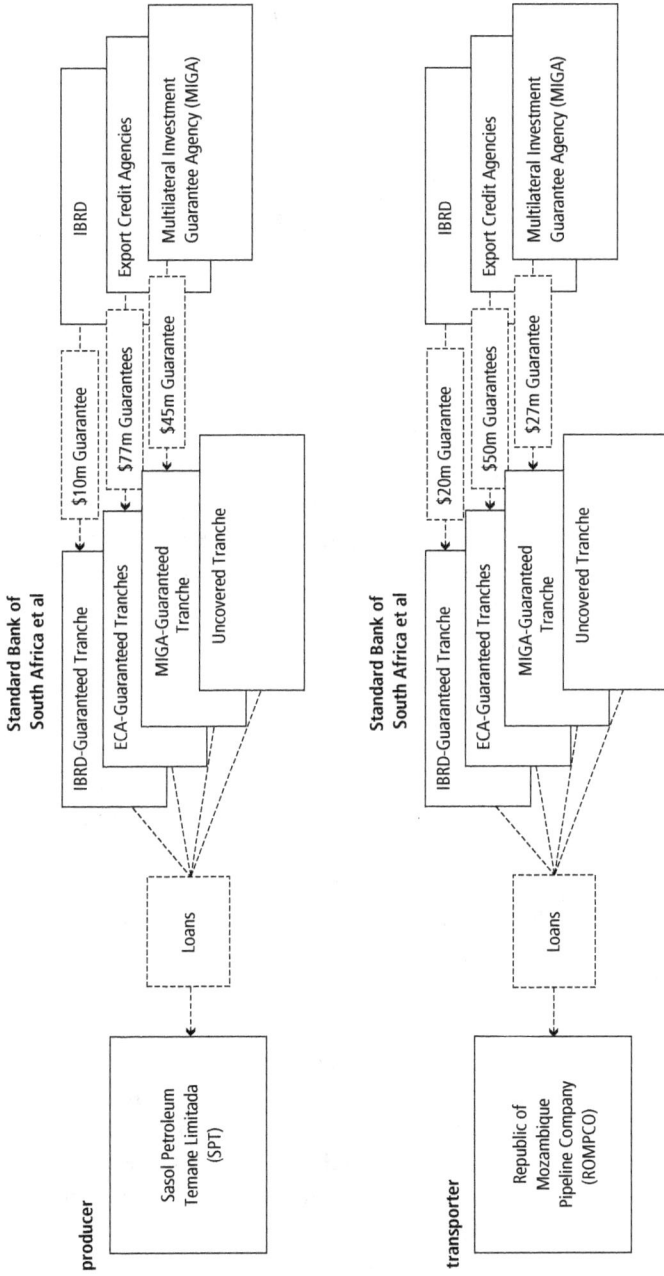

- commercial insurance and financial market hedging products (covering narrowly defined risks):
  - business interruption insurance
  - foreign currency hedging products
  - interest rate hedging products.

Partial risk guarantees and credit insurance often are provided by multilateral institutions, such as the World Bank Group, or by bilateral development institutions, such as KfW Entwicklungsbank; but there also are some notable private companies providing political risk insurance (the top five being AIG, Chubb, Sovereign, Zurich, and Lloyds). Partial credit guarantees and credit insurance are available from multilateral and bilateral agencies and from private commercial suppliers of RMIs. Insurance and financial market hedging products are offered by private suppliers, and are used widely in infrastructure projects.

Eligibility criteria for RMIs from noncommercial sources vary from being completely open to being highly restrictive. Bilateral agencies tend to focus on companies and banks from their own countries. For example, the U.S. Overseas Private Investment Corporation (OPIC) provides partial risk insurance or loan guarantees to U.S. companies or to projects with at least 25 percent of the equity being owned by a U.S. investor.

National export credit guarantee agencies have been established to provide guarantees on exports from their own countries or on exports by companies of national origin operating outside the home country. For example, the Italian export credit agency, SACE, which is involved as coguarantor in the Southern Africa Regional Gas Project, provides various forms of insurance for exports of goods and services by Italian companies based either in Italy or abroad.

Table 4.6 provides details of two sample RMIs available from the World Bank Group. The table presents the parameters that need to be considered in relation to RMIs. These parameters include different eligibility criteria, types of risk coverage, varying tenure, and maximum amounts that can be covered; and the fees that are involved. As illustrated for the case of the IBRD partial credit guarantee, in many cases some form of counterguarantee is required, this typically being a sovereign guarantee.

Given the dominance of state-owned enterprises in the gas sectors of Southeast Europe, it is worth noting that the availability of RMIs is not limited to private sector projects. As noted in table 4.6, instruments such as the World Bank's IBRD partial credit guarantee are specifically oriented to supporting public sector investment projects. For governments, access to RMIs

- catalyzes private financing of infrastructure projects
- provides access to commercial banks and capital markets

Table 4.6   Details of Sample Multilateral Risk Mitigation Instruments from the World Bank Group

Sample instrument	IBRD partial credit guarantee	MIGA political risk insurance
RMI type	Debt guarantee	Investment guarantee
Eligible borrowers, investments, and projects	Sovereign or public borrowers for new investments (private entities can be considered)	New cross-border investments that are developmental, viable, and sustainable
Risk types covered	Guarantee backs government/SOE obligations: covers private debt against public sector failure to meet specific project obligations	Coverage as needed against currency inconvertibility and transfer restrictions, expropriation, war and civil disturbance, and/or breach of contract
Tenure	No specific limit	Up to 15 years (20 years, in exceptional cases)
Maximum amount	No specific limit	Up to 90% of equity and 95% of shareholders' loans and related debt; up to $200 million (more if needed, through reinsurance and coinsurance)
Initiation, processing, and front-end fees	None	Application fee, $5,000–10,000; processing fee, $25,000
Standby fee	25 basis points per year on a present value basis	May be charged on undisbursed amount of approved guarantee
Guarantee or insurance fee	50 basis points per year on a present value basis	Case-by-case basis
Host country requirement	Counterguarantee required from member-country (World Bank Articles requirement)	Host country approval required
Web site	www.worldbank.org/guarantees	www.miga.org

Sources: Compiled from Matsukawa and Habeck (2007) and Sinclair (2005).
Note: IBRD = International Bank for Reconstruction and Development; MIGA = Multilateral Investment Guarantee Agency; RMI = risk mitigation instrument; SOE = state-owned enterprise.

- reduces the cost of private financing to affordable levels
- reduces government risk exposure by passing commercial risk to the private sector
- encourages cofinancing of large infrastructure projects.

The corresponding advantages for the private sector are that providing RMIs

- mitigates risk that the private sector does not control
- opens new markets
- lowers the cost of financing
- improves project sustainability.

Box 4.3 details the financing structure of the West African Gas Pipeline Project. The crucial risk element in the project is the adherence of the main offtaker (the Volta River Authority of Ghana) to its take-or-pay commitments to purchase the gas. Three different agencies agreed to provide political risk coverage. Should the guarantees ever be called, there are differing pro-rata sharing arrangements, depending on the circumstances of the default.

When the project first was proposed, there was skepticism that the complex WAGP project, spanning four countries with poor country risk ratings, would ever reach financial closure. Securing political risk guarantees and insurance was an important step in ensuring that the project would go ahead. The World Bank's involvement was important in giving confidence in the economic and financial viability of the project, the application of adequate standards of transparency, and good practices in respect to environmental and social safeguards.

Conclusions on Institutional Issues

In conclusion, we consider the types of gas projects in the region and the corporate structure for the proposed EC Gas Transmission Ring.

Types of SEE Regional Gas Projects

Summarizing what has been presented thus far in this chapter, obstacles to the implementation of regional gas projects usefully may be addressed in terms of these three interrelated aspects:

1. **National gas markets**—Gas markets must be strengthened within the SEE region, with the immediate challenge being to pursue road maps agreed with the EC Secretariat to ensure rapid attainment of the gas market conditions laid out in the Gas Directive.
2. **Cross-border framework**—Harmonization of operational procedures, standardization of the third-party access waiver application procedures (as

BOX 4.3

Risk Mitigation Instruments in the West African Gas Pipeline Project

Countries: Benin, Ghana, Nigeria, Togo
Project costs: $590 million
RMI type: Partial risk guarantee, partial risk insurance
RMI providers: International Development Association, Multilateral
                    Investment Guarantee Agency, Zurich/Overseas Private
                    Investment Corporation
RMI beneficiary: West African Gas Pipeline Company (equity investments,
                    shareholder debt)
RMI amount: $250 million (42% of total)
Financial closure: 2005

Two special purchase vehicles were established for this project: West African
Gas Pipeline Company Limited (WAPCo) was formed to build, own, and operate the gas pipeline; and N-Gas Ltd. is a trading company formed to buy the
gas at the source, transport it through the pipeline, and sell to the main foundation customers. The $590 million initial project cost is financed by direct
equity and shareholder loans to WAPCo from the sponsors, a mixture of
state-owned and private oil companies.

The main legal agreements for the West African Gas Pipeline project are
an international project agreement among the four countries and WAPCo;
gas transport agreements between WAPCo and N-Gas; and gas sales agreements between N-Gas and the foundation customers, which are the Volta
River Authority (VRA) of Ghana and Communauté Electrique du Bénin.
Ghana has provided a government consent and support agreement that
unconditionally and irrevocably guarantees the performance obligations of
VRA to N-Gas and WAPCo.

The risk guarantee structure is illustrated in the figure included in this
box. Partial risk guarantees from the International Development Association
($50 million), the Multilateral Investment Guarantee Agency ($75 million),
and Steadfast/Zurich ($125 million, reinsured by the Overseas Private Invest-
ment Corporation) all cover payments owed by the government of Ghana if
VRA should fail to meet its obligations. The International Development Association guarantee is structured to cover the government's termination payment to WAPCo.

(continued on next page)

Box 4.3 (Continued)

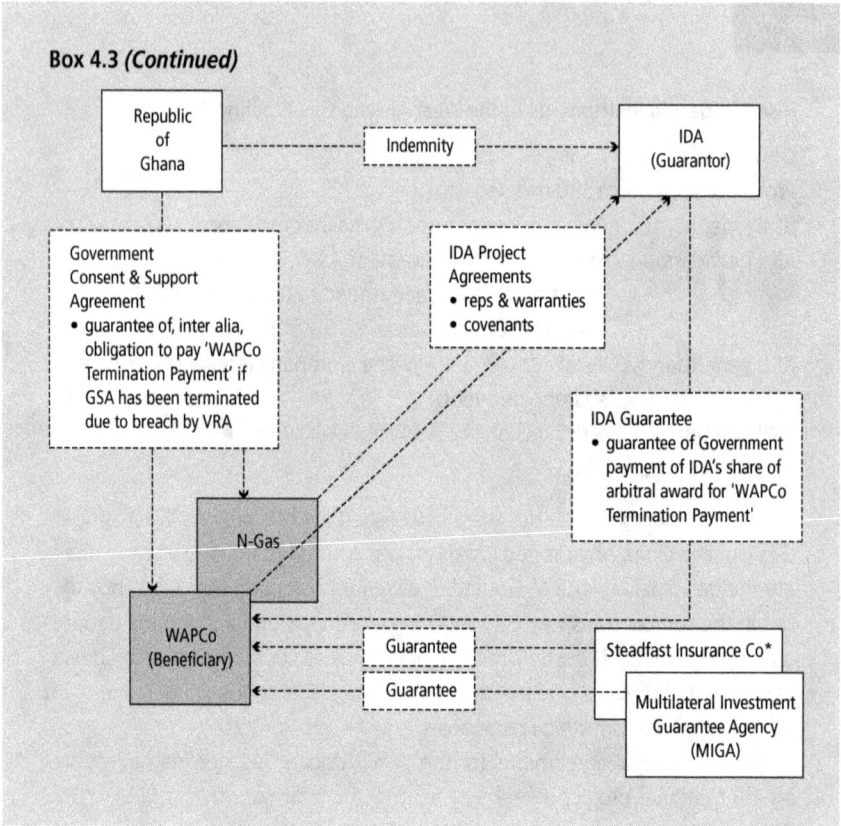

Source: Compiled from Matsukawa and Habeck (2007), Maweni (2005), and Sinclair (2005).

laid out in the EC's NGIIR), and adoption of a single operator (the TPO) for a regional gas project are needed.

3. **Financing**—Good project design is needed, including an institutional structure to minimize public sector exposure to risks, careful structuring of the interlocking contracts required for a cross-border gas project, and negotiation of a package of RMIs to ensure financial closure while minimizing the cost of financing.

This Southeast Europe Regional Gasification Study has identified benefits that SEE countries can reap by intensifying regional cooperation in a mix of projects ranging from relatively modest bilateral projects to reinforce existing or to build new transmission lines, to the ambitious proposals for the EC Gas Ring. On the face of it, the rational approach would be to schedule projects so as to move progressively toward completing the ring.

However, from the viewpoint of accelerating SEE gasification, the earlier the ring is in place, the better. This is because the EC Ring would link currently ungasified areas with mature gas markets. Such linking would facilitate supply diversity and provide favorable prospects for security of supply, including through access to regional underground storage facilities. The ring would foster regional cooperation by promoting constructive interdependence among seven markets of the region.

For this reason, while not underplaying the importance of smaller regional gas projects, it is relevant to consider what will be required to implement a project of the size and complexity of the proposed EC Ring. Having seven markets involved is important in terms of maximizing the benefits; but from an institutional viewpoint, it greatly increases the challenges of structuring and financing the project. One of the main themes of this discussion of institutional issues has been that an increase in the number of countries more than proportionately increases the difficulties of financing and implementing a regional gas project.

Moving to the seven-country EC Gas Ring project thus strengthens the case for urgent attention given to aligning national gas markets with EU norms and harmonizing operational and third-party access waiver procedures in cross-border contexts. With regard to the other issues, the key starting point for defining the cross-border framework, identifying a transmission project operator, and negotiating financing is to establish an institutional structure for the EC Gas Ring project. The pros and cons of the structure that currently is proposed are presented in the next section of this chapter.

EC Ring Corporate Structure
In considering an appropriate structure for the EC Gas Ring project, a pertinent project to analyze is the Nabucco pipeline project. That project involves five markets largely located in the SEE region. The corporate structure that has been established for Nabucco is one centered on a holding company, the Nabucco Gas Pipeline International GmbH (Nabucco International), with five Nabucco national companies as subsidiaries. As shown in figure 4.6, Nabucco International will raise all the necessary financing and contract with the national companies to build and maintain the sections of the pipeline in their territories. All gas transport rights will be vested in the transmission operator (Nabucco International), which will provide a one-stop-shop for the users of the pipeline. The Nabucco partners each hold equal shares in Nabucco International.

Would a similar structure be useful for the EC Gas Ring? This possibility is illustrated in figure 4.7, where it is assumed that the ring partners would be the transmission companies in each of the markets. In markets presently without gas (Albania, Kosovo, and Montenegro), the electricity transmission

Figure 4.6   Nabucco Pipeline Corporate Structure

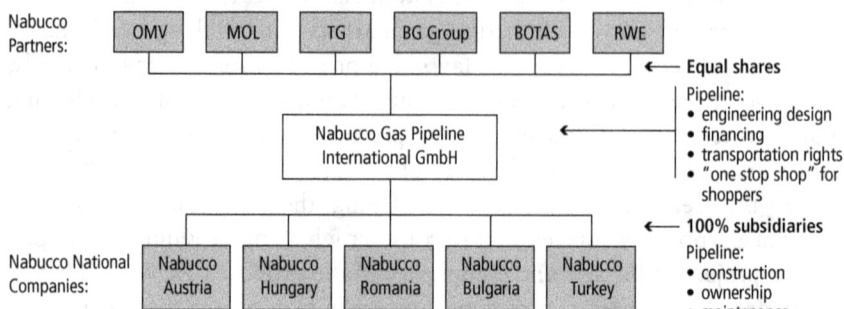

Source: Nabucco Gas Pipeline International GmbH, http://www.nabucco-pipeline.com/company/company-structure/index.html.

owner might use its accumulated experience and knowledge of EU transmission requirements to take on the transmission of gas. There is a precedent for this in the National Grid Transco in the United Kingdom, which is responsible for both electricity and gas transmission. However, other possibilities would be to include an existing energy company that would take on gas transmission or a new company formed for that purpose. New EC Gas Ring subsidiary companies would be needed in each market to build, own, and maintain the relevant segments of the ring.

Some possible advantages and disadvantages of adopting the Nabucco corporate structure for the EC Gas Ring (ECGR) Regional Gas Pipeline Company would be these:

- Advantages
  - Autonomy—The ECGR Regional Gas Pipeline Company would be an autonomous entity, acting independently of its parent companies and protecting those companies from project risks.
  - **Transmission project operator**—The company would be the TPO, providing a one-stop-shop for users.
  - **Subsidiary companies**—These would be local companies in each market, set up to respond to local requirements.
  - **Concentrated financing effort**—In all likelihood, it would be efficient for the company to negotiate financing for the entire project.
- Disadvantages
  - **Joint financing**—This could mean financiers setting terms for the entire project on the basis of the most risky participants, thus raising costs overall.

Figure 4.7 Replicating Nabucco Corporate Structure for the EC Gas Ring

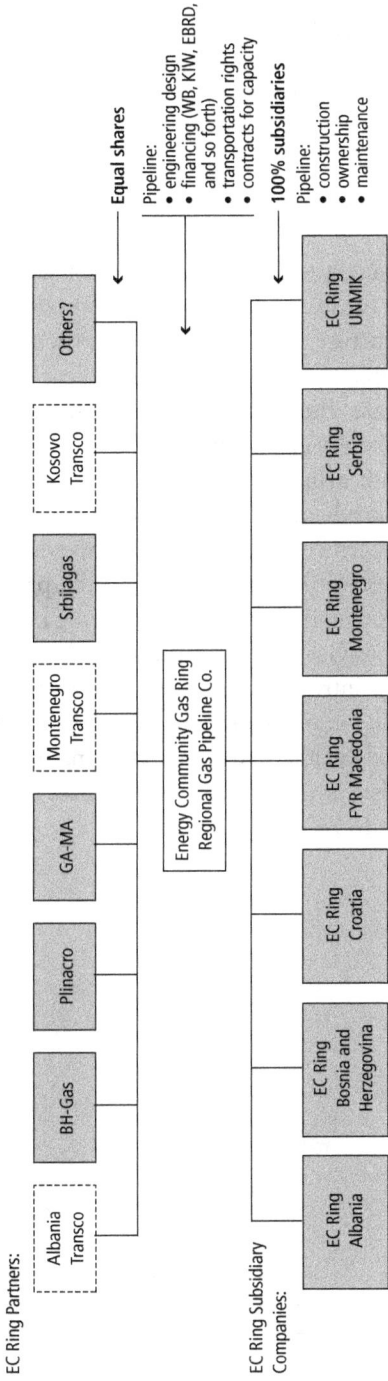

EC Ring Partners:

Albania Transco — BH-Gas — Plinacro — GA-MA — Montenegro Transco — Srbijagas — Kosovo Transco — Others?

Energy Community Gas Ring Regional Gas Pipeline Co.

Equal shares

Pipeline:
- engineering design
- financing (WB, KfW, EBRD, and so forth)
- transportation rights
- contracts for capacity

100% subsidiaries

Pipeline:
- construction
- ownership
- maintenance

EC Ring Subsidiary Companies:

EC Ring Albania — EC Ring Bosnia and Herzegovina — EC Ring Croatia — EC Ring FYR Macedonia — EC Ring Montenegro — EC Ring Serbia — EC Ring UNMIK

Source: Nabucco Gas Pipeline International GmbH, http://www.nabucco-pipeline.com/company/company-structure/index.html.
Note: EBRD = European Bank for Reconstruction and Development; EC = Energy Community; KfW = KfW Entwicklungsbank; UNMIK = United Nations Interim Administration Mission in Kosovo; WB = World Bank.

- **Sharing the commercial benefits of the ring**—Having equal shares in the ECGR Regional Gas Pipeline Company and the regional companies as 100 percent subsidiaries (so that all profits are pooled in the holding company) implies that EC Ring partners will have equal shares in the profits of operating the ring, irrespective of levels of investment and of activity in the different territories. Even if this is agreed at the start of the project, it is an issue that may not prove to be acceptable over time.

On the second disadvantage, there is reason to doubt whether equal shares ever would be acceptable for EC Gas Ring partners. In the case of Nabucco, all of the project infrastructure is to be newly constructed (although in the initial phases, it will be able to operate with limited capacity using existing infrastructure). By contrast, the EC Gas Ring might include segments of existing pipelines. How these segments will be handled is yet to be resolved, but this is likely to have a bearing on the view of participants about how the project is to be shared to produce an equitable outcome.

Perhaps the disadvantages could be overcome by adapting the concept. For example, it might involve negotiating around the problem of different country risk levels with potential financiers, and having nonequal shareholdings in the ECGR Regional Gas Pipeline Company. A mix of common and preferred shares could be introduced to retain the equal-shares basis and combine this with flexibility in the manner in which dividends are allocated.

The EC Gas Ring would be inherently more challenging than the Nabucco project because it involves a larger number of countries and a greater variation in levels of adherence to EC commitments.

5.

CONCLUSIONS AND KEY FINDINGS

This concluding section of the report does not attempt to provide a summary of the whole study. Its more limited aim is to highlight a small number of key findings that might have a strong influence on the future gasification of the Southeast Europe (SEE) region.

Economics of Gasification

The SEE markets are small in terms of current and future gas consumption. Their current size makes the prospect of developing and financing infrastructure for new gas consumption more challenging. The city distribution case studies have shown that expansion of distribution generally will be economical under current conditions, provided the gas can be brought into the region at reasonable cost.

Increased gasification requires large up-front investments in transmission infrastructure to bring the gas to the markets concerned. Conversely, up-front investment in transmission infrastructure requires creditworthy offtakers with a sufficiently large quantity of demand immediately after the completion of construction (anchor loads) to make the investment economical and bankable. This is the "chicken-and-egg" problem that faces much new infrastructure.

The problems applies in Southeast Europe, especially to completely new pipelines for markets currently without any gas (all of Albania, Kosovo, and Montenegro; most of the former Yugoslav Republic of Macedonia; and much of southern and western Serbia, Bosnia and Herzegovina, and southern Croatia). It also applies to the construction of additional capacity for markets already served to some extent by gas (Bosnia and Herzegovina, Croatia, and Serbia).[1] This means that gasification of new areas is more likely to start with gas supply to large loads (like power generation) than to start with city gas distribution schemes on their own.

One solution to render gas transmission projects economical and bankable is to coordinate parallel up-front investments in gas-fired power stations to bring them online at the same time that the gas pipeline becomes operational. Distribution investment can follow the establishing of transmission infrastructure, building the smaller loads on top of the power generation anchor load. In this approach, gas and power development are closely linked. Therefore, we have paid considerable attention to the updated Generation Investment Study ([GIS]; SEE Consultants 2007), which provides the reference power development scenarios for the region.

The updated GIS shows that modestly increased use of gas in the power sector is economical in the SEE region; but that the quantity of gas-fired power generation is highly sensitive to the future gas price, especially compared with the price of coal/lignite. In the scenario described as a "fully interconnected power system without any transmission constraints and partial environmental compliance,"[2] 2,100 megawatts of new gas-fired combined-cycle gas turbine generation capacity is required in the period up to 2020. Based on the generation expansion schedule in the updated GIS, and reflecting high gas prices, we estimate that those plants would require about 1 billion cubic meters (Bcm) of gas a year from 2010, 1.6 Bcm from 2013, 2.2 Bcm from 2017, and 2.6 Bcm from 2019.

In the high gas price scenario of the updated GIS, the economically optimum level of gas-fired plant capacity falls to 1,300 megawatts by 2020. Those plants would be estimated to need just 0.6 Bcm a year from 2010 and 1.0 Bcm from 2020. The gas price assumptions in the former scenario are a little lower than current gas border prices, and a little lower than the high gas price scenario in the present study. The gas prices in the updated GIS high price scenario are based on an assumption of a weighted basket of crude oil at $100a barrel, and are very much higher than both current gas border prices and the high gas price scenario in the present study.

In the updated GIS carbon price scenario, using $20 per tonne of carbon dioxide, the economically optimum level of gas-fired capacity increases enormously to 7,900 megawatts. Those plants would be estimated to

---

[1] Bulgaria has sufficient capacity on its transmission ring to expand the use of gas with new spur lines and distribution investments. The main need in Romania is rehabilitation of the old gas transmission infrastructure.

[2] This is updated, based on Scenario B/Case 2A2 of the original Generation Investment Study.

require 4.3 Bcm of gas annually from 2010, increasing to 6.2 Bcm from 2011, 6.8 Bcm from 2012, 8.8 Bcm from 2013, 9.4 Bcm from 2015, and 9.8 Bcm from 2018.

In the updated GIS's very high gas price scenario, it is clear that the power sector gas demand would be too small to stimulate investment in new transmission capacity. Therefore, the three plants (2 × 500 megawatts plus 1 × 300 megawatts) either would be located near existing transmission infrastructure with sufficient available capacity, or would not be developed at all because they could not gain access to gas. In either case, increased gasification would not be catalyzed.

In contrast, the carbon price scenario would require very large investments in gas transmission capacity in the region; and it would require access to capacity upstream of the region, in addition to the investments in the power plants themselves. Access to the gas would be the constraining factor. It seems unlikely that the power sector in the region will be faced with a hard financial price for carbon dioxide emissions by 2020. However, it is possible that the Kyoto Protocol flexibility mechanisms may make it possible for some gas-fired developments to access the value of reduced carbon dioxide emissions.

In reality, development of gas-fired power generation is very unlikely to follow exactly the economically optimal plant construction sequence and buildup of load resulting from the WASP[3] model runs in the updated GIS. To make the gas investments viable in the first place, our key finding is that some of the gas-fired generation capacity scheduled for later years would need to be brought forward (and some non-gas-fired plants correspondingly would be slipped back in the schedule) to provide a minimum of 2.0–2.5 Bcm of anchor demand from the first year of operation of the new gas transmission infrastructure.

To achieve that outcome, governments in each market would have to develop a policy for gas distribution in advance of the development of the transmission infrastructure, so that investors are prepared for the development of distribution networks without delay when the gas is available on the transmission system. This preparation might include, for example, concessioning distribution licenses with requirements to develop networks and connect customers at a certain rate after the transmission system is in place.

The Energy Community Gas Ring:
A Cooperative Regional Vision for Gas Development
Coordinated development of transmission infrastructure will benefit all of the markets in the region (most of which are individually tiny potential gas

---

[3] WASP is the Wien Automatic System Planning model, developed by the International Atomic Energy Agency.

markets by European standards) by making it possible to achieve economies of scale. The concept of the Energy Community (EC) Gas Ring provides a vision for such development. The ring would deliver a large number of benefits and enhanced regional economic and technical cooperation, including

- aligning naturally with the principles of the Stability Pact for Southeast Europe[4]
- establishing physical infrastructure to enable the realization in the gas sector of the aims of the Energy Community Treaty[5]
- creating strong practical economic incentives for countries currently without gas to implement the terms of the Energy Community Treaty with respect to gas (which otherwise would be a "paper exercise")
- enabling the pipeline infrastructure to be sized just large enough to deliver gas to the initial anchor loads (which may be along a linear configuration prior to completion of the ring)
- enabling incremental development of transmission capacity with each additional injection point, as and when required to serve subsequent growth in demand
- combining the demand of seven regional markets (including six main cities)
- directly linking seven SEE gas markets with the gas markets of four European Union neighbors—Bulgaria, Greece, Hungary, and Romania
- delivering gas deep into currently ungasified areas
- enabling flexibility in the development of SEE regional transmission infrastructure with respect to major proposed pipeline developments, such as Nabucco, the Turkey-Greece-Italy pipeline, the trans-Adriatic pipeline, the Georgia-Ukraine-European Union-White Stream-pan-European gas pipeline

---

[4] ". . . [T]he Stability Pact for Southeast Europe is the first comprehensive conflict-prevention strategy of the international community, aimed at strengthening the efforts of the countries of Southeast Europe in fostering peace, democracy, respect for human rights and economic prosperity. The Stability Pact provides a framework to stimulate regional co-operation and expedite integration into European and trans-Atlantic structures. . . . Working Table II [of the Pact's secretariat, located in Brussels, deals with issues of] economic reconstruction, cooperation and development matters . . ." (http://www.stabilitypact.org/).

[5] The first page of the treaty recalls ". . . the contribution of the Stability Pact for Southeast Europe . . . has as its core the need to strengthen co-operation amongst the states and nations of Southeast Europe and to foster the conditions for peace, stability and economic growth . . . " (http://www.stabilitypact.org/energy/Treaty.en05.pdf).

- enhancing both diversity and technical security of supply
- facilitating regional SEE gas trading in the future
- linking all of the connected markets to regional underground storage
- synchronizing with the development of gas-fired power plants.

Phased Development of the EC Ring

Because transmission capacity increases with each additional injection point added to the ring—as and when required to serve subsequent growth in demand—the ring concept allows for the initial pipeline infrastructure to be configured as a linear system to deliver gas directly to the initial anchor loads. Therefore, pipelines may be sized just large enough to serve the initial anchor loads (which have a high load factor, allowing further economies on pipeline diameter) plus the first few years of subsequent demand growth before the completion of the full ring configuration and the addition of new injection points.

That approach contrasts markedly with linear-radial system development, where the pipeline would need to be sized to serve medium- to longer-term demand projections. Linear-radial design has obvious disadvantages in terms of up-front capital cost and increased financial risk. The savings in pipeline sizing for the ring largely offset the cost benefits of "telescoping" from large diameters down to small diameters along a linear-radial pipeline system. The ring concept also offers increased flexibility for future development. A major advantage is that there are numerous possibilities for phased development, and the concept is sufficiently flexible to be adapted to whichever upstream project developments and gas supply options emerge. One possible phased development approach is described below.

These are the actions to be taken in the initial phase:

- Develop about 2,000 megawatts of gas-fired power generation capacity in Albania, southern Croatia, FYR Macedonia, and Montenegro
- At the same time, construct the southwestern section, Skopje-Tirana-Podgorica-Dubrovnik (possibly as part of the Ionian-Adriatic pipeline project), northward and parallel to the coast to join the Croatian gas transmission extension planned to Split and southward toward Metkovic.
- Either strengthen the connection from the Bulgarian transmission ring westward to an entry point on the future ring near Skopje in FYR Macedonia; or connect, via the Greek gas grid, northward to an entry point in Albania and FYR Macedonia (possibly as part of the trans-Adriatic pipeline project).

In the second phase, these are the actions to be taken:

- Develop distribution networks in Albania, southern Croatia, FYR Macedonia, and Montenegro to build demand for gas delivered via the first-phase transmission infrastructure.
- Complete the southeastern corner of the EC Ring, Skopje-Pristina-Nis.[6]
- Complete the northwestern section of the EC Ring, Metkovic-Mostar-Sarajevo-Belgrade, to close the ring, using the existing Belgrade-Nis pipeline, subject to future replacement of this section, when needed, at the same pipeline diameter as the rest of the EC Ring (or possibly looping to create the same effect).
- Manage seasonal swing on the EC Ring (as distribution volumes build up) by connecting the underground storage facility at Banatski Dvor to the EC Ring, via the Serbian gas transmission system, providing an entry point for Russian gas delivered via Ukraine and Hungary.

In the third phase, these actions should be taken:

- Develop distribution networks in Bosnia and Herzegovina, Kosovo, and southern and western Serbia.
- When necessary, loop the existing Nis-Belgrade pipeline to reinforce the eastern section of the EC Ring.
- Access additional volumes and increase the capacity of the ring, when required, by connecting to the EC Ring from an offtake point near Belgrade on the pan-European gas pipeline (when it is built).
- Access additional volumes and increase the capacity of the ring, when required, by connecting the EC Ring to the Nabucco pipeline (either via the Bulgarian ring and Doupnitsa-Nis, or from an offtake point near Nabucco compressor station 11 in Romania across to a point near Belgrade in Serbia)
- Manage additional seasonal swing and increase the winter peak capacity of the ring by developing underground storage in Albania.

Access to Upstream Pipeline Capacity to Supply the EC Ring

Initially, the EC Ring would require just enough upstream capacity to meet the anchor loads. Analysis of capacities on the Greek natural gas transmission system suggests that there is more than enough entry capacity (including

---

[6] If the pan-European gas pipeline has been completed by this time, completing this corner will close a larger loop via the existing Belgrade-Nis pipeline to northern Croatia and down the Croatian coast to the first phase of the EC Ring. If the Blue Line pipeline has been completed by this time, this section may be able to close a larger loop via the Blue Line infrastructure to the Croatian system and back down the Croatian coast to the first phase of the EC Ring.

existing capacity from the Revithoussa liquefied natural gas terminal in the entry capacity to the Greek grid) to meet an annual demand of 2.0–2.5 Bcm for power stations on the EC Ring.

Diversity of Gas Sources of Supply

Completing the EC Ring with connections from upstream transmission pipeline infrastructure delivering gas to various entry points on the ring would open up a wide range of contracting sources for gas volumes to buyers of wholesale gas in Southeast Europe. These sources would include

- Mediterranean market liquefied natural gas via Revithoussa, (possibly swapped with Russian gas to manage and economize transmission flows)
- Algerian pipeline gas or an Italian market mix of gas sources (possibly swapped with Russian gas under a backhaul transmission contract through the Italy-Greece Interconnector)
- Azeri or other Caspian gas (or a mix of Caspian and Russian gas) via a direct offtake from Nabucco in Bulgaria or Romania
- Azeri or other Caspian gas via a direct offtake from a point on the pan-European pipeline near Belgrade
- Russian gas through expansion of the existing corridor via Ukraine and Hungary and through northern Serbia to an entry point near Belgrade
- Russian gas from an offtake point on the Blue Line near Nis or Belgrade
- Russian gas from the Nord branch of Gazprom's proposed South Stream project via Romania to an entry point near Belgrade, via the Bulgarian ring to an entry point near Nis, or from the Sud branch of Gazprom's proposed South Steam project via Bulgaria to an entry point near Nis, Skopje, or Tirana.

Institutional and Regulatory Framework to Realize the Regional Ring Concept

The EC Treaty provides the blueprint for implementing the institutional and regulatory framework in each market. It would be very surprising if such implementation were not a prerequisite to qualify for international financial institution and donor funding of new gas infrastructure and commercial financing. Drafting and enacting a gas law and developing the associated secondary legislation, regulations, and technical rules take time. To avoid unnecessary delays to increased gasification in Southeast Europe, therefore, each government should move to implement fully the provisions of the EC Treaty within the legal system of its market. This applies even in markets where currently there is no natural gas industry.

The prospects of actual gas infrastructure development, based around a clear regional development vision to bring gas deep into currently ungasified markets and ungasified parts of other markets, should serve as a major incentive to implementation of the requirements of the EC Treaty to which the governments of the SEE markets are signatories.

Roles of Public and Private Sector Players in Realizing the Gasification Vision

Gas transmission infrastructure is essential, and can play a vital catalyzing role in increasing gasification in the SEE markets. Development of regional transmission infrastructure fits well within the aims and objectives of the Stability Pact. In the energy sector, the EC Treaty is an important part of the Stability Pact. But without physical transmission infrastructure to allow gas to be delivered to the markets of Southeast Europe, even the full implementation of the requirements of the EC Treaty will not bring any tangible benefits to the people in markets currently unserved by gas.

Therefore, there is a major potential role for public financing of transmission to kick-start the increased gasification of Southeast Europe. Institutions that would be expected to take an interest in financing gas transmission in the region include the World Bank, KfW Entwicklungsbank, the European Bank for Reconstruction and Development, the European Investment Bank, and the European Union. Furthermore, these international institutions and donors are in the best positions to manage the country risk with the involvement of such organizations as the Multilateral Investment Guarantee Agency.

Power plants clearly will be required to provide the large, up-front, high load factor demands that are necessary to make investments in transmission economical and bankable. The updated GIS shows economic potential for several thousand megawatts of gas-fired combined-cycle plants in the region, under some likely scenarios in the next few years. Many private sector generation companies are highly experienced in the development of such plants, and there are well-established business models for independent power plants. This is an area suitable for private financing, possibly with some financial involvement of such institutions as the European Bank for Reconstruction and Development (which can lend or take an equity position in such investments) and the International Finance Corporation (the private sector arm of the World Bank).

Gas distribution infrastructure can be developed only when the transmission infrastructure is in place. Distribution-connected customers are far more numerous than are transmission-connected customers (such as power stations); and individually, they are much smaller. Their load tends to build up more gradually over time, as gas penetrates new markets. Distribution is very suitable for private sector investment, as a number of countries have shown. But distribution development needs a suitable regulatory model, typically involving concessions to provide investors with confidence that they can earn a return on their up-front capital investments. Regulatory models exist for concession licenses (three countries in the region have private distribution licensees/concessionaires) designed to provide developers with a financial incentive actually to invest in the distribution network and connect new customers at an agreed rate over time. Leveraging private sector financing in those parts of the system where the private sector is best able to contribute will enable scarce public sector financing, together with donor support, to be focused on the remaining areas.

APPENDIX A

FUTURE RUSSIAN GAS PRICES

The Russian Federation already is a supplier of natural gas to Southeast Europe (SEE) markets, as illustrated in table A.1. However, much of the supply is under rolling one-year contracts, which do not provide a basis for the markets to make significant investment in additional gas infrastructure. This appendix

- reviews the factors that are likely to determine the price at which Russia may agree to supply natural gas to Southeast Europe under a long-term contract
- discusses some of the security-of-supply issues that will affect prices and that SEE markets should consider
- proposes a price basis for potential investors in gas infrastructure in the SEE region to use when evaluating possible investments.

Context

To begin, it is necessary to consider the current situation regarding Russian gas supply to Europe to provide a context for the discussion and initial conclusions in this report. At the time of writing, the future volume and price of Russian gas exports are major concerns of many European policy makers, analysts, and gas industry managers. European Union (EU) countries are becoming increasingly concerned about the ability of Russia to sustain its current volumes of natural gas exports while supplying contracted new volumes via the cross-Baltic North-European Gas Pipeline (NEGP). This view is reinforced by recent presentations by Lukoil and others.

Table A.1   Russia Gas Supply to SEE Markets

Market	Imports from Russia (Bcm/y)	Notes
Albania	0	None
Bosnia and Herzegovina	0.38	None
Bulgaria	3.20	Includes transit fee gas
Croatia	1.13	None
Kosovo	0	None
Macedonia, FYR	0.08	None
Montenegro	0	None
Romania	5.70	Includes transit fee gas
Serbia	2.15	Includes Montenegro
Total (approximate)	12.50	None

Sources: BP 2005; EIA 2003; Economic Consulting Associates' research.
Note: SEE = Southeast Europe.

The traditional European view of Russian gas exports is this: Exports = Production + Imports – Internal consumption. Thus, the European gas industry and European politicians increasingly are looking for reassurance from Gazprom and the government of Russia to demonstrate that both internal demand and export volumes can be met, before committing to higher prices for extending existing Russian gas supply contracts.

The major uncertainties involve the level of gas consumption in the internal Russian market and how it will change over time. In June 2006, Anatoly Chubais, head of the state-controlled electricity utility RAO UESR, called for an increase in internal gas prices and, hence, gas supply to the Russian market to avoid electricity shortages in coming years. Chubais's statements have achieved their first objective in that energy supply to the internal Russian market now seems to be given much more attention than before.

During the first week of September 2006, Prime Minister Mikhail Fradkov signed a decree setting up an experimental domestic gas exchange for the country's independent gas producers and the export monopoly Gazprom to sell gas at unregulated prices. As Gazprom explains it,

> Gazprom and independent producers have been selling gas at the Mezhregiongaz electronic trading platform (ETP) since November

2006, in compliance with the Russian Government Decree "On Experimental Gas Sales via the Electronic Trading Platform" and the Russian Industry and Energy Ministry Order "On Experimental Gas Trading via the Electronic Platform."

As part of the experiment Gazprom was entitled to sell up to 5 billion cubic meters of gas at free prices. Independent producers could sell the same amount of gas at free prices.

In 2008 the amount of gas approved for ETP was increased to 7.5 billion cubic meters for each party. Based on the 2008 results a total of 6.1 billion cubic meters of natural gas was marketed at the Mezhregiongaz ETP, including 3.1 billion cubic meters by Gazprom and 3 billion cubic meters by independent producers. The bulk of the gas (86 per cent) was purchased by electric power generating companies. (Gazprom, http://www.gazprom.com/marketing/russia/)

Also during the first week of September 2006, Minister for Economic Development and Trade German Gref called for the introduction of transparent conditions for nonstate natural gas producers to gain access to the national pipeline system.

That call was followed closely by reports that Gazprom will have to disclose to independent producers the available capacity in its network, according to a draft resolution from the Federal Antimonopoly Service. The reported rules require Gazprom to declare its own capacity when calculating spare capacity in the system, and they require independent producers to adopt a nomination procedure.

Later in September 2006, the Russian government declared that internal gas prices for commercial consumers would have to increase significantly, but increases for the population and communal enterprises would be moderate.

The above developments suggest that a process of major change in the Russian gas market has begun. Although the process is still at an early stage, this process could follow the same path toward regulated third-party access to gas transmission pipelines as that taken in the EU. However, the internal Russian energy market has a number of distortions that prevent energy prices to consumers moving in direct relationship with costs.

Also, on July 31, 2006, President Vladimir Putin signed into force a new law that enshrined Gazprom's monopoly over gas exports from Russia.

Projections of Russian gas export prices and volumes need to be seen against the background described above.

Figure A.1 Gas Supply Price Factors

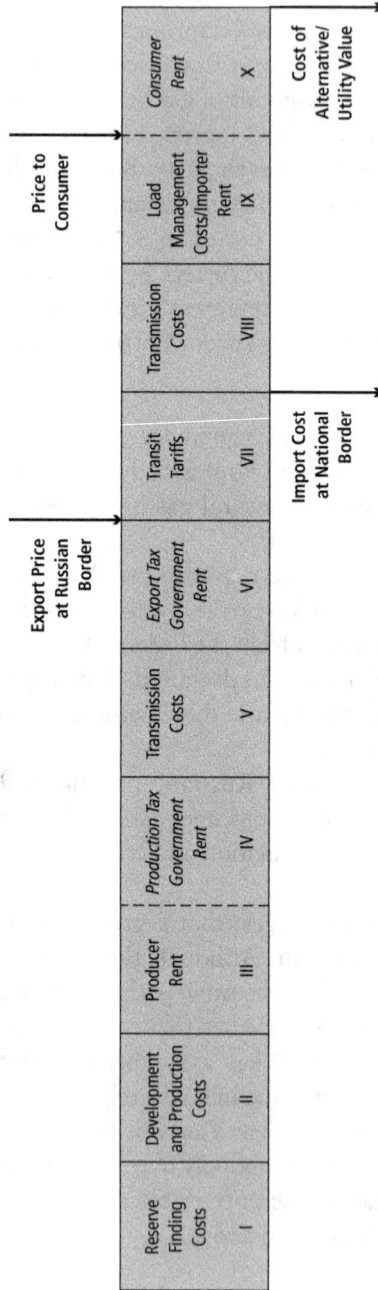

Reserve Finding Costs	Development and Production Costs	Producer Rent	Production Tax Government Rent	Transmission Costs	Export Tax Government Rent	Transit Tariffs	Transmission Costs	Load Management Costs/Importer Rent	Consumer Rent
I	II	III	IV	V	VI	VII	VIII	IX	X

Export Price at Russian Border

Price to Consumer

Import Cost at National Border

Cost of Alternative/ Utility Value

Source: Authors' illustration.
Note: Roman numerals indicate steps in the value chain.

Key Gas Price Factors

In considering future gas prices, each element in the gas supply chain is considered separately, as shown in figure A.1.

Reserve-Finding Costs

The reserves legacy "inherited" by the Russian gas industry is such that finding costs will be close to zero for some years. In 2003, the reserves-to-production ratio for the Urals Federal District (which includes West Siberia, Yamal-Nenets, and the Yamal Peninsula) was more than 70 years, as illustrated in table A.2.

Current projections of natural gas production from this region are set out in table 3.28. However, independent producers clearly have the ability to develop and produce much greater volumes of natural gas—given a price incentive and access to Gazprom's transmission system.

Development and Production Costs

Estimates of long-run marginal cost (LRMC) in Russian gas production have been made on the basis of available project-by-project data. The projected costs include value added tax on capital expenditure, because of the difficulties of recovering it; and they reflect a 12 percent real rate of return on investment. Generally, development in Russia is becoming ever more expensive. Because the commissioning dates for specific gas fields are uncertain, the LRMC production cost information has been grouped by categories of fields, location, and geology. Table 3.28 shows future peak gas production in Russia with an estimated cost.

Producer Rent

As noted above, the LRMC production costs in table 3.28 reflect a 12 percent real rate of return on investment, which is considered to be the required

Table A.2   Urals Federal District Reserves/Production Ratio, 2003

Producer	Reserves (Bcm)	Production (Bcm/y)	Reserves/ Production ratio (years)
Gazprom	27,665	490	56.5
Independent producers	12,575	58	216.8
Total	40,240	548	73.4

Source: Energywise Consultants.
Note: Bcm/y = billion cubic meters per year.

rate of return on all Gazprom's investments. Independent producers, such as Novatek and Itera, may hope for a higher rate of return, but they settle for this rate. The Russian oil companies, however, are unlikely to settle, in the first instance, for a 12 percent real rate of return on their investment in gas production when they have the alternative of investing in oil production. Also, the Russian oil companies increasingly are investing outside Russia, and may well consider they already have enough Russian government risk.

Nonetheless, it seems likely that the Russian government will be able to persuade the Russian oil companies to produce and deliver more gas to the internal market in return for granting some form of access to Gazprom's pipelines.

It is interesting to note that Ministry of Industry and Energy representatives have claimed that the level of independent (non-Gazprom) production would make no difference to the level of gas exports.

Production Tax—Government Rent

The mineral production tax (NDPI), introduced in 2002, replaced all previous special taxes in gas production and gas excise tax. The NDPI rate for gas initially was defined ad valorem (16 percent, or approximately Rub 23.4 per thousand cubic meters [Mcm]). Since January 1, 2004, however, natural gas extraction also has been taxed at a fixed rate per unit of output. The initial rate of Rub 107/Mcm represented a roughly fivefold increase on the old ad valorem rate, and the rate later was increased to Rub 147/Mcm of produced gas. A zero-rate NDPI applies to subsurface sites located in eastern Siberia, the Nenets district, on the Yamal peninsula, on the continental shelf, and in the Azov and Caspian seas.

Although no major changes in gas taxation policies are under discussion in the Russian government or legislative institutions, some changes are anticipated. First, the NDPI rate is likely to increase for the following reasons:

- A rate set as a fixed value with no indexation naturally needs some adjustment, even if there are no price increases.
- By 2005, gas prices in the Russian market reached a level at which domestic gas sales stopped being loss generating for the main supplier. By 2007, new investments were the only element of Gazprom's costs still covered by Gazprom export revenues. Continued gas price increases in the domestic market mean that the range of the gas price rent available to be captured by the state is likely to expand.
- In 2009, the Ministry of Finance was reported to be proposing an increase in the rate for 2010.

Second, it may well be that the single rate of the NDPI tax is replaced with a rate that varies for different gas fields, along the lines introduced for oil fields. It seems likely that such arrangements for gas fields will be introduced for these reasons:

- Some of the largest gas fields reached a high degree of depletion, thus objectively causing their costs to rise.
- Gas production operations move to more difficult/marginal regions, thus requiring additional costs to set up infrastructure.
- There is a rising quantity of objects that will be developed as self-standing investment projects with the assistance of external investors, thus excluding any possibility for cross-subsidies.
- The zero-rate NDPI on the areas bearing a higher cost of gas already recognizes the principle and establishes the precedent for differentiated tax rates.

Existing opinions on this issue reflect the common stance that it would be feasible to apply the oil industry differentiation model to gas fields. This suggests that the current single NDPI rate would act as a maximum applicable rate, and tax allowances in the form of reduction factors would be used for marginal fields. In other words, the presently discussed idea for the NDPI tax to be applied at various rates would not result in further gas price increases.

Transmission Tariffs

It seems likely that Russia will retain a two-tier system of transmission tariffs, with exports being priced at the LRMC of a new transmission pipeline and the internal market benefiting from depreciated long-installed pipelines. However, the need to rehabilitate and expand the capacity of the network means that the cost differential will not be so great—although this may not be reflected in tariffs.

Export gas transmission from Nadym-Pur-Taz fields westward is not associated mainly with the construction of new export pipelines; rather, it requires some costs for the relevant gas fields to get connected to the existing transmission system.

Pipeline construction costs on the Yamal Peninsula are expected to be high, equivalent to $2.50/Mcm per 100 kilometers on the basis of a 12 percent real rate of return. For much of the route to Russia's western border, however, $1.00/Mcm per 100 kilometers traditionally has been used as the cost of new transmission for planning purposes—although costs in Russia are increasing all the time as steel prices increase and buoyant demand enables higher margins to be achieved.

Also, as the price of gas in the destination market increases, so does the cost of the gas consumed en route. That is why there is significant interest in improving the efficiency of Russia's gas transmission compressors.

Although they are subject to all of the factors discussed above, total gas transportation costs to Russia's western border have been estimated as follows:

- from the Urengoi complex (3,700 kilometers), on a "new pipeline" basis: approximately $37/Mcm
- from the Yamal Peninsula to Russia's western border (Torzhok): $45–$50/Mcm.

Export Tax—Government Rent

Export customs duty ("export tax") is the fundamental instrument by which the government of Russia raises revenue from gas exports and differentiates between export gas prices and those in the internal market. Since January 1, 2004, the rate has been set at 30 percent of the customs gas price and, as far as is known, there are no plans to change this rate. However, some changes can be anticipated. A general stance in the state regulation of the Russian gas sector, as emphasized by then-President Putin on several occasions, is and will continue to be aimed in the future at providing protective measures for the national economy and domestic market against volatility in international prices. This means that the export customs duty is likely to stay in use as a regulator of domestic market prices and as an arrangement to capture the price rent of gas. However, it also may mean that the rates of the customs duty will vary, depending on the changing relationship between international and domestic market prices.

A key consideration is the difference in the regulatory approach to rates of the customs duty between natural gas and crude oil. According to the federal law "On Customs Tariff," Russian government resolutions are required to set the list of export commodities that are subject to collection of the customs duty and the rates of the duty. In addition, that law contains a procedure for calculating the rate of customs duty for crude oil, which sets a scale of maximum rates to be applied. As a result, the government can deviate only downward from this scale. Regarding natural gas, however, the law provides no caps or floors, leaving it to the government to set the rate of duty to be applied.

It has been suggested that "discretionary discounts" may be available for gas-importing countries that support Russia's aims and objectives in international forums. Although this is a difficult area to predict, there have been some tendencies for the "political" element in gas prices to diminish.

Changes in the government pricing policies implemented by Gazprom show that, in recent years, there has been a gradual transition to applying "normal" pricing formulas in the relationships with all countries importing Russian gas supplies. We believe such policy changes are the result of transitional period necessities, whereas any difference in specific price formulas can be explained by the presence or lack of extra benefits for Gazprom activities in a given market of the importing country.

Transit Tariffs

Gas transit issues between Russia and the Ukraine during the winter of 2005/06 dramatically raised concerns about natural gas security-of-supply issues in Western and Central European countries.

On January 4, 2006, Russia and the Ukraine reached an agreement to end their dispute. A five-year contract was signed, although with gas prices set only for the next six months. In the deal Gazprom "secured the hefty price hikes it had been demanding, raising the cost for its supply" to $230/Mcm to the Russian-Swiss company RosUkrEnergo. After mixing Russian gas with a two-thirds quantity of cheaper supplies from Central Asia, RosUkrEnergo resold it to Ukraine at a price of $95/Mcm. The parties also agreed to raise the tariff for transit from $1.0937 to $1.6000/Mcm per 100 kilometers—a price fixed to 2010 and to be paid in cash.

Elsewhere, Gazprom has negotiated transit tariffs individually with countries. However, the following have been reported widely:

- The "European" gas transmission tariff is $2.00-$2.50/Mcm per 100 kilometers.
- In 2003, Gazprom was paying Moldova a gas transit tariff of $2.50/Mcm per 100 kilometers.
- In 2004, Gazprom was paying $2.34/Mcm per 100 kilometers in Poland, when it owned an interest in the pipeline.

Even with the recent significant increase in the Ukraine's tariff rate, the rate remains less than those of other countries. At the same time, Ukraine has received Russian gas imports at prices that are lower than European market-parity prices.

With the cross-Black Sea Blue Stream pipeline, Gazprom has an alternative route to SEE markets, and it has been said to be interested in participating in the Nabucco pipeline. Nabucco Gas Pipeline International is amenable to 20–30 percent of the Nabucco capacity being used to deliver Russian gas. The delivery point inevitably will affect the total transit cost.

Table A.3   Transit Costs

Transit	Approximate distance (km)	Transit cost over total distance (2006 $/Mcm)
Ukraine/Moldova	1,000	25.00
Romania/Bulgaria	500	12.50
Total	1,500	37.50

Source: Authors' compilation.
Note: km = kilometers; Mcm = thousand cubic meters.

Ultimately, although the cost of transit must be recovered through the price paid for importing gas from Russia, SEE gas markets will pay a delivered price, which may be based on a specified nominal route. However, it will be for Gazprom to worry about the complexities of the actual route and the way in which overall transit costs affect overall gas export netbacks.

Nonetheless, it can be assumed that Gazprom will need to recover something like $2.50/Mcm per 100 kilometers in the delivered price of natural gas. This is shown in table A.3.

Transmission Costs

It can be assumed that transmission costs within the purchasing country will be set in accordance with the prevailing regulatory framework.

Load Management Costs

Load management is likely to become increasingly complex as consumers become more concerned about security-of-supply issues and, therefore, willing to pay for some "insurance" against supply interruption resulting from increased development and use of both physical and financial instruments.

In response to the concerns raised by the dispute with the Ukraine, Gazprom is known to have expressed interest in developing gas storage facilities in or adjacent to the markets it supplies to provide a more complete gas supply "service."

Security-of-Supply Considerations

As noted above, the European gas industry is becoming increasingly concerned about Russia's ability to sustain export volumes as internal Russian gas demand increases. Imperfections in the internal Russian energy market currently do not provide incentives for the necessary investment in energy efficiency (particularly in electricity and heat generation) or in gas development for the internal market.

Part of the issue is perception. To Western European eyes, it would be unthinkable for the Russian government to maintain gas exports to Europe while reducing gas deliveries to its internal market. However, as former German Chancellor Gerhard Schroder noted at the ceremony to start construction of the NEGP, "Russia has always met its contractual gas supply obligations to Europe." Russian government representatives state the same: "Export contracts will be fulfilled, with the internal market balancing overall supply with demand."

As table A.4 shows, a number of existing gas export contracts are due to expire over the next 10 years. Thus, there is an ongoing process by which importers and Gazprom are extending existing gas supply contracts in return for higher prices earlier. It has been reported that both E.ON Ruhrgas and Gaz de France recently have extended their Russian gas supply contracts; and there are some indications of a "scramble" by existing importers to lock in long-term gas supplies in return for higher prices now.

Export Gas Price Indexation

Historically, prices for natural gas delivered under long-term contracts to Western and Central Europe are indexed to a formula that uses a moving average of gas oil and fuel oil prices in Northwestern Europe. As a result, the average export gas price correlates with the price of these refined oil products, although with some lags because of the moving average. The lag typically is 45–90 days (based on a time base for the moving average of 90–180 days).

Although Gazprom has stressed the confidentiality of its gas export contracts, the indexes generally are thought to be based on 30 percent gas oil and 70 percent fuel oil (according to the nearest reference market). For Southern Europe, that market is Mediterranean cargoes. The 70 percent fuel oil link may be divided equally between light and heavy fuel oils.

The price of gas oil rose 1.97 times in 2000–05, and the price of fuel oil increased 1.65 times over the same period; those increases caused the average export gas price to grow 1.76 times (see table A.5 and figure A.2).

The formula applies to the indexation, whereas the base price traditionally has been the result of negotiation and incorporation of many different factors. Nonetheless, there is every indication that prices are being recalibrated to a base reflecting 30 percent gas oil and 70 percent fuel oil. Furthermore, at current prices, this is very close to the EU projection of a 1.3 ratio for crude oil to natural gas, as shown in table A.6.

Table A.4   Known Long-Term Russian Gas Contracts with Europe

Importing country	Contracting party	Maximum amount (Bcm/y)	Contract period begins	Contract period ends	Notes	Amount contracted for, 2005 (Bcm/y)	Amount contracted for, 2010 (Bcm/y)	Amount contracted for, 2015 (Bcm/y)	Amount contracted for, 2020 (Bcm/y)	Amount contracted for, 2025 (Bcm/y)	Amount contracted for, 2030 (Bcm/y)	Comments
Austria	OMV	6.50	1984	2024/25	None	6.50	6.50	6.50	6.50	6.50	n.a.	None
Bulgaria	Bulgargaz	3.00	2005	2010	None	3.00	3.00	n.a.	n.a.	n.a.	n.a.	None
Czech Rep.	Unknown	9.00	1998/99	2015/16	None	9.00	9.00	9.00	n.a.	n.a.	n.a.	None
Denmark	DONG Energy	1.00	2011	2031	NEGP	n.a.	n.a.	1.00	1.00	1.00	1.00	None
Finland	Gasum	8.10	Unknown	2025	Extended	5.10	5.10	6.10	6.70	6.30	n.a.	Assumed = Demand
France	GDF Suez	8.00	Unknown	2015/16	None	8.00	8.00	8.00	n.a.	n.a.	n.a.	None
France	GDF Suez	2.50	Unknown	2012/13	None	2.50	2.50	n.a.	n.a.	n.a.	n.a.	None
France	GDF Suez	1.50	Unknown	2012/13	None	1.50	1.50	n.a.	n.a.	n.a.	n.a.	None
Germany	E.ON Ruhrgas	13.00	Unknown	2015/16	None	13.00	13.00	13.00	n.a.	n.a.	n.a.	None
Germany	WINGAS	13.50	1998	2030	None	13.50	13.50	13.50	13.50	13.50	13.50	None
Germany	Verbundnetz Gas	12.00	Unknown	2017/18	None	12.00	12.00	12.00	n.a.	n.a.	n.a.	None
Germany	E.ON Ruhrgas	9.00	2011	2036	NEGP	n.a.	n.a.	9.00	9.00	9.00	9.00	None
Germany	WINGAS	9.00	2011	2036	NEGP	n.a.	n.a.	9.00	9.00	9.00	9.00	None
Any country	Gazprom	8.00	2011	2036	NEGP	n.a.	n.a.	8.00	8.00	8.00	8.00	None
Greece	DEPA	2.24	Unknown	2013/14	None	2.24	2.24	n.a.	n.a.	n.a.	n.a.	None
Hungary	MOL	11.00	1996/97	2015/16	None	11.00	11.00	11.00	n.a.	n.a.	n.a.	None

Importing country	Contracting party	Maximum amount (Bcm/y)	Contract period begins	Contract period ends	Notes	Amount contracted for, 2005 (Bcm/y)	Amount contracted for, 2010 (Bcm/y)	Amount contracted for, 2015 (Bcm/y)	Amount contracted for, 2020 (Bcm/y)	Amount contracted for, 2025 (Bcm/y)	Amount contracted for, 2030 (Bcm/y)	Comments
Hungary	GDF Suez	0.40	1996/97	2015/16	None	0.40	0.40	0.40	n.a.	n.a.	n.a.	None
Italy	Snam	7.40	1996/97	2027	Recently extended	7.40	7.40	7.40	7.40	7.40	n.a.	None
Italy	Snam	8.00	1998/99	2027	Recently extended	8.00	8.00	8.00	8.00	8.00	n.a.	None
Italy	Snam	5.50	Unknown	2027	Recently extended	5.50	5.50	5.50	5.50	5.50	n.a.	None
Italy	Unknown	5.60	2008/09	2018/19	None	5.60	5.60	5.60	n.a.	n.a.	n.a.	None
Italy	Edison	2.00	2000	2020	None	2.00	2.00	2.00	2.00	n.a.	n.a.	None
Italy	Enel	3.00	2005/06	2025	None	3.00	3.00	3.00	3.00	3.00	n.a.	None
Netherlands	Gasunie	4.00	2001/02	2015/16	None	4.00	4.00	4.00	n.a.	n.a.	n.a.	None
Poland	Polish Oil and Gas Co.	12.50	1996	2021	None	12.50	12.50	12.50	12.50	n.a.	n.a.	None
Romania	Romgaz	7.50	2005	2010	None	7.50	7.50	n.a.	n.a.	n.a.	n.a.	None
Slovak Rep.	SPP	9.00	1997/98	2008/09	None	9.00	n.a.	n.a.	n.a.	n.a.	n.a.	None
Slovenia	Geoplin	0.70	1992/93	2015	Extended	0.70	0.70	0.70	n.a.	n.a.	n.a.	None
Estonia	EESTI Gaas	1.70	2000	2005	None	1.20	n.a.	n.a.	n.a.	n.a.	n.a.	Assumed = Demand

(continued on next page)

Table A.4 Known Long-Term Russian Gas Contracts with Europe *(Continued)*

Importing country	Contracting party	Maximum amount (Bcm/y)	Contract period begins	Contract period ends	Notes	Amount contracted for, 2005 (Bcm/y)	Amount contracted for, 2010 (Bcm/y)	Amount contracted for, 2015 (Bcm/y)	Amount contracted for, 2020 (Bcm/y)	Amount contracted for, 2025 (Bcm/y)	Amount contracted for, 2030 (Bcm/y)	Comments
Latvia	Latvijas Gaze	3.40	Unknown	2015	None	2.40	2.40	2.90	n.a.	n.a.	n.a.	Assumed = Demand
Lithuania	Lietuvos Dujos	6.20	Unknown	2015	None	4.50	4.50	5.10	n.a.	n.a.	n.a.	Assumed = Demand
Total EU-25		194.24	n.a.	n.a.	None	161.04	150.84	163.20	92.10	77.20	40.50	None
Croatia	INA	1.20	Unknown	2010	None	1.20	1.20	n.a.	n.a.	n.a.	n.a.	None
Croatia	INA	1.50	2010	2030	None	n.a.	1.50	1.50	1.50	1.50	1.50	Requested by INA
Serbia	Srbijagas	2.12	2005	2010	None	2.12	2.12	n.a.	n.a.	n.a.	n.a.	None
Bosnia and Herzegovina	BH-Gas	0.38	2005	2010	None	0.38	0.38	n.a.	n.a.	n.a.	n.a.	None
+ Non-EU SEE markets		199.44	n.a.	n.a.	None	164.74	156.04	164.70	93.60	78.70	42.00	None

Source: Authors' compilation.

Note: Bcm/y = billion cubic meters per year; EU = European Union; n.a. = not applicable; NEGP = North-European Gas Pipeline; SEE = Southeast Europe.

Table A.5   European Oil Product Prices and Russian Gas Export Gas Prices, 2000–05

Fuel	2000	2001	2002	2003	2004	2005
Gas oil[a] *($/bbl)*	34.4	29.2	27.8	34.0	46.8	67.7
Fuel oil[a] *($/bbl)*	23.7	18.5	21.8	25.8	25.0	39.2
Natural gas (average price)[b] *($/Mcm)*	85.9	101.0	85.7	106.0	109.0	151.1
Natural gas (for Europe)[c] *($/Mcm)*	101.9	120.2	99.0	124.3	126.2	181.3

Sources: International Energy Agency's *Oil Market Report;* Russian State Customs Committee, Gazprom; Russian State Statistics Committee; Energywise Consultants.
Note: bbl = barrel; Mcm = thousand cubic meters.
a. Prices for gas oil and fuel oil (sulfur content up to 1 percent), according to the International Energy Agency's *Oil Market Report,* at Rotterdam.
b. Average price for Russian gas exports, according to Russian State Customs Committee.
c. Average price for gas exported to countries that are not members of the Commonwealth of Independent States, estimated on the basis of data from the Russian State Customs Committee, Gazprom, and the Russian State Statistics Committee.

Figure A.2   European Oil Product Prices and Russian Export Gas Prices, 2000–05

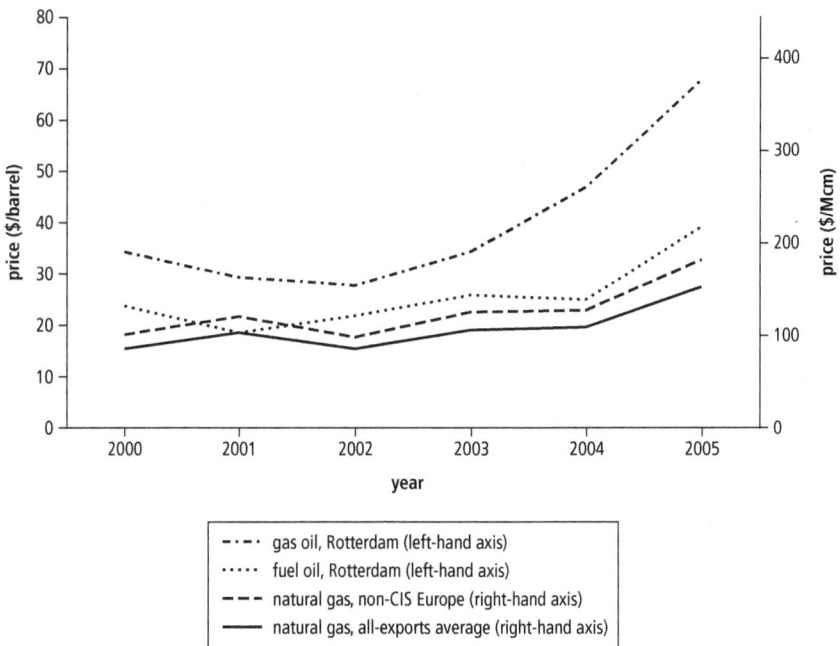

Source: Energywise Consultants.
Note: CIS = Commonwealth of Independent States; Mcm = thousand cubic meters.

Table A.6　Crude Oil and Petroleum Product Prices, September 29, 2006

		MJ/kg NCV	MJ/kg NCV
Crude oil ($/bbl)	63.00		
Barrels per tonne	7.5		
Crude oil ($/tonne)	472.50	41.88	19.79
Gas oil ($/tonne)	550.00	42.63	23.45
Fuel oil ($/tonne)	290.00	40.38	11.71
Gas oil (%)		30	7.03
Fuel oil (%)		70	8.20
Total gas price			15.23
Oil/gas price ratio			1.30

Source: Authors' compilation.
Note: bbl = barrel; MJ/kg = megajoules per kilogram; NCV = net calorific value.

The Link between Oil and Gas Prices

There has been a view in Europe that "with increasing gas-to-gas competition, gas prices are decoupled from oil prices in the second part of the
projection period as the difference between both prices becomes larger."[1]
However, this view seems less realistic following the security-of-supply concerns raised by the Russia/Ukraine gas transit dispute that occurred from
December 2005 to January 2006, and the similar but larger-scale dispute
of December 2008 to January 2009; and with growing experience of the
EU Emission Trading System now quantifying the environmental benefits of
natural gas over other fossil fuels.

For Russia, retaining the link with oil products has two advantages:

1. It does not require any change or rethinking of its traditional contractual
   approach.
2. Remembering how Ruhrgas used to boast about how it captured rent by
   pricing its gas to consumers just below their gas oil opportunity cost, Russia effectively can do the same thing now.

However, recognizing that gas prices increasingly incorporate an environmental premium (whereas oil markets well may continue to be volatile), the
Russian government has indicated a wish for a floor on the price of natural

---

[1] Quoted from the 2005 EU scenario.

gas exports, based on crude oil or petroleum product prices. Although this floor is subject to negotiation, indications are that Russia will not agree to any floor below the equivalent of $50 a barrel of crude oil.

That expectation also would be consistent with the minority (but growing) view that natural gas prices will be decoupled from oil prices but will rise relative to oil prices as a result of the increasing environmental premium of gas over oil products.

LIQUEFIED NATURAL GAS SOURCES OF INTEREST

Egypt

Egypt has 1.89 trillion cubic meters (Tcm) (66.7 trillion cubic feet [tcf]) of proven reserves, and it has probable reserves of 3.4 Tcm (120 tcf) (Norton Rose 2006).

Presently, there are two liquefied natural gas (LNG) schemes in Egypt (map B.1):

1. ELNG[1] owns and operates the LNG plant at Idku. The LNG project operates on a tolling basis. The LNG from train 2 had been destined to go to Brindisi, Italy; but because that terminal is unlikely to go forward, the LNG will go initially to Lake Charles in the United States. This means that the sellers have to take full U.S. price risk.
2. Damietta is operated by SEGAS.[2] All of train 1 is destined for European markets, including a new French terminal at Fos Cavaou.

There are several possibilities for additional Egyptian gas to supply LNG export terminals, including BP's Ruby 2 field and RWE A's discovery at Raven.

---

[1] ELNG involves the BG Group, Petronas, the Egyptian Natural Gas Holding Company, the Egyptian General Petroleum Corporation, and GDF Suez

[2] SEGAS is 80 percent owned by Union Fenosa Gas (a joint venture between Union Fenosa and ENI), with the Egyptian Natural Gas Holding Company and the Egyptian General Petroleum Corporation each holding 10 percent stakes.

Map B.1   Egyptian LNG

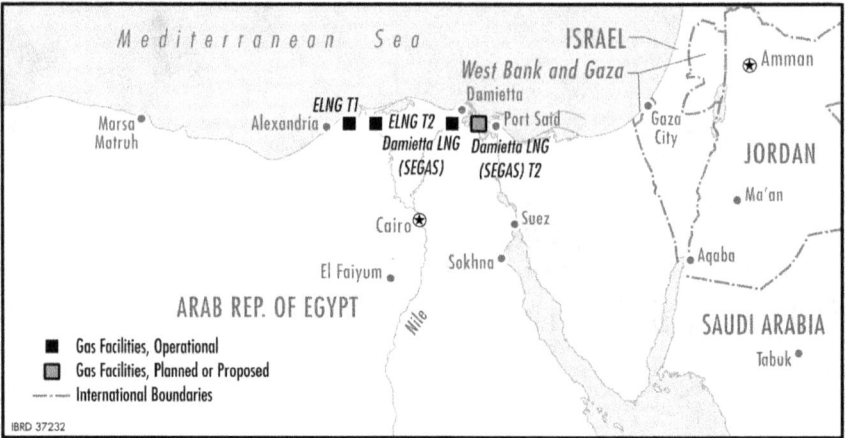

Sources: World Bank, compiled with reference to Norton Rose Global Gas, *LNG Export Report,* December 2006.
Note: LNG = liquefied natural gas.

In the LNG business, RWE corporately is attempting to build a position akin to that of Union Fenosa. However, an independent third LNG project is unlikely to move ahead quickly. Recent statements from the Egyptian government suggest that it currently is looking to support only two major LNG streams.

Libya

Libya has estimated proven reserves of 1.49 billion cubic meters (Bcm) (52.6 tcf). Libyan experts believe the reserves could be as high as 2.8 Tcm because much of the territory remains unexplored. The government is hoping to develop two further greenfield LNG schemes (map B.2) (involving Shell and BP) and to extend the export of piped gas (Norton Rose 2006).

Although the country began exporting LNG in 1971, there still is only one operating plant (at Marsa El Brega). This plant was built in the 1960s by Exxon. Although the three trains have a combined annual capacity of 2.3 Mt (megatonnes), the plant is operating at only 25–30 percent of capacity because of technical limitations. Shell issued tenders in 2006 for a major three-year overhaul and possible expansion to 3.2 Mt a year in phase 2. LNG currently is sold to Enagas in Spain.

BP is reported to have entered into a memorandum of understanding to explore and produce gas' and if this is successful, the gas would be exported as LNG to Europe, the United States, or both.

Map B.2   Libyan LNG

Sources: World Bank, compiled with reference to Norton Rose Global Gas, *LNG Export Report,* December 2006.
Note: LNG = liquefied natural gas.

Algeria

Algeria has proven reserves of 4.58 Tcm (161.7 tcf) (Norton Rose 2006). Skikda was the world's first LNG terminal (map B.3), starting up in 1964. Three of the six trains were destroyed in an explosion in 2004, and the remaining trains were affected. The three destroyed trains will be replaced by one large train. The engineering procurement and construction contract was awarded in March 2007, and work began in July of that year. Originally planned to be in operation by 2009, in March 2009 (with construction 20 percent complete and procurement 70 percent completed), the plant was expected to be in operation by 2013. There are three other plants at Arzew (with annual capacities of 7.8 Mt, 8.8 Mt, and 4.0 Mt).

Qatar

An alternative to obtaining LNG supplies from North Africa might be the to getting them from he Middle East, most likely Qatar (map B.4). Qatar has estimated proven natural gas reserves of 25.78 Tcm (910.1 tcf). It is the third-largest LNG exporter in the world, with 10 percent of the world's known gas reserves.

There are two LNG plants in operation—Qatargas and Rasgas—both supplied with gas from the country's north field (the world's largest non-associated gas field).

Map B.3 Algerian LNG

Sources: World Bank, compiled with reference to Norton Rose Global Gas, *LNG Export Report*, December 2006.
Note: LNG = liquefied natural gas.

There are several different major projects in Qatar:

- Qatargas I (Qatar Petroleum, Total, ExxonMobil, Marubeni, and Mitsui) has a "debottlenecked," annual capacity of 9.5 Mt.
- The $12.8 billion Qatargas II project (Qatar Petroleum, ExxonMobil, and Total) is expected to deliver its first cargoes in 2008 to Northern Europe, the United Kingdom, and the United States. The annual capacity is 15.6 Mt.
- Qatargas III (Qatar Petroleum and ConocoPhillips) is due to start up in 2008/09, supplying as much as 7.8 Mt a year to the Gulf of Mexico.
- Qatargas IV (Qatar Petroleum and Shell) is due to start up in 2010/12, supplying 5 Mt a year to Europe and North America.
- Rasgas (Qatar Petroleum, ExxonMobil, KORAS, Itochu, and LNG Japan Corporation) has an annual capacity of 6.6 Mt and supplies LNG to Kogas, Japan.
- Rasgas trains 3 and 4 (known as Rasgas II) (Qatar Petroleum and Exxon-Mobil) have a total annual capacity of 9.4 Mt and supply LNG to Edison (Italy), Endesa (Spain), and Petronet (India).
- Rasgas train 5 (also called Rasgas II) is a third train with an annual capacity of 4.7 Mt, and it supplies Taiwan (China), Distrigas (Belgium), and Endesa (Spain).

Map B.4   Qatar LNG

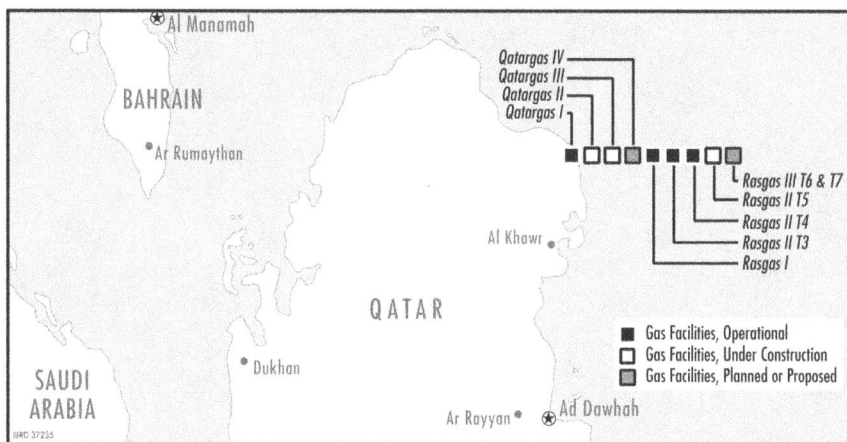

Sources: World Bank, compiled with reference to Norton Rose Global Gas, *LNG Export Report,* December 2006.
Note: LNG = liquefied natural gas.

Qatar also has enormous further potential to develop gas for export. In fact, the growth in exports has been so rapid that the authorities imposed a temporary moratorium on further major development until 2008. This is affecting both LNG and GTL. This is unlikely to mark a major change in development policy. To date, Qatar has not indulged in much short-term switching of LNG supply to take advantage of arbitrage opportunities; but, recently, it announced that it would divert to the United States a significant volume of supply from Qatargas III from the second phase of the South Hook terminal in the United Kingdom—presumably because it felt that netbacks would be higher from sales in North America. As stated above, Qatar accepted a netback pricing basis for LNG pricing at South Hook that is related to the prevailing price of gas at the National Balancing Point rather than a traditional pricing formula.

METHODOLOGY FOR CALCULATING PIPELINE COSTS

Engineering Cost Estimates for Regional Transmission

The engineering cost estimates for the regional transmission branches begin with the demand projections to 2025, presented in chapter 2, and the deductions for indigenous production and existing supply to give the projected incremental import requirements. The notional branch transmission pipelines under each major pipeline supply scenario in the section of chapter 3 titled "Gas Sources of Potential Interest to Southeast Europe" have been designed to meet those import requirements. The annual volumes and engineering capital cost estimates also shown there can be used as the basis for calculations of the transmission economics.

Peak Flows/Design Capacities

The design capacities of all of the regional branch pipelines are based on estimated daily peak flows corresponding to the projected annual volumes in 2025, with the assumption of 65 percent annual load factor. The implied load factors for distribution design are much lower (on the order of 25 percent), so underground storage close to the load centers would be required to achieve a 65 percent annual load factor on the transmission system.

Pipeline Diameters, Compression Requirements, and Capital Costs

A projected annual volume, together with an annual load factor, gives a peak daily flow that can be used to select the necessary pipeline diameter.

Table C.1 Pipeline Diameters and Compression Requirements

Nominal Diameter		Gas flow at 100% load factor			Pipeline construction cost				CS/	OS	BMS	PRMS
					Easy		Hard					
(mm)	(inches)	Hourly (Mcm)	Daily (Mcm)	Yearly (Bcm)	($M per 200 km)	($M per km)	($M per 200 km)	($M per km)	200 km ($M)	($M)	($M)	($M)
200	8	20	480	0.175	29	0.145	41	0.205	1	5	3	3
250	10	40	960	0.350	38	0.188	53	0.263	2	5	3	3
300	**12**	**60**	**1,200**	**0.438**	**46**	**0.230**	**64**	**0.320**	**3**	**5**	**3**	**4**
350	14	80	1,920	0.701	54	0.270	75	0.375	4	5	3	4
400	16	110	2,640	0.964	63	0.314	87	0.434	6	5	3	4
450	18	150	3,600	1.314	74	0.372	101	0.507	7	5	3	4
500	20	200	4,800	1.752	83	0.414	113	0.564	10	5	4	5
550	22	250	6,000	2.190	94	0.471	127	0.636	12	5	4	5
600	**24**	**310**	**7,440**	**2.716**	**106**	**0.530**	**142**	**0.710**	**15**	**5**	**4**	**5**
650	26	390	9,360	3.416	119	0.593	158	0.788	19	5	4	5
700	28	480	11,520	4.205	128	0.639	170	0.849	24	5	4	5
750	30	570	13,680	4.993	141	0.706	186	0.931	25	5	4	5
800	32	670	16,080	5.869	155	0.776	203	1.016	29	5	4	5
850	34	790	18,960	6.920	170	0.849	221	1.104	30	5	4	5
900	**36**	**910**	**21,840**	**7.972**	**185**	**0.924**	**239**	**1.194**	**35**	**5**	**4**	**5**
950	38	1,050	25,200	9.198	195	0.976	252	1.261	40	5	4	5
1,000	40	1,200	28,800	10.510	211	1.055	271	1.355	46	5	5	5
1,050	42	1,350	32,400	11.830	233	1.167	296	1.482	51	5	5	6
1,100	44	1,510	36,240	13.230	244	1.222	310	1.552	57	5	5	6

Source: Penspen calculations.

Note: Bcm = billion cubic meters; BMS = border metering station; CS = compressor station; km = kilometers; Mcm = thousand cubic meters; mm = millimeters; OS = offtake station; PRMS = pressure reduction and metering station. Major-size steps (every 12 inches) are set in boldface type.

The diameters were selected, based on the assumptions of a 60-barg maximum operating pressure and a maximum flow velocity of 10 meters per second.

Penspen calculated the maximum hourly flow rate for pipelines increasing in 2-inch (50-millimeter) nominal diameter steps, as shown in table C.1. Also shown in that table are Penspen's estimates of the unit capital cost and capital cost per 200-kilometer section; the estimates of the capital expenditure required for compressor stations each 200 kilometers; and the capital cost for offtake stations, border metering stations, and pressure reduction and metering stations.

Figure C.1, which plots the maximum hourly flow for each diameter of pipeline and for selected diameters, indicates the equivalent annual flow at 100 percent load factor. The flow estimates were arrived at by Penspen, using engineering calculations. As the figure shows, these fit extremely closely to a quadratic curve, which has been extrapolated here up to 56 inches in diameter. With these suction and delivery pressure assumptions used for the smaller diameters, a 56-inch-diameter pipe would be able to deliver just less than 24 Bcm a year. The Nabucco pipeline is being designed at 56 inches, with a design pressure of 100 barg and an annual capacity of 32 Bcm.

Figure C.1 Maximum Hourly and Annual Flow Rates Versus Pipeline Diameters

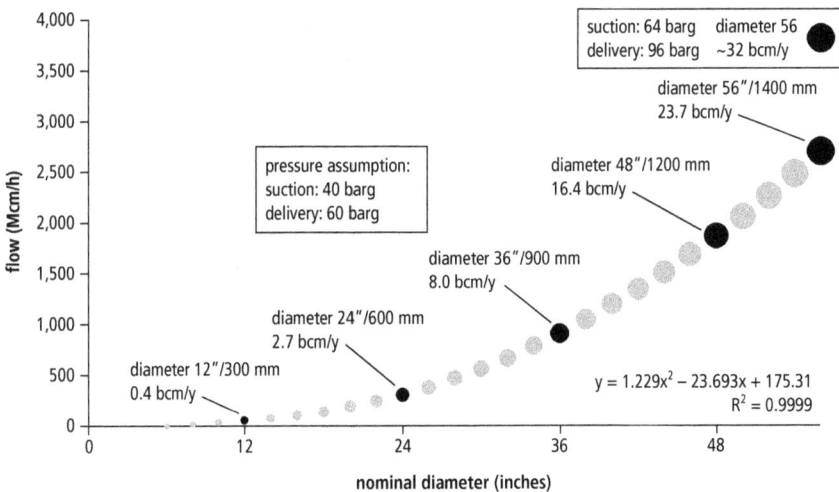

suction: 64 barg   diameter 56
delivery: 96 barg   ~32 bcm/y

diameter 56"/1400 mm
23.7 bcm/y

pressure assumption:
suction: 40 barg
delivery: 60 barg

diameter 48"/1200 mm
16.4 bcm/y

diameter 36"/900 mm
8.0 bcm/y

diameter 24"/600 mm
2.7 bcm/y

diameter 12"/300 mm
0.4 bcm/y

$y = 1.229x^2 - 23.693x + 175.31$
$R^2 = 0.9999$

flow (Mcm/h)

nominal diameter (inches)

Source: Economic Consulting Associates' illustration, based on Penspen calculations.
Note: Bcm/y = billion cubic meters per year; mm = millimeters; Mcm/h = thousand cubic meters per hour.

Figure C.2   Unit Costs by Pipeline Diameter for Easy and Hard Terrain

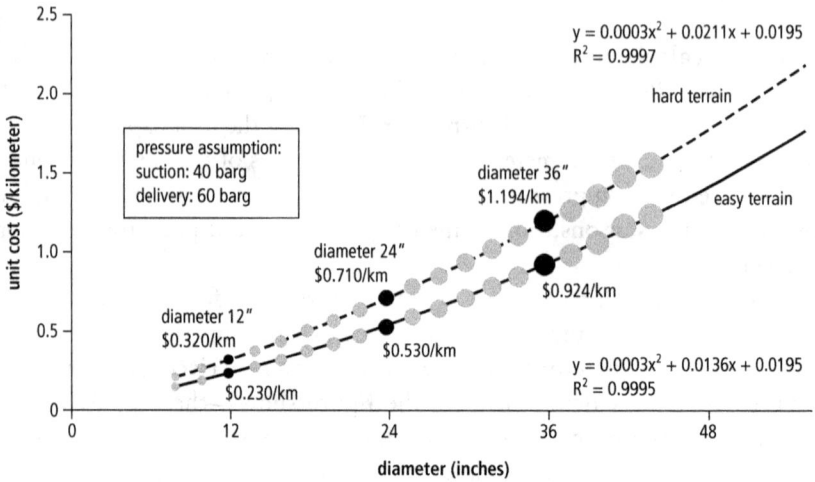

Source: Economic Consulting Associates' illustration, based on Penspen calculations.

Figure C.2 shows the corresponding unit costs for laying pipelines of each diameter in easy terrain (level ground, with soil that allows easy trenching) and in hard terrain (rocky and mountainous routes that require blasting). These cost estimates also have been built from the bottom up, using engineering calculations; and the results fit very closely to quadratic curves.

APPENDIX D

DETAILED TRANSMISSION PIPELINE ROUTES

This appendix provides detailed descriptions of the original branch transmission pipeline concept configurations under each major transmission and gas supply scenario for the Southeast Europe (SEE) markets, described in overview form in the section titled "Transmission Pipeline Supply Routes and Scenarios" in chapter 3. We emphasize that these branch concepts are not least-cost development plans, which would be beyond the scope of the present study. They were not based on an optimal expansion analysis nor were they stress-tested for sensitivities against all of the possible options.

Regional Transmission Branches under Each Scenario
Table D.1 shows the conceptual possibilities for supply routes to the nine SEE markets, including new transmission branches. This table shows existing imports with **+**. Where there is a combination of indigenous supply and imports, the two sources are each shown with ◆ and ▲. The markets that potential new pipelines would pass through are indicated with *. Likely branches are indicated (●), as are less likely braches (■).

Mapping Transmission Routes to Gas Sources
Table D.2 maps these routes to the sources of gas. The top-left corner of the matrix shows Russian gas delivered via existing and possible future routes. The central (shaded) block of the matrix shows the competing gas sources that would be delivered to market via pipeline routes. The lower-right corner of the matrix shows gas from sources that could be delivered via liquefied natural gas.

Table D.1 Existing and Future Supply Routes into the Nine SEE Markets

Supply/ route to SEE market	Location Direction	Northern		Central		Southern			Eastern	
		Croatia	Bosnia and Herzegovina	Serbia	Montenegro	Kosovo	Albania	Macedonia, FYE	Romania	Bulgaria
Indigenous	↓	◆		◆					◆	
via Ukraine	↓	◀	+	◀					◀	+
Blue Line option 1	↖ ↙	*	●	*	■	●	■	■		*
Blue Line option 2	↖ ↙	*	●	*	●	*	●	*		*
South Steam Nord	↖ ↓			●					*	*
South Stream Sud	↓	■	■	●	●	●	*	*		*
Nabucco	↖	●	■	●	■	●	■	■		*
Georgia-Ukraine-EU White Stream	↓	■	■	●					*	●
Pan-European gas pipeline	↓	*	●	*					*	●

Supply/ route to SEE market	Location	Northern		Central			Southern		Eastern	
	Direction	Croatia	Bosnia and Herzegovina	Serbia	Montenegro	Kosovo	Albania	Macedonia, FYE	Romania	Bulgaria
Ionian-Adriatic pipeline	↖	*	●		*		*	*		
Trans-Adriatic pipeline	↙				●	●	*	●		
Italy-Greece Interconnector	↙				■	■	●	●		
Revithoussa LNG	↗ & ↖				●	●	●	●		●
Adria (Krk) LNG	↗ & ↖	●	●							

Source: Authors' compilation.

Note: ✚ = existing imports; ◆ = existing indigenous gas; ▲ = existing balance imported; ✱ = future; ● = potential future branch; ■ = less likely future branch; EU = European Union; LNG = liquefied natural gas.

Table D.2 Supply Routes, by Source

Route	Russian	Caspian	Trans-Caspian	Middle East and Egypt	North Africa, including Egypt
Via Ukraine	▲	—	—	—	—
Via Blue Stream	▲	—	✱	—	—
Blue Line	●	—	✱	—	—
South Stream	●	—	✱	—	—
Nabucco	✱	●	✱	●	—
Georgia-Ukraine-EU White Stream	—	●	✱	—	—
Pan-European gas pipeline	—	●	✱	—	—
Italy-Greece Interconnector	✱	●	✱	✱	■
Ionian-Adriatic pipeline	✱	✱	✱	—	■
Trans-Adriatic pipeline	✱	✱	✱	—	■
LNG	—	—	—	■ or ●	■ or ●

Source: Authors' compilation.
Note: — = unlikely or not applicable; ▲ = existing; ● = future; ■ = future backhaul; ✱ = maybe; EU = European Union; LNG = liquefied natural gas.

Turkmenistan currently needs to deliver its gas via Russia because of the absence of alternative transmission infrastructure from Turkmenistan to European markets. This situation effectively gives Russia market control of Turkmen gas and access to a large share of the rent on that gas (which also currently transits Uzbekistan and Kazakhstan as it passes around the northern end of the Caspian Sea before transiting Russia and then Ukraine).

In theory, Turkmen gas could diverge from this route in Russia, enter Blue Stream, and transit Turkey either via Nabucco or a parallel route to Southeast Europe. However, it seems unlikely. When the Nabucco pipeline is in place, Turkmen gas will have a potential route to market through the Islamic

Republic of Iran around the southern shore of the Caspian Sea. There is an existing pipeline corridor from the Khangiran field in the far-northeast area of the Islamic Republic of Iran around the southern shore of the Caspian Sea, joining a corridor to Erzurum in Turkey. The diameter, operating pressure, and physical condition of that pipeline are not known; and, in any case, the capacity probably would need to be increased to deliver substantial quantities of gas from Dauletabad to the Nabucco inlet. But it would be expected to provide a more direct route (and surely one with a lower economic cost) for gas delivered to Southeast Europe from the fields in southern Turkmenistan (particularly Dauletabad) than would the existing pipeline routes passing north of the Caspian Sea and then turning south through Blue Stream. Improvements in the political situation in Turkmenistan would facilitate use of this route. Potential barriers to the route include the economics of delivering Iranian gas directly to Turkey, relative to the economics of transiting Turkmen gas through the Islamic Republic of Iran and the nature of commercial and political links between Iran and the Russian Federation.

The most direct route for Turkmen gas to Europe would be via the previously proposed trans-Caspian pipeline. Two challenges are widely thought to have presented obstacles to this pipeline being built—one economic, the other commercial-political. The economic challenge is the existence of large quantities of low-cost gas in Shah Deniz, essentially at the downstream end of the proposed pipeline. To date, most observers have expected that Azerbaijan would prefer to exploit its own resources fully before facilitating transit of Turkmen gas. The commercial-political issue relates to the unresolved international legal status of the Caspian Sea. The international Law of the Sea facilitates the development of pipeline infrastructure. But Russia's position is that the Caspian Sea is a lake, not a sea. Infrastructure developments in lakes are not governed by the Law of the Sea; rather, they require the consent of all the littoral states (including, in this case, Russia). Not all of the littoral states agree that Russia can veto construction of a gas pipeline across the Caspian Sea between two other states on environmental or other grounds.

Spur Lines from the Russian Gas System to SEE Markets

Spur lines from the extremities of the Russian gas system, or system reinforcements plus spur lines to the SEE markets, have been developed and priced. The pricing methodology is as described for the projected international gas transmission pipelines.

Russian gas is distributed from existing nodes, reinforced as necessary back into the Russian gas system to a point where assessed capacity is sufficient to support the gas offtake through the system to the SEE regional gasification study (RGS) markets.

Distribution networks were developed conceptually to connect the target cities and were sized for the 2025 city and country gas demands, resulting in three networks and three spur lines to remote locations. Maps have been developed on a background of satellite imagery to show distribution systems and spur lines to remote locations. The configurations of the branches or "legs" that make up each spur line are explained here:

- Leg 1—Bulgaria to Macedonia and Albania: As noted in table D.3, gas is abstracted from the Bulgarian gas ring at Doupnitsa, south of Sofia, and transported to Skopje and Tirana (with spur lines to Tetovo and Elbasan). No reinforcement to the Bulgarian ring was made to support the gas demands of Albania and the former Yugoslav Republic of Macedonia. The pipeline between Bulgaria and Skopje will loop, in part, the existing pipeline to Skopje and will share with it the 2025 hourly flow of 352 Mcm.
- Leg 2—Serbia to Kosovo and Bulgaria: To support the gas flows in Leg 2, the supply is taken back to Belgrade, and the existing pipeline to Nis is looped over its full length. Gas is distributed from Nis to Pristina (with a spur off to Leskovac), and then from Pristina to Kosovo Mitrovica. A separate spur line runs northwest from Nis to Vidin in Bulgaria (see table D.4).
- Leg 3—Serbia to Bosnia and Herzegovina, Croatia, and Montenegro: Gas to supply Bosnia and Herzegovina, Croatia, and Montenegro is abstracted

Table D.3 Network in Bulgaria, FYR Macedonia, and Albania

Pipeline	Peak flow (Mcm/h)	Diameter (inches)	Length (km)
Doupnitsa to Skopje	352	24	139
Skopje offtake	101	n.a.	n.a.
Macedonia total	198	n.a.	n.a.
Skopje to Tetovo spur	190	20	39
Tetovo offtake	36	12	22
Tetovo spur to Tirana	154	20	130
Tirana offtake	81	n.a.	n.a.
Tirana to Elbasan	18	10	35
Elbasan offtake	18	n.a.	n.a.
Albania total	154	n.a.	n.a.

Source: Penspen analysis.
Note: km = kilometers; Mcm/h = thousand cubic meters per hour; n.a. = not applicable.

Table D.4　Network in Serbia, Kosovo, and Bulgaria

Pipeline	Peak flow (Mcm/h)	Diameter (inches)	Length (km)
Belgrade to Nis	220	22	215
Nis to Leskovac spur	185	20	29
Leskovac offtake	15	12	30
South Serbia offtake	52	n.a.	n.a.
Leskovac spur to Pristina	152	18	75
Pristina offtake	101	n.a.	n.a.
Pristina to Kosovo Mitrovica	20	10	35
Kosovo Mitrovica offtake	20	n.a.	n.a.
Nis to Vidin	35	12	116
Vidin offtake	16	n.a.	n.a.

Source: Penspen analysis.
Note: km = kilometers; Mcm/h = thousand cubic meters per hour; n.a. = not applicable.

at Belgrade with upstream reinforcement back to Kekskemet in Hungary, where the system capacity is assessed to be sufficient to support the 2025 gas demand. From Belgrade, the distribution network will supply Sarajevo (with a spur line to Uzice and Banja Luka), and then Mostar to Metkovic where the line bifurcates to Split in Croatia and Niksic and Podgorica in Montenegro (see table D.5).

Supply to SEE from Existing Russian Gas Supply Routes

The gas transmission and distribution networks that were developed during the period of the Council for Mutual Economic Assistance trade alignments have seen very little development since the secession of the former satellite countries in the SEE region. Of the SEE RGS countries, only Romania had significant indigenous gas resources (which now are in decline). In any event, the Romanian system served only Romanian demand, with no export to the SEE countries.

In addition to gas transport and distribution to the SEE countries, export pipelines for Russian gas transit Romania and Bulgaria to deliver gas to Turkey and Greece. These pipelines are considered separate entities from the transmission and distribution systems in Romania and Bulgaria, although their domestic transmission and distribution networks are connected to and fed by the export pipelines.

Table D.5　Network in Serbia, Bosnia and Herzegovina, Croatia, and Montenegro

Pipeline	Peak flow (Mcm/h)	Diameter (inches)	Length (km)
Kekskemet to Szeged	500	30	88
Szeged to Belgrade supplementary flow	500	30	182
Belgrade to Uzice spur	346	28	72
Uzice offtake	14	10	75
Central Serbia offtake	105	n.a.	n.a.
Uzice spur to Sarajevo	346	28	139
Sarajevo offtake (existing)		n.a.	n.a.
Sarajevo to Zenica	94	16	62
Zenica offtake	30	n.a.	n.a.
Zenica to Banja Luka	40	12	92
Banja Luka offtake	40	n.a.	n.a.
Sarajevo to Mostar	172	20	83
Mostar offtake	25	n.a.	n.a.
Mostar to Metkovic	147	18	37
Metkovic to Split	87	16	116
Split offtake	67	n.a.	n.a.
Metkovic to Niksic	60	16	138
Niksic offtake	12	n.a.	n.a.
Niksic to Podgorica	48	12	50
Podgorica offtake	26	n.a.	n.a.

Source: Penspen analysis.
Note: km = kilometers; Mcm/h = thousand cubic meters per hour; n.a. = not applicable.

Gas that transits Russia to supply the SEE RGS region (Russian gas) enters the region via the major international pipelines that traverse Romania, Bulgaria, Hungary, and Slovenia. Russian gas presently penetrates the SEE target area almost to the Adriatic. However, these pipelines are at the very extremity of the system; generally, they are of small diameter and low transportation capacity, as shown in table D.6.

Table D.6 Estimated Capacity of the Russian Pipeline Network in the SEE Region

Country	Present Capacity to Country (Mcm/h)	Location of extremity of Russian-supplied system	Pipeline diameter at extremity (inches)	Assessed maximum capacity at extremity (Mcm/h)
Croatia	200	Sisak	20	200
Bosnia and Herzegovina	80	Sarajevo	18	80
Serbia	540	Nis	18	150
Bulgaria	1040	Kyustendil	20	200
Macedonia	90	Skopje	20	90

Sources: Penspen analysis of data from Gas Infrastructure Europe (Bosnia and Herzegovina, Croatia, and Serbia) and of assessed data (Bulgaria and FYR Macedonia).
Note: Mcm/h = thousand cubic meters per hour; SEE = Southeast Europe.

The capacity of the Russian gas system to forward additional large quantities of gas to Southeast Europe is limited. To assess deliverability of the Russian system for its connection to the SEE markets, the gross onward flow is compared with the assessed maximum capacity at the particular system extremity. If the gross additional flow is less than 25 percent of the assessed maximum capacity, the end point is deemed to be capable of delivering the additional flow. If the gross additional flow is more than 25 percent, the additional flow is taken upstream in the Russian system at a location from which it can be supported. Spur pipelines to SEE demand centers have been sized and their costs determined as described above.

Map D.1 shows notional branch pipelines from the existing Russian-connected transmission system.

Table D.7 presents the volumes, peak flows, pipeline diameters, total lengths, and engineering estimate of capital expenditures for the pipelines and facilities (compressor stations, MLO, border metering stations, and pressure reduction and metering stations).

Offtake from the Blue Line

Map D.2 shows a schematic chart for the Blue Line project. Blue Line is an extension of the Blue Stream gas project that supplies Russian gas. If it came to fruition, the pipeline would transfer gas to the European Union (EU) via Bulgaria; and it is expected to transit Serbia, Bosnia and Herzegovina, Croatia, Slovenia, and Italy. Table D.8 shows the key data for the branches under the Blue Line scenario.

Map D.1   Notional Regional Branch Transmission Lines, Russian Gas Scenario

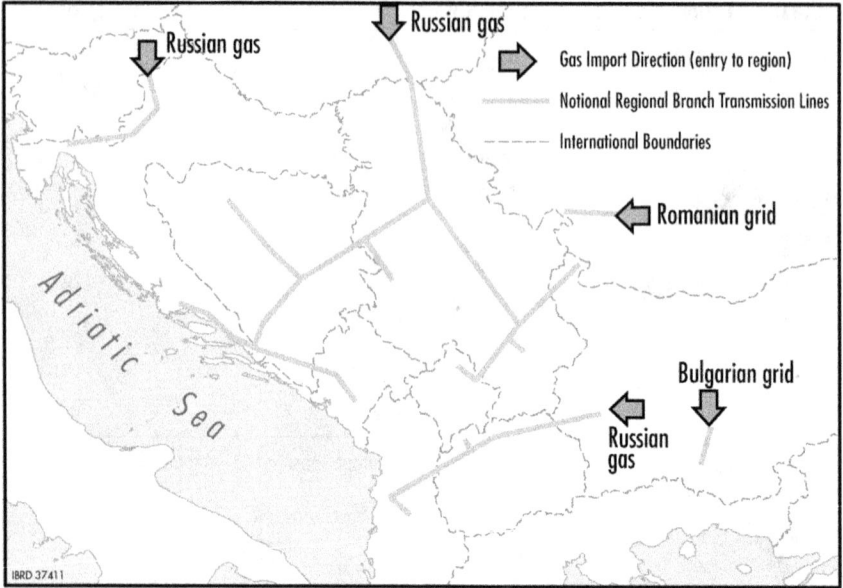

Source: World Bank.

Map D.2   Notional Regional Branch Transmission Lines, Blue Line Scenario

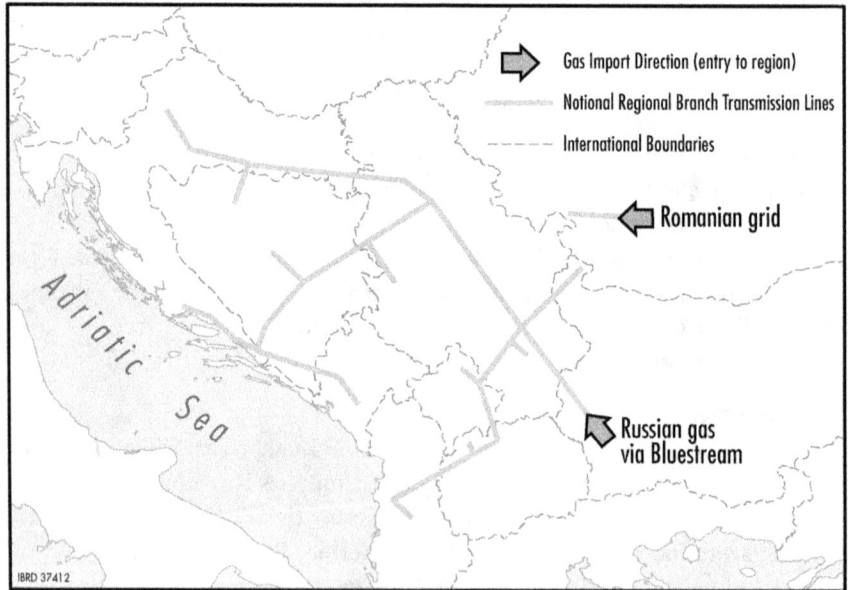

Source: World Bank.

Table D.7 Notional Regional Branch Transmission Lines, Russian Gas Scenario

					Capital expenditure		
Branch markets	Volume (Bcm/y)	Peak flow (Mcm/h)	Diameter (inches)	Total (km)	Pipelines ($M)	Facilities ($M)	Total ($M)
Gazprom Inlet 1: Skopje-Tetovo-Elbasan-Tirana spur line							
Bulgaria/Macedonia FYR/ Albania	2.00	352	10–24	365	170	54	224
Gazprom Inlet 2: Belgrade-Sarajevo-Split-Podgorica spur line\-Nis-Kosovo Mitrovica-Leskovac-Vidin spur line							
Serbia/Bulgaria/Kosovo/ Montenegro/Croatia/Bosnia and Herzegovina	2.85	500	10–30	1,634	775	141	916
Gazprom Inlet 3: Rogatec-Zagreb-Karlovac-Rijeka							
Croatia	0.56	99	16	204	64	13	77
Gazprom Inlet 4: Filasi-Turnu Severin							
Romania	0.13	23	12	75	17	0	17
Gazprom Inlet 5: Azenovgrad-Smolyan							
Bulgaria	0.04	7	10	55	10	0	10
Total	5.59	--	10–30	2,333	1,037	208	1,245

Source: Penspen analysis.

Note: Bcm/y = billion cubic meters per year; km = kilometers; Mcm/h = thousand cubic meters per hour; n.a. = not applicable.

Table D.8 Notional Regional Branch Transmission Lines, Blue Line Scenario

| Branch markets | Volume (Bcm/y) | Peak flow (Mcm/h) | Diameter (inches) | Total (km) | Capital expenditure | | |
					Pipelines ($M)	Facilities ($M)	Total ($M)
Blue Line: Pristina-Skopje-Tirana-Elbasan\Sarajevo-Mostar-Metkovic-Niksic-Podgorica\-Split							
Serbia/Bulgaria/Kosovo/ Montenegro/Croatia/Bosnia and Herzegovina	7.24	1,271	1,0-42	2,166	1,232	169	1,401

Source: Penspen analysis.

Note: Bcm/y = billion cubic meters per year; km = kilometers; Mcm/h = thousand cubic meters per hour.

Offtake from Nabucco

Map D.3 illustrates the Nabucco pipeline, which is proposed to supply Caspian gas to Western Europe by transiting via Turkey, Bulgaria, Romania, Hungary, and Austria. Of all the pipeline options, Nabucco is the most advanced in terms of feasibility and developer consortiums. Spur line investments directly associated with the Nabucco pipeline can be broken into three discreet sections. Table D.9 shows the key data for the branches under the Nabucco scenario.

Offtake from the Turkey-Greece-Italy Pipeline

The Turkey-Greece-Italy (TGI) pipeline route—of which the Italy-Greece Interconnector (IGI) is a part—is another pipeline project that aims to transfer Caspian gas to markets in Europe via Turkey, through Greece, and then into southern Italy. However, there is apparent potential for offtake to branch transmission lines that could supply the nearby markets of Southeast Europe, including Albania, Bosnia and Herzegovina, Croatia, and Montenegro. Map D.4 shows the IGI section of the TGI pipeline route, as well as the potential transmission branch pipeline opportunities. Table D.10 shows the key data for the branch under the TGI scenario.

Map D.3   Notional Regional Branch Transmission Lines, Nabucco Scenario

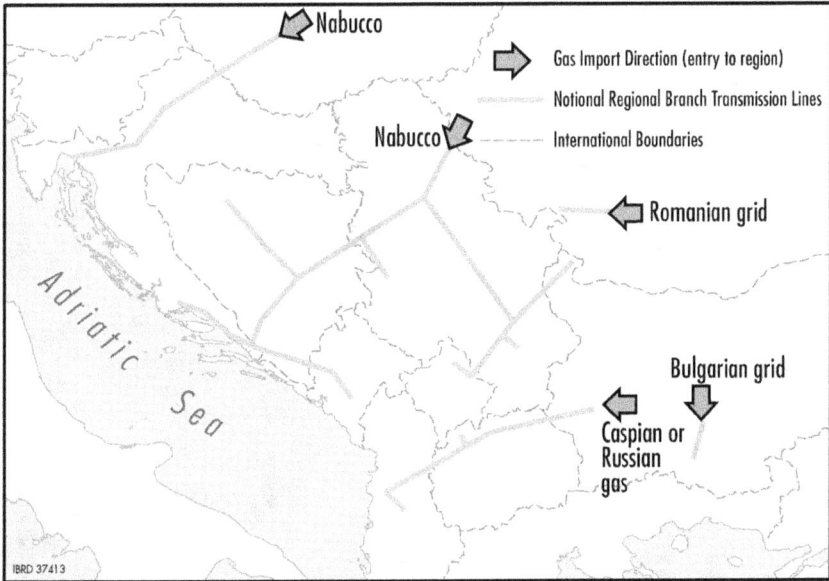

Source: World Bank.

Table D.9 Notional Regional Branch Transmission Lines, Nabucco Scenario

Branch markets	Volume (Bcm/y)	Peak flow (Mcm/h)	Diameter (inches)	Total (km)	Pipelines ($M)	Facilities ($M)	Total ($M)
Nabucco Inlet 1: Skopje-Tetovo-Elbasan-Tirana spur line							
Bulgaria/Macedonia, FYR/							
Albania	2.00	352	10–24	365	170	54	224
Nabucco Inlet 2: Belgrade-Sarajevo-Split-Podgorica spur line							
Romania/Serbia/Bulgaria/							
Kosovo/Montenegro/							
Croatia/Bosnia and							
Herzegovina	4.03	707	10–34	1,496	692	129	821
Nabucco Inlet 3: Szekesfehervar-Zagreb-Karlovac-Rijeka							
Croatia	0.56	99	16	204	64	13	77
Nabucco Inlet 4: Filasi-Turnu Severin							
Romania	0.13	23	12	75	17	9	26
Nabucco Inlet 5: Azenovgrad-Smolyan							
Bulgaria	0.04	7	10	55	10	8	18
Total	6.76	–	10–34	1,593	954	213	1,167

Source: Penspen analysis.

Note: Bcm/y = billion cubic meters per year; km = kilometers; Mcm/h = thousand cubic meters per hour; n.a. = not applicable.

Map D.4　Notional Regional Branch Transmission Lines, TGI Scenario

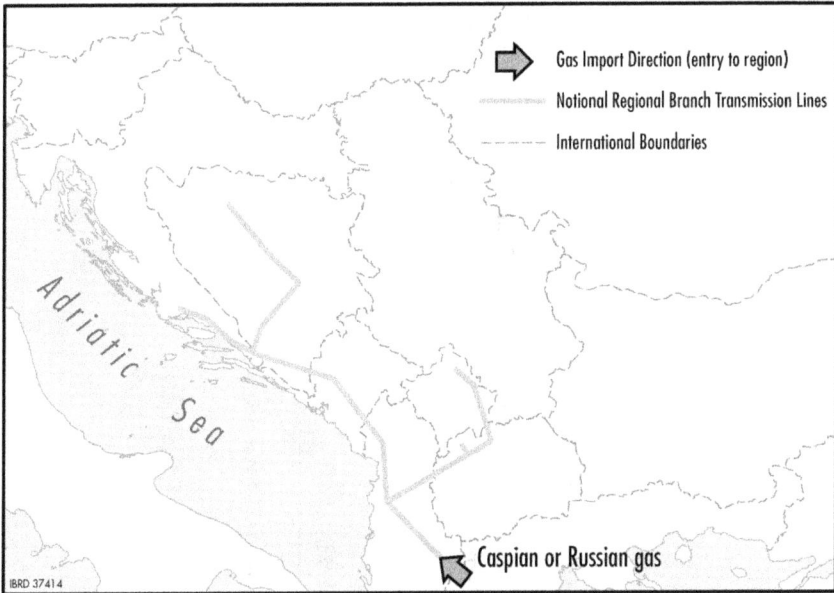

Source: World Bank.
Note: TGI = Turkey-Greece-Italy pipeline.

Offtake from the Trans-Adriatic Pipeline

The trans-Adriatic pipeline (TAP) connects to existing infrastructure near Thessaloniki, Greece, at the point where the existing pipeline delivering Russian gas to Greece via Bulgaria converges with the new Turkey-Greece pipeline. TAP's proposed route passes through Greece, across Albania and the Adriatic Sea, and enters southern Italy near Brindisi. At least in theory, TAP would be able to deliver either Caspian gas transiting through Turkey or Russian gas transiting Romania and Bulgaria.

The notional spur lines from TAP (map D.5) would follow the route Elbasan-Tirana-Podgorica-Nicsic-Metkovic\-Split\-Mostar-Sarajevo-Zenica-Banja Luka. Table D.11 shows the key data for the branch under the TAP scenario.

Offtake from the Georgia-Ukraine-EU White Stream

The Georgia-Ukraine-EU (GUEU) pipeline is proposed to transfer Caspian gas to Europe via Ukraine by a pipeline similar to Blue Stream built in the depths of the Black Sea (map D.6). The GUEU pipeline would deliver gas to Constanta and/or the Crimean peninsula. The SEE RGS would allow

Table D.10 Notional Regional Branch Transmission Lines, TGI Scenario

					Capital expenditure		
Branch markets	Volume (Bcm/y)	Peak flow (Mcm/h)	Diameter (inches)	Total (km)	Pipelines ($M)	Facilities ($M)	Total ($M)
TGI: Grevena-Elbasan-Tirana-Podgorica-Niksic-Metkovic\-Split\-Mostar-Sarajevo-Zenica-Banja Luka							
Albania/Kosovo/ Montenegro/Croatia/Bosnia and Herzegovina	2.78	488	12–30	1,244	723	122	845

Source: Penspen analysis.
Note: Bcm/y = billion cubic meters per year; km = kilometers; Mcm/h = thousand cubic meters per hour; TGI = Turkey-Greece-Italy pipeline.

Map D.5 Notional Regional Branch Transmission Lines, TAP Scenario

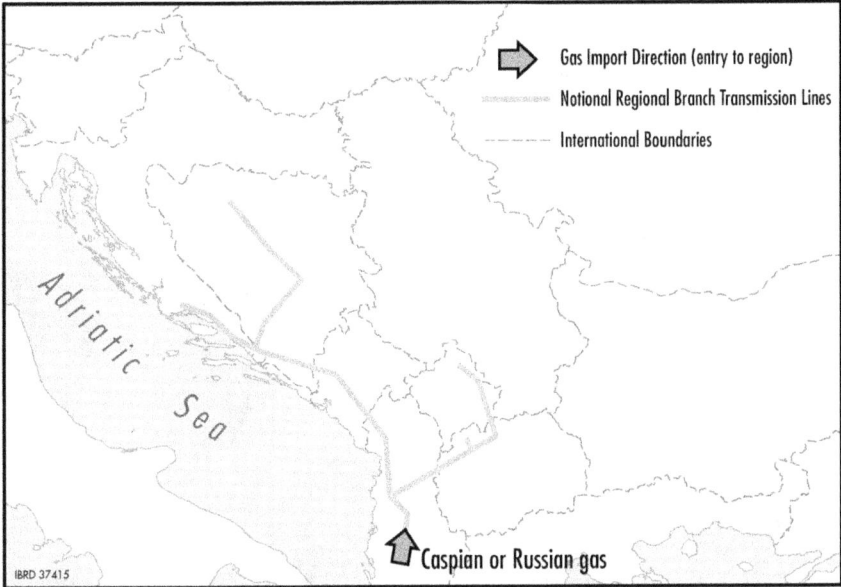

Source: World Bank.
Note: TAP = trans-Adriatic pipeline.

Map D.6 Notional Regional Branch Transmission Lines, GUEU Scenario

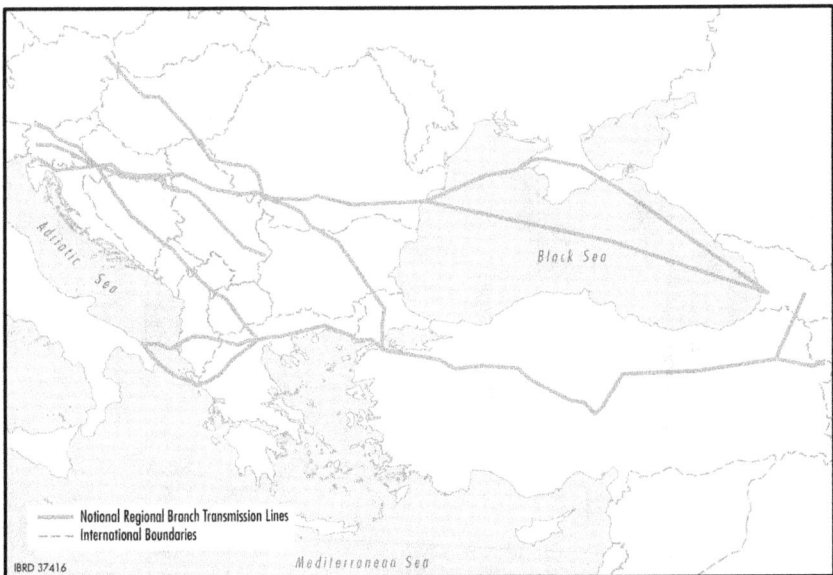

Source: World Bank.
Note: GUEU = Georgia-Ukraine-European Union pipeline.

Table D.11 Notional Regional Branch Transmission Lines, TAP Scenario

| Branch markets | Volume (Bcm/y) | Peak flow (Mcm/h) | Diameter (inches) | Total (km) | Capital expenditure | | |
					Pipelines ($M)	Facilities ($M)	Total ($M)
TAP: Elbasan-Tirana-Podgorica-Niksic-Metkovic\-Split-Mostar-Sarajevo-Zenica-Banja Luka							
Albania/Kosovo/							
Montenegro/Croatia/Bosnia							
and Herzegovina	2.78	488	12–30	862	481	83	564

Source: Penspen analysis.
Note: Bcm/y = billion cubic meters per year; km = kilometers; Mcm/h = thousand cubic meters per hour; TAP = trans-Adriatic pipeline.

Table D.12 Notional Regional Branch Transmission Lines, GUEU Scenario

| Branch Markets | Volume (Bcm/y) | Peak Flow (Mcm/h) | Diameter (inches) | Total (km) | Capital expenditure | | |
					Pipelines ($M)	Facilities ($M)	Total ($M)
GUEU: Nikolayev-Tiraspol-Onesti-Negru Voda							
Romania/Bulgaria	6.76	1,187	20–42	836	633	168	801

Source: Penspen analysis.
Note: Bcm/y = billion cubic meters per year; GUEU = Georgia-Ukraine-European Union pipeline; km = kilometers; Mcm/h = thousand cubic meters per hour.

for onward transportation to tie-ins for Romania and Bulgaria. Existing domestic gas systems in Romania and Bulgaria would provide onward transportation.

The GUEU pipeline project itself is expected to cost more than $4 billion when fully developed. Table D.12 shows the estimates for the branch from the GUEU pipeline.

Promising Regional Transmission Branches

A preliminary assessment has been made of the most promising regional transmission branch for each market. Map D.7 shows the most economically attractive and promising regional branch pipeline projects—that is, the option that could deliver new gas to each market at the lowest cost. These branches are

- a branch from Nabucco near Timosoara, supplying
  - central Serbia, western Serbia (including Uzice), and southern Serbia, (including Leskovac)
  - Vidin, Bulgaria, via Serbia
  - Pristina and Kosovo Mitrovica via southern Serbia
  - Banja Luka, Zenica, and Mostar, Bosnia and Herzegovina, via Serbia

Map D.7   Most Economically Attractive Regional Branch Pipelines

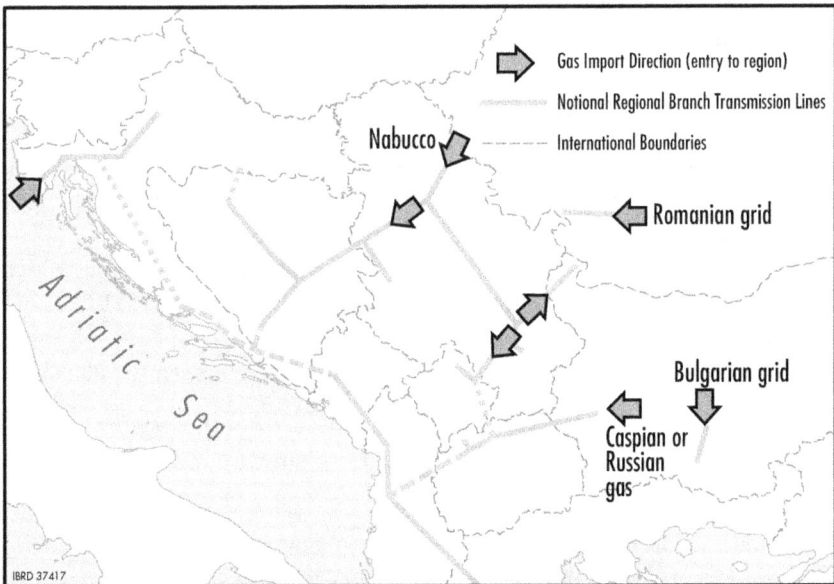

Source: World Bank, Penspen pipeline designs adapted by ECA.

- a branch from the Bulgarian ring near Doupnitsa, supplying Skopje and Tetovo, FYR Macedonia
- a branch from the IGI in Greece (or from TAP in Albania), supplying Tirana and Elbasan, Albania, and Podgorica and Niksic, Montenegro.

Drobeta Turnu Severin and Horezu in Romania would be supplied directly from the Romanian grid, with no need for regional transmission branches. Similarly, Smolyan, Bulgaria, would be supplied directly from the Bulgarian grid.

Table D.13 summarizes these investments. It includes a total of $1.18 billion of capital expenditure on 1,865 kilometers of transmission lines, ranging from 34-inch main pipelines to 10-inch spur lines. The pipeline capital expenditure totals $992 million and facilities (compressors, border metering and regulating stations, and so forth) total $188 million. The regional branch pipelines from the Nabucco project for Bulgaria, Romania, Serbia, Kosovo, and Bosnia and Herzegovina total $710 million; the regional branch pipelines from the IGI project for Albania and Montenegro total $372 million; and the regional branch from the Bulgarian ring for FYR Macedonia totals $98 million.

Adding the costs from the Plinacro development plan for the spur line to Split will increase the total. A review of the pipeline design capacities to account for the reconfiguration from selecting a combination of parts from each major pipeline scenario is likely to lead to a slight reduction in capital expenditure, relative to the costs in table D.13.

There are several variations of the above branches, but their economics have not been analyzed. These variations are indicated with dotted lines in map D.7. They would involve supplying

- Pristina and Kosovo Mitrovica, Kosovo, via Skopje in FYR Macedonia (following the alignment of the old pipeline), with a new pipeline that could be interconnected later to the Serbian system at Nis
- Banja Luka, Bosnia and Herzegovina, via a pipeline from Croatia, which subsequently could be connected to Zenica (as planned by BH-Gas and Plinacro)
- Split from the Croatian system (as already under development by Plinacro).

The pipeline sections that have been removed from the original indicative designs are indicated with long dashed lines in map D.7. The following points are important to note:

- The effect of removing those sections from the designs (apparently because alternative branches provide more economic supply) has not been analyzed. Removing sections from the ends of the original branch pipeline designs will reduce the flows somewhat all the way upstream in the pipe-

Table D.13. Summary of the Most Promising Regional Branch Transmission Projects

Market	Investments	Diameter (inches)	Length (km)	Capital expenditure		
				Pipeline ($M)	Facilities ($M)	Total ($M)
Total	Regional branch from Nabucco	10–34	1,285	587	123	710
Romania	Timisoara-Serbia border	34	125	60	18	78
Serbia	-Belgrade-Nis-Leskovac/ Uzice	12–34	654	309	62	371
Kosovo	-Pristina/-Kosovo Mitrovica	10–18	68	19	7	26
Bulgaria	-Vidin/-Smolyan	12	107	22	11	33
Bosnia and Herzegovina	-Sarajevo-Zenica-Banja Luka/-Mostar	12–28	331	177	25	202
	Plinacro development plan					
Croatia	Karlovac-Split					
Total	Regional branch from Italy-Greece					
	Interconnector	24–30	442	325	47	372
Montenegro	ALB border-Podgorica-Niksic	24–28	105	41	10	51
Albania	Greece-Albania border-Elbasan-Tirana-Montenegro	28–30	337	284	37	321
	Regional branch from Bulgarian ring					
Macedonia, FYR	Doupnitsa-Skopje-Tetovo	12–28	138	80	18	98
Total	All projects	10–34	1,865	992	188	1,180

Source: Economic Consulting Associates' economic analysis, based on Penspen engineering analysis.
Note: km = kilometers. This is a preliminary assessment, and it is subject to revision.

line. This may mean that a diameter of the pipeline required becomes smaller than in the original indicative design. Such an outcome would reduce the capital cost of the projects slightly, but may result in incremental transmission costs that are slightly higher than the costs that have been calculated at each node for the interim regional branch pipeline designs.

- The projects indicated here are contingent on at least two of the major pipeline projects proceeding: Nabucco (or Blue Line) and the IGI (or TAP). Because these pairs of projects (one south to north, the other east to west) are complementary, their going forward is considered a reasonable assumption.

- In the near term, if loads in some markets are initially small, it may be possible to make use of existing infrastructure for several years and thus delay investment in the pipelines described here. However, the addition of significant anchor loads will require that new pipelines be developed.

Spur Lines to Other Locations

The target cities of Rijeka, Turnu Severin, Horezu, and Smolyan are supplied by standalone spur lines from the nearest gas network (see table D.14). For the Romanian cities of Turnu Severin and Horezu, physical connection to Russian gas is unlikely. However, Russian gas could be supplied by substituting it for gas entering Romania from Khust to Satu Mare.

The pipeline supply to Rijeka is sized to transport an assessed volume of gas to other consumption centers in northern Croatia; it originates from the Rogatec node in Slovenia.

Table D.14   Spur Lines to Remote Locations

Pipeline	Peak Flow (Mcm/h)	Diameter (inches)	Length (km)
Rijeka			
Rogatec to Zagreb	99	16	55
Zagreb to Karlovac	70	16	52
Karlovac to Rijeka offtake	34	16	97
Turnu Severin			
Filasi to Turnu Severin offtake	23	12	75
Horezu			
Romanian Ring to Horezu offtake	2	10	50
Smolyan			
Azenovgrad to Smolyan offtake	7	10	55

Source: Authors' compilation.
Note: km = kilometers; Mcm/h = thousand cubic meters per hour.

PROSPECTS FOR UNDERGROUND GAS STORAGE IN SOUTHEAST EUROPE

General Overview

The following locations have been identified as potential underground gas storage (UGS) facilities suitable to support an integrated natural gas supply and distribution system in Southeast Europe:

- Banatski Dvor, depleted field under development for UGS in Serbia
- Okoli, depleted field UGS capacity expansion in Croatia
- Benicanci, depleted field development to UGS facility in Croatia
- Tuzla-Tetima, potential salt cavern UGS in Bosnia and Herzegovina
- Divjaka, depleted field with UGS development potential in Albania
- Dumrea, potential salt cavern UGS in Albania.

Serbia

Banatski Dvor, currently under development, is the only UGS facility expected to be developed in Serbia in the immediate future. Several other depleted oil and gas fields exist in Serbia, some of which have been identified in desk reviews by Serbian geologists as having the potential for redevelopment as UGS facilities. But given Banatski Dvor's quite large potential capacity, relative to the Serbian gas system demand, and the financial constraints of the Serbian gas sector, there are no definite plans to develop these structures as underground storage in the near term. The demand for storage services from sites in Serbia may increase if the country's system is developed in such a way that it becomes more interconnected with neighboring countries; and especially if Serbia becomes part of a major international gas transport route (for example, one of the branches of South Stream), for which supporting storage services would be valuable.

Detailed technical information about Banatski Dvor was not available to this study because it is one of the assets that have been subject to confidential commercial negotiations between the Serbian government with respect to Gazprom's purchase of a majority holding in NIS and Srbijagas. However, there are some data in the public domain, and it has been possible to make calculations based on reasonable assumptions and estimations to provide cost estimates for the analysis.

During the period of economic sanctions imposed on the former Yugoslavia in the 1990s, the former gas field of Banatski Dvor was depleted to a larger extent than initially planned; and it exhibits a water drive. As a consequence, the reservoir is in the early stages of cushion gas replacement, which must be done gradually over a number of years. During this period, some winter withdrawals will be possible. For the winter period 2008/09, the storage facility is expected to be able to support the gas supply system for several days in extreme cold weather conditions. The first regular gas withdrawal phase is planned for 2009/2010, with a working gas volume of 100 million cubic meters (MMcm).

When the storage reservoir is developed fully, the working gas volume will amount to 800 MMcm. The daily injection and withdrawal capacity then will be 5–7 MMcm and 7–11 MMcm, respectively. The complete filling of the reservoir to the planned working gas volume of 800 MMcm (with the corresponding cushion gas volume in place) is expected to last approximately 10 years.

Croatia

Croatia successfully has been operating a depleted gas field at Okoli as a UGS facility for three decades. The main parameters are

working gas volume	580 MMcm
cushion gas	470 MMcm
maximum daily injection capacity	3.8 MMcm
maximum daily withdrawal capacity	5.8 MMcm
number of production wells	22
average well depth	1,780 m
porosity	approximately 16 percent

permeability	12–25 millidarcies
compression capacity	4 units, 2.8 megawatts each
	• suction pressure, 30–38 bar
	• discharge pressure, 190 bar
	• hourly compression rate, 40 Mcm
	• gas-motor driven
remarks	two blocks with different reservoir characteristics

Croatia has the following two options for extending its natural gas storage capacity

Okoli Depleted Oil Field Storage Capacity Expansion   This is a depleted gas field in a separate reservoir. Because the potential storage horizon is significantly deeper and completely separated from that already in use, the development of Okoli 2b would be no extension of the existing storage facility, but instead the construction of a completely new facility. The expected parameters are

working gas volume	400 MMcm
cushion gas	350 MMcm
daily maximum withdrawal capacity	4.0 MMcm
number of production wells	13
average well depth	2,100 meters

These are the advantages:

- Reuse of existing infrastructure is possible.
- Connection to pipeline grid already exists.

These are the disadvantages:

- There is very low reservoir pressure. (A large volume of cushion gas is required, and low pressure hampers the drilling of new wells.)
- There is low permeability.

Benicanci Depleted Oil Field Redevelopment   This is a depleted oil field with the presence of active water drive. The reservoir is characterized by several bulges that preferably can be used for the generation of the gas "bubbles."[1] The specific conditions (two-phase gaseous and liquid flow with three different media—oil, gas, and water) are very complex. This means that it is not possible to develop the structure quickly. The developer, therefore, would be constrained to gradually develop the reservoir for storage over a period of approximately 15 years. Expected parameters are

working gas volume	500–2,000 MMcm
cushion gas	450 MMcm in the initial phase
maximum daily withdrawal capacity	6.2 MMcm
number of production wells	8
average well depth	1,080 meters
porosity	approximately 8 percent
permeability	300 millidarcies
remarks	brecciated rock material from limestone and dolomite (combined porous and fissured)

So far, no decision has been made about which of those two options is more desirable. A two-year Benicanci pilot project involving 2 wells with injection of 200 MMcm will study injection and withdrawal behaviors.

Bosnia and Herzegovina

The construction of salt caverns in the salt formation of Tuzla-Tetima is the only potential opportunity identified with potential underground storage capacity in Bosnia and Herzegovina.

The possibility of leaching salt caverns for natural gas storage has been studied by the Rudarski Institute, Tuzla, in 2002. In the related prefeasibility study, the possibility of four caverns (each with a net geometrical volume of 120,000 cubic meters and a total working gas storage capacity of 60 MMcm) has been proved. The salt formation allows for the construction of several more caverns, but the remaining salt resources definitely are reserved by government decision for industrial salt production.

---

[1] Gas injected into each part of the structure would push the oil upward and outward and push the water downward and outward, forming a "bubble" of gas.

The concept of leaching the storage caverns is based strongly on the presumption that the outcoming brine will be processed by the salt mine. Because privatization of the salt mining company has not been decided and a reliable execution of the leaching operation is uncertain, the start of the storage project remains pending.

According to the prefeasibility study, the expected parameters are

working gas volume	50 MMcm
cushion gas volume	12 MMcm
number of caverns	4
geometrical net volume of caverns	$4 \times 120,000 \text{ m}^3 = 480,000 \text{ m}^3$
minimum cavern pressure	2.5 MPa
maximum cavern pressure	12.5 MPa
maximum daily withdrawal capacity	1.9 MMcm
maximum daily injection capacity	0.5 MMcm
remarks	difficult hydrogeological conditions in the overburden; recompression of the outcoming gas in the final withdrawal phase might be necessary

Albania

Based on a potential annual gas demand in Albania of 1 billion cubic meters, Albanian oil and gas sector experts estimate a future market need for a working gas volume of 150 MMcm.

The following two potential UGS locations have been identified and considered.

Divjaka Depleted Gas Field Conversion Divjaka was exploited between 1960 and 1980, and it is practically empty. In that time period, approximately 1,300 MMcm of natural gas had been produced. The Divjaka field consists of 25 different reservoir layers, each 4–6 meters thick, in the depth interval from 2,000 to 2,600 meters. There is no water drive.

The information provided regarding the productivity is inconsistent. On one hand, a porosity value of 16–20 percent and a permeability value of 153 millidarcies were given—values that would indicate a rather good reservoir performance. On the other hand, it was said that the field had been exploited by 70 production wells, corresponding to an average daily productivity rate of 2,650 square cubic meters per well—a very low rate.

The possibility of gas storage in the Divjaka field has been investigated by a feasibility study, but the study itself was not accessible.

Dumrea Salt Dome—Leaching of Salt Caverns   The salt dome at Dumrea is a large diapir covering a surface area of approximately 250 square kilometers. The salt mirror is mostly at a depth of 2,000 meters. The overburden is karstic to a large extent, and consists of gypsum and anhydrite. The salt reaches down to 6,000 meters. The salt volume is estimated to amount to 1,400 cubic kilometers.

The salt quality seems not to be the best for solution mining (15 percent of insoluble material, with occurrence of potash salt). A few wells already have been drilled. It is expected that the salt dome may outcrop closer to the surface in some locations, although this is yet to be established. Presumably based on that assumption, a feasibility study performed in the 1990s focused on storage caverns operated in the pressure range of 80–200 bar. That pressure range implies that the caverns have been planned in the depth interval of approximately 1,150–1,500 meters. The study itself was not accessible.

Frakulla Depleted Gas Reservoir   The depleted gas reservoir of Frakulla is too small to be considered as an underground storage reservoir. So far, 106 MMcm have been produced by two production wells.

Storage Concepts and Scenarios, by Country

The information obtained has differing degrees of detail, often is limited, and sometimes is either inconsistent or unreliable. There also are many uncertainties in terms of both technical and commercial parameters (costs for purchase of land, infrastructure development, connection to pipeline grids and utilities, local price levels for services, and so forth). To make the storage concepts and scenarios to be developed comparable to each other, they will be developed on an identical basis with the same degree of accuracy. The general approach to presenting the information is as follows:

- general description of the storage scenario
- postulates regarding the main subsurface storage volume and performance parameters
- consequences regarding the extension of the number of production wells/caverns
- technical sketch of an appropriate surface facility
- time schedule for different activities and cost estimation.
  For seasonal storage, the following information may be included:
- injection period (from April to October)—for identifying the dimensions of the injection compressor capacity, 120 days was assumed

- withdrawal period (from December to March)—for identifying the performance dimensions of the withdrawal trains, a time period of 90 days was assumed.

For cushion gas, specific investment costs of €0.40 per square cubic meter are assumed.

The time schedules and cost estimations are based on the assumption that all planning and design work has been performed, a positive decision was made, and investment will start at the beginning of 2009 (first year).

The investment and operating costs for leaching are estimated on the basis of recent experiences in comparable projects in Central Europe, slightly reduced with respect to the lower price level in Southeast Europe. No price escalation has been taken into account.

Serbia: Banatski Dvor

According to public information and taking into account a one-year delay in project implementation, the time schedule for developing Banatski Dvor shown in table E.1 may apply.

For stage 1, the surface facilities already have been installed. The process of pressurizing with cushion gas is under way. When a cushion gas volume of 250 MMcm has been reached, the maximum daily withdrawal capacity will amount to approximately 2 MMcm, and the maximum daily injection capacity will be approximately 1 MMcm.

Just to reach a working gas volume of 800 MMcm and a withdrawal rate of 7–11 MMcm a day, it is estimated that 17 additional wells will have to be drilled.

Based on this information, the scenario presented in table E.2 may apply for developing stages 2 and 3.

Croatia: Okoli 2b Depleted Field

No information could be obtained regarding the reservoir behavior of the Okoli 2b formation, and a possible time schedule to develop that storage to its full planned capacity could not be calculated. It is known that the current reservoir pressure is very low, and that might cause problems when drilling new wells. Another important factor is that new wells will have to penetrate the existing storage formation. Doing so requires additional technical measures, and demands that drilling be done only if the storage reservoir is at high pressure. Therefore, prices for drilling new wells are uncertain:

- If mud loss in the new storage formation can be avoided by the use of precipitants, a per-well price of €5.7 million would be expected.

Table E.1 Injection and Production Plan, Banatski Dvor

Year		Cycle	Injection (MMcm)	Production (MMcm)	Cushion gas (MMcm)	Pressure (bar)	Stage
2008	I	Injection	50	n.a.	n.a.	91.7	
2008/09		Production	n.a.	0	50	91.7	
2009	II	Injection	200	n.a.	n.a.	113.7	
2009/10		Production	n.a.	100	150	104.9	
2010	III	Injection	250	n.a.	n.a.	131.1	1: 16,000 MWh
2010/11		Production	n.a.	200	200	110.7	average for full cycle
2011	IV	Injection	300	n.a.	n.a.	140.9	
2011/12		Production	n.a.	250	250	114.8	
2012	V	Injection	300	n.a.	n.a.	143.8	
2012/13		Production	n.a.	300	250	113.5	
2013	VI	Injection	400	n.a.	n.a.	147.0	
2013/14		Production	n.a.	300	350	116.0	
2014	VII	Injection	450	n.a.	n.a.	152.1	
2014/15		Production	n.a.	350	450	116.3	2: 38,000 MWh
2015	VIII	Injection	550	n.a.	n.a.	157.7	average for full cycle
2015/16		Production	n.a.	400	600	117.4	
2016	IX	Injection	700	n.a.	n.a.	159.7	
2016/17		Production	n.a.	500	800	113.0	
2017	X	Injection	800	n.a.	n.a.	159.0	3: 58,000 MWh
2017/18		Production	n.a.	800	800	91.9	for full cycle

Source: Srbijagas.
Note: MMcm = million cubic meters; MWh = megawatt-hours; n.a. = not applicable.

Table E.2 Estimated Development Costs, Banatski Dvor

Stage	Year	Activities	Investment cost (€M)
1	2009	100 MMcm cushion gas	40.0
	2010	50 MMcm cushion gas	20.0
	2011	50 MMcm cushion gas	20.0
2	2012	Drilling of 3 new wells	12.0
		Construction of an additional injection/ withdrawal train with a daily injection capacity of 2.0 MMcm and a daily withdrawal capacity of 3.5 MMcm	26.9
	2013	Drilling of 3 new wells	12.0
		100 MMcm cushion gas	40.0
3	2014	Drilling of 3 new wells	12.0
		Construction of an additional injection/ withdrawal train with a daily injection capacity of 2.0 MMcm and a daily withdrawal capacity of 3.5 MMcm	26.9
		100 MMcm cushion gas	40.0
	2015	Drilling of 4 new wells	12.0
		150 MMcm cushion gas	60.0
	2016	Drilling of 4 new wells	12.0
		200 MMcm cushion gas	80.0

Source: Authors' compilation.
Note: MMcm = million cubic meters.

- If mud loss is serious and cannot be abated in the traditional manner, then underbalanced drilling would have to be applied. That is neither standard nor state-of-the-art practice. The price for a well drilled with that technology would be expected to amount to €7.2–8.3 million.

For the purposes of deriving a storage development scenario, the following assumptions are made:

- The storage will be developed continuously over three years to the full capacity of 400 MMcm working gas volume and 350 MMcm of cushion gas volume.

Table E.3 Estimated Costs for Notional Development Plan, Okoli 2b

Year	Activities	Related investment and operation costs (without price escalation) (€M)
First	Drilling of 4 new wells	22.8
	Construction and commissioning of the gas storage surface facilities	88.0
Second	150 MMcm cushion gas (100 MMcm working gas)	60.0
	Drilling of 4 new wells	22.8
Third	100 MMcm cushion gas (250 MMcm working gas)	40.0
	Drilling of 5 new wells	28.5
Fourth	100 MMcm cushion gas (400 MMcm working gas)	40.0

Source: Authors' compilation.
Note: MMcm = million cubic meters.

- The maximum reservoir pressure would amount to 210 bar.
- Thirteen additional wells would be drilled. For the cost estimate, a progressive approach would be applied by assuming a specific per-well price of €5.7 million see table E.3.
- The surface facilities would consist of one injection train (suction pressure, 30 bar; maximum discharge pressure, 190 bar; 10.7 megawatts) and two withdrawal trains. The daily injection capacity would be 3.0 MMcm and the daily withdrawal capacity would be 4.4 MMcm.

The energy consumption for a full cycle amounts to approximately 31 megawatt-hours.

Croatia: Depleted Field Benicanci

The main problem in Benicanci is the reservoir conditions (two-phase flow with three media). Experience regarding conversion of a former oil field into a gas storage reservoir is limited. If the pilot test that INA intends to undertake succeeds, the following concept may apply:

- gradual development of the storage reservoir to full capacity over 15 years in three construction stages (somewhat similar to Banatski Dvor)

Table E.4 Estimated Costs for Notional Development Plan, First Stage, Benicanci

Year	Activities	Investment cost (€M)
2009	50 MMcm cushion gas for testing	20.0
2010	100 MMcm cushion gas for testing	40.0
2011	50 MMcm cushion gas for testing	20.0
	Decision on further investment	
2012	Planning and design activities	n.a.
2013	Drilling of 2 new wells	6.0
	Construction of 1 injection train with a daily capacity of 2.0 MMcm; and 2 withdrawal trains, each with a daily capacity of 3.1 MMcm	90.0
2014	Drilling of 2 new wells	6.0
	Injection of 50 MMcm cushion gas (approximately 200 MMcm working gas)	20.0
2015	Drilling of 2 new wells	6.0
	50 MMcm cushion gas (approximately 300 MMcm working gas)	20.0
2016	Drilling of 2 new wells	6.0
	Construction of an additional injection train with a daily capacity of 2.0 MMcm	14.1
	100 MMcm cushion gas (approximately 500 MMcm working gas)	40.0

Source: Authors' compilation.
Note: MMcm = million cubic meters; n.a. = not applicable.

- The first construction stage characterized by
  - working gas volume of approximately 500 MMcm and cushion gas volume or approximately 450 MMcm
  - average daily injection capacity of 4.0 MMcm and average daily withdrawal capacity of 6.2 MMcm
  - drilling of eight additional wells to reach the planned performance
  - implementation carried out over the time period 2013–16 (see table E.4).

If Benicanci is suitable for development as a storage reservoir, the surface facilities must be capable of separating longer-chain hydrocarbons from the gas withdrawn. The commercial revenues obtained from these separated higher hydrocarbons would not be expected to compensate for the additional costs of processing; and they are not considered significant, given the magnitude of uncertainty around the present estimations.

Bosnia and Herzegovina: Tuzla-Tetima

The Rudarski Institute has studied the possibility of leaching salt caverns for natural gas storage. A related prefeasibility study proved the possibility of four caverns, each with a net geometrical volume of 120,000 cubic meters, having a total working gas storage capacity of 60 MMcm.

Table E.5. Estimated Costs for Notional Development Plan, Tuzla-Tetima

Year	Activities	Related investment and operation costs (without price escalation) (€M)
First	Drilling of 2 cavern wells, 1 with extended coring and 1 with reduced coring	6.3
	Start of leaching operation, 2 caverns parallel	
Second	Leaching operation, 2 caverns parallel	
	Drilling of 2 cavern wells with reduced coring	6.0
	Construction and commissioning of the gas storage surface facilities	42.0
Third	First-gas filling of 2 caverns (total of 25 MMcm working gas)	4.0
	6 MMcm cushion gas, as investment	2.4
	Start of leaching operations, 2 caverns parallel	
Fourth	Leaching operation, 2 caverns parallel	n.a
Fifth	First-gas filling of 2 caverns (total of 25 MMcm working gas)	4.0
	6 MMcm cushion gas, as investment	2.4

Source: Authors' compilation.
Note: MMcm = million cubic meters; n.a. = not applicable.

In case of a positive decision to develop the storage capacity, it has been agreed that the investment and operating costs of leaching the caverns (for the leaching plant and related infrastructure) are to be borne by the salt producer. These are commercial arrangements, but they reasonably reflect the underlying economics because the revenues from salt production cover the costs of leaching the caverns, leaving only the incremental costs of subsequent development of the caverns for gas storage. The storage operator would have to bear the costs for the wells, for completion for gas storage operation, for first-gas filling, for the cushion gas, and for the gas storage surface facilities (see table E.5).

These are the salt cavern parameters:

cavern diameter	50 meters
cavern height	70 meters
cavern net volume	0.12 million m^3
minimum pressure	25 bar
maximum cavern pressure	128 bar
working gas volume	15 MMcm
cushion gas volume	3 MMcm

These are the parameters for the leaching process:

number of caverns simultaneously in leaching	2
total hourly fresh water flow rate	approximately 150 m^3
hourly flow rate per cavern	75 m^3
time for creation of two cavities	approximately 19 months
cavern well with extended coring (one)	3.3 €M
cavern well with reduced coring (three)	3.0 €M
well completion and first-gas filling per cavern	2.0 €M

The expected performance of the gas storage facility would be

daily gas withdrawal capacity	1.9 MMcm
daily gas injection capacity	0.5 MMcm

The surface facilities are proposed to consist of one gas injection/gas withdrawal train encompassing

- one compressor (suction pressure, 25 bar; discharge pressure, 130 bar; hourly flow rate, 20,000 square cubic meters)
- one gas heating station and pressure reduction/pressure control
- one gas dehydration unit with two glycol regeneration units (one redundant regeneration unit)
- filters, valves, internal piping, and so forth
- metering station
- control room.

Albania: Depleted Field in Divjaka

For Divjaka, the following assumptions are made on the basis of discussions with local experts in Albania:

- The reservoir performance is rather low.
- The reservoir is nearly empty.
- Seventy wells have been necessary in the plateau production phase (0.15 MMcm/d).

The amount of cushion gas required, the gas working volume that is possible, and the design approach chosen within the technically feasible parameters would affect the actual development scheme for Divjaka, as shown in table E.6.

The optimum approach for redeveloping Divjaka as a UGS facility is not clear from the limited information available. However, when thinking about drilling new wells in Divjaka, the following aspects have to be taken into account:

- The wells will have to be quite deep (2,000–2,600 meters)—and therefore expensive.[2]
- The reservoir pressure is low, so specific measures will have to undertaken to keep the mud column stable while drilling (even after loading with cushion gas). These measures will prompt additional costs (as much as 50 percent more).

---

[2] The costs for one well, without specific measures for mud loss prevention, will range from €6 million to €7 million. A few years ago, eight wells were considered by the Albanians to reach efficiency in Divjaka. In the meantime, the prices for drilling services and casings have gone up drastically.

Table E.6. Alternative Technical Development Options, Divjaka

	Cushion gas volume			
	Low		High	
Working gas volume	Low	High	Low	High
Visualization of working gas, cushion gas pressure, and performance over the withdrawal cycle				
Maximum pressure	Low	High	High	Higher
Minimum pressure	Low	Low	Slightly lower	High
Withdrawal performance[a]	Low	High to low	Approximately constant	High to medium
Additional wells required	None	Many	None or few	Several
Cushion gas costs	Low	Low	High	High
Compression for withdrawals	Yes	Yes	No	No

Source: Authors' compilation.
a. Performance over the withdrawal cycle.

- The number of existing production wells is still large, so the resulting maintenance costs in the future will be high. Each additional well will increase these costs.
- Even if drilling of horizontal wells is considered, the incremental contribution of one or several new wells to the overall performance of the storage facility will be rather small.

All of those factors explain why the concept "rather high cushion gas volume and rather low working gas volume" is assumed for the purposes of this report.

Regarding storage parameters, the following assumptions are made:

working gas volume	60 MMcm
cushion gas volume	170 MMcm
number of existing wells	70
number of additional wells	0

upper pressure level	approximately 130 bar
lower pressure level	approximately 110 bar
daily withdrawal capacity	0.50 MMcm
daily injection capacity	0.35 MMcm

Reduction of the pressure level would result in an adequate reduction of working gas volume. Increase of the pressure level would result in a drastic deterioration of the working gas-to-cushion gas ratio and an increase of the cushion gas volume.

The proposed storage concept has the following advantages:

- no additional wells to be drilled
- nearly complete reuse of the infrastructure (for example, field lines, gas dehydration and metering units, filters)
- short time needed for implementation.
  The main disadvantage are
- high cushion gas volume
- quite small working gas volume
- low discharge rate
- quite high operating costs because of the high pressure level.

The surface facilities will consist of existing gas production facilities, with an additional train for gas injection (compressor):

- one compressor (suction pressure, 40 bar; discharge pressure, 125 bar; 0.5 MMcm/d)
- one gas heating station and pressure reduction/pressure control
- one gas dehydration unit with glycol regeneration
- one metering station
- filters, valves, internal piping, and so forth
- control room.

The time schedule presented in table E.7 is based on the described assumptions.

The energy consumption for a complete cycle would be approximately 5,000 megawatt-hours.

Albania: Construction of Salt Caverns in Dumrea

The Albanian market's expected future demand for storage is estimated to be 150 MMcm. That working gas volume could be stored in two salt caverns of approximately 500,000 cubic meters each. A corresponding storage

Table E.7   Divjaka Notional Development Plan

Year	Activities	Related investment costs (€M)
First	Construction and commissioning of the surface facilities (1 injection train and two withdrawal trains)	39.0
Second	Injection of 80 MMcm cushion gas	32.0
Third	Injection of 80 MMcm cushion gas	32.0
Fourth	Injection of 10 MMcm cushion gas and 60 MMcm working gas, start of gas withdrawal operation	4.0
Fifth	First gas withdrawal cycle	n.a.

Source: Authors' compilation.
Note: MMcm = million cubic meters; n.a. = not applicable.

plant would cover the national demand only. This will be treated below as the "national variant." That variant provides the storage capacity for the long-run Albanian demand.

The salt dome of Dumrea, however, offers potential for more and larger caverns. In that case, storage capacity would exceed the national demand, but could support an integrated trans-Balkan gas system. This option will be treated below as the "transit variant."

For Dumrea, the following assumptions are made:

- Some locations can be identified where the salt mirror is shallow enough that salt caverns can be leached in the depth interval 1,150–1,500 meters.[3]
- The flow rate of the water supply for leaching is practically unlimited (from the nearby Devoll River or several lakes).
- Brine disposal is a critical issue. For Dumrea, two options are prospective:
  1. It can be injected into karstic formations at the boundary of the salt dome. Six drilled wells are available, but will have to be inspected and recompleted for brine injection. No brine treatment is necessary. The injection wells are likely to exhibit a good injection performance. Three wells are estimated to be sufficient for brine injection. This option might be the best solution for the national variant.

---

[3] The salt mirror in Dumrea normally is expected at a depth of 6,000-7,000 meters. This is too deep for storage caverns. Therefore, it is necessary to find a location where the salt mirror is significantly more shallow. If that is not possible, gas storage in salt caverns will be impossible at Dumrea.

2. The brine could be processed in a salt production plant. Annual salt production capacity would be approximately 1,000,000 tons. This option requires continuous, high-quantity brine production over decades, and so is applicable for the transit variant only. That variant provides large storage capacity and high performance, but it will take approximately 10 years before the first storage capacity is available.

"National Variant" of Salt Caverns in Dumrea   These are the salt cavern parameters:

cavern diameter	55–60 meters
cavern height	200 meters
cavern net volume	0.50–0.57 million m^3
minimum pressure	90 bar
maximum cavern pressure	215 bar
working gas volume	65–75 MMcm
cushion gas volume	45–53 MMcm

These are the parameters for the leaching process:

number of cavern simultaneously in leaching	2
total hourly fresh water flow rate	300 m^3
hourly flow rate per cavern	150 m^3
time for creation of two cavities	approximately 3.5 years
number of brine injection wells (reuse)	3
blanket	nitrogen

These are the specific costs for the leaching operation:

cavern well with extended coring	4.0 €M
test, recompletion of brine injection well	0.9 €M
leaching plant	14.1 €M
operating/leaching cost per cavern	5.6 €M

These are the specific costs for gas storage operation:

well completion and first-gas filling per cavern	2.3 €M
cushion gas per cavern	26.0 €M

Table E.8   Dumrea Notional Development Plan, National Variant

Year	Activities	Related investment and operation costs (without price escalation) (€M)
First	Drilling of 2 cavern wells with extended coring	8.00
	Inspection, repair, and testing of 3 brine injection wells	2.70
	Construction and commissioning of the leaching facilities, with infrastructure (including costs for dismantling)	12.31
Second to fifth	Leaching operation, 2 caverns parallel	5.62
Fourth to fifth	Construction and commissioning of the gas storage surface facilities	44.00
Fifth	First-gas filling of first cavern (total of 120 MMcm working gas)	2.32
	50 MMcm cushion gas, as investment	20.00
Sixth	First-gas filling of second cavern (total 120 MMcm working gas)	2.32
	50 MMcm cushion gas, as investment	20.00
	Dismantling of the leaching plant, plugging and abandonment of the brine injection wells	2.40

Source: Authors' compilation.
Note: MMcm = million cubic meters.

The draft on the surface facilities and the time schedule (table E.8) relate to leaching of two caverns in parallel, each with 150 cubic meters per hour and brine disposal into the subsurface. The surface facilities consist of one injection train and two withdrawal trains (compressor with suction pressure, 30 bar; maximum injection pressure, 200 bar).

The energy consumption for a complete turnover would be approx 14,000 megawatt-hours.

"Transit Variant" of Salt Caverns in Dumrea These are the salt cavern parameters:

cavern diameter	70–80 meters
cavern height	200–300 meters
cavern net volume	1.00–1.15 million m³
minimum pressure	90 bar
maximum cavern pressure	215 bar
working gas volume	130–150 MMcm
cushion gas volume	90–105 MMcm

These are the leaching process parameters (salt production):

number of caverns simultaneously in leaching	4
total hourly fresh water flow rate	400 m³
hourly flow rate per cavern	100 m³
time for creation of four cavities	approximately 8 years
blanket	nitrogen

In this case, it is understood that leaching of the caverns is the responsibility of the salt producer. The salt producer has to bear the investment costs of the leaching, brine treatment, and salt production plant and the related operation costs. The storage operator has to bear the costs of the wells, the completion for gas storage operation, the first-gas filling, the cushion gas, and the gas storage surface facilities.

The storage would be developed in stages, with each stage encompassing four caverns and requiring a corresponding extension of the surface facilities.

Injection and withdrawal performance of each construction stage will amount to 6.0 MMcm per day and 2.0 MMcm per day, respectively.

The specific costs to be borne by the storage operator are these:

cavern well with extended coring, two pieces at the beginning of the project	4.0 €M
cavern well with reduced coring, when the knowledge about the salt structure is more profound	3.5 €M
cavern well completion for gas storage operation and first-gas filling operation (without cushion gas)	2.5 €M
cushion gas per cavern (100 MMcm)	40.0 €M

The surface facilities for each construction stage will consist of two injection and two withdrawal trains, each equipped with

- one compressor (suction pressure, 30 bar; discharge pressure, 200 bar; 8.3 megawatts)
- one gas heating station and pressure reduction/pressure control
- one gas dehydration unit with glycol regeneration
- filters, valves, internal piping, and so forth.

Metering and control room are part of the first construction stage, and will apply for the other stages as well.

The following storage development scenario is based on the assumption that two construction stages will be performed, each stage putting four new caverns in operation. The time schedule and cost estimation relate to leaching of four caverns in parallel, each with 100 cubic meters an hour, and brine delivery to the salt production plant. The costs to be borne by the storage operator are presented in table E.9.

At the different construction stages, the energy consumption for a total turnover would be

- *first construction stage:* approximately 12,500 megawatt-hours
- *second construction stage:* approximately 25,000 megawatt-hours.

Just to have an idea about the expected costs related to the brine treatment and salt production plant, the following figures are given:

- *investment cost for the leaching plant*—approximately €26.5 million; energy consumption, approximately 0.7 megawatts
- *salt production plant investment cost*—approximately €42.5 million; energy consumption, approximately 17.5 megawatts
- *leaching cost per cavern*—approximately €17.0 million
- *energy consumption for salt production*—approximately 150 kilowatt-hours per ton of salt.

Table E.9 Dumrea Notional Development Plan, Regional/Transit Variant

Year	Activities	Related investment and operation costs (without price escalation) (€M)
1st	Drilling of 2 cavern wells with extended coring and 2 cavern wells with reduced coring	15.0
	Construction and commissioning of the leaching and salt production plant	
2nd to 9th	Leaching operation, 4 caverns parallel	
	Construction and commissioning of the gas storage surface facilities (first stage)	80.2
	Drilling of 2 cavern wells with reduced coring	7.0
10th	First-gas filling of 2 caverns (total of 280 MMcm working gas, plus cushion gas)	5.0
	200 MMcm cushion gas, as investment	80.0
	Drilling of 2 cavern wells with reduced coring	7.0
11th	First-gas filling of 2 caverns (total of 280 MMcm working gas, plus cushion gas)	5.0
	200 MMcm cushion gas, as investment	80.0
12th to 19th year	Leaching operation, 4 caverns parallel	
	Construction and commissioning of the gas storage surface facilities (second stage)	45.2
30th	First-gas filling of 2 caverns (total of 280 MMcm working gas, plus cushion gas)	5.0
	200 MMcm cushion gas, as investment	80.0
21st	First-gas filling of 2 caverns (total of 280 MMcm working gas, plus cushion gas)	5.0
	200 MMcm cushion gas, as investment	80.0

Source: Authors' compilation.
Note: MMcm = million cubic meters.

APPENDIX F

CITY DISTRIBUTION CASE STUDIES

Table F.1 Available Data on Natural Gas Consumption

Data description	Belgrade	Novi Sad
Heating degree days	2,520	2,680
Design temperature	−15°C	−20°C
Natural gas consumption	cm/y	cm/y
Poor-quality pre-1970 flats	1,168	1,270
Typical pre-1970 flats	1,065	1,155
Typical modern flats	746	793

Source: Authors' compilation.
Note: cm/y = cubic meters per year.

Table F.2 Engineering Cost Estimate Results for City Distribution Case Studies

| Market | Capital or other city | Data source | Offtake | | | Distribution network | | Subtotal, by city ($M) | Industrial and commercial connections ($M) | Residential connections ($M) | Residential installation ($M) | Total, by city ($M) |
			Offtake station ($M)	Spur ($M)	CGS ($M)	HP ($M)	MP ($M)					
Albania	Tirana	Local	5	n.a.	5	14.7	30.4	55.1	0	124.9	25.0	**205.1**
	Elbasan	Local	5	11.2	4	4.0	6.9	31.1	0	28.4	5.7	**65.2**
Bosnia and Herzegovina	Banja Luka	Local	5	31.9	4	8.1	11.4	60.4	0	46.9	9.5	**116.7**
	Zenica	Local	5	23.9	4	2.0	5.1	40.0	0	20.9	4.1	**65.0**
	Mostar	Local	5	2.6	3	3.5	5.9	20.0	0	16.5	3.2	**39.7**
Bulgaria	Kardjali	Local	1	13.2	4	0.6	4.4	23.2	0	18.1	3.6	**44.9**
	Vidin	Local	5	18.4	4	1.4	7.7	36.6	0	21.7	4.3	**62.6**
	Smolyan	Local	1	13.2	3	2.3	5.2	24.7	0	21.0	4.2	**49.9**
Croatia	Split	Local	5	56.2	4	7.4	16.4	89.0	0	46.0	9.2	**144.2**
	Rijeka	Local	1	52.5	4	3.7	10.3	71.5	0	42.3	8.5	**122.3**
Kosovo	Pristina	Generic	5	n.a.	5	7.5	27.2	44.7	0	111.7	22.3	**178.7**
	Kosovo Mitrovica	Local	5	11.2	4	3.3	5.9	29.4	0	24.4	4.9	**58.6**

Market	Capital or other city	Data source	Offtake			Distribution network			Industrial and commercial connections ($M)	Residential connections ($M)	Residential installation ($M)	Total, by city ($M)
			Offtake station ($M)	Spur ($M)	CGS ($M)	HP ($M)	MP ($M)	Subtotal, by city ($M)				
Macedonia, FYR	Skopje	Local	5	n.a.	5	14.8	27.2	52.0	0	111.5	22.3	**185.9**
	Tetovo	Local	5	4.1	3	1.2	3.2	16.5	0	8.9	1.8	**27.2**
Montenegro	Podgorica	Generic	5	n.a.	4	3.5	6.7	19.2	0	27.7	5.5	**52.5**
	Niksic	Generic	5	7.9	4	2.7	6.5	26.1	0	18.3	3.7	**48.0**
Romania	Drobeta Turnu Severin	Local	5	25.6	4	2.3	7.2	44.1	0	29.1	5.9	**79.1**
	Horezu	Local	5	8.2	3	n.a.	0.7	16.9	0	2.0	0.5	**19.3**
Serbia	Leskovac	Generic	5	11.2	4	1.7	3.9	25.8	0	15.8	3.2	**44.8**
	Uzice	Generic	5	18.4	4	1.2	2.8	31.4	0	11.2	2.2	**44.8**
SEE 9	20 cities	Total	88	309.7	79	86	195.0	758.0	0	747.0	150.0	1,654.0

Source: Penspen analysis.

Note: CGS = city gate station; HP = high pressure; MP = medium pressure; n.a. = not applicable; SEE 9 = nine markets of Southeast Europe

APPENDIX G

PRIVATE FINANCING

Figure G.1   Forms of Public-Private Participation in Infrastructure

Centralized/state-owned service provider	Fully public (centralized) responsibility for all investment, financing, and operations
Subcontracting	Public service provider directly subcontracts to a private firm for technical and commercial services. Public service provider owns all assets; and remains responsible for costs, revenues, and profits. Contractor is responsible only for own labor and material costs.
Administrative services contract	Public service provider carries out all investment and collects revenues; contractor is responsible only for costs related to defined services.
Management operating contract	Public service provider carries out all investment. Contractor is responsible for costs and revenues; therefore, has operating profit responsibility.
Asset rental/leasing contract	Public service provider carries out all (or most) investment, and leases or rents assets to contractor. Contractor is responsible for costs and revenues; therefore, has responsibility for operating profit and assets maintenance.
BOT or concession	A project company is responsible for a specific project's investment, costs, revenues, and profits; its corporate aim is to be profitable over the concession period. Public service provider ensures that technical standards are met.
Joint-venture company	A joint-venture company has responsibilities similar to those of a BOT/concession. Public service provider may be a shareholder in a joint venture, and provides technical regulation. Risk is mitigated by the public sector partner, but there are inherent conflicts of interest.
Fully private company	Fully private (decentralized) responsibility for all investment, financing, and operations, with independent regulation.

Source: Compiled by Economic Consulting Associates, using various sources.
Note: BOT = build-own-transfer.

Project Financing Structural Models

Project financing structures are more complex when they involve more than one country and cross-border investments. Depending on the ownership and configuration of cross-border projects, different structural models might need to be investigated to allocate the risk in the most effective way to facilitate project financing. Here are some alternative models:

- *Model 1: Project promoter is a large, cash-rich entity*—In this case, the project probably would be self-financed initially, with the option of refinancing when the project cash flow had been proved.
- *Model 2: Project is owned wholly or predominantly by state enterprises*—Sovereign debt guarantees by all of the countries involved would be essential, with additional risk mitigation instruments from international financial institutions and export guarantee agencies to bring the project to financial closure.
- *Model 3: Project has participation by the private sector as an investor*—An even more elaborate set of risk guarantees probably would be necessary to secure project financing.
- *Model 4: Project is broken down into national components*—Rather than having a single special-purpose entity for executing a unified project, another option is for each pipeline segment to be financed by the country concerned.

The South Caucasus pipeline project is a combination of models 1 and 3. The fourth model is the approach being discussed for the Nabucco project. It has the advantage of minimizing the cost of finance for each segment. That is dissimilar to models 2 and 3, in which there is a danger that the financing for the entire project will be based on the most adverse risk conditions in any of the component segments. The fourth model also facilitates the participation of certain key international financial institutions, such as the World Bank, which are able to lend only to countries and for which a segmented approach may ease the financing of a regional project.

In all but the first model, if the projects are to reach financial closure, risk mitigation roles will have to be assumed by governments and donors, international financial institutions, and bilateral agencies. Governments will have to make equity investments and/or offer sovereign guarantees. The support agencies will have to offer instruments such as partial risk guarantees, political risk insurance, and export credit agreements. Figure G.2 illustrates the type of structure that is likely to be required for the case of a single project company (models 2 and 3).

Figure G.2   Illustrative Project Financing Structure

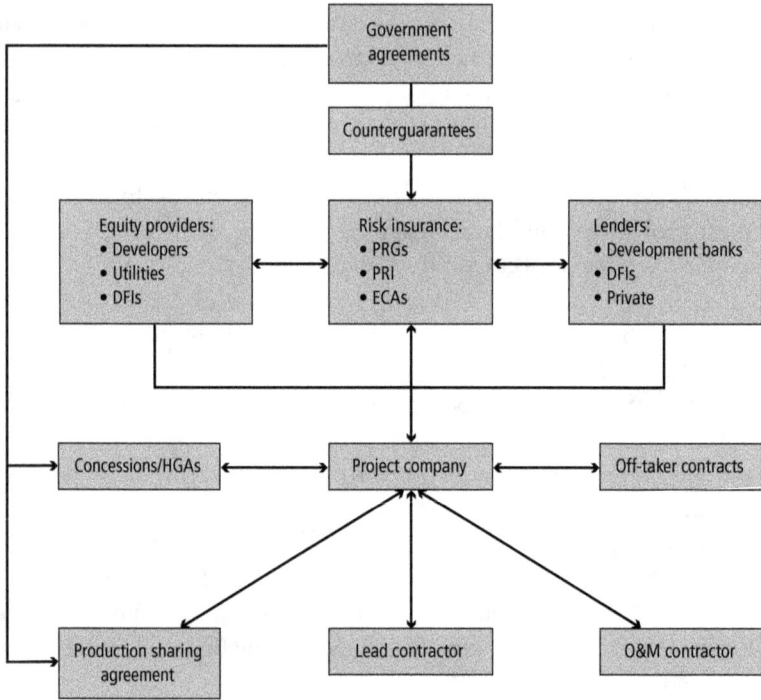

Source: Authors' illustration.
Note: DFI = Development Financial Institution; ECA = export credit agreement; HGA = host government agreement; PRG = partial risk guarantee; PRI = political risk insurance.

REFERENCES

BP. Various years. *Statistical Review of World Energy.* London: BP. http://www.bp
.com/statisticalreview.

Bros, Thierry. 2007. "How Much Extra Spot Gas Is There?" *Gaz d'aujourd'hui* 131
(4): 41–44.

Carnevalini, Rosita. 2008. "Role of Regulators in Relation to a Regulated/Negoti-
ated Access to Storage Facilities." Presentation to the Seventh Meeting of the Joint
Working Group on Gas Infrastructure and Regulation, Belgrade, Serbia, September 11.

CEER (Council of European Energy Regulators). 2005. *Investments in Gas Infra-
structures and the Role of the EU National Regulatory Authorities.* Brussels, Belgium: CEER.

EIA (Energy Information Administration). 2003. "World Natural Gas Data." U.S.
Department of Energy, Washington, DC. http://www.eia.doe.gov/iea/ng.html.

———. 2008. *International Energy Outlook 2008.* Washington, DC: U.S. Department of Energy.

Ghiosso, Ivan. 2006. "Regulation and Development of Natural Gas Interconnection
Facilities in Europe." http://www.tu-dresden.de/wwbwleeg/events/enerday/2007/
Pres/Ghiosso_pres.pdf.

GIE (Gas Infrastructure Europe). 2006. "Gas Transmission Europe Map, Operational Procedures—Information by Entry Point, Provisional Version, August."
Brussels, Belgium. http://www.gie.eu.com/maps_data/index.html.

———. 2009. "GSE Storage Map and Dataset, April 2009 Version." Brussels, Belgium. http://www.gie.eu.com/maps_data/storage.html.

Harris, Frank, and Gavin Law. 2007. "Seller's Market for LNG Set to Last: A Perspective from Wood Mackenzie." In *Fundamentals of the Global LNG Industry,
2007,* 16–18. London: Petroleum Economist.

Hurd, D. 2005. "Global LNG: Key Themes and Choices." Deutsche Bank, Frankfurt, Germany.

IEA (International Energy Agency). 2008. *World Energy Outlook 2008.* Paris: Organisation for Economic Co-operation and Development.

———. Various years. *Oil Market Report.* Paris. http://omrpublic.iea.org/.

Ilex. 2006. *Gas Security of Supply: The Effectiveness of Current Gas Security of Supply Arrangements-An Energy Consultation.* London: Department for Business, Innovation, and Skills. http://www.berr.gov.uk/files/file34563.pdf.

INOGATE (Interstate Oil and Gas Transport to Europe). 2003. "Projects of Pan-European Interest, Proposed Priority Axes for Natural Gas Pipelines." Kiev, Ukraine.

Kaufmann, Daniel, Aart Kraay, and Massimo Mastruzzi. 2007. "Governance Matters VI: Aggregate and Individual Governance Indicators for 1996–2006." Policy Research Working Paper 4280, World Bank, Washington, DC.

Kessler, Robert A., Jeff A. Dietert, Ruairidh Stewart, and Molly T. Reeves. 2005. *Liquefied Natural Gas.* Houston, TX: Simmons & Company.

King and Spalding. 2006. *LNG in Europe: An Overview of European Import Terminals.* Houston, TX: King and Spalding.

Lewisch, Christoph. 2006. "LNG Terminal in the Adriatic Sea." Presentation to the Mini Gas Forum," Vienna, Austria, October 13.

———. 2007. "The LNG Terminal in the Adriatic Sea: An Attractive Option Enhancing the Security of Gas Supply." Presentation to the Mini Gas Forum, Vienna, Austria, May 11.

Matsukawa, Tomoko, and Odo Habeck. 2007. *Review of Risk Mitigation Instruments for Infrastructure Financing and Recent Trends and Developments.* Washington, DC: World Bank.

Maweni, Joel. 2005. "Taking Advantage of the Latest Financing Sources and Techniques for Infrastructure Investment." Presentation to the SADC Regional Electricity Investment Conference, Windhoek, Namibia, September 20.

Norton Rose. 2006. *Global Gas: LNG Exports Report.* London: Norton Rose.

Oxford Analytica and Aon. 2007. "Political and Economic Risk Map." Oxford, UK: Aon.

Rehbinder, Maria. 2006. "Preliminary Report—Gas: Presentation of DG Comp's Findings." Energy Community, Brussels, Belgium, February 16.

SEE (Southeast Europe) Consultants Ltd. 2007. *Development of Power Generation in South East Europe: Update of Generation Investment Study, Final Report.* 2 vols. Washington, DC: World Bank.

Sinclair, Scott. 2005. "World Bank Group Financial Instruments for the Oil and Gas Sector." Presentation to the Joint Organization of the Petroleum Exporting Countries/World Bank Workshop on Global Gas Flaring Reduction, "Tools for Flaring Reduction: Financing, Clean Development Mechanism (CDM), Data Collection and the Standard." Vienna, Austria, June 30–July 1. http://go.worldbank.org/142SKE5RV0.

Thomadakis, Michael, and Gerasimos Avlonitis. 2007. "An Insight Into the Role of LNG in the Greek and the SEE Gas Markets." Presentation at the EU Gas Regulation Focus Day following the Commercial Strategies for LNG Regas Terminals-Europe 2007 Conference, London, July 11t.

UNDP (United Nations Development Programme). 2006. *Human Development Report 2006: Beyond Scarcity: Power Poverty, and the Global Water Crisis.* New York: UNDP.

www.ingramcontent.com/pod-product-compliance
Lightning Source LLC
Chambersburg PA
CBHW060959280326
41935CB00009B/759